Gender, Class, and Freedom
in Modern Political Theory

Gender, Class, and Freedom in Modern Political Theory

Nancy J. Hirschmann

PRINCETON UNIVERSITY PRESS

PRINCETON AND OXFORD

Copyright © 2008 by Princeton University Press
Published by Princeton University Press, 41 William Street, Princeton, New Jersey 08540
In the United Kingdom: Princeton University Press, 3 Market Place, Woodstock, Ox-
fordshire OX20 1SY

Library of Congress Cataloging-in-Publication Data

Hirschmann, Nancy J.
Gender, class, and freedom in modern political theory / Nancy J. Hirschmann.
p. cm.
Includes bibliographical references and index.
ISBN 978-0-691-12988-4 (cloth : alk. paper)—ISBN 978-0-691-12989-1 (pbk. : alk. paper)
1. Liberty—Philosophy. 2. Constructivism (Philosophy). 3. Sex role—Political aspects.
4. Women's rights. 5. Social classes—Political aspects. 6. Feminist theory. I. Title.
JC585.H484 2008
320.01′1—dc22   2007019955

British Library Cataloging-in-Publication Data is available

This book has been composed in Sabon

Printed on acid-free paper. ∞

press.princeton.edu

Printed in the United States of America

10 9 8 7 6 5 4 3 2 1

#13677802D

*For my parents, Audrey Eleanor Soos Hirschmann
and William Frederick Hirschmann*

Contents

Acknowledgments

BECAUSE THIS BOOK originated in two lengthy chapters of my previous book, *The Subject of Liberty: Toward a Feminist Theory of Freedom*, that were subsequently excised to become this book, there is some duplication of thanks for this book, and in a sense everyone I thanked there would need to be thanked here. But I will limit myself to those who had a relatively direct relationship to the present book, and hope that nobody will feel slighted. Isaac Kramnick, Will Kymlicka, and Joan Tronto all read those two original chapters and provided important feedback; the latter two in particular urged me to remove those chapters from *The Subject of Liberty* and turn them into a separate book, advice for which I am grateful. Brooke Ackerly provided very helpful guidance on the entire revised manuscript for the present book (with apologies for ignoring her urging that I include Rawls). A number of anonymous reviewers also deserve to be thanked for careful, detailed readings, insightful commentary, and multiple helpful suggestions on the entire manuscript. I regret that their identities were not revealed to me so that I could thank them by name. Kirstie McClure and Gordon Schochet read the Locke chapter in the form of a related paper and provided useful and elucidating suggestions. Joanne Wright read the Hobbes chapter and provided similarly useful feedback. Rogers Smith read a paper on Mill that dovetailed with my Mill chapter, and his comments on that paper helped me with the chapter here. Keally McBride also read that Mill paper as well as the Hobbes chapter and offered helpful comments. That I did not follow some of the suggestions made to me by all of these fine readers is my own failing, as are any flaws that remain in the book. A special note of thanks goes to Paul Guyer for lending me the prepublication manuscript of his excellent new translation of Kant's *Observations on the Beautiful and Sublime*.

I also thank my graduate students at the University of Pennsylvania, particularly those who participated in my seminar on Locke and Mill during the final stages of the book, for several valuable insights into my own reading of the texts. Extremely valuable research assistance was offered by Craig Ewasiuk, particularly on the Mill chapter. Craig's dissertation work on Hobbes also prompted me to rethink certain aspects of my argument in chapter 1. Kate Moran constructed the bibliography and tracked down references. The College of Arts and Sciences at the University of Pennsylvania provided me with research funds when I joined Penn, and later the R. Jean Brownlee Endowed Term Chair, which helped defray various research expenses associated with this book. Thanks also to colleagues in the Political Science Department and the Women's Studies Program at the University of Pennsylvania for providing a cordial atmosphere in which to do my work, with particular thanks to Rogers Smith, Anne Norton, Andrew Norris, and Ellen Kennedy.

Finally, thanks to my husband, Chris Stoeckert, for help in ways that cannot be measured. The book is dedicated to my parents, Audrey and Bill Hirschmann, to whom I owe more than a mere book, or even several books, can possibly repay.

Portions of chapter 2 originally appeared as Nancy J. Hirschmann, "Intersectionality before Intersectionality Was Cool: The Importance of Class to Feminist Interpretations of Locke," in *Feminist Interpretations of John Locke*, ed. Nancy J. Hirschmann and Kirstie M. McClure (University Park: Pennsylvania State University Press, 2007); reprinted by permission of the press.

Gender, Class, and Freedom
in Modern Political Theory

THE PURPOSE OF THIS BOOK is to examine the concept of freedom in five key canonical figures: Hobbes, Locke, Rousseau, Kant, and Mill. The importance of the concept of freedom is, I assume, self-evident to readers of this book: it is clearly a, if not the, key concept of the modern canon. Defining "the canon" of modern political theory in terms of these five figures, rather than Hume, Hegel, Marx, Nietzsche, or any number of other figures, is justified because of their centrality to at least the West's understanding of freedom, and particularly to Western political theory arguments about freedom; they are all key figures in modern liberalism, which is arguably the ideology that has been responsible for translating the political theory ideal of freedom into the common collective consciousness of the modern West. For Hobbes, Locke, and Rousseau, the "natural freedom" of the state of nature posited by each theorist has had profound effects on how we understand, think about, and talk about freedom in the West today.[1] Mill made vital contributions to this understanding in his famous defense of individual liberty of conscience and speech, and his articulation of the notion of a zone of privacy into which the state may not intrude. Kant, perhaps better known as a moral philosopher who posited the "categorical imperative," also defended liberal freedoms such as freedom of speech in his political writings and is associated by many scholars with social contract theory and the liberal tradition. As the ensuing chapters will demonstrate, I do not always agree with these dominant readings, but these readings make the selection of these five theorists obvious and central for anyone writing on freedom.

In one sense, then, this book is a very traditional work of political theory: it selects some major canonical figures, examines their texts, analyzes their arguments, and develops an account of freedom out of that. But it is not traditional in the three related themes that I use to guide my reading of the texts: Isaiah Berlin's typology of negative and positive liberty in its historical, rather than analytic, dimensions; the idea of social construction; and the place of gender and class in the concept of freedom. At first glance, the first and third might not seem that untraditional: but instead of justifying those themes here in summary fashion, I will break down my introduction to this book along the lines of those three themes, to present the reader with a picture of how I see the argument unfolding, and why I believe that this argument poses a challenge to the mainstream to take up a set of issues and questions that it has tended to resist.

NEGATIVE AND POSITIVE LIBERTY IN THE WESTERN CANON

By taking up the "historical, rather than analytic dimensions" of Berlin's typology, I mean to argue that Berlin's typology is historically inaccurate as an account of the canonical theorists, though it is conceptually important to understanding what those theorists argue. That distinction may be too subtle, even confusing, for some, but it is important. In his famous essay "Two Concepts of Liberty," Berlin argued that negative liberty embodied the Western liberal notion of doing what I want without interference from others. It defined the free individual as a desire-generating and -expressing being who was able to act on those desires without being prevented by other individuals, groups, or institutions. Not only was desire individual, but it was not a matter for discussion: I want what I want. The issue for freedom evaluators is to determine whether anybody or anything is trying to prevent me from pursuing that desire. Freedom is thus defined as an absence of external barriers to doing what I want. "By being free in this sense I mean not being interfered with by others. The wider the area of non-interference, the wider my freedom." For negative liberty, "frustrating my wishes" is the delimiting factor of freedom.[2] The classic statement of negative liberty is often associated with Hobbes: "By liberty, is understood, according to the proper signification of the word, the absence of external impediments: which impediments, may oft take away part of man's power to do what he would."[3] And indeed, Berlin cites Hobbes and other "classical English political philosophers" such as Mill, Bentham, and Locke as the key proponents of this view.[4]

By contrast, positive liberty referred to the idea that freedom is not consistent with pursuing bad or wrong desires, but only true desires; and it allowed for various ways in which others, and particularly states, could "second-guess" individuals' desires and decide which desires were consistent with their true ends. It thus allowed for "internal barriers," which might prevent me from pursuing those true desires, or perhaps from even understanding what they were. This sets positive and negative liberty apart from the very start. A key element of negative liberty was to presuppose ability; that is, if I am unable to do something, such as "jump ten feet into the air," then I cannot be said to be unfree to do it; nobody or nothing is preventing me.[5] The limitation is internal to me; I am unable, not unfree. By contrast, positive liberty allowed for the provision of enabling conditions to help me realize my true desires, such as wheelchair ramps that will allow me to attend classes and obtain a university degree. In this, ironically, the internal/external divide is turned on its head, because negative liberty holds that all abilities must be contained within me, whereas positive liberty allows that abilities can come from external sources. But this adheres to the competing notions of the individual that the two models operate from: the radical individualism of negative liberty holds that abilities and desires—the source of free will—are internal to the self, and come only from the self; external factors are what pose potential barriers to the free self. The social or communitarian self of positive liberty holds that abilities and desires are themselves social, that external factors can help maximize freedom, and that the inner forces of desire and will are grounds of struggle, potentially threatening to liberty. Berlin identifies Kant, Rousseau, Hegel, Marx, and T. H. Green as key figures of positive liberty.[6]

These models may seem to present an extreme dichotomy, which should give us pause. For Berlin himself, in several places in his essay, suggests this is not his intention. For instance, he talks of the positive and negative "senses" of liberty, rather than "models."[7] He explicitly states that he is not posing them as a dichotomy, and even criticizes those who have made the typology appear dichotomous. He recognizes that each of the two concepts is problematic, and "liable to perversion into the very vice which it was created to resist."[8] In fact, he goes so far as to say that his only point is to show that they are "not the same thing."[9]

But at the same time, he notes that the ends of the two "may clash irreconcilably."[10] The political context in which Berlin articulated these concepts, namely the Cold War, motivated him to champion negative liberty and show positive liberty in the worst light possible; practically speaking, positive liberty was the current danger. "Hence the greater need, it seems to me, to expose the aberrations of positive liberty than those of its negative brother," and particularly "its historic role (in both capitalist and anti-capitalist societies) as a cloak for despotism in the name of a wider freedom" was a matter of practical contingency.[11] But the result was to dichotomize the two "senses" of freedom into, as the famous essay is titled, "two *concepts* of liberty."

Berlin's initial characterization of the two concepts demonstrates this superficial gloss of the two as related while masking an underlying dualism. He claims that the two concepts of liberty are structured by two questions, answers to which "overlap"; namely, "What is the area within which the subject—a person or a group of persons—is or should be left to do or be what he is able to do or be, without interference from other persons?" versus "What, or who, is the source of control or interference that can determine someone to do, or be, this rather than that?"[12] But of course the second question is already skewed toward a narrow construal of positive liberty as authoritarianism and obscures many other important features that the ideal of positive liberty includes, such as enabling conditions or conflicts among my desires. If he had posed a different question as emblematic of positive liberty—such as "How do I know that what I want is really what I want, how can I figure that out, and can others help me?" or perhaps "How can my abilities be enhanced to enable me to do or be other kinds of things?" or "What is the role of relationship and community in understanding and creating my 'self' that has the desires it has?"— the ensuing discourse in political philosophy might have unfolded differently. These questions not only are less biased toward a predetermined judgment about the value of positive liberty, but also much more accurately capture the arguments of the theorists, such as Rousseau, Kant, Comte, and Green, whom Berlin classifies as positive liberty's champions.

In other words, Berlin's account of positive liberty is inadequate, if not inaccurate and unfair. He posits positive liberty as a caricature, in which all my wants have to be reconciled into some sort of master plan: "a correctly planned life for all," which will produce "full freedom—the freedom of rational self-direction—for all." This then requires that one's plan follow "the one unique pattern which alone fits the claims of reason"; and he condemns what he considers this "slaughter of individuals on the altars of the great historical ideals," which is done in "the belief . . . that there is a final solution."[13] But while that may be a fair account of what was happening in the Soviet bloc when he wrote the essay, that is not what positive liberty theory actually requires, if one attends to the arguments offered by Rousseau, Kant, Marx, and the other theorists Berlin cites as proponents of positive liberty. Thus, while chastizing critics who accuse him of setting up a dichotomy, Berlin himself uses dichotomous language throughout the essay to characterize what he considered "opposite poles."[14] Berlin clearly uses political theory to shadow contemporary issues, aligning negative liberty with liberal democracies and positive liberty with the totalitarian states of the communist Soviet regime.

But the typology that he developed had a profound transhistorical influence on political philosophies of freedom that emerged in the second half of the twentieth century, and even those who have rejected it find themselves unable to shake loose of its influence. I maintain that this is because they have grabbed the wrong end of the stick in identifying the weaknesses of Berlin's argument, ignoring its contributions to philosophical and everyday understandings of the concept. To be specific, the primary attacks on Berlin's typology by contemporary theorists have generally been made in terms of the analytic content and logic of the typology. Gerald MacCallum's is the best known, arguing that every incident of freedom contains a tripartite relationship between an agent, a desire (including desired actions and conditions), and conditions that restrain: "[F]reedom is thus always *of* something (an agent or agents), *from* something, *to* do, not do, become, or not become something."[15] According to MacCallum, negative and positive liberty theorists are really each only talking about "one part of what is always present in any case of freedom."[16] The crux of the debate between the two is not actually freedom per se according to him, but rather other kinds of values that they believe are important to political society and social relations.[17] Freedom can be defined along the lines of these various values, but that does not alter the meaning of freedom as a triadic relation between agents, desires, and constraints.

As John Gray suggests, however, MacCallum's formula is from the start biased in favor of negative liberty; for instance, he includes "preventing conditions" in his triad, but not "enabling" ones.[18] Furthermore, the role that "rationality" plays in his argument similarly presupposes a negative liberty framework. But I think that the real trouble with MacCallum is that his dismissive claim that "every freedom *from* is also a freedom *to*" demonstrates a superficial grasp of Berlin's argument and misses the true strength of the typology. Berlin's categorization of freedom into these two camps reveals a tension between two aspects of freedom, but not the aspects that MacCallum suggests.

Specifically, it is a tension between the outer dimensions of freedom and the inner dimensions. By outer dimension I mean forces, institutions, and people who prevent me from doing what I want, as negative liberty maintains, as well as those who help me achieve the ability to do what I want, as positive liberty includes. By internal dimensions, I mean desire (including aversions as well as appetites), will, subjectivity, and identity, which can be a source of freedom or frustrating to it. These internal aspects of freedom are generally ignored, or at least taken for granted, by negative liberty: I want what I want when I want it, it does not really matter why I want it. Desire is the limiting condition of freedom, but it is not appropriately a matter for freedom evaluation; as Hobbes put it, "one can, in truth, be free to *act*; one cannot, however, be free to *desire*."[19] Positive liberty, by contrast, is quite concerned with these aspects, for why I want something is an important part of determining whether a desire is "true" or "false." Hence Charles Taylor argues that we must "discriminate among motivations" and that obstacles to doing what we want "can be internal as well as external." But positive liberty sometimes errs on the other side, as Berlin suggested, assuming that we can definitively declare what a true desire is, and whether the agent is expressing it. The individual can be "second-guessed," as Taylor put it. This second-guessing leads critics like Berlin to worry that positive liberty has "totalitarian" implications; the state can require citizens to act against their apparent interests in favor of their "true" interests, but such "true" interests often reflect the selfish interests of state leaders. The pinnacle of such duplicity is seen to lie in Rousseau's comment that citizens can be "forced to be free."[20]

The concepts of negative and positive liberty that Berlin originally developed display some variety from theorist to theorist, but I maintain that this division between external and internal factors is a key difference between them.[21] Even the commonly repeated, if superficial and reductive, claim that negative freedom is "freedom from" whereas positive liberty is "freedom to" captures this notion: the former implies an absence or removal of external obstacles, whereas the latter implies enabling conditions to enhance achievement. But in the process of articulating these various internal and external aspects of freedom, the typology is also conceptually and politically useful in the differing models it suggests of what it means to be a human being, even if Berlin himself did not acknowledge this. Or more accurately, although Berlin sees that the conception of the self, and hence of desire, is important to the typology, the models of the self he posits are straw men. Focusing on positive liberty's notion of "higher" and "lower" desires, with the former's ability to control the latter as key to freedom, Berlin maintains that "the divided self" is the starting point for positive liberty, the state being necessary to "unify" these selves by saving themselves from false desires. By contrast, negative liberty operates from a notion of the self as unified from the start, and accepts the conscious self as the final determiner of choice. Freedom may be measured by how many options are available to me, but nobody can force me to choose an option and still claim that I am free.

This, however, is a problematic construction, for it not only relies on a caricature of positive liberty, it also ignores the complex psychology of choice. In the introduction to *Four Essays on Liberty*, Berlin frets that, in the original version of "Two Concepts of Liberty," the definition of negative liberty as "doing what I want," or fulfilling desire, is vulnerable to my simply reducing "what I want" in the ascetic vein; that is, I could simply not want what I cannot have, rein in my desires, and thereby enlarge my freedom.[22] Berlin therefore concludes that although freedom is "constituted by the absence of obstacles to the exercise of choice,"[23] choice is an "objective" rather than subjective notion; freedom requires "a range of objectively open possibilities, whether these are desired or not. . . . It is the actual doors that are open that determine the extent of someone's freedom, and not his own preferences."[24] The presence of options themselves, objectively defined, is key to freedom; I may not want many, or even any, of the other alternatives available, but I am nevertheless freer than if there was only one option. If choice is paramount in the definition of freedom, then the more choices I have, the freer I am. Negative liberty is measured by the options that are open to me, whether I want them or not.

This modification of his definition of freedom poses the somewhat absurd paradox that I am freer when I have twenty options, none of which I want, than if I have three, all of which I would like. After all, the whole point of seeking to maximize options is the underlying assumption that humans have desires and want to fulfill them. Without that assumption, freedom would be unnecessary, and there would be no point to defining freedom in terms of available options.[25] So Berlin does a little sleight of hand in the attempt to "clarify" his argument and backs away from the true challenge to negative liberty, which is that I can often be confused, conflicted, and perhaps even unaware of what I really want. But until I identify and express my desires, we cannot begin the process of evaluating my freedom, much less say that freedom is relevant.

The centrality of desire to both positive and negative liberty highlights the obvious claim that how we understand the self is vital to the conceptualization of freedom. Indeed, I believe that one of the most important contributions of Berlin's typology is its identification of two different models of the self at work in the history of political thought. But rather than the unified self versus the divided self, which Berlin invokes, I mean the individualist self versus the social self. Specifically, negative liberty operates from an assumption that individuals are disconnected and self-contained. Clear lines are drawn between inner and outer, subject and object, self and other. All others pose potential limitations on my pursuit of what I want; in its extreme forms, such as Hobbes's state of nature, all others are actively hostile, not just potentially so. But in its more modified form, negative liberty's assertion of the self's ability to control her life, her destiny, by making her own choices, is a key aspect of what we in the West commonly think it means to be human. Despite the ability of language to communicate our thoughts and feelings, and despite the fundamental human ability to build communities and families, we are irreducibly separate from others, each with our own thoughts and desires. Positive liberty, by contrast, sees the self as innately social and immersed in social relations, such that the individual cannot be understood outside of those relations. In its extreme forms, self and other become merged, the collective overtakes the individual. But in its more moderate versions positive liberty's assertion of the need to understand that the individual of negative liberty becomes who she is in and through social relations is an equally key aspect of what it means to be human.

These two sides of humanity, the individual and the social, are juxtaposed by the typology, and that is unfortunate; Berlin inadvertently falls into the trap he identifies, of reducing humanity to a caricature. If we do not see the two models as mutually exclusive, but rather as interactive, the typology affords an understanding of humanity that is much more complex than Berlin himself realized. It is this complex understanding of humanity that is necessary to understand the meaning of freedom.

Thus the problems with Berlin's typology have little to do with his conceptualization of freedom. Rather, they have to do with the issue of categorization. In particular, the typology as Berlin presents it is inadequate as a *descriptive* account of canonical liberty theory. This is a fact that nobody has systematically demonstrated. That is, canonical theorists do not divide up along positive and negative liberty lines. Berlin is correct, however, in identifying the various *aspects* of freedom as guided by internal and external factors. It is my contention that most canonical theorists actually display elements of *both* positive and negative liberty. Efforts, therefore, to squeeze theorists into one or the other model—for instance, that Hobbes or Mill is the quintessential negative libertarian, Rousseau the standard-bearer for positive liberty—distort not only the canonical theories, but the concept of freedom itself, including what is useful and instructive about the typology.

Indeed, Berlin himself is the theorist who comes closest to admitting that the typology does not neatly fit the modern canon; he recognizes that Locke and Mill display elements that cohere with positive liberty, Rousseau and Kant elements that adhere to negative liberty. But he then proceeds to ignore his own cautionary notes. This set the stage for misunderstanding the typology and for its misapplication to canonical theory. But using the typology as a loose frame for analyzing the canonical theories considered here helps us see that even if MacCallum misread what Berlin's typology was about, his bottom line was correct: all theories have elements of both models in them. Thus, unlike most contemporary critics, who maintain that the typology is conceptually flawed, my argument instead challenges the opposition constructed between the two models, as well as the effort to characterize canonical figures along the oppositional lines of the dichotomy Berlin posed. While historically inaccurate as a description *of* the canon, I maintain, the typology nevertheless has conceptual importance for understanding the notion of freedom that emerges *from* the canon. This conceptual importance relates to the fundamentally political insights Berlin provides into how theories of freedom deploy different conceptions of humanity. Because Berlin himself did not do more than make passing references to the canon—though his essay did include all five theorists covered in the present book as prominent figures in the history of liberty theory—it might be thought that my claim is unfair, that I am setting up a proverbial straw man. But my point in the chapters that follow will be not to demonstrate that each of them is not simply one or the other kind of theorist, but rather to focus on the way in which positive and negative liberty elements work together in their theories to construct a particular understanding of the concept of freedom.

An important challenge to my claim is offered by Phillip Pettit. Pettit argues that Berlin's typology misses some key points about the history of freedom theory in the modern canon, and that his definition of negative liberty as "freedom from interference," and of positive liberty as "self-mastery," misconstrues how many canonical theorists conceptualized freedom. Berlin's attribution of negative liberty to Hobbes, Locke, and Mill ("the pantheon of modern liberalism") and positive liberty to Kant and Rousseau (whom Pettit labels "continental romantics") distorts the fact that the idea of liberty as noninterference was actually promoted by the American antirevolutionaries, who wanted to defend the interests of the crown. By contrast, revolutionaries such as James Madison and Thomas Paine promoted a republican ideal of "freedom as nondomination." By extension, their ideological forefathers, such as John Locke, similarly conceptualized freedom in such terms. The negative/positive typology, thus, is not an accurate reflection of the modern canon.[26]

Pettit offers the republican ideal of freedom as nondomination to contemporary thinkers as an alternative, "third" approach to freedom. This third way lies in "the philosophical space left unoccupied by the distinction between negative and positive liberty." Pettit defines domination as "a particular power of interference on an arbitrary basis." The key issue of domination, Pettit argues, is "being subject to arbitrary sway: being subject to the potentially capricious will or the potentially idiosyncratic judgment of another." Nondomination thus entails "escape from the arbitrary." Freedom as nondomination, according to Pettit, combines the negative liberty notion of "absence" with the positive liberty notion of "mastery," to define nondomination as "the absence of mastery by others." But this is more than "the rule of your own private will," which he associates with negative liberty, because he posits the state as a positive institution for the establishment of nondomination and the protection of citizens from mastery by others.[27]

Pettit's conception of freedom as nondomination accurately captures key historical strains in liberty theory, particularly concerning the theorists considered in this book. It bears especially strong adherence to Locke's "freedom from arbitrary authority," as well as Mill's conception of freedom from government interference. It also captures certain analytic elements, because domination increases the chances of an individual's actions and choices being restrained or "interfered with." And clearly, my own conceptualization of freedom that I articulated in *The Subject of Liberty* shares important elements with Pettit's notion of freedom as nondomination, particularly the way in which it seeks to expand the concept of "barrier" beyond the deliberate, purposeful action of identifiable agents.[28] But although Pettit's conception is interesting, important, and useful, it does not make Berlin's conceptualization obsolete or irrelevant to canonical theory. For we must acknowledge the firm grip that Berlin's typology has on contemporary freedom theory, which has not taken up Pettit's reformulation. Pettit's argument is that negative liberty, as noninterference, introduced by Hobbes, was then forgotten until the American Revolution, when the Tories took it up to argue that colonists would be no more free under their own republic than under the British crown. Then, thanks to Jeremy Bentham, who opposed the American and French revolutions, it entered into popular discourse.[29] But why would it enter popular discourse if it did not already say something true about how people saw their experiences? Pettit does not explain. What gives Pettit's argument such vigor is how against the grain it runs: yet the fact that it does run against the grain, that the dominant orientation in political theory is to stay with Berlin's typology, suggests a tenacity of negative and positive liberty that at the very least implies its coherence with lived experiences of freedom and unfreedom. It is not just the orneriness of intellectuals loath to change their ideas, or the intransigence of political theory to new ways of thinking, that explains the persistence.

Furthermore, Pettit's definition of domination as subjection to arbitrary power is too limited. In defining domination as the power to interfere, he argues correctly that even if such interference does not occur, domination can still persist: it is the *power* to interfere, not the interference itself, that establishes domination. For example, the fact that a woman is not beaten every day does not mean that she is not dominated by her husband on the days that she is not beaten. However, the distinction he makes between domination and interference cannot be pushed too far; for domination could not be domination if there was not at least some interference. If the power to interfere were never enacted, the domination would lose its power: if her husband never beat her, her fear of him would eventually lessen, boundaries would be pushed, and domination would cease to be a factor in the relationship (assuming, of course, that other sorts of interference, such as repeated threats or other surrogates for violence, are not enacted instead).[30] Similarly, one might argue that many, perhaps even most, women are not sexually assaulted, they are not sexually harassed, they do not experience obvious discrimination: they are not "interfered with" in that way.[31] And yet the fact that a significant number of other women are "interfered with" is sufficient to exert dominating force over the remaining women. If *no* men ever assaulted *any* women, if *no* men ever harassed *any* women, if *no* men ever discriminated against *any* women, then the power of domination would thereby weaken. Pettit's contrast between interference and domination is thus too strong, because he construes interference too narrowly and individualistically.

At the same time, domination can be, indeed often is, not arbitrary at all, but systematic and predictable. It is, moreover, often grounded in a variety of principles, such as tradition, religious doctrine, and biology, such as when women's sexuality becomes the justification for male superiority. Obviously, I do not endorse such a view of sexuality, and examples like this are precisely what tempts one to agree with Pettit's labeling of such a reason "arbitrary" on the basis that, as he argues, nonarbitrariness requires a certain level of democratic access and "the permanent possibility of effectively contesting" a tradition, practice, rule, or law.[32] But while strongly supporting the role of democracy, equality, and participation in power structures in establishing an adequate theory of freedom, I am not sure that I would call the lack of these things "arbitrary," rather than simply not liberal, or not feminist, or not egalitarian.[33] Domination is most difficult to resist when it is not arbitrary but systematic, part of an elaborate system of rules and principles, interpreted in such a way as to exclude from consideration alternative readings and interpretations. A liberal or a republican might call such exclusion "arbitrary," but a fundamentalist, for instance, would say that it is not, that it adheres to a closed system of rules, much as liberalism could be claimed to do.

At any rate, although participation itself is fundamental to freedom, it cannot ensure nondomination; as Mill argued, if patriarchal society has done its job properly, women will have learned that an essential aspect of femininity is to adopt a mode of passivity and deferral. So what then? What about women who do not press charges against abusers, either because they have no means of support, having left employment when they had children, or because they have internalized a cultural belief that they are responsible for the relationship? This is why couching a theory of freedom in terms of nondomination requires a simultaneous consideration of social construction, as I will argue shortly.

Pettit could answer this objection by focusing on "all of us who identify with western style democracy," who "naturally assign to the notion of freedom" great "importance," thereby eliminating the fundamentalist from the discussion.[34] But of course, if this assignment is "natural," why is it limited to people in Western democracies? I doubt that Pettit believes that evolutionary migration ensured that those whose natures favored democracy migrated to North America and western Europe, while those of other natures occupied Africa and Asia. By contrast, the social constructivist argument can readily explain why it is that those in Western democracies define freedom in a particular way and assign it a particular importance in their understanding of how the world should work, just as it can explain other ideological orientations of other societies and cultures. For the point of social construction is to turn people into the kinds of individuals who do not *see* their domination, who internalize the set of norms and values that normalize their lack of power. In modern Western political thought, including the republican theories on which Pettit relies, that particularly meant women, laborers, the poor, and less obviously (because less frequently acknowledged) non-Europeans.

So while I agree with Pettit that "the positive-negative distinction has served us ill in political thought," I disagree with how it has disserved political theory.[35] Although his argument is grounded in the history of the concept, his critique is conceptual: there are not just two concepts of freedom, he argues, but three. And like other attempts to create some "third concept of liberty," Pettit depends on a simplified account of the "two concepts" that it supposedly supplants. Negative liberty is more than noninterference, and positive liberty is more than self-mastery, as I have argued above. And in fact, Pettit's account of nondomination borrows considerable elements from each model, if we understand those models to be more complex and richer than their critics generally allow. Consider, for instance, Pettit's claim that "the republican view that the laws create people's freedom" is evidence that the theorists in question adhere to "freedom as nondomination." I do not dispute that Locke's view of law as "the direction of an intelligent agent to his proper Interest" has republican elements. But it is also an example of the ways in which positive liberty is evidenced in his theory.[36] Furthermore, Pettit juxtaposes Locke's view to Hobbes, for whom he believes "law is always itself an invasion of people's liberty, however benign in the long term."[37] Yet I will show that Hobbes, too, took an ambiguous position on law, displaying positive liberty elements: in words that foreshadow Locke, Hobbes notes that "the use of Lawes . . . is not to bind the People from all Voluntary actions; but to direct and keep them in such a motion, as not to hurt themselves by their own impetuous desires, rashnesse, or indiscretion as Hedges are set, not to stop Travellers, but to keep them in the way."[38] But Hobbes, in Pettit's view, is by no means a republican. So the categories of republican and not-republican start to become a bit arbitrary and skewed, much as happens when theorists try to put the canonical figures into Berlin's typology as either negative or positive liberty theorists.

Hence, I argue that it is more useful to recognize that both negative and positive liberty are important to all of these theories—indeed that it is virtually impossible not to incorporate at least some aspects of each model. In this, though my argument in this book involves a critique of Berlin's typology, it also involves a defense of it. I accept that the two models present contrasting views of freedom; what I reject is the idea that any given theory of freedom is one or the other. Rather, the models identify important features that are found in most theories of freedom, features that pertain to different aspects of human life and different visions of what a human being is.

THE SOCIAL CONSTRUCTION OF FREEDOM

An important aspect of the conceptual importance of Berlin's negative and positive liberty typology relates to a second theme I explore in this book, and to which I have already alluded, namely the *historical deployment of social constructivism in canonical theory*. Social constructivism is the idea that who we are is not natural but rather the product and function of social relations: who we are, how we see and understand ourselves, how we see and define our interests, preferences, and desires, are all shaped by various constellations of social and institutional practices, customs, organizations, and institutions that make up our social "reality." By showing us, through his articulation of positive liberty, that internal factors are important to freedom, Berlin opened the way (again without realizing it) to understand that many canonical freedom theorists intimately involved themselves in studying issues of the will, desire, identity, and subjectivity. These issues lend themselves to a social constructivism argument, because the question of why I want what I want is a question that allows for the interaction and integration of the individual and the social, an understanding of how what is supposedly internal is externally generated, influenced, produced, and interpreted. Positive liberty gives the idea of social construction a purchase in freedom theory then, but social constructivism is what enables me to argue that the dichotomy between internal and external that typically characterizes the typology is itself false.

As I argued in *The Subject of Liberty*, desire—the foundation and starting point of freedom, as I have already suggested—is socially constructed. Women, for instance, are expected to have children, to care for men and children, and to participate in an entire range of activities that are seen as appropriate to the gender identity of femininity. But moreover, an essential dimension of femininity is not merely to engage in such behaviors, but to *want* to do so. As a result, many women are individuals who have been raised from childhood to think of themselves in particular ways that are more conducive to certain choices rather than others: for instance, if girls are acculturated to motherhood and wifehood in heterosexual marriage, the desire to be child-free, to engage in a profession traditionally reserved for men, or to have a sexual and romantic relationship with a woman becomes difficult (though obviously not impossible) to identify to oneself, even more to express and act on. A significant aspect of the feminist movement has been to undercut the "oppressive socialization" that women are subjected to in male-dominant society, to "liberate" their desires from patriarchal stricture.[39]

However, social construction goes beyond such processes of what would most likely be called "socialization." For these ways of channeling individuals to particular roles, activities, and preferences take place in a plane of consciousness that merges the psychological with the physical, the symbolic with the material, language with feeling. In fact, there are three different ways of talking about social construction, which I believe interact as three "layers" of a complex social process.[40] The first layer constitutes ideology, a system of knowledge claims or beliefs about a category of people, such as women, that supposedly represents "truth" but often in fact elides it. For instance, the idea that women are naturally nurturant and biologically destined to be mothers, that this designation accompanies a lack of rational skills and an overdevelopment of emotion, is a recognizable theme in the history of political thought. Its truth has been challenged and rejected by many, and one might be hard-pressed to find many people in the early twenty-first century who adhere to the view that women are incapable of rationality.[41] But the power of ideology to distort the truth and to represent reality through a particular conceptual ordering of social relations creates an understanding of categories of people, social relations, institutions, and practices that pervades broad segments of the population.

This layer of social construction is the one most people associate with the term. Catherine MacKinnon deploys this mode most obviously, arguing that men actively do things to women to turn them into sexual beings who wish to be abused.[42] The "construction" is as close to literal as one can get: women are made as men want them made. But this rather crude notion of social construction reduces the complexity of the process. For ideology not only distorts "reality"; it also produces concrete, material effects on the social phenomena it (mis)describes, in a process I call "materialization," the second layer of social construction. The idea of materialization is that ideology provides a rationale for structuring social relations, practices, and institutions in ways that ensure that the ideology is sustained. For instance, if one takes the ideological belief that women are irrational as a reason to deny women education, one will fulfill one's own expectations by increasing the likelihood that most women will fail to develop the skills of rational thinking. If one takes the ideological belief that women should be wives and mothers to justify the exclusion of women from professions and employment, most women will end up focusing their energies on finding a husband and having children.

The third layer of social construction is "discourse," which involves the way in which language develops to explain, describe, and account for this material reality and its underlying ideology. This is the aspect of social constructivism most closely allied with poststructuralism, and it centrally involves the idea that language produces reality, rather than merely describes it. Language is not simply a mirror of nature, reflecting an independent reality, but it produces the things that we see, because "what we see" must be translated in our brains in order for us to understand it. We cannot make sense of material reality without language, and in the act of making sense of it, we change it and make it real. This layer of social construction tends to be associated with poststructuralists, with Judith Butler usually seen as its main proponent.[43] Of course, to say that language is central to meaning does not entail that we can simply make things up, that language has no anchor to physicality, as critics of poststructuralism are wont to complain. But it does mean that "empirical reality" is not independent of language, perception, and interpretation: humans can have no direct apprehension of the physical world except through the interpretive structures of language. Empirical existence cannot make sense outside of discourse, but discourse must also be guided by existence, including the history of specific relevant discourses. Physical reality is not an illusion any more than it is self-evident; we have to explain it, interpret it, even instantaneously, but always through language, ideas, concepts.

These three layers of social construction—ideology, materialization, and discourse—operate in an interactive dynamic rather than a linear relationship. Ideology produces materialization, which shapes discourse, but discourse also makes it possible to formulate ideology and makes it possible for materialization to occur. The three are in a triangular relationship, each one relating directly to the other two, as well as indirectly through it to the other. Thus, for instance, the liberal ideology of social contract theory that men are "naturally" free and equal created a way of seeing and understanding human beings that shaped political institutions, normative practices, and social relations. It affected the meaning of gender and class, as conflicts over women's individuality and rights emerged in a context of an increasingly submerged and subtle form of patriarchy, and as relations between landowner and laborer transformed into one between capitalist and worker. Similarly, one's interpretation of a particular social phenomenon like "domestic violence" does not produce, from whole cloth, that experience; how people talk about it is shaped by the empirical reality. But that empirical reality has in turn already, through a long history of thinking about it and acting on those thoughts, been shaped by discourse and ideology. It would be naïve, if not simplistic, to say that when we see a particular man hit a particular woman, that act has not been shaped by a long history of discourses and ideological framings of masculinity and femininity: legal rights of marriage, police power, state authority, attitudes about the household division of labor, social roles within heterosexual relationships, men's homosocial power formations, property, and individualism all construct the gendered character of power. Moreover, individual practice—the "micro" level of social construction—occurs within a "meso" level of institutional, cultural, legal, and social practice, and a "macro" level of conceptual categories, such as the meaning of gender, race, and class. These levels of micro, meso, and macro cut across the three layers of ideology, materialization, and discourse.[44]

The interaction of these various layers, levels, and dimensions of social construction indicates the degree of "totality" that social constructivism maintains. It is thereby distinct from theories of "oppressive socialization," which operate on an implicit assumption that there is a "natural" person underlying the layers of socialization we experience; if the socialization could be removed, that theory goes, the natural self would emerge and everything would be fine. Social constructivism denies this underlying person, claiming that social construction is something that operates at the level of language and knowledge as well as practice, and imbues every aspect of our existence, so that we become the beings we are with the desires we have. As Kathy Ferguson puts it, "it is not simply that [we are] being socialized; rather, a subject on whom socialization can do its work is being produced."[45] Furthermore, these forces provide us with our powers as much as our limitations—a possibility that oppressive socialization theory excludes—because its constitution of "reality" is what makes it possible to desire, choose, and act. In other words, social construction is not merely a limitation on who we are, as if it were some false distortion of the "true" self. It is the only way that one can become a self. And although a different construction of women in the seventeenth, eighteenth, or nineteenth century might have been preferable from a feminist perspective, the fact remains that history unfolded through the particular construction that it did, which produced desires, identities, roles, options, and self-understandings. So social construction has "positive" as well as "negative" implications for meaning, identity, and choice.

Obviously, gender is not the only aspect of identity and desire that is socially constructed; class, race, and sexuality are the most obvious and commonly discussed in contemporary theory, though the present book will not consider the latter two in any detail. And women are not the only individuals constructed by gender. For instance, work on domestic violence shows that social discourses of romantic love feed ideals of masculinity that could lead some men to behave in abusive ways. Such ideals lead men to make choices that are contrary to their interests, self-defeating, or otherwise "inauthentic" in the positive liberty sense. Such choices range from capitulation to the conventional ideological role of family breadwinner who is excluded from involvement in his children's lives to controlling and abusive behavior toward his children and partner. But conforming to patriarchal ideology also leads to external barriers, such as when men are violent toward other men, or when such violence leads to incarceration. This construction perpetuates the inner/outer, self/other dichotomy that is located at the heart of negative liberty's individualistic conception of the self: for the conception of who I am as a man leads me to "choose" violent behavior, instead of seeing that this choice has been constructed for me. For instance, the fact that the devotees of most professional sports teams and violent video games are male can hardly be attributed to testosterone, but rather to the learning of masculinity in American culture. What we do not see is the way that such choices and desires have been constructed for us through the learning of gender.[46]

Most contemporary freedom theorists do not take the social construction of desire into account. Though phenomena such as "brainwashing," "hypnosis," or "manipulation" are sometimes acknowledged, the more complex and common process by which beliefs can be caused by a combination of external forces working interactively with other internal aspects of the subject is generally ignored. Particularly in negative liberty theories, the general assumption is that the self is whole and complete, that the inner will is fully intact, that I can be "influenced" only by things that appeal to my passions and interests, and that only things completely external to me—such as a hypnotist—can interfere with my desire, will, and liberty. Beliefs, mistaken or not, that I take into myself are never seen as barriers to my will, but rather part of it, internal to me. Positive liberty, by contrast, with its notion of true and false desires, in principle allows for a social constructivist dynamic. But by claiming that there is one true will, determined by objective principles of virtue or truth, it often similarly denies the complex process of social construction by which individual identity is constituted by and within particular social contexts. "Second-guessing" is the most hated aspect of positive liberty, because of its totalitarian "mind control" associations. But social constructivism reveals that second-guessing is to some extent unavoidable, always and already part of every understanding of freedom because always already part of the nature of desire. We can never be completely sure that what we want is what we really want, because human psychology ensures that we can never be sure of *why* we want something.

In the present book, I demonstrate that as an intellectual, social, and political process and phenomenon, social constructivism is an important aspect of canonical political theory. Because contemporary theorists often write as if social constructivism was invented by Foucault, this apparently basic and unremarkable argument has a potentially radical force. It also has a powerful potential to unsettle standard readings of canonical works, which are seen as fundamentally dependent on theories of human "nature" that guide their prescriptions for government and politics. Social constructivism suggests not only that these theorists created their understanding of human nature and their visions for political society out of their own contemporary frameworks, but calls into question whether human "nature" is really as important to political theory as the accepted wisdom would have it.

In the holy trinity of social contract theory, for instance—Hobbes, Locke, and Rousseau—the conception of human nature ostensibly plays a foundational role. Postulating a "state of nature" into which individuals were once born, these theorists developed arguments about what men's fundamental nature was like: if one stripped away all laws, government, social institutions, customs, organized religions, and philosophical and moral systems, one would be able to see what man was in his essence. The result was somewhat different for each in the details, of course, as delineated in the chapters that follow. But all three theorists shared significant elements in their state of nature theories: all men were naturally free and equal; such freedom and equality inevitably resulted in competition for goods, respect, and recognition; the conflict to which such competition unavoidably gave way resulted in the institution of government. Such governments logically had to come into being through contract, because the voluntary choice of men was the only way in which institutionalized association, structures of authority, laws, and systems of punishment could be created that respected the fundamental and natural freedom and equality of all men, coming full circle. Indeed, an important (though not the only) rationale for government was to preserve and enhance the freedom and equality that nature, though creating such qualities in men, could not sustain.

The dominance of such naturalist readings of social contract theories and particularly of their understandings of freedom make them difficult to challenge, but I believe that these theorists actually employ social constructivism. They do not merely posit pre-given individuals who must navigate a world of external restraints and blockages to the expression of their "passions and interests," but rather concern themselves with the social construction of desire and will. This is particularly evident for the concept of freedom, as a persistent theme in all of these social contract theories is a tension between free choice and the right choice. That is, in seeking to create a justification and foundation for government that respects natural freedom, the theories all base political legitimacy on individual choice: if I am naturally (and negatively) free, then choice, or consent, is the only way that I can have a limitation on my freedom that is simultaneously an expression of that very same freedom. As Hobbes puts it, there can be "no obligation on any man which ariseth not from some act of his own; for all men equally are by nature free."[47]

Thus free choice—freedom in the negative liberty sense—is central. But because these theorists are equally concerned with what such free individuals might choose, they also seek to construct men through social institutions and practices that will make them want to choose what the theorists think they should choose: freedom in the positive liberty sense of making the "right" choice that reflects my "true" will. Because such institutions and practices are decidedly social, and hence presuppose civil government, the naturalism of the state of nature is obviously challenged, if not contradicted outright. In the chapters that follow, I trace the ways in which the respective theorists actually produce the subjects that they claim to be describing. I show that social construction occurs in modern political theories of freedom in several related ways.

The first, most obviously, is the literal construction of the text. That is, political theory involves an ideological and discursive creation of a particular way of seeing and understanding the world. The way in which "man" or "humanity" is conceptualized, the definition of freedom, the relationship of law to freedom, and the role and purpose of the state are all literally constructed through the writing of these political theory texts that are read by, and in turn influence, audiences of particular genders, classes, nationalities, and time periods. The textual conceptualizations that deployed a new discourse and vocabulary about the human condition, the meaning of humanity, and society in turn contributed to the creation of a new ideology of liberal capitalism, as freedom was defined in such a way so as to exclude women and laborers de facto, if not de jure. Such exclusion, apparently at odds with the premises of "human nature" on which they were founded, contained internal inconsistencies, if not downright misrepresentations of women and the poor.

How these entities are defined by each theorist entails an interpretation of empirically observable phenomena, but such interpretation is filtered through a set of political beliefs, attitudes, and desires: that is, descriptions of how people *do* behave is in part a function of the theorist's view of how people *should* behave. Hence, all men are declared to be naturally free because the theorist wants them to be free; the descriptive character of the statement obscures its deeply normative sentiment. Freedom is thereby defined along the lines of the particular way the theorist wants men to be and fed into the different forms of government they prefer. Ideology thus plays a key role in the social construction of political theories of freedom.

But the theories also prescribe institutions, laws, policies, and practices that will coerce and socialize individuals and create their identities, their moral sensibilities, and their epistemological frameworks. And in this, political theory "materializes" itself into concrete effects. These texts were read by men of power, who were influenced or persuaded by these theories to translate their ideas into policy or law. Some theorists, like Locke, were directly tied to such men (the Earl of Shaftesbury), and indeed their theories reflected the ideas of their politically active patrons. Others, like Mill, were themselves officeholders and politically active. Some texts, such as Rousseau's *Emile*, were "best-sellers" and influenced daily practice at the popular level. Thus, in various ways, political theories have concrete material effects on the construction of individuals and society. Education for "virtue" or "character," such as we find in Rousseau's or Locke's theories, is the most obvious, though often overlooked by political theorists. The forms of government that a theorist favors are less obvious but no less crucial: the ways in which laws are made and the relationship that various citizens are said to have with their rulers reflect the theorist's idea of what it means to be a person, of course, but also produce that definition and make it real: if a government is established on the basis of popular elections, for instance, that electoral process will impact on the people participating in it, as Mill suggested. Public policy similarly constructs people in immediately material ways: poor-law policies, laws regarding men's authority in the family, women's social, political, and legal relationship to property, and moral codes of sexual behavior all materialize ideology into concrete reality, shaping and changing individuals' lives, understandings of who they are and their place in the world, and what "reality" is.

More subtle constructions emerge through the definition of social institutions such as the family; these institutions, and the ways in which they are conceptualized through language, produce roles and identities for men and women that in turn define the citizen. How the private sphere is envisioned affects how it is organized: family structure, women's role in the family, their relation to their husbands through law and social policy, all have concrete effects on what a woman is and the kind of life she leads. Rousseau is the most obvious here, for he structures a vision of the family that completely segregates women from politics, cities, and indeed the public sphere altogether, to produce women who are modest, chaste, and subservient to men. Other theorists may be less obvious, but are no less effective in their constructions of gender, as I will show in the chapters that follow. Discourse, ideology, and materiality thus interact through the texts themselves, through the ideas put forth in the theories that circulate through the political and social realms, and through the social institutions and practices that emerge out of or are reinterpreted by the theories. A new ideology created new institutions, practices, and relationships, such as the bourgeois family and mercantilist economy, that made the ideology true: as women, who at the beginning of the seventeenth century often participated along with husbands in the public economy, were pushed out of the economic sphere and into the home, the meaning of the family, the private and public, of women themselves, shifted and developed to reflect the ideology's ideals.[48] Educational treatises and policies turned to the production and reinforcement of the ideological and moral ideals that underwrote these social relationships, in many ways furthering the divide between the genders and classes, in other ways making that divide more vulnerable to collapse. This in turn created different ways of thinking about women and laborers that led to constructions of new policies (like poor-law reform or laws regarding women's property rights) that further solidified the ideological and linguistic meanings. Social construction thus occurs at many levels in the modern canonical theories of freedom.

As I will argue in the chapters that follow, particularly significant for freedom in this complex interaction of ideology, materiality, and discourse are the ways in which the theories discussed here, ostensibly dedicated to free choice, construct citizens and other subjects to make very particular choices, a tension I identify between the individual's "own choice" and the "right choice."[49] The architecture of their theories of government and morality all require that the individuals who constitute these governments and political societies display particular features and express particular desires that the theorist needs them to have and express. This uniformity of character that the theories expect of citizens, as well as of noncitizens such as women and the poor, indicates a conceptualization of freedom and choice that contains a particular content, as in positive liberty, and yet adheres steadfastly to specific notions of process, as in negative liberty. But it also means that the possibility of transgression, of difference, though ostensibly encouraged, as in Mill's theory, or rejected, as in Rousseau's, is in reality effectively contained.

The Gender Politics of Freedom

This containment is demonstrated in various aspects of the theories, but one of the ways in which it is most apparent is in the treatment of women. Accordingly, my third theme is the *significance of gender* to understanding freedom as a historical, philosophical, and political concept. By analyzing the relationship of women in these canonical theories to the theory and practices of freedom—ranging from women's ability to make choices to women's education to their legal status as citizens and property holders to their relation to labor and markets—I am able to demonstrate that many of the incoherences and inconsistencies in canonical theories of freedom are at least linked to, and often most readily illustrated by, the theorists' respective views on women, namely, their human, civic, social, and familial status.

Gender particularly relates to Berlin's typology when one reads the canonical figures, for my analysis of gender's place in these theories supports my critique of the dichotomy between negative and positive liberty. Consideration of gender reveals that many of these theories not only deploy both positive and negative models, thus challenging the dualism often attributed to them, but demonstrate a dualistic theory of freedom in another sense: a negative liberty of rights in the public sphere, exclusively for men, positive liberty in the private sphere, where obedience and subordination of the will are cultivated and learned by everybody, though often in gender-specific ways. The deployment of both positive and negative models of freedom is, as will be shown, much more complicated than this, of course; it is not a simple public/private, male/female, negative/positive dichotomy, because women are often denied both kinds of freedom. Women are obviously restricted from pursuing desires, but they are also subjected to the constraints of positive liberty, because they are seen as creatures with inferior wills. Furthermore, though men are the primary agents of negative liberty, positive liberty is relevant to men when considering how men are educated to want the right things in order to prepare them for citizenship. But because both models are deployed in this two-tiered fashion inflected by gender, as well as class, canonical theorists appear to present them, and later theorists can interpret them, as opposed. When considering gender, we can see how interdependent they actually are.

This third theme might not seem as controversial as the other two, for increasing numbers of political scientists see the relevance of gender to the history of political thought as fairly old hat, dating back to Susan Moller Okin's *Women in Western Political Thought* through Carole Pateman's *The Sexual Contract* to the "Rereading the Canon" series.[50] But to many mainstream political theorists, political scientists, and philosophers, gender is still at best an afterthought, a sideline to historical analysis of the "major" themes and issues of the canonical texts. It is not that such theorists are actively hostile to feminism (though some still are), but that they do not see feminism as having anything to do with "real" political theory. It has long been one of the central aims of my academic writing to change such attitudes by demonstrating that feminism is a method, a way of conceptualizing social relations that reveals aspects of social and political life that are otherwise not seen, such as power dynamics in the family, or the ways in which the denial of equal rights to women is a more profound denial of women's full humanity.[51] In the present book, I am less directly concerned with methodological issues than I am with a basic argument about substance: gender matters to *all* political theory. By incorporating gender into the analysis of freedom offered by this book, I demonstrate that gender is an important aspect *of* the mainstream of political theory, not an aside; and that if the mainstream is to be truly "mainstream," and not narrowly focused on the experiences and interests of a small group of white men, then it must attend to gender, as well as race and class.

My social construction theme leads us to see that part of what is constructed by these theories of freedom is a particular form of masculine identity that is required of all proper "subjects" of liberty. Men are the quintessential "individuals" of modern negative liberty theory because they are able to be disconnected from others in the public sphere as heads of families—specifically, because they are intimately connected to others in the private sphere, particularly women and children who are dependent on them and under their control. This connectedness supports the gendered character of positive liberty as well, for the communities on which the general will or common good depends, depend in turn on women's subordination to men, who are once again freedom's appropriate "subjects" even as women are its "objects." Women's unfreedom is thus in some ways the precondition for men's freedom. Indeed, women's unfreedom is in some ways a precondition for political theory's ability to define and conceptualize freedom, both as the absence of external impediments (because women are restrained more than men by law and social practice) and as the realization of virtue or true desire (because women's behavior is a frequent focus). I say "in some ways" because increasing women's freedom is also of varying concern to some theorists, as fluctuating recognition of women's status as individuals and citizens is made. Additionally, gender is not the only factor affecting the modern conception of freedom; but it is a crucial part of the equation that is generally left out. Gender relates not only to the material conditions of freedom, but to the ways in which discourse and ideology operate to construct modern understandings of freedom as a concept and as a lived experience.

Certainly, the gender of the theorists most likely affected, even shaped, their theories, much like other aspects of their locations in the social matrix of culture, race, class, education, historical epoch, and nation. And their understandings of freedom may likely have been motivated to some extent by gender-related concerns. In my argument, however, I am less concerned whether gender is "foundational" in the "causal" or even "animating" sense than I am with the various ways in which gender intersects with freedom to give it the particular shape that it has. For instance, as I previously discussed, gender is a marker for different kinds of freedom, which adhere in various ways to the ideals of negative and positive freedom. But although seeing this tiered conception of freedom is made possible by attending to gender, as well as to class, that is quite different from arguing that gender or class caused this division. Whether attitudes and conceptualizations of gender led theorists to theorize freedom in the way they did, or whether they simply sought to fit women into their theories because gender posed particular challenges to their conceptualizations that they needed to get around, is not something that can be definitively answered. In every chapter—one dedicated to each of the five theorists— I show how their treatment of women is related to their respective constructions of the concept and practice of freedom, and show that gender is important to the concept itself. But although gender is foundational to freedom in important ways, it is not "the" foundation; it is only part of the foundation. Many of the features that nonfeminist theorists traditionally identify are also important, such as emerging capitalism or industrialization, war and succession, religious conflict, changing cultural patterns, and other social phenomena.

That is, I am not using the concept of freedom to plumb a particular question about gender. Rather, the purpose of my analysis is to understand the concept of freedom, and my analysis of women and gender serves that thematic aim. There are many aspects to the concept of freedom that I analyze that do not obviously connect to gender. Each chapter begins with a detailed account of the fundamentals of freedom for each theorist, with gender and class brought in later to elucidate certain aspects of the theory, or because they highlight particular problems with it. Gender, then, is not central in the way that it typically is in works that call themselves "feminist," and in that sense, one might say that this book is the least feminist work I have thus far published. But that would only be the case if one took feminism as an all-or-nothing ideology, rather than an intellectual framework for analysis. Although I do not wish to underplay the importance of gender, it is part of the point of this book to argue that gender must be considered *along with* these other things, by feminists and nonfeminists alike. I hope it demonstrates that gender need not be the core element of analysis in order to still be relevant, important, and worthy of attention. More precisely, the notion of "gender" itself needs to be broadened to include other aspects of experience like race and class, family structure, and economic system; "the core" should never be reduced to a simplistic category.

Hence, in several of the chapters I show ways in which class biases similarly influence the theorists' conceptions of liberty. Moreover, I argue that gender and class need to be considered in tandem in many cases, particularly Locke and Mill. The idea of "intersectionality" has been a prominent concept in contemporary feminist theory, namely the idea that the different vectors of identity and power marked by gender, race, class, and sexuality need to be considered simultaneously in order to generate intellectually plausible and politically effective theories. When theorizing about "women," it is argued, feminists cannot afford to ignore the fact that black and white women experience similar phenomena differently—

such as domestic violence—because of their race, or sexuality, or class.[52] Few feminists, however, despite repeatedly calling for intersectionality, actually achieve it in their own work, particularly when dealing with the history of canonical political thought. Certainly, in most mainstream political theory that considers canonical work, it is extremely uncommon to find any of these various categories considered at all, much less in tandem with each other, and feminist analysis is a significant improvement in our understanding of the canon. But even those feminist theories tend to treat "women" as an undifferentiated category; although we invoke the importance of race, class, and sexuality in contemporary analysis, as soon as we reach back before the late twentieth century, it seems that once again "all the women are white,"[53] not to mention middle-class.

The ostensible reason for this could be that the majority of women in canonical political thought *are* white and middle-class: the wives and daughters of the men who were the primary subjects of political theory. It is rare to find a single comment made about women of color in the works of many Enlightenment theorists. Admittedly, they did not live in the "multicultural" milieu in which many westerners live today; but that hardly should have made them less aware of racial difference, with the advent of African slavery, as well as the encounters with Native Americans and Caribbeans that were taking place in the New World. Kant made some brief references to Native American women in his *Anthropology*; Mill an oblique reference to African American female slaves in *The Subjection of Women*. Rousseau similarly made passing recognition of "savages" in *The Origin of Inequality*.[54] References in Locke's work to Africans of either gender are extremely scarce, thus causing a number of scholars to abandon the attempt to develop a definitive argument about his views on slavery.[55] Even the work that historians—and very few of them, at that—have offered attests more to the milieu in which theorists like Locke wrote, rather than any definitive claims about the theorists' lives and experiences themselves.[56] Just as it may be the case that women's failure to show up on a theorist's radar screen is not owing to women's absence from history, but rather to the theorist's inattention, contempt, and dismissiveness toward women, so it is likely that a theorist's inattention to race is the mark of his racism, for he does not even see race as worthy of his notice. It is thus understandable that feminist political theorists have not addressed the possible intersections of race and gender in the canonical work: there is simply too little material to work with.

However, class issues were considered at somewhat greater length by theorists such as Mill, Marx, and Kant, and less overtly, though no less significantly, by Locke and Rousseau, and to a more obscure extent by Hobbes, as a number of commentators have shown. Foremost among these was C. B. Macpherson, whose idea of "possessive individualism" held that in state of nature theory people were focused on acquisition. The supposedly natural individuals at the heart of Hobbes's and Locke's theory were, Macpherson argued, the bourgeois individuals of emerging capitalism: white, propertied, middle- to upper-class.[57] By locating these theories at the dawn of capitalism, possessive individualism theorized an ontology for a new historical era and world order. People were constructed—in the sense that the theories conceptualized and defined humans—as "individuals" in the most extreme sense of the term: as innately separate from other people, even hostile and antagonistic to them. In the interest of challenging hierarchical, agnatic obeisance, these theorists denied any and all natural bonds of community; relationships could be established only by formal agreement, the result of individual choice. Hence, government could be legitimately founded only by a "social contract," or an explicit agreement between governments and the people they were to govern. This myth of contractual obligations, Macpherson argued, obscured the relationships of inequality on which they were based; what made it possible for bourgeois "individuals" to be such was the hidden existence of propertyless laborers.

The theory of possessive individualism gave feminists a useful entry point for considering gender, because of course the white propertied possessive individuals of which Macpherson spoke were decidedly male. And moreover, those bonds that were most arguably natural, namely the family, were removed from the public sphere by definition, and women were assigned exclusively to that realm of the family. In this sense, Macpherson provided a sort of template for feminist analysis: by arguing that underneath the language of "free and equal" individuals in a state of nature lay very unequal beings who were not at all universal or natural but rather situated in particular social and economic relationships in a particular historical era, Macpherson showed us that the state of nature arguments provided a mask to hide a class bias. Feminists subsequently argued that this language also masked a gender bias. But the ways in which these two stories of gender and class intersect has not been addressed by political theorists.

Thus, to argue that freedom is gendered does not mean that gender is the only thing that interpreters need to look at. Class, the context set by historical events, other texts written by the author that are not obviously related to his or her concept of freedom are all important as well, and are considered in my argument. Furthermore, to say that freedom as a concept is based on masculine experience, that it is structured to defend masculine interests, does not mean that the concept of freedom does not, much less cannot, apply to women. To say that would presuppose a dichotomy between the male and female gender that feminists have long challenged: difference is not necessarily dichotomy, even if some aspects of gendered experience seem more at odds than others. Women can and do act freely in a variety of ways, if under constrained conditions. Neither does the argument that freedom is gendered mean that freedom is straightforward, that women or men are either completely free or unfree. Insofar as freedom is based on a set of interests that only men—not all men, but few if any women—could access at the time when the theories were written, such as selecting one's representatives through a limited electoral process, women are thereby excluded. But when conditions change and women can access those interests—for instance, by gaining suffrage—disadvantages to women will not necessarily disappear; hence women's suffrage has not produced gender equity in public office or in many public policies, such as welfare, abortion, sexual harassment, pay equity, Social Security for homemakers, or child care for working mothers. The same holds true for excluded groups of men.

❏ ❏ ❏

It should be clear by now that social constructivism, gender, and Berlin's typology interact in the argument in a variety of ways. The Enlightenment theorists, by placing human agency and individualism at the core of politics, problematized state authority, which is invested in controlling people. Starting from the premise of individual agency, doing what I want—what I choose—is central to the theories of Hobbes, Locke, and Mill. And although Rousseau and Kant link freedom with morality and apparently independent criteria of virtue, rationality, and goodness, both clearly hold that individuals must choose the good, rational, or virtuous in order to be truly free; they cannot have such goodness thrust upon them without violating freedom. Indeed, one could argue that such choice was more important for these theorists than it was for Hobbes, Locke, and Mill, who similarly held that people had to make the right choices, but were apparently so uneasy about that possibility that they rather disingenuously hid the reality of choicelessness behind the rhetoric of consent or, in Mill's case, democracy.

Certainly it would be a mistake simply to label such theories authoritarian, for the primacy of individual choice was nevertheless a core theoretical concept, even if these theorists could not figure out how to realize it consistently in their plans for the state. Instead, I am arguing, they reconciled the tension between individual agency and state authority by providing choice for certain segments of the population and controlling others, particularly white women, nonlanded laborers, the poor, and implicitly men and women of color. Such control, if it is to be consistent with the ideology of choice, must be masked, and this occurs most effectively if the state controls individuals to such an extent that they are not aware of being controlled; that is, if they are constructed to accept the disciplinary power of the state as a key expression of their desires. The state, thus, is successful only because, or insofar as, social practices and social formations like the family can construct identities, subjectivities, and desires in ways that feed state interests. This is why freedom must be considered in its "internal" as well as "external" dimensions, for it requires us to understand how we have come to be the citizens we are in the twenty-first century. Understanding that process of becoming, including its origins in the modern era, is central to understanding the concept of freedom.

Each of the theorists considered in the following five chapters obviously handles this set of issues differently. I do not propose a single formula that fits all of these theorists, and I have not selected these five because they cohere to a particular pattern. Clearly, certain similarities will emerge as I explore the three themes I have articulated, and certain patterns of argument may recur. Indeed, what may be most sobering is the degree to which the same issues repeat themselves. Although that may be reassuring to some political theorists, who can take it as evidence that modern Western political theory has achieved truth, it will be more depressing to feminists and other progressives, who can see it as evidence of the persistence of class and sex bias. This bias is particularly disturbing in the early twenty-first century, when "freedom" has become a term of ideological doublespeak, bandied about by irresponsible and duplicitous political leaders. This makes it especially important to gain a fuller and more accurate understanding of some of the major historical figures responsible for founding contemporary assumptions and beliefs about the concept. Freedom may not be the *most* important ideal to humanity, or even the most fundamental, but it is nevertheless central to understanding who we are. It is my hope that this book may contribute to that project in some small way.

CHAPTER ONE

Thomas Hobbes

DESIRE AND RATIONALITY

HOBBES IS ONE OF THE first of the early modern political theorists to focus on liberty as a central element of his theory of human nature and of politics. Quentin Skinner notes that as Hobbes's work progressed throughout his life, he became more and more concerned with defining liberty as a key intellectual project, culminating in *Leviathan*.[1] And Hobbes is a central figure taken up by any number of contemporary freedom theorists. But Hobbes also may present a strong challenge to the notion that all of the modern freedom theorists utilize both negative liberty and positive liberty arguments, for he is often taken to be the classic example of a negative libertarian, as Richard Flathman and others have noted. He also may seem to challenge my social constructivist thesis, for the naturalism that Hobbes deploys is an extreme form of biologism. C. B. Macpherson argues in his introduction to *Leviathan* that Hobbes conceptualized humans as appetitive machines who sought their perpetual motion; freedom was thereby defined in reference to this motion. That is, people are free to the extent that external barriers do not inhibit them from pursuing their desires, and hence interfere with or even cease their motion. Hobbes says, "By *liberty*, is understood, according to the proper signification of the word, the *absence of external impediments*: which impediments, may oft take away part of man's power to do what he would."[2] And in chapter 21, he says, "Liberty, or freedom, signifieth (properly) the *absence of Opposition*; (by Opposition, I mean external Impediments of motion;) and may be applyed no lesse to Irrationall, and Inanimate creatures, than to Rationall. For whatsoever is so tyed, or environed, as it cannot move, but within a certain space, which space is determined by the opposition of some externall body, we say it hath not Liberty to go further" (261).

As Flathman notes, Hobbes often fails to discriminate between agents who take purposive actions and objects that would (normally) behave in certain ways but for restraints;[3] in his "proper signification" of freedom, Hobbes's reference to water that "falls freely" as an illustration of the meaning of the term supports the notion of a purely descriptive account of freedom (*Leviathan*, ch. 4, 189; ch. 21, 263). Freedom for Hobbes centers on motion, regardless of what intention that motion serves—

whether I am stretching my arms in a yawn or reaching out to strangle you—or what its genesis. Freedom for Hobbes is also distinguished from ability, or "power," and this criteria is similarly applied to animate and inanimate beings alike. Thus a stone that "lyeth still" is no more unfree than "a man . . . fastned to his bed by sicknesse," because both simply lack the ability to move (*Leviathan*, ch. 21, 262); it is as much the property of stones not to be able to move under their own force as it is for someone with a bad case of flu to be unable to rise from her bed. What prevents them from motion lies within themselves, and freedom concerns the absence or presence of strictly external obstacles.

Nevertheless, the realm of humanity, and hence what most philosophers call human action and agency, is the focus of Hobbes's *Leviathan*, and as such this naturalistic formulation of freedom needs to be explained as it specifically pertains to humans and their actions. Skinner maintains that the two key elements of Hobbes's conception of freedom involve having the power to act and being unimpeded in using that power, for "An agent forfeits his liberty if an external force renders him either powerless to act or powerless not to act in some particular way."[4] In the move from nature to civil society, however, the impediments to the use of certain powers have a more complicated relationship to freedom; for humans and their abilities are importantly constructed by the elements that Hobbes builds into his understanding of the social contract and its formation, including the institutions and social forms that underlie it, such as the family.

The Will to Freedom

Hobbes's central definition of "*A* free-man *is he, that in those things, which by his strength and wit he is able to do, is not hindered to doe what he has a will to*" (*Leviathan*, ch. 21, 262). As Skinner points out about Hobbes's argument, however, it is not merely being unimpeded from doing or obtaining something I want that defines freedom; I must also be permitted to "forebeare" from doing something if I so will.[5] By this means the idea of choice, of choosing my actions, is important to freedom for Hobbes. Desire may be a physical reflex to particular stimuli, and all people may have desires that manifest themselves in similar ways and propel them to similar kinds of behavior. But the content of desire, what particular individuals do and do not desire in particular instances, varies greatly from person to person, a diversity almost beyond calculation. As Hobbes says, "the similitude of *Passions*, which are the same in all men, *desire, feare, hope*, &c" does not dictate a "similitude of *the objects* of the Passions, which are the *things desired, feared, hoped* &c: for these the constitution individuall, and particular education do so vary, and they are so easie to be kept from our knowledge" ("The Introduction," 82–83). Freedom thus requires that each can choose which desires to pursue.

Our inability to know the content of others' desires means that Hobbes draws strict boundaries between the internal and the external aspects of freedom, as discussed in the previous chapter. Not only are the impediments to motion external to the self, but only action, the external expression of the self, can be impeded. That is, freedom pertains to my acting, or refraining from acting, *on* my appetites and aversions; it does not pertain to my forming desires in the first place. The latter Hobbes calls "the will," and particularly in his exchange with Bishop Bramhall, he scornfully dismisses the idea that we have control over the will, or that the will is even an appropriate subject of the concept "liberty." Free will for Hobbes consists in being "free to do if he will," not being "free to will."

> No man can determine his own will. For the will is appetite; nor can a man more determine his will than any other appetite, that is, more than he can determine when he shall be hungry and when not. When a man is hungry, it is in his choice to eat or not eat; this is the liberty of the man. But to be hungry or not hungry, which is that which I hold to proceed from necessity, is not in his choice.[6]

Will is the function of desire, and desire simply comes to us; it is not something that we consciously choose. I did not choose to love chocolate ice cream and detest spinach; I just do, even though those tastes run contrary to good health. I choose only whether and how to fulfill (or deny) my desires, whether to forgo the ice cream and eat the spinach despite my desires. "One can, in truth, be free to *act*; one cannot, however, be free to *desire*."[7]

One might take issue with Hobbes right from the start, for most of us think that hunger, as a basic biological drive, is on a different plane than desires for money or fame, which one can discipline oneself to desire or not, as the case may be. But Hobbes would disagree. The notion of man as an appetitive machine, with "a perpetuall and restlesse desire of Power after power, that ceaseth onely in Death" (*Leviathan*, ch. 11, 161) deploys a mechanistic model of desire. Civilized academics may be more skilled than primitive humans at channeling or even restricting their desires for glory, for instance (perhaps even scorning it on the reasoning that if nobody likes my work, I must be on to something), but Hobbes would say that we have simply exercised our liberty to resist the impulse for fame—an impulse that we nonetheless have. For what Hobbes calls "glory" would seem to be as biologically basic as hunger, part of the psychology that God or nature has hardwired into humans to ensure their survival in the nasty and brutish state of nature. Hobbes might argue that we have confused ourselves, and that if we thought clearly, we would acknowledge that all of us seek professional recognition and respect, but those who claim to eschew it have simply built up defensive rationalizations to cover over their disappointment and frustration in being denied it; or perhaps they think that a nonchalant response to recognition simply enhances their glory.

Despite his concern with "the proper signification of words" throughout the *Leviathan*, however, Hobbes is involved in more than a semantic debate; he is trying to get us—his readers—to think methodically about the categories and concepts we use, so that we can demarcate clearly one concept from another. "Seeing that *truth* consisteth in the right ordering of names in our affirmations, a man that seeketh precise *truth*, had need to remember what every name he uses stands for; and to place it accordingly" in his speech; "the right Definition of Names . . . is the Acquisition of Science" (*Leviathan*, ch. 4, 105–6). It is particularly imperative that words such as "freedom" be defined precisely and used correctly, for they have important political consequences; muddled thinking about such concepts produces muddled thinking about politics, leading to either "erroneous Doctrines" or "Ignorance" (ch. 4, 106).

This striving for precision indicates Hobbes's quest to develop a "science of politics," as well as what has been called his "methodological individualism";[8] as Hobbes says, "the first cause of Absurd conclusions I ascribe to the want of Method; in that they begin not their Ratiocination from Definitions" (*Leviathan*, ch. 5, 114). But his definition of freedom certainly coheres with an atomistic way of thinking. Freedom is an either/or proposition for Hobbes, not a matter of degree. In response to John Bramhall's claim that angels are freer than humans, Hobbes says, "it cannot be conceived that there is any liberty greater than for a man to do what he will. One heat may be more intensive than another but not one liberty than another. He that can do what he will has all liberty possible, and he that cannot has none at all."[9] I cannot be more or less free: either I can do what I want, or I cannot. And that "can" is strictly defined by the limits of my inherent ability; for me to complain that I am unfree because I want to fly from the roof of my house and cannot do so would involve a nonsensical use of the term "freedom." I am physically unable to fly, and therefore my desire is not the proper subject of the concept "liberty." I must have a power in order to make its nonexercise a question of freedom; but having a power itself is not the same thing as freedom. Unfreedom is not a lack of power, but an external impediment to my using the powers that I have. Of course, in this particular example, nobody and nothing restrains me from *trying* to fly, that is, from jumping off my roof, except my own fear of injury. But fear only compels the will, not the body, so the fact that fear prevents me from jumping only means that, in fact, I do not want to jump.

Hobbes's debate with Bramhall over free will elucidates his view of what makes something voluntary in this sense of selecting among desires. According to Hobbes, Bramhall thinks that not every spontaneous action is necessarily voluntary; for Bramhall, "voluntary presupposes some precedent deliberation, that is to say, some consideration and meditation of what is likely to follow."[10] He is wrong in this, Hobbes maintains, for there is always some level of "reflection" or "deliberation" in actions; we are aware that we are doing them. For example, "he that kills in a sudden passion of anger shall nevertheless be justly put to death, because all the time, wherein he was able to consider whether to kill were good or evil, shall be held for one continual deliberation; and consequently the killing shall be adjudged to proceed from election."[11] The fact that background knowledge of right and wrong underlies all action constitutes sufficient "deliberation" for Hobbes. Striking someone in the "heat of the moment" of anger is not like a sneeze or hiccup.

Deliberation, in other words, is not necessarily a careful and ponderous process of weighing options and choosing the most rational outcome. Or rather, for Hobbes, a "rational" choice is not one that coheres, in Kantian terms, with a higher law; rather, it is one that gives me what I want. If I seem to be torn between two desires, all that deliberation consists in is a vacillation between "contrary appetites," and between appetite and aversion, weighing the balance of whether doing something would help me or hurt me, and what would help me more or hurt me less. In other words, all action is a product of choices that we make, and all that the will consists in is the final desire that we have: so "in all deliberations, that is to say, in all alternate succession of contrary appetites, the last is that which we call the will."[12] Hobbes articulates this more fully in *Elements of Law*, where he explains that

> external objects cause conceptions, and conceptions appetite and fear, which are the first unperceived beginnings of our actions: for either the action immediately followeth the first appetite, as when we do anything upon a sudden; or else to our first appetite there succeedeth some conception of evil to happen unto us by such actions, which is fear, and which holdeth us from proceeding. And to that fear may succeed a new appetite, and to that appetite another fear, alternately, till the action be either done, or some accident come between, to make it impossible; and so this alternate appetite and fear ceaseth. This alternate succession of appetite and fear, during all the time the action is in our power to do or not to do, is that we call *deliberation*.[13]

That it *withholds* us, rather than *prevents* us, or *impedes* us, indicates the difference between persuasion and physical restraint, between making a choice under nonideal circumstances and being prevented from acting on one's choice, between the inner realm of will and the outer force of restraint. The inner realm, according to Hobbes, is extremely robust and is clearly demarcated from the outer forces. Hobbes even uses the word "compel" in a way that seems not to contradict freedom, for the compulsion simply provides a very forceful reason for deciding to do or not to do something. Being tied by ropes is not compulsion, but restriction. You could be compelled to walk by the fact that someone is pulling on the ropes and you will otherwise be dragged, but this compulsion does not change the fact that you prefer walking to being dragged. Thus, "when a man is carried to prison he is pulled on against his will, and yet goes upright voluntarily, for fear of being trailed along the ground: insomuch that in going to prison, going is voluntary; to the prison, involuntary" (*Elements*, 1.12.3). Compulsion only impacts on the will, which can never be the subject of freedom; "fear makes him willing to it, as when a man willingly throws his goods into the sea to save himself, or submits to his enemy for fear of being killed. Thus all men that do anything for love or revenge or lust are free from compulsion, and yet their actions may be as necessary as those which are done by compulsion; for sometimes other passions work as forcibly as fear."[14]

This meaning of compulsion explains why Hobbes maintains that fear is compatible with freedom: if a robber threatens to kill me if I refuse to hand over my wallet, I act freely in choosing to give up my money in order to save my life. Fear has only given me a reason for making a particular choice that expresses my immediate desire. Neither is necessity incompatible with freedom; such a claim for their incompatibility would make no sense, because "every act of mans will, and every desire, and inclination proceedeth from some cause, and that from another cause, which causes in a continuall chaine (whose first link [is] in the hand of God the first of all causes) proceed from *necessity*. So to him that could see the connexion of those causes, the *necessity* of all mens voluntary actions, would appeare manifest" (*Leviathan*, ch. 21, 263).

Indeed, completing the division between internal and external factors in his conception of freedom, Hobbes suggests that when external factors affect my will or desires—which happens all the time—they do not thereby impede my liberty; "extrinsical causes that take away endeavor [i.e., my wanting and trying to do something] are not to be called impediments; nor can any man be said to be hindered from doing that which he had no purpose at all to do." So if my threat to hit you if you leave the room results in your deciding that you do not want to leave the room, I have not restricted your freedom. "Extrinsical" factors that prevent me from doing what I want impede my liberty—such as when I push you away from the door and physically prevent you from leaving the room—but not those that cause me to change what I want, as a threat of such violence may do. Even "when a man is compelled . . . to subject himself to his enemy or to die, he still has election left, and a deliberation to think which of the two he can best endure."[15]

This compatibility between freedom and fear may be the biggest problem for most contemporary readers thinking of coercive dilemmas. For instance, according to the logic of Hobbes's argument, a battered woman who is trying to decide whether to leave her abusive spouse will "vacillate," in Hobbesian terms, between desires to avoid injury (which could lead her to leave) and desires to avoid poverty (which might lead her to stay if she is unemployed and the mother of small children). It is not, in Hobbes's mind, that she wants two mutually exclusive things at the same time, or even that she wants a third option that is not available, but rather a vacillation between different desires for different available options. Feminists and others would balk at such an account, arguing that her choice is coerced, and hence not much of a choice at all. But Hobbes would say that the woman's fear of her husband's violence simply gives her a reason to leave, and her fear of homelessness, poverty, and losing her children to foster care are reasons to stay. Her decision to stay, he might argue, is therefore not a product of coercion but rather a product of deliberation and expression of her will: if she views poverty as a greater threat to her existence than his violence, she therefore has a greater aversion to it. It is up to her to choose, however; as long as he is not physically restraining her or throwing her out the door, she is free.[16] His violence impedes her liberty when he uses it to prevent her from leaving, but it does not impede her freedom if it makes her want to stay for fear of angering him or because he threatens to sue her for child custody by charging her with abandonment. Much as Hobbes parses the various aspects of the prisoner's decision to walk to avoid being dragged, perhaps he would say "insomuch that in staying in an abusive marriage, staying is voluntary; in the abuse, involuntary."

FREEDOM AND OBLIGATION: FROM CHOICE TO CONTRACT

This compatibility between freedom and fear also underlies the rationale for Hobbes's social contract, and implicitly questions whether women are parties to it. Certainly on its face, the question of whether *anyone* is an actual "party" to Hobbes's social contract would seem to be gender neutral. For if "The propounding of benefits and of harms, that is to say, of reward and punishment, is the cause of our appetite and of our fears, and therefore also of our wills" (*Elements*, 1.12.6), then, like the abusive spouse, all that the Leviathan does is change our fears and appetites; rather than being afraid of people killing me for the food I have gathered, I am afraid of punishment by the sovereign if I were to take someone else's food. So by making and enforcing positive laws, the sovereign "gives imprudent and vain-glorious subjects new and powerful motivations to discharge obligations they know they already have" by "annul[ing] the justification that the temperate otherwise have for 'obeying' the laws of nature only *in foro interno*."[17] That is, Leviathan shapes our will, it does not thwart it; "so a man sometimes pays his debt, only for *feare* of Imprisonment" (*Leviathan* ch. 21, 262). Accordingly, in civil society, laws can be obeyed to avoid punishment, or broken with sanction, as an individual chooses, depending on his assessment of benefits and harms. And of course women would seem to have just as much to fear in the state of nature, and hence just as much reason to leave it, as men. But Hobbes's treatment of gender is somewhat complicated and ambiguous.

My analogy between the battered woman and the average subject of Leviathan takes on particular relevance in light of Gordon Schochet's interpretation, for he posits the patriarchal family as the origin of civil society in Hobbes's theory, and the authoritarian patriarch as the model for the sovereign. In spite of his abstract individualism, Hobbes noted the need for society. Indeed, in *De Cive*, foreshadowing contemporary feminist arguments, Hobbes admits that "it is true indeed, that to man by nature, or as man, that is, as soon as he is born, solitude is an enemy; for infants have need of others to help them to live, and those of riper years to help them to live well. Wherefore I deny not that men (even nature compelling) desire to come together."[18] What he did deny was that humans could establish and maintain society without a central authoritarian power. His portrait of humans as acquisitive machines that seek their perpetual motion dismissed the possibility of natural society or relationship; and yet he does suggest in several places that we have some ability to form "confederacy with others" in the state of nature. Schochet maintains that such confederacies take the form of families, which not only exist in the state of nature but provide the only plausible foundation for "Commonwealths by Institution," or the social contract (as opposed to "Commonwealths by Acquisition," or conquest). Such confederacies do not stem from sociability, however, but are limited by self-interest; once a superior power is destroyed, for instance, individuals in a confederacy may not be interested in sustaining the alliance, or they might fight over the succession of power and produce a state of war. Even families have their origin in lust—hardly a stable emotion—not in sympathy, natural sociability, or even love (*Elements*, 1.9.15–16). Hobbes indicates that people can and do love each other, but such emotions arise out of the regularity of contact that families make possible; they do not themselves found families. According to Schochet, rather, what gives families stability is the effective use of power by a patriarch.[19] Thus, the existence of families in the state of nature does not in itself undercut the strong individualism, and its accompanying distrust and hostility, commonly attributed to Hobbes.

This may be why, at the same time that he posits such confederacies and government by institution as a function of free choice, Hobbes also declares that obligation—including, implicitly, the obligation to obey the sovereign—is "inconsistent" with liberty (*Leviathan*, ch. 14, 189). Hobbes has to figure out a way to create obligation in order to secure the harmony that is necessary to end the "nasty, brutish, and short" state of nature (ch. 13, 186). If men are to preserve the essence of their humanity, they must preserve their freedom; relationships threaten that freedom because there is no assurance that the other person will not try to harm you (the classic "prisoner's dilemma" attributed to Hobbes but arising out of game theory). The particular kind of relationship civil society entails—namely, obedience to authority that can punish disobedience—means that the danger of direct connection between people is modified by a direct connection with the sovereign; my connection to other people in fact occurs *through* the sovereign, who now mediates social relations. While in the state of nature I might be killed for breaking a contract with my neighbor, I have an equally good chance (indeed, perhaps even a better one, particularly if she is enough of a trusting fool to have performed her part of the contract first) of killing her, and hence of getting something for nothing. But the vast power of the state—and before the state, according to Schochet, of the patriarchal head of the family—greatly increases the odds against me, and indeed reduces them sufficiently so that obedience is always in my interest. This is what makes relations with others predictable and reliable.

The state does this, of course, by instituting laws, which spell out for individuals what they may not do. In the classic liberal formulation that Mill was to articulate explicitly two centuries later, what the law prohibits are actions that infringe on the liberty of others, thus in theory producing at least an even trade, if not a net gain, of liberty for the self. Unlike Mill, however, Hobbes favors deterrence over retribution as the primary point of law: "The intention of the law is not to grieve the delinquent for that which is past and not to be undone, but to make him and others just that else would not be so."[20] This makes the relation of law to liberty in Hobbes's account somewhat ambiguous, as I mentioned in my introduction when discussing Pettit's reading of Hobbes on this issue. On the one hand, Hobbes writes as if law is nothing but a restriction on liberty: a necessary restriction, of course, and one of which all rational men admit the necessity, but a restriction nonetheless. Thus, Hobbes says that many liberties "depend on the silence of the Law. . . . In cases where the Soveraign has prescribed no rule, there the Subject hath the liberty to do, or forbeare, according to his own discretion" (*Leviathan* ch. 21, 271). Law provides a set of parameters around our natural tendency to act however we wish; we are free within those parameters, but the parameters are themselves limitations on freedom; for "whatsoever is . . . environed, as it cannot move, but within a certain space, which space is determined by the opposition of some externall body, we say it hath not Liberty to go further" (ch. 21, 261). Hence "the Right of Nature, that is, the naturall Liberty of man, may by the Civill Law be abridged, and restrained: nay, the end of making Laws, is no other, but such Restraint; without the which there cannot possibly be any Peace" (ch. 26, 315).

At the same time, however, in other passages Hobbes seems to suggest that law is not a limitation on freedom at all, but rather the condition under which freedom is possible; "the use of Lawes . . . is not to bind the People from all Voluntary actions; but to direct and keep them in such a motion, as not to hurt themselves by their own impetuous desires, rashnesse, or indiscretion as Hedges are set, not to stop Travellers, but to keep them in the way" (*Leviathan*, ch. 30, 388). Indeed, so consonant with liberty is law that in certain parts of the *Leviathan* Hobbes even seems to reject outright the idea that law restricts liberty: "if we take Liberty, for an exemption from Lawes, it is no lesse absurd, for men to demand as they doe, that Liberty, by which all other men may be masters of their lives." Without law, Hobbes says, we would not in fact be free, but rather subject to the unpredictable wills of others. Thus "the Liberty of a Subject, lyeth therefore only in those things, which in regulating their actions, the Soveraign hath praetermitted" (ch. 21, 264), such as to buy and sell, contract with other individuals, eat as one likes, live where one likes, and so forth.

Although the former view of law as limiting freedom would seem to fit Hobbes's notion of freedom as absence of external impediment to motion, the latter view of law as facilitating freedom coheres with his claim that liberty is compatible with fear and necessity. Indeed, Hobbes offers as an example of the compatibility of fear and freedom "all actions which men do in Commonwealths, for *feare* of the law, are actions, which the doers had *liberty* to omit" (ch. 21, 263). This matches "the logic of leviathan" (to borrow Gauthier's phrase), for what might be an example of an occasion when I was not at liberty to obey the law, that is, when my breaking the law could be seen as an unfree action? The only case might be when my choice is to break the law or die; but by analogy to Hobbes's robbery example, it would seem I still have a choice and must be seen as acting freely. Otherwise, Hobbes leaves open the possibility of coercion with regard to the law that he closes in regard to all other venues. Thus, Skinner notes that although "there is no doubt that the force of law serves to limit our liberty as subjects," nevertheless "the liberty of such agents to act as their judgment and reason dictate will not in the least be infringed by their obligation to obey the law. The dictates of reason and the requirements of law will prove to be one and the same."[21]

The apparent contradiction this poses—the point of law is to restrain natural liberty, but law does not actually impede our liberty—derives in part from the specificity of Hobbes's concept. Rather than a general notion of "a free man," Hobbes says (despite his own use of this term throughout his writings), we can talk only about being free to *do* specific things. Hence, law limits my freedom to kill you, but not my freedom to engage in commerce; and because the latter is what I want to do anyhow, this choice structure is what I want. The fact remains that I am no longer free to kill you, but it becomes unimportant. Even this resolution is incomplete, however, because of course I really *am* free to kill you in civil society; it is just that I will likely be punished for it and therefore most likely do not want to do it. Hence, returning to the *Leviathan*'s opening definition of liberty—"By LIBERTY is understood, according to the proper signification of the word, the absence of external impediments: which impediments, may oft take away part of man's power to do what he would"—the word "part" directs our attention to the rest of that passage, often ignored: "but cannot hinder him from using the power left him, according as his judgement, as reason shall dictate to him" (*Leviathan*, ch. 14, 189). Impediments prevent me from taking specific actions, but few impediments prevent me from taking all possible actions; they do not make me an unfree *person*.

Law is consistent with freedom, then, because having law is in my interest. Because it is in my interest, then by definition I act freely when I obey it, according to Hobbesian logic. Hobbes reconciles this reasoning with the simultaneous assertion that law *limits* liberty by deploying the mechanism of consent. Perhaps it is testimony to the danger he sees in connection and relationship, but in the move from the state of nature to civil society Hobbes argues that consent is the only legitimate foundation for the sovereign's authority. For consent is the only way to preserve the essence of humanity, natural freedom. In a social contract, all agree to alienate certain of their liberties to a sovereign who will in turn oversee everyone's behavior. What makes this legitimate is that people *choose* to enter into this contract; the limitation of their liberty that the contract imposes is thus also an expression of their liberty—even, perhaps, its ultimate expression. Political obligation can exist only by the exercise of will, "there being no Obligation on any man, which ariseth not from some Act of his own; for all men equally, are by Nature Free" (*Leviathan*, ch. 21, 268).

This radical notion of individual will and choice works well with Hobbes's abstract individualism, and yet the status of this apparently radical choice is once again somewhat paradoxical. For Hobbes's argument sets up such consent and choice as an inescapable logical requirement. Given that the paramount desire of humans is to live, then we must logically want whatever will achieve that end; this is the essence of the first two laws of nature (*Leviathan*, ch. 14, 190). By constructing the state of nature in anarchic terms, Hobbes is able to maintain flatly that the sovereign is the only effective and reliable means to this end. Hence, consent to authority is something we must want, and this is true whether we realize it or not; anyone who chooses to violate his own interests "is not to be understood as if he meant it" (ch. 14, 192). Thus, all are obligated to the contract, for "as well he that *Voted for it*, as he that *Voted against it*, shall *Authorize* all the Actions and Judgements, of that Man, or Assembly of men, in the same manner, as if they were his own" (ch. 18, 229).

Hobbes thus sets up what I have called a "rational fiat."[22] That is, we are compelled to consent to the social contract because we have no practical choice in the matter; it is the only choice we can rationally make. The logic of Hobbes's construct is that no one can rationally commit to the social contract, because distrust is necessary to survival in the state of nature; how could such innately suspicious and antagonistic beings ever agree on anything, let alone to give up their right to kill their enemies? Yet all are logically compelled to choose the social contract, because it is the only way to escape the uncertain state of nature. Indeed, Hobbes implies not only that such agreement is possible, but even that there is some kind of prior social compact among men predating the covenant with the sovereign, when he defends the logical necessity of majority rule:

> because the major part hath by consenting voices declared a Soveraigne; he that dissented must now consent with the rest; that is, be contented to avow all the actions he shall do, or else justly be destroyed by the rest. For if he voluntarily entered into the Congregation of them that were assembled, he sufficiently declared thereby his will (and therefore tacitely covenanted) to stand to what the major part should ordayne. (*Leviathan*, ch. 18, 231)

Thus, Skinner maintains that the compact is not with the sovereign per se, but with other men who agree among themselves to appoint a sovereign.[23] But this scenario, too, would have to employ a rational fiat. For the trust necessary to found this congregation requires the very sovereign authority that is supposed to be the result of the congregation. Furthermore, the possibility is not even considered that an individual might "enter the congregation" just to see what is going on and what kind of a solution can be developed before agreeing to be part of this decision-making body.

Or rather, it is not considered in *Leviathan*. In *The Elements of Law*, which was written earlier, Hobbes explicitly maintained that "though thus assembled with intention to unite themselves, they are yet in that estate in which every man hath right to everything" and moreover, that "every man's hand, and every man's will, (not so much as one excepted) [must] have concurred thereto. . . . [W]hensoever therefore any man saith, that a number of men hath done any act: it is to be understood, that every particular man in that number hath consented thereunto, and not the greatest part only" (*Elements*, 2.1.2). By the time Hobbes composed *Leviathan*, however, the difficulties of obtaining unanimous agreement may have appeared too great to allow for such conditional assemblage.[24] In the later text, Hobbes indicates that everyone is automatically included in the "agreement," for the only alternative to it is the state of war, which all seek to avoid. Hence, there, in contrast to the *Elements*, Hobbes declares that "whether he be of the Congregation, or not; and whether his consent be asked, or not, he must either submit to their decrees, or be left in the condition of warre he was in before; wherein he might without injustice be destroyed by any man whatsoever" (*Leviathan*, ch. 18, 232).

As a practical matter, of course, how this "congregation" could have been established in the first place is a puzzle, given the total lack of trust among individuals in the state of nature. Schochet suggests that because heads of families—patriarchs—are already experienced in ruling smaller groups of people and maintaining peace among them, they are the likely members of such a congregation, and hence the only possible parties to the compact. If this is correct, then one could imagine that once these patriarchs have hammered out an agreement among themselves, the members of their respective families would be the potential "dissenters" to whom Hobbes refers in the passage above; they may be unhappy with what their patriarch has worked out, Hobbes could be saying, but because they have long benefited from the security he has provided, they are not really in a position to challenge his transfer of everyone's right, including much of his own authority, to a single sovereign. But Hobbes also seems to suggest that the "congregation" and its "dissenters" refers to the immediate grouping engaged in the actual contract negotiations. Moreover, how he imagines these patriarchs to come together and agree is still at issue. For if what Hobbes says is correct, and what we do by simply showing up at the meeting is to authorize all the actions of the sovereign who is selected at the meeting, then logically I thereby authorize him to imprison me for not voting for him in the first place. Indeed, I could paradoxically authorize him to kill me. That is, though I cannot transfer that right to anyone, by failing to abide by the majority's decision I place myself in a state of war with the newly selected sovereign, which entitles him to kill me if he can. That could be the reasoning that leads Hobbes to assume that all will in fact agree. But the very same reasoning would more likely lead to everyone's nonparticipation in the first place, as the most likely outcome of my disagreement is death, and that is not a risk I would willingly take.

Indeed, although Hobbes outlines the social contract as an example of "government by Institution," the only realistic scenario that could bring this social contract into being would have to be "government by Acquisition," that is, conquest by a neighboring country with an already established governing force that could subdue a people and *then* propose a contract. (Or perhaps one of the larger and better-organized families could wage war on another family.) This would be analogous to the thief holding a gun to your head and offering "your money or your life," with one significant difference: there is no going back. That is, once the thief's back is turned, the fact that I "chose" to give him my money does not nullify my right to turn around and try to construct a new "agreement" by turning the gun on him, thus creating a strong incentive for him to "choose" to give the money back. By contrast, once I have agreed to the sovereign's authority, Hobbes says, I can never alter the contract. Perhaps this is because the sovereign's ability to establish a military force means that I can never get the "gun" away from him. But it also could be because such a contract is ongoing and never ultimately completed, whereas the contract with the thief is completed as soon as I turn over my money and he turns to go without killing me.

That is, the social contract is a "covenant." Although covenant is a *kind* of contract—hence the legitimacy of the term "social contract" to describe Hobbes's theory—a contract is defined by Hobbes as a "mutual transferring of Right" that is immediate: I agree to exchange my barrel of apples for a bushel of your corn, and we exchange at the same time. Or I give you my wallet, and you put your gun away. By contrast, a covenant involves a promise of future performance, and therefore involves trust, whether the agreement is that "one of the Contractors, may deliver the Thing contracted for on his part, and leave the other to perform his part at some determinate time after. . . . Or both parts . . . contract now, to performe hereafter." In either case, covenant requires that the party performing in the future "in the mean time be trusted" (*Leviathan*, ch. 14, 193). The social contract is obviously this specific kind of contract, namely, a covenant, because the sovereign's protection of life is ongoing; just because he has preserved your life today does not mean you do not need him to preserve it again tomorrow. Moreover, you can never prove that he has not fulfilled his part of the bargain until you are staring death in the face; at which point, Hobbes indicates, I am free to enter a new agreement with my would-be slayer.[25]

But the foundation for such trust is the very same feature that makes acquisition a more likely foundation of the "contract" than institution: namely, the fact that the sovereign has an army to back him up. Contracts of acquisition "differeth from Soveraignty by Institution, onely in this, That men who choose their Soveraign, do it for fear of one another, and not of him whom they Institute" (ch. 21, 252). Because trust is impossible in the state of nature, the chicken-and-egg problem plagues the transition to civil society: trust is necessary for the sovereign to be instituted, but trust cannot be given until the sovereign is instituted. If, as Hobbes indicates, fear backs up the trust that underlies that social contract, then a fully formed state mechanism, including an army or police force, must be in place at the very moment of the contract's inception. Otherwise, just as I can try to get my money back from the thief once his back is turned, there is no reason for people not to try to subdue the sovereign once *his* back is turned. In *Elements*, in fact, Hobbes says

> Covenants agreed upon by every man assembled for the making of a commonwealth, and put in writing without erecting of a power of coercion, are no reasonable security for any of them that so covenant, nor are to be called laws; and leave men still in the estate of nature and hostility. For seeing the wills of most men are governed only by fear, and where there is no power of coercion, there is no fear, the wills of most men will follow their passions of covetousness, lust, anger, and the like, to the breaking of those covenants, whereby the rest, also, who otherwise would keep them, are set at liberty, and have no law but from themselves. (2.1.6)

In other words, one needs to establish an entire state apparatus, or at least a police force, when the sovereign takes power, or else the social compact is meaningless, and people remain in a state of nature. The ready-made state provided by the conquest scenario ensures that the sovereign's back is in effect *never* turned; and it is this that provides people with a reason for "voluntarily" keeping the contract. This conquest scenario, however, actually begs rather than answers the question of how the social contract comes into being "by Institution," for it entirely sidesteps the question of how Hobbes might hypothesize the initial formation of the conquering society in the first place; it is a problem of endless regression.

The only way for completely antisocial people to unite is by fiat, rational or not. But, Hobbes maintains, that does not mean that such a fiat is at odds with choice, because necessity and liberty are compatible. Although this may seem conveniently circular, it also perfectly illustrates Hobbes's abstractly individualist conception of freedom, key to which is that people do not depend on the will of others either in acting on their desires or in formulating them. Passions and interests come from inside the self, and thus are immune from infringements of outside powers. Action to satisfy desires may be thwarted, but the desires themselves cannot *logically* be interfered with: by definition, I am the only one who can have my own desires and passions. This natural nondependence on the will of others, and the natural givenness of the passions (as well as their alleged diversity among men) is what makes us human. Thus if obligation and obedience in Hobbes's theory are prudential, humans' rational capabilities nevertheless enable them to see that: and Hobbesian man will always freely choose to do whatever is prudent—even if such choice seems to be coerced.

Warrior Women, Invisible Wives

This ambiguity over choice, the social capabilities of humans, and the nature of trust is particularly relevant to the question of women's relationship to freedom. And indeed, considering the place of gender provides significant insights into the apparent paradoxes I have identified about freedom and choice, even as it reveals others. As I have noted already, Gordon Schochet's groundbreaking work on patriarchalism in the social contract theory of the early-modern period in England points out that "sovereignty by acquisition . . . includes patriarchal power" for Hobbes. Indeed, Schochet suggests that patriarchy is the foundation for states of both sorts. Moreover, he points out "that patriarchal power is derived not from the [natural] right of the father but from the tacit or projected consent of the child to be bound by the governance of his parent(s) and from the fourth law of nature, the law of gratitude."[26] Once again, Hobbes collapses the distinction between force and choice. The family, in Schochet's reading, plays a vital role in Hobbes's theory, for it is the only way in which states can possibly get their start, by either path. Thus, the "state of nature" actually contains families, on this reading, in which rules of primitive civil society prevail: "It was as if the state of nature extended only to the door of the household but did not pass over the threshold, for Hobbes claimed that there was private property in the family but not in the state of nature. There can only be private ownership where there is sufficient security, a qualification that precluded the state of nature. But a family, Hobbes wrote, 'is a little city.' " The logical structure of the state of nature, on this reading, involved a population of heads of families, or patriarchs, who were the individuals engaged in a state of war of all against all and who were the parties to any kind of social contract. "Operationally, then, the elemental social unit for Hobbes was not the individual but the family."[27]

Such a reading of Hobbes certainly challenges the more conventional reading of him as an "abstract individualist," which feminists generally follow. It thereby saves Hobbes from a significant feminist criticism, namely, the supposedly isolated state of natural man, where all relationships are contractual; and it introduces a more plausible understanding of human "nature" as deeply situated in social relations, particularly families.[28] Schochet points out that such patriarchalism persists despite the overt antipatriarchalism of Hobbes's theory of political legitimacy, but he never explains *why* the family should take a patriarchal form for Hobbes. Or more specifically, because it was clear why it would take an *authoritarian* form, he never explains why men should be the ones to head these natural families. Joanne Wright further argues that Hobbes "disrupted gender norms" for "instrumental" purposes "to undermine patriarchalism as a political theory,"[29] further raising the question as to why men should be the authoritarians. And yet Hobbes's concern for order brings him to a specifically patriarchalist conclusion, of rule specifically by the father, not the mother, even if that was not his specific intent.

According to Wright, Hobbes's position is puzzling, because the social context in which Hobbes wrote was quite radical from a feminist perspective: "the 1640's in particular witnessed an unusually high rate of women's public religious activity that also led to such political acts as the petitioning of Parliament." She notes that "during the civil war and Interregnum, women engaged in religious debates, preaching, prophesying, speaking and writing according to their consciences. Such acts were deliberately public." Though the explicit issue of gender equality was not always in evidence, substantial numbers of women, particularly Levellers, presented petitions to Parliament and employed an explicitly political "language of rights and liberties to defend their cause"; they "argued openly against clergy and male church members in a way that was considered beyond the pale for a woman." But at the same time, "the gender order of the seventeenth century was premised on classical, Aristotelian, and Biblical notions of women's inferiority in strength and reason." Hobbes, of course, disliked Aristotle, and despite frequent references to the Bible in all his major works never cites it in specific reference to gender. But the point, as Wright puts it, is that in Hobbes's time there was "an increasing gap between what was thought about women and women's behavior."[30]

According to Sara Mendelson and Patricia Crawford, this cultural ambivalence thematizes the socioeconomic context for women as well. Women in Hobbes's time were relatively active politically and economically, according to them, a situation that declined toward the end of the century. Though women had primary responsibility for what are still considered "traditional" women's duties of child care and household management, women of different classes participated in economic production.

Women engaged in a wide variety of activities, including some of the least well paid and respected, such as knitting and bone lace making, running alehouses (often unlicensed, because women were denied licenses on the basis of sex), and serving as "searchers," who would "examine bodies during epidemics of plague to discover the causes of death." Women of the "middling classes" fared better, though the impact of gender as a category of explicit limitation grew with economic status; women assisted their husbands' businesses, and engaged in midwifery, medical healing (though not as doctors), and teaching; they "ran inns, kept shops, and engaged in a range of crafts and trades," though unmarried women had somewhat greater freedom to pursue a wider variety of trades, hold apprenticeships, and train their own apprentices. Married women also had less freedom to spend the money that they earned, or even inherited, because husbands were legally entitled to all such income. Women were also able to write and publish as economic activities, though denied the status of professional authors.[31]

Class divisions certainly impacted on gendered experience and in turn shaped it. Yet women of the lower classes experienced less gender segregation of labor: "the higher the social level, the more rigid were the divisions between men's and women's work. The lower the status, the more likely it was to find men and women engaging in similar tasks." Thus, women of the middle and upper classes were more likely to be engaged in time-consuming domestic household management, including "brewing and distilling," laundry (which even women in royal families were expected to supervise at home), dairy management, spinning and textiles, and "physick," or medical care.[32]

Women's participation in the trades was therefore limited by gender, because women were restrained by their household responsibilities in the consistency with which they could participate in their own or their husbands' trades. But there were more obvious blockages as well. Women often were not trained as apprentices, which compromised their ability to run trades. And by law, women working in their husbands' trades did so as "servants."[33] Widows or married women who worked in different trades from their husbands as *femes sole* had greater freedom and power. But in general, women's status declined vis-à-vis the marketplace as the century progressed, so that by Locke's time "paid work of any kind was becoming socially taboo for women of the common gentry and above." The situation of women, work, and property will be revisited in the following chapter, but what is interesting about Mendelson and Crawford's account is the relative power and equality that women seemed to have in Hobbes's era. Some women even voted before 1642, especially leading up to the Civil War, a practice that was not explicitly outlawed until Locke's era.[34]

We do not know Hobbes's specific thoughts on such matters, but this social context provides a useful framework for evaluating his ambiguity on the subject of women. Hobbes at first provides a view of women that is radically different from his contemporaries, such as Filmer. Like men, women start out perfectly free and equal in Hobbes's state of nature; just as the physical or mental inferiority of some men to others is fairly evened out by the fact that no one can dominate another for long, so women, to the extent that they may be physically less strong than most men, will not thereby be dominated for any sustained period. Indeed, they have as much chance at mental superiority as physical inferiority: "there is not always that difference of strength or prudence between the man and the woman, as that the right [of "Dominion" over each other] can be determined without War."[35] Women are free, like men, to do whatever they want within the realm of whatever they can actually achieve. As Carole Pateman notes, "in Hobbes' state of nature female individuals can be victors in the war of all against all just as often as male individuals." However, she continues, "he remains silent . . . about the status of any men who come under women's power."[36] Indeed, even though he allows that "universally, if the society of the male and the female be such an union, as the one have subjected himself to the other, the children belong to him or her that commands,"[37] it seems doubtful, from his writings, that Hobbes thinks women would gain consistent dominion over men, despite his references to the subordination of male spouses to female monarchs. In *Elements*, Hobbes refers to queens to illustrate the point that "because sometimes the government may belong to the wife only, sometimes also the dominion over the children shall be in her only" (2.4.7). But in *De Cive* and *Leviathan*, his use of queens is to serve as the exception that proves the rule of men's dominion. Further, he seems to drop the claim that women who are not queens might hold dominion in marriage: unless they are queens, either women are married and subservient to men or else they are not married at all.

Indeed, in Hobbes's civil society, women seem to drop out of the picture altogether, and become invisible. For Hobbes defines a family as "a man and his children; or of a man and his servants; or of a man, and his children, and servants together" (*Leviathan*, ch. 20, 257), as women seem to disappear from the scene. And in *De Cive*, Hobbes says, "A *father* with his *sons* and *servants*, grown into civil person by virtue of his paternal jurisdiction, is called a *family*" (9.10). In his earlier *The Elements of Law*, women are mentioned in the definition of family; "the whole consisting of the father or the mother, or both, and of the children, and of the servants, is called a FAMILY." But even here, he immediately follows this with: "wherein the father or master of the family is sovereign of the same and the rest (both children and servants equally) subjects," once again relegating mothers to invisibility.[38] The question is, how did they become so?

Within the state of nature, because of women's overall equality with men in physical strength and "wit," women are not naturally under men's dominion, and indeed seem to be on an equal par with men. Particularly significant to this equality is men's and women's "dominion" over children, the matter on which Hobbes devotes most of his attention to gender. In the state of nature there is no marriage, there being "no lawes of Matrimony"; but given "the naturall inclination of the Sexes, one to another, and to their children" (*Leviathan*, ch. 20, 253), men and women will have some occasion to negotiate with each other in relation to the children they produce. Hobbes notes that "there be always two that are equally parents: the Dominion therefore over the child, should belong equally to both." However, he also notes that this "is impossible; for no man can obey two Masters" (ch. 20, 253). Accordingly, whereas dominion in civil society is generally granted to men because of custom (though Hobbes never speculates on how such customs arose), in the state of nature dominion over each child is to be determined by contract, which may grant dominion to the man or to the woman, or even divide the children among them, as the Amazons supposedly contracted to keep female babies and sent males back to their fathers (ch. 20, 254). But given the difficulty, if not impossibility, of enforceable contracts in the state of nature,[39] Hobbes notes that "If there be no Contract, the Dominion is in the Mother," because without matrimonial laws governing the sexual activity of women, paternity is uncertain. Once this dominion is established, mothers gain an even firmer foothold by "nourishing" the child, rather than "exposing" it and leaving it to die; hence, children owe obedience to her, and her claim to "natural" dominion is stronger than the man's (ch. 20, 254).

Hobbes goes on in this vein to say that if one member of a couple is subject to the other prior to a child's birth, the child is under the latter's dominion, and this can refer to men or women, "as when a Soveraign Queen marrieth one of her subjects" (*Leviathan* ch. 20, 254). When two monarchs of different kingdoms produce a child, dominion is determined again by contract, or in the absence of contract, by residence (that is, the parent who is ruler of whichever of the two countries the parents and child reside in has dominion). Furthermore, bucking a common theoretical tactic in the seventeenth and eighteenth centuries, he nowhere uses the Bible to justify wives' subservience to husbands, even in his references to Adam and Eve, and even though he cites scripture to justify the subservience of sons, daughters, and "maid servants" (ch. 20, 258–60).

At the same time, Hobbes seems to express a considerable degree of gender inequality in his theory. For instance, in his thoughts on succession, he says that "a Child of his own, Male, or Female, be preferred before any other, because men are presumed to be more inclined by nature, to advance their own children, than the children of other men; and of their own, rather a Male than a Female; because men, are naturally fitter than women, for actions of labour and danger" (*Leviathan*, ch. 19, 250). And in *De Cive*, he adds that sons are preferred "because for the most part, although not always, they are fitter for the administration of greater matters, but specially of wars" (9.16). Similarly, in *Elements of Law* Hobbes notes that "generally men are endued with greater parts of wisdom and courage, by which all monarchies are kept from dissolution, than women are; it is to be presumed, where no express will is extant to the contrary, he preferreth his male children before the female. Not but that women may govern, and have in divers ages and places governed wisely, but are not so apt thereto in general as men" (2.4.14). Hobbes also remarks that "for the most part, a man hath more than a woman" the "advantage of so much strength" (*Elements*, 2.4.2).

Hobbes might be forgiven for "preferring" males, even though it does seem to contradict outright what he has already said about the relative equality of strength and wit among all people, including women. The degree of difference in strength and fitness could not be great, as women can get along fine in the state of nature without male protection. Perhaps once we leave the state of nature, small differences in strength make a bigger difference to social utility and commodious living, though Hobbes does not actually say that. Thus, Hobbes's gender discrimination may be subtle, but no less effective than that of other, more overt sexists such as Rousseau.

This subtlety leads to sometimes conflicting readings of Hobbes on the major issue that concerns feminist interpreters, namely women's status in the family, and accordingly for my own purposes, their power and freedom. For women's natural dominion over children is automatically transferred if mothers become subject to other people, such as husbands. Without matrimonial law, marriage "contracts" would be as unenforceable as other kinds of contracts; and as I have already argued, stable long-term relationships are very difficult to establish and maintain in the state of nature, being founded on lust or other short-term interests. However, marriage does exist in civil society, and it takes a patriarchal authoritarian form. The question, then, is: Why? And how?

NATURAL FREEDOM, CIVIL CONTRACT

As I have already indicated, most feminist commentators—as well as the few nonfeminist ones who have paid any attention to the family—believe that marriage exists in the state of nature and that it takes a patriarchal form in that state: that is, that women are subordinated to men in nature.

But although Hobbes makes offhand references to the ways in which laws commonly determine father-right over mother-right, and seems to accept marriage as a given in civil society, he leaves open, without any direct explanation, the larger and prior question of why marriage is necessary in the first place.

This may be because the logic of his argument contradicts the institution of marriage, and particularly patriarchal marriage in which women are subordinate to men. Hobbes's arguments about contracts for dominion over children contain a certain circularity that goes beyond the paradoxical character of contracts in the state of nature. That is, contracts over children are not only unenforceable without a sovereign, just like other contracts; they are virtually unimaginable. That is, if there were no long-term sexual relationships in the state of nature prior to childbirth, then men and women would have absolutely no cause—or even opportunity—to enter into contracts over children, as a woman would be long gone before she knew she was pregnant, making it impossible for a man to know that he fathered a given child, or even to be able to draw the logical association between copulation and birth. And unless the woman is already subordinate to the man, she has no reason to let him know, as that provides him with a motive to seek dominion over the child. This is something that most commentators have overlooked.[40]

The fact that Hobbes does postulate such contracts, however, indicates that he must believe that marriage, or something resembling it, exists naturally, even despite the absence of matrimonial law in the state of nature. But if Schochet is correct that such families are patriarchal, then Hobbes has defined away women's contracting abilities before he has even declared them in his text. Hobbes's abstract individualism notwithstanding, he acknowledges some ability of natural beings to form communities: in the state of nature, "no man can hope by his own strength, or wit, to defend himselfe from destruction, without the help of Confederates" (*Leviathan* ch. 15, 204). And in his exchange with Bramhall, Hobbes declares, "It is very likely to be true, that since the creation there never was a time in which mankind was totally without society."[41] He cites this as the major reason why people might want to keep covenants in the state of nature, for those who do not keep them will be unable to form such alliances. But it also suggests why people might want to establish marriage contracts.

Or rather, it suggests why *men* would want such contracts. Because women have natural dominion over children in the absence of contracts to the contrary, owing to the care they take in preserving a child's life, a natural "confederacy" is built into the relationship between mother and child: "it is to be presumed, that he which giveth sustenance to another, whereby to strengthen him, hath received a promise of obedience in consideration thereof. For else it would be wisdom in men, rather to let their children perish, while they are infants, than to live in their danger or subjection, when they are grown" (*Elements* 2.4.3). Similarly, in *De Cive* Hobbes says, "If therefore she breed him, because the state of nature is the state of war, she is supposed to bring him up on this condition; that being grown to full age he become not her enemy; which is, that he obey her" (9.3). Although dominion can be brought about by conquest, as contracts can, it can also be gained through generation, according to Hobbes (*Leviathan*, ch. 20, 253). Generation is not the same as the "institution" by which contracts can be created, for generation involves the creation and maintenance of a human being. Generation is the condition that makes "contracts by institution" possible. Dominion by generation does involve a kind of contract, however; "begetting" a child does not in and of itself create dominion, but rather "the Childs Consent, either expresse, or by other sufficient arguments declared" (*Leviathan*, ch. 20, 253). Though older children can expressly consent, obviously infants cannot, as they lack language. By the time the child attains the age of speech, and later reason, she is already deeply indebted to her caretaker. In the state of nature, Hobbes has indicated, this caretaker is most likely to be the mother. Thus, mothers and children could work together to subdue individual men, who have no such natural confederacies and who are owed no such deep obligations of loyalty as the child owes the mother. At best, he can only form confederacies by contract with other men, and in the state of nature, contracts are unreliable. So, women are likely to be in a superior position vis-à-vis men in the state of nature.

Recognizing this power women have over children and the strength advantage such confederacy gives them, men would logically want to get in on the act. But how? Marriage contract is the logical answer; but because such contracts must logically violate women's best interests—a woman would have to give up some of her natural dominion over both herself and her children unless men agreed to be subservient—then patriarchal marriage contracts would not likely be made by "institution" in the state of nature. Women would have no reason to seek out such contracts, or subordinate themselves to men if they could negotiate different terms.

That leaves "acquisition," specifically conquest. Women's invisibility in the family—indeed, the fact that they partake in "families" at all—could be a function of the "right of succession to paternal dominion," which occurs by "conquest" rather than by "institution." Hobbes maintains that when someone is vanquished, in order to avoid death he or she will contract to be a servant (*Leviathan*, ch. 20, 255). In this, of course, it is not the conquest itself that produces the right of dominion, Hobbes says, but the covenants that the victor is able to exact from the vanquished under duress. It is in this specific way—not the simple fact of a patriarchal head—that the family is "a little Monarchy" (ch. 20, 257). In Hobbes's description of a family as "a man and his children; or of a man and his servants; or of a man, and his children, and servants together" (ch. 20, 257), the absence of the wife's mention could be attributed to a semantic inclusion of her as a "servant," which Hobbes defines as anyone "who is obliged to obey the commands of any man before he knows what he will command him," a description that could easily cover wives in patriarchal marriage.[42] As Schochet maintains, "Authority over the child in the state of nature belonged to anyone who had the power to kill it. In the first instance this person was always the mother, and the patriarchal title originated in power over her, not in the inherent rights or superiority of either males or fathers."[43] That is, even though patriarchy is "rule by the father," his rule over the children is accessed through his ruling over the mother, who becomes his servant. This might seem to contradict Hobbes's earlier egalitarian views on the ability of women and men to contract equally for dominion of their children, but as Hobbes has just indicated, conquest and contract are not mutually exclusive; indeed, contract is what gives value to conquest. So perhaps women's willingness to agree to contracts of patriarchal marriage must be read in the context of Hobbes's belief that women will always make such contracts from the position of the vanquished, not the victor.

This is a position with which many feminist commentators seem to agree, in different ways. Carole Pateman, for instance, attributes women's submission—or the fact that supposedly free and equal women always seem to lose to men the battles for conquest—to the fact that they are mothers. "When a woman becomes a mother and decides to become a lord and raise her child, her position changes; she is put at a slight disadvantage against men, since now she has her infant to attend to. Conversely, a man obtains a slight advantage over her and is then able to defeat the woman he had initially to treat with as an equal. . . . Mother-right can never be more than fleeting." It is because of this prior subjection, she maintains, that the sexual contract precedes and indeed founds the social contract, which is formed specifically and exclusively by men: "If free and equal women could enter the original contract there is no reason whatsoever why they would agree to create a civil law that secures their permanent subjections as wives. Matrimonial law takes a patriarchal form because *men* have made the original contract."[44] Most other feminist commentators agree that women's subordination occurs in the state of nature prior to the social contract, for similar reasons: pregnancy makes women vulnerable to attack; having infants makes women even more vulnerable to attack; women want to care for their children, even though it makes them vulnerable; women are simply less strong than men regardless of reproductive status; women are less hostile and atomistic than men and thus are not as aggressive as men.[45]

If that is the case, however, then Hobbes's comments suggesting women's equality, and their natural superiority in terms of the dominion of children, need to be reevaluated. For rather than equal partners to a reciprocal contract, it would seem that women are either vanquished, and hence contract with men to be servants, or else they are not vanquished and do not enter into contracts at all.[46] It may be for this reason that the chapter in which women's potential dominion over children is discussed is titled "*Of Dominion* PATERNALL, *and* DESPOTICAL" (*Leviathan*, ch. 20, 251); and indeed throughout the chapter Hobbes includes mother-right under specifically "paternal dominion," either introducing a radically different meaning of the term, or apparently oblivious to the contradiction he poses.

Such treatment of women would cohere with Hobbes's other references to women in several passages—veiled references, at that—where he seems to liken women to property. For instance, in quarrels of competition in the state of nature, men "use Violence, to make themselves Masters of other men's persons, wives, children, and cattell" (*Leviathan* ch. 13, 185). "Of things held in propriety, those that are dearest to a man are his own life, & limbs; and in the next degree, (in most men,) those that concern conjugall affection; and after them riches and means of living" (ch. 30, 382). Hobbes also notes in several places that rape is a way for men to attain honor, being one way to attain dominion over another man's property; thus, "the ancient Heathen did not thinke they Dishonoured, but greatly Honoured the Gods, when they introduced them in their Poems, committing Rapes, Thefts, and other great, but unjust, or unclean acts" (ch. 10, 156). He further maintains that "forcible rapine, and fraudulent surreption of one anothers goods" are among the acts to which natural man is prone, and which the sovereign must outlaw (ch. 30, 383). Such remarks prompt Karen Green to remark that women are "treated as booty, rather than enemies, in war."[47]

This reading lends support to Schochet's interpretation; women exist in the state of nature not in the free and equal status that Hobbes originally describes, but in families where they are "property," or at least "servants." This conclusion is supported by one of Hobbes's most telling passages, where he refers to "the Fathers of families, when by instituting a Common-wealth, they resigned that absolute Power" of life and death over children. His point here is to insist that fathers are still owed "honour due unto them for [providing children's] education" (*Leviathan* ch. 30, 382), but what stands out is that, as Schochet has maintained, Hobbes is asserting that parties to the original contract are male heads of families explicitly, and not merely implicitly. Women would seem to be obliterated from the social contract except via the consent of their "lords"; for in consenting to the authority of my lord, I automatically consent to his consent to a superior lord, that is, the sovereign.

Why, however, would Hobbes write so ambiguously on the issue of women's freedom and equality with men? To understand this requires a rethinking of some of the central claims in the dominant feminist accounts. In the first place, I maintain that mother-right is *not* a disability in Hobbes's state of nature, but a power: and indeed it is *because* it is a power that men are compelled to conquer women. There is no reason to assume, as Pateman and others do, that caring for a child makes a woman less able to defend herself unless we radically alter Hobbesian assumptions, according to which a woman would abandon an infant if she found that it jeopardized her security. Or more likely, given that abandoning it would allow someone else to nourish it and thereby claim its allegiance, she would probably kill it. The idea proffered by Pateman and others that "when a woman becomes a mother and decides to raise her child," such a decision is irrevocable, is simply unsupported by Hobbes's text. A woman would simply revoke her decision as soon as it put her life in danger. Indeed, Hobbes says that the parent who raises the child and thereby gains dominion over it "may alienate them, that is, assign his or her dominion, by selling or giving them in adoption or servitude to others; or may pawn them for hostages, kill them for rebellion, or sacrifice them for peace, by the law of nature, when he or she, in his or her conscience, think it to be necessary" (*Elements*, 2.4.8). This is hardly a vision of nurturant motherhood that seems to be assumed by most feminists.

Pateman asserts that having a child is such a liability that if Hobbesian women were truly rational egoists, they would never raise children in the first place—indeed, they would never have them—which, she claims, points out the illogicality of Hobbes's argument, because the human race would cease to exist.[48] But not only does that ignore the short-term self-interest of Hobbesian men and women—lust, after all, is the foundation of attraction between men and women, according to Hobbes, thus ensuring that children would always be born[49]—it also underplays the instrumental value that children can serve adults in the state of nature. After all, why are children seen as an asset in the first place? The most obvious answer is confederacy and obedience; if children owe obedience to parents out of obligations of gratitude for keeping them alive, such obligations are a rich source of power.

In other words, a more likely scenario than abandoning or killing the child is that, under the power of confederacy, the mother and child would work together to defeat the man, as I suggested previously. Children would not need to be very old to serve as useful confederates, after all; a two-year-old could distract an adult, a five-year-old could steal unobtrusively. The view that infants are burdens pure and simple, placing women at such a disadvantage that cannot be overcome, coheres in an odd way with romantic visions of childhood and motherhood that did not pertain in Hobbes's day but rather developed in the eighteenth and nineteenth centuries.[50] In Hobbes's formula, rather than being a liability, motherhood provides a natural source of power that would give women a strategic advantage over men. Accordingly, motherhood cannot be the cause of woman's downfall in the way Pateman and other feminists maintain.

As I have already argued, however, motherhood does provide men with greater motivation to conquer women, because they thereby gain dominion over children at the same time. Understanding men's *motivation* to conquer women, however, still does not explain how men come to be *successful* in their conquests to the point that patriarchy is established as a general practice. Green, in saying that women are "booty rather than enemies," suggests that "women have little to gain by attempting to vanquish men" because men, viewing women as a resource to provide further offspring, "have little motivation to kill women."[51] This argument does not accurately reflect Hobbesian psychology, however. It is true that, because women can have dominion over children without involving men at all, there is less motive for women to seek dominion over men for this purpose. But there are many other purposes that could be served by women's vanquishing men—as means to another good such as honor or glory, or to obtain what goods a man has, not to mention self-defense, including defense against slavery. At any rate, the fact that a man has reasons not to kill a woman does not mean that she can trust him not to do so; and though enslavement is preferable to death on Hobbes's formula, freedom is further preferable, and a woman has every reason to kill her male captor when she can and reclaim her children. After all, once a man can claim dominion over a woman's child, its advantage to her diminishes, and she has little self-interest in keeping it alive; as long as she is under a man's dominion, her children belong to him, not her. She should only care about keeping them alive if she thinks that eventually she can reclaim them, or their lives serve her interests in some other capacity. So the question of how men as a group are uniformly successful in subjugating women as a group is left unanswered.

My interpretation on this point leads to a second, related, and perhaps more important issue on which I disagree with the apparent feminist consensus. Namely, *marriage does not precede the social contract, but follows from it*. The fact that women would never, as Pateman maintains, "agree to create a civil law that secures their permanent subjections as wives" misses a central point: marriage is a *product of* civil law. When we consent to the social contract, we consent to everything the sovereign decides, and we do not have a say about what laws the sovereign passes. We have no idea ahead of time whether he will decree mother-right or father-right, monogamy or polygamy, or even any family structure at all.[52] All we know is that, as individuals in the state of nature, we are miserable and desperate for relief, a relief that can only come through a "confederacy" that is seemingly impossible to maintain without a common authority over us. Even women's "natural" confederacy with children might have a certain degree of uncertainty; children can always be ungrateful and turn on their caregiver, as wrong as this might be in Hobbes's view. Given this, it makes sense within Hobbes's theory for women to consent to the social contract, the above passage about "fathers" consenting to the social contract notwithstanding. Indeed, that passage does not necessarily have to be interpreted to mean that *only* fathers consent. He could be arguing that *when* fathers consent, they do not give up the right to gratitude from children, but that does not preclude mothers from similarly consenting and similarly retaining the right to gratitude. Admittedly, the question as to why Hobbes refers to fathers and not mothers is suspicious, but as I have noted, Hobbes includes mothers' authority under the term "paternal."

The more important point is that, only then, *after* women have consented to the social contract, could women's subjugation come into play. That is, it is logical for a sovereign concerned with order and security to command an authoritarian family structure, for in this way the sovereign channels men's natural desire for dominion into a formal structure that feeds the sovereign's interests: that is, the sovereign need not control everyone directly, but only heads of families, who in turn would keep their respective family members in line. Without an authoritarian family structure, the danger of people's interactions in daily commerce and the like degenerating into civil chaos is much greater; families could provide a structure of discipline, habituating men and women to obedience and curbing their natural hostility and distrust. Thus, rather than predating the social contract, I maintain that the family is a by-product of the social contract, created by the sovereign to maintain order.

However, why a *patriarchal* authoritarian family structure? This makes less logical sense from the perspective of order, though perhaps it is logical enough. Given men's envy of women's natural dominion over children, and given their continued desire for "honor," which includes dominion over other people, particularly over children but also over women through means that include rape and adultery, it would make sense for the sovereign to write laws establishing father-right in order to secure peace among men. Patriarchal matrimonial law would thus help secure peace by establishing territorial or property rights over women—and perhaps even more important, over the products of women's bodies, namely children—which the sword of Leviathan now upholds.[53] The feminist objection that women would not consent to such subordination—such an obvious problem in the state of nature—dissolves in civil society, for such consent would not have to be "given" in any express way; it would automatically follow from women's original consent to the sovereign. In this, the family does for women what the social contract does for men; it takes away their ultimate natural powers. That the social contract alone is insufficient to tame women's powers—that the sovereign must also authorize the patriarchal family—is the only relevant difference between the sexes. For rather than being inferior in the state of nature, women are at least potentially, if not actually, superior.

It is this natural superiority that casts into doubt the idea that women as a group are subordinated to men as a group in nature. Certainly one could argue that women would make themselves worse off by failing to consent to patriarchal marriage, because the general disruption caused by men's fighting over them and their reproductive ability creates a general situation of disorder in which women could also be killed, even by accident. This danger could be enough to justify their voluntary submission. Such reasoning, however, is weakened by the fact that the men engaged in such contests are more likely to kill *each other*, thereby leaving women in a superior position to then force the remaining men to submit. Indeed, it is puzzling why Hobbes did not recommend matriarchy from the start, because that would remove much of men's motive for dominion over women, and hence a major source of conflict. Hobbes's reference to the minor disadvantages women supposedly have compared with men, such as weeping, demonstrates the weakness of his argument when it comes to differentiating among citizens in terms of gender. Although Hobbes can use the rational fiat to claim men's consent to the sovereign because the state of war unconditionally threatens all, women's consent to men's dominion cannot be rationally deduced in the state of nature because reproduction does not threaten women. Or, to be more precise, to the degree that reproduction does threaten women, the family cannot protect them. Thus, although the picture Hobbes seems to draw indicates that the family predates the social contract as Schochet and others argue, the logical tenets of his theory do not require it, nor even assert it with any consistency: the social contract, instead, must predate the family.

Hobbes's explanation in *De Cive* of how "dominion passes from the mother to others" supports my argument. There are four ways: if the mother "exposes" the infant, and abandons its care; if the mother is taken prisoner; if she becomes "a subject under what government soever," because the sovereign has dominion over her child as he or she does over everyone living in the relevant territory covered by the sovereignty; and "if a woman *for society's sake* [emphasis added] give herself to a man on this condition, that he shall bear the sway" (9.4–5). The first two ways pertain most obviously in the state of nature, but the latter two pertain to civil society. The third way particularly does so, as Hobbes is saying that if a woman consents to a sovereign, then her children are contained in that consent, and the sovereign can give them to a man he then designates as her husband. But it is the fourth way that is the most interesting. It suggests that women recognize that their reproductive and sexual capacities are a source of conflict among men, who can only be civilized through gaining patriarchal dominion, as I have previously argued. But more significantly, it suggests that women can give up their individual good for the good of the whole. This could possibly serve as evidence of the "altruism" that Green posits, but it is more likely evidence of the social contract predating patriarchy. For there is no "society" prior to the contract, and hence no "good" of society. Thus, submitting to patriarchal marriage "for society's sake" could happen *only* after a social contract was formed; or at best, it could happen concurrently with the social contract's formation. Because Hobbes rejects the idea of *summum bonum* (*Leviathan*, ch. 11, 160), the good of this society has to be order and peace, the first law of nature; but without the surety of a superior power that the sovereign ensures, it would be irrational and contrary to self-interest for women to give over such powers to men without more of a guarantee than a simple reassurance from a single man. As Hobbes notes, "the mutual aid of two or three men is of very little security; for the odds on the other side, of a man or two, giveth sufficient encouragement to an assault. And therefore before men have sufficient security in the help of one another, their number must be so great, that the odds of a few which the enemy may have, be no certain and sensible advantage" (*Elements*, 1.19.3). Such reasoning might lead natural woman to prefer the protection of a sovereign to that offered by confederacy with her children. But Hobbesian woman does not strike one as the type to be beguiled by such a trade with a single man, because she could probably do a better job of protecting herself. Or, even if she could not, she would *believe* that she could, for people in the state of nature suffer from the fault of "Vainglory, a foolish over-rating of their own worth" (*Leviathan*, ch. 27, 341). That is, they believe that they are superior to others, even if they are not so in fact.[54] That is one of the charcteristics that makes the state of nature so dangerous.

If, as Green suggests (and others imply), women are in fact limitedly altruistic because of their propensity to care for children, even when that means servitude to a man, then Hobbes's whole foundation of rational egoism goes up in smoke. Women's voluntary subordination is much more acceptable, however, if we assume that the social contract is already in place; in such a context, it might behoove a woman to give up her dominion, and her struggle to gain dominion, for the sake of calming conflicts between men. Or rather, she consents to do so by virtue of the fact that the sovereign, whom she has authorized, commands it. In theory, of course, Hobbes has to allow the possibility that the sovereign could just as readily legislate matriarchal families where women have power and dominion over men; men, after all, seem to be the troublemakers who need controlling. But this, Hobbes says with a matter-of-fact shrug, just does not seem to have happened very often, if at all ("for the most part Common-wealths have been erected by the Fathers, not by the Mothers of families"[*Leviathan* ch. 20, 253]). In this oft-cited sentence, however, he is not *recommending* father-right and patriarchy as much as *observing* it.[55] That is, women "consent" to men's dominion just as men "consent" to their own imprisonment when they break the law; in both cases, they consent by virtue of the fact that they have consented to the sovereign's authority. But of course such "explanation" is made possible only by virtue of Hobbes's normative framework, wherein he clearly endorses women's subjugation as more conducive to social order and peace.

The implications of all this for freedom might seem quite obvious. Women are naturally as free as men in the state of nature and civil society alike: the fact that men usually have dominion over women does not make the latter less free. And it is the desire for dominion, not liberty per se, that produces the state of war (*De Cive*, 10.8). Women's freedom depends only on their choice or consent, which is the expression of their will. If women are subject to more constricted experiences because of men's dominion, then their decision structure may be different than men's. But because they consented, one way or another, to men's dominion, it does not make sense in Hobbesian terms to say that they are "less free" than men. Within a narrower or wider range of options, what determines my freedom for Hobbes is whether I am able to act on the desire I have in the "final deliberation." As I discussed earlier, if a battered woman must decide between leaving her spouse and living in poverty on the one hand or remaining subject to abuse and maintaining a higher standard of living on the other, she must decide which of these options she prefers to avoid. The fact that her spouse does not have to make such a choice does not affect her ability to decide for herself.

But most contemporary readers would find this argument a bit disingenuous, and might be forced to dismiss Hobbes altogether if that was really the only conclusion that could be drawn from his work. Along with women's invisibility in the family, we must assume, comes a loss of freedom, particularly given women's subservient status in the family in civil society. Even if they are as free as men in the state of nature, in civil society women are considerably less free than men. Not only are they subject to the sovereign, as men are, but they are subject to their husbands. Hence, despite the fact, cited earlier, that women managed to gain some economic power in Hobbes's seventeenth century, they could not legally control the money they earned or inherited; a woman engaging in her husband's trade on her own (rather than as his servant) could even be subject to prosecution. Women were denied poor relief by parishes who sought to remove single women from their jurisdiction and tried to make them ineligible in other ways; and household service was the major outlet for women's economic support, an employment that made them vulnerable to sexual assault with little recourse to the protection that the law is supposed to provide under the social contract.[56] Such economic and social inequality forces women, by the sovereign law, to depend on individual men.

Is such dependence necessarily incompatible with freedom, however? In the *Elements*, Hobbes says, "Freedom . . . in commonwealths is nothing but the honour of equality of favour with other subjects, and servitude the estate of the rest. A freeman therefore may expect employments of honour, rather than a servant. And this is all that can be understood by the liberty of the subject. For in all other senses, liberty is the state of him that is not subject" (*Elements*, 2.4.9). Freedom in civil society thus bears hardly any resemblance to Hobbes's central definition in *Leviathan*: "the absence of . . . external Impediments of motion" (ch. 21, 261). That meaning of freedom would seem to apply only to the state of nature, which everyone gives up under the social contract. The sovereign presumably grants certain subjects more favor to do what they want, but it is not an entitlement, and therefore not "freedom," which is linked to "right." Hobbes calls consenters to the social compact "freemen," but this is not because choosing the sovereign gives them any rights over him. Rather, under the social contract, "liberty is not any exemption from subjection and obedience to the sovereign power, but a state of better hope than theirs, that have been subjected by force and conquest." Even by this more limited understanding of civil freedom as "the honour of equality of favour with other subjects," however, women still fall short, making up "the rest" for whom "servitude [is] the estate" (*Elements*, 2.4.9).

If, as I suggested earlier, freedom in civil society is both defined and restricted by law, then women's freedom, like men's, depends on the law. And if those laws unilaterally grant men dominion over women, so that their lives are determined by men's desires, preferences, and actions, then their liberty is more proscribed than men's. Just as Hobbes seems torn between men's radical freedom and his fear of what they will do with that freedom, he seems similarly torn between women's radical freedom as individuals and what their radical freedom might do to men, particularly given women's considerable power to form alliances that not only exclude men, but threaten them. In short, as evidenced by the anarchic picture he paints of the state of nature, Hobbes is afraid of what people will do with their freedom. Though Wright may be correct that Hobbes displays less "anxious masculinity" than other Enlightenment figures,[57] he nevertheless displays considerable "anxious humanity"; that is, he is worried about all human beings, both male and female. But although all must give up their natural freedom in order to have a secure society, it is clear that women must give up more of that freedom. That women have more natural power than men—rather than less, as the popular feminist reading suggests—the power to give life as well as the power to take it away, necessitates greater restraint. Furthermore, it is clear that women give up that freedom specifically to the end of greater freedom for men: within Hobbes's zero-sum formulation of liberty, the smaller the "environ" or "certain space" (*Leviathan*, ch. 21, 261) within which women can move, the larger the space for men. The sovereign determines those spaces by matrimonial law, and Hobbes indicates in most cases that the sovereign will see the advantages of constructing those laws to give husbands power over wives. Just as Hobbes begins natural men in the most radically free state and ends them up in the most repressive political regime, so does he start women in the most radically free and equal position and land them in the most authoritarian patriarchal families. The formation and terms of the marriage contract provide a direct echo of Hobbes's argument concerning the formation and terms of the social contract; though I would maintain, in contrast to Pateman and others, that what is echo and what is original is less than certain.

The logic of women's lesser freedom can thus be explained by the pragmatic aspects of Hobbes's theory. It may be true in some sense that people have more absolute liberty in the state of nature, but people can also see that such liberty is not worth very much to them in their "nasty, brutish and short" lives. They must spend so much time defending what they have that they are prevented from seeking other things they want. Thus, Hobbes notes that of the "two general grievances" of man in civil society, "loss of liberty" is inconsequential, because in the state of nature

> a subject may no more govern his own actions according to his own discretion and judgment, or (which is all one) conscience, as the present occasions from time to time shall dictate to him; but must be tied to do according to that will only, which once for all he had long ago laid up, and involved in the wills of the major part of an assembly, or in the will of some one man. But this is really no inconvenience. For, as it hath been shewed before, it is the only means by which we have any possibility of preserving ourselves. (*Elements*, 2.5.2)

Hence, people freely act to curtail their liberty when a powerful leader affords them an opportunity to establish order and security for their lives and possessions. In this regard, Hobbes could be taken as saying that liberty, while the most fundamental natural quality of humanity, is not the most important one; security and order are immensely more important than freedom, and for that reason we *give up* liberty to the sovereign in exchange for such security.

In invoking "the Histories, and Philosophy of the Antient Greeks, and Romans" Hobbes maintains that what is important, and what he is concerned to promote, "is not the Libertie of Particular men; but the Libertie of the Commonwealth" (*Leviathan*, ch. 21, 266). The commonwealth then limits individual freedom to maintain order. The social contract is reciprocal in that both sovereign and subject receive something of importance to them, but what they receive is nonparallel and nonreciprocal: obedience and dominion on the one hand and protection on the other. Thus, on this reading, whereas the social contract is the *result of* individual free choice, namely, consent, individual freedom does not lie at the heart of what the contract is *about*; rather, the object of the contract is order and security. In this sense, Hobbes can be seen to decenter liberty; freedom is not an end in itself, but rather a means to other things that are of greater importance, such as security.

But if security is the primary goal of government, then why does Hobbes structure his theory such that people need to consent to the social contract? Why does there need to be a *contract* at all? Divine right, it would seem, would be as logical and sensible a formula as any, a useful myth that could be part of what the sovereign "teaches" his subjects to believe, to keep people in line. Or if Hobbes does not wish to accept divine right, then why does he not argue for hereditary monarchy on the basis of simplicity in succession, since moments when a sovereign dies are the most fraught with dangers of instability, rather than on the "fact" that people "prefer" their own sons and other family members? Indeed, why not, as Hume argued, simply say that we should obey whatever government is in power? In his remarks about government by acquisition or conquest, Hobbes basically does argue that, but he still insists that we will consent to whatever power shows its force to us and that this consent is what obligates us. By contrast, Hume's authoritarian theory of political legitimacy and allegiance is based on a *rejection* of consent as the foundation of government, and this rejection is really the only position consistent with authoritarianism.[58]

These questions are clarified and reinforced by the consideration of gender, because the same question is posed, with greater specificity: why should women submit to patriarchal marriage and subordinate themselves to a husband? Though gender clarifies the questions, however, it does not clarify the answer, as I have shown, for the logic of women's consent is even less self-evident than that of average male citizens. Assuming that gender is deployed instrumentally by Hobbes, as Wright suggests, we can postulate that Hobbes uses the family to lay out the logic and rationale of such consent; but that still does not tell us why he seeks to employ this logic. In this regard, Stanlick may be correct that women's subservience to men in the family serves as the fundamental model of subservience of all men and women in the social contract.[59]

THE SOCIAL CONSTRUCTION OF FREEDOM

As these questions suggest, central aspects of Hobbes's theory seem contradictory, or at least paradoxical, particularly from a negative liberty perspective, and particularly in his conception of choice. The absolutism of the social contract is especially problematic. I am obligated by my own consent whether or not I have actually agreed; for instance, if I am one of those "that Voted against it." I am similarly bound if I "agreed" unwittingly; say that I show up at the congregation, highly skeptical, and before I know it my presence is taken to authorize the new sovereign to put me in jail for not giving him my enthusiastic endorsement. Moreover, even though the "loss of liberty" in civil society is not really that great a loss—because natural freedom is not worth much in a natural state of insecurity and fear—nevertheless "it *appeareth* a great inconvenience to every man in particular, to be debarred of this liberty, because every one apart considereth it as in himself, and not as in the rest" (*Elements*, 2.5.2, emphasis added). Not only do people misunderstand what liberty is, according to Hobbes; they also overvalue it, because they are atomistic individuals and cannot think in terms of either the collective interest or their own long-term rational self-interest.

It is because most people are confused in their thinking about freedom that Hobbes deploys his "rational fiat," which compels people logically to choose what Hobbes thinks they actually should choose. Whatever I do, the benefits of civil society over the state of nature compel me to consent implicitly. Hence, "contract by inference" entails "whatsoever sufficiently argues the will of the contractor" (*Leviathan*, ch. 14, 193–94), and one can always assume that the individual wills his survival. This feature lends positive liberty elements to his theory. Given the rational egoism of Hobbesian man, and given that men's supreme interest of staying alive can be met only through the social contract with the sovereign, people are logically compelled to consent. It would be irrational and contrary to their individual interests for them not to, because only the sovereign can enforce the laws of nature and ensure that they check men's unbridled and conflicting passions. And anyone who acts to make herself worse off (as I would if I refused consent to the sovereign) can be assumed not to know what she is doing.

Why do I say this is positive liberty, however? I say this because of the social constructivist character of Hobbes's argument, in which he crafts a civil society that is structured to compel individuals to make particular choices and have certain desires. Portraying Hobbes as a social constructivist might seem to be a difficult case to sustain, because citizens only have to fear the sovereign sufficiently to obey the law and keep order. After all, does it really matter what people are like, or how they will behave naturally, if an absolute sovereign can keep everyone in line with the sword of Leviathan? "People flourish in Monarchy" not because of the sovereign's right to rule per se, but rather "because they obey him" (*Leviathan* ch. 30, 380). On this reading, Hobbes does not need to care what people are actually like; it is sufficient that enough people are likely to be hostile and aggressive without a sovereign to reign them in. It is the possibility of violence that justifies his belief that all really do consent whether they realize it or not. In this light, Hobbes does not need to "produce" people in any particular way to make this happen.

But the problem with this line of thinking is that citizens' obedience cannot be exacted through force alone; the sword of Leviathan cannot be everywhere at once. The problem that perpetually faces students of Hobbes is how fear can be such an effective motivator when the state is limited in its ability to control people on a daily basis. If fear is my sole reason for obedience, then it is logical to assume that I will disobey whenever I have reason to believe I will not get caught—which might logically be quite often. Instead, Hobbes hits on a much more efficient, and effective, answer: namely, to create people to want the very order that the sovereign is to impose, to "tame" natural man into civil man and substitute one set of desires for another within the framework of rational egoism. As Stephen Holmes puts it in his introduction to *Behemoth*, Hobbes believed that "to govern human beings you must govern their opinions; and if you cannot do this by force or threat of force, you must find other means." Hence, "The ultimate source of political authority is not coercion of the body, but captivation of the mind. The subjective or psychological basis of authority provides the core of Hobbes's political science."[60]

Hobbes's constructivism operates in several ways. A significant dimension of it lies in the logic of his argument. Gauthier describes Hobbes as engaging in a "resolutive-compositive" methodology, in which ideas, concepts, and phenomena are broken down into their component parts and then rebuilt by placing their parts together once again, much as one takes apart a watch to understand the workings of each part of the mechanism and then puts the parts together again in order for the mechanism to work.[61] Hobbes seeks to align himself with mathematicians, and the structure of his argument with the principles of geometry: "So the Geometrician," Hobbes says, "from the construction of Figures, findeth out many Properties thereof; and from the Properties, new Ways of their Construction, by Reasoning." And "nothing is produced by Reasoning aright, but generall, eternall, and immutable Truth" (*Leviathan*, ch. 46, 682). Similarly, in his critique of Thomas White's *De Mundo*, Hobbes maintains that in all other fields of science besides geometry, "some have spoken more plausibly than others have; but none of them has taught anything that was not open to question."[62] His critical posture suggests to the reader that Hobbes himself is engaged in a scientific effort of the mathematical sort.

It is thus with the rigor of geometrical proof that Hobbes executes his argument to compel his readers to agree that he is right. In this, despite positing a radical notion of natural freedom to do whatever one is able, Hobbes also demonstrates a significant concern about the bad choices people might make. He thereby, as I have shown, binds them to an absolute sovereign who can make the right choices for them, but does so through a conception of consent that substitutes hypothetical choice for actual; given the "nasty, brutish, and short" state of nature (*Leviathan*, ch. 13, 186), anyone voting against the social compact "is not to be understood as if he meant it" (ch. 14, 192). Accordingly, as I noted earlier, "as well he that *Voted for it*, as he that *Voted against it*" (ch. 18, 229) gives consent to the compact. Similarly, as I also noted earlier, Hobbes declares that law will "direct and keep [people] in such a motion, as not to hurt themselves by their own impetuous desires, rashnesse, or indiscretion as Hedges are set, not to stop Travellers, but to keep them in the way" (ch. 30, 388). By requiring people to make the choices Hobbes wants them to make, he constructs "man" in a way to make such restriction voluntary: we freely choose to limit our freedom. This construction of freedom shapes the ability of subjects to see and define themselves, their options, and their relation to the social context in which they live.

The logical compulsion at work in Hobbes's reasoning ties to a second and perhaps more complicated constructivist aspect of his argument, which lies in his use of language and the way that he defines his terms; for "the first use of language, is the expression of our conceptions, that is, the begetting in one another the same conceptions that we have in ourselves" (*Elements*, 1.13.2). Hobbes maintains that there are "four legitimate ends of speech." First is narration of events, which he calls "history." Second is "rhetoric," which means "to move our hearer's mind towards performing something." Third is "to glorify [certain] deeds and, by celebrating them, to hand them down to posterity," which he calls "poetry." And fourth is "to teach, i.e. to demonstrate the truth of some assertion universal in character." It is the last of these that has the closest relation to truth; for teaching involves "explaining the definitions of names in order to eliminate ambiguity . . . [and] deducing necessary consequences from the definitions," which he calls "logic" (*De Mundo*, 1.2). And logic is the proper domain of philosophy, in all its various forms; in addition to "geometry and arithmetic, which are usually combined under the name of mathematics," there are "ethics or moral philosophy," which "concerns the passions, the manners and the aims or purposes of men," and "politics or civil philosophy," which "concerns human society and discusses civil laws, justice and all the other virtues." But all kinds of "philosophy should . . . be treated logically, for the aim of its students is not to impress [others], but to know with certainty. So philosophy is not concerned with rhetoric. . . . philosophy is not to do with history, and much less with poetry, for the latter relates deeds of great moment, and it deliberately sets aside truth" (*De Mundo*, 1.3).

The juxtaposition of philosophy with rhetoric and history raises some legitimate questions about what work Hobbes is himself engaged in. In dealing with concepts, particularly, the "compositive" part of Hobbes's argument involves interpretation and reconstruction: he puts together a picture that does not, from the reader's perspective in the twenty-first century, objectively cohere with "reality" but rather with how Hobbes sees that reality, even if he thinks that how he sees it is the right way. In this, he illustrates the point that I made in the previous chapter, that social constructivism is an inevitable function of language. We apprehend the world in and through language; physical or material entities that we encounter must be given meaning in our minds through language in order for us to make sense of the world. Similarly, all words, even as signifiers of concrete things in an apparently direct correlation, such as a tree or a rock (as opposed to a more esoteric concept such as happiness), are themselves abstractions: all rocks and trees are different from one another, yet there is a collection of ideas that we hold in our minds that makes the use of those words to describe certain objects acceptable to others. Hobbes himself seems to acknowledge this when he maintains that "' perception' is to do not with things themselves but with the words and terms by which we express our judgment about things. So it is said to be of universals. Things are not universals, but names are" (*De Mundo*, 4.1). But the abstraction involved in this process means that the use of these words could and likely does have an interpretive component as well as a descriptive one, such as when I have to decide whether something is large enough to be a rock, or is more accurately called a pebble. And such interpretation leads to normative elements in terms of how one classifies things in the world.

When one considers more abstract entities, such as justice, freedom, or obligation, the interpretive and normative components of language take on even greater importance. Consider, for instance, that Hobbes defines freedom to exclude the formation of will; as I discussed earlier, in Hobbes's exchange with Bramhall, it is precisely by constructing the will as constituted by acting (or refraining from acting) on desire, and not as a process of forming desire, that Hobbes is able to exclude the will from his definition of freedom. His construction of equality in mental and physical terms, rather than more abstractly in terms of rights, similarly produces a particular understanding of humanity and creates specific premises that enable him to draw the conclusions he does about the necessity of an absolute monarch. Though Hobbes claims that philosophy should be allied with logic, and should lead to "certainty" of knowledge, the way in which he defines the "proper signification" of his terms, the way in which he produces meaning, constructs an interpretive framework that compels the reader to agree with his argument.[63] He is trying to construct meaning, a particular way of understanding and living in the world, to produce agreement that his way is the best way. It thus appears to the twenty-first-century reader that Hobbes seeks "to move our hearer's mind towards performing something,"which is the meaning of rhetoric, not philosophy (*De Mundo*, 1.2). In particular, he wants us to move our minds toward obedience.

Thus, an important part of Hobbes's constructivism is the "story" that he tells his reader, and the picture of reality that he seduces, if not subdues, his reader into accepting. But this further ties into a more proactive construction of citizens through civic education; the "begetting in one another the same conceptions" that I cited earlier as "the first use of language" is what Hobbes calls "teaching." Education is an important though submerged and subtle theme in Hobbes's writings. But education ties to the significance of language in the construction of reality, the different forms of language and ways in which it is used. Of particular concern to Hobbes is the way in which most education is conducted in his contemporary society; rather than "truth," which is deduced by scientific method, students are offered "opinion" that is not grounded in facts. One of the axes Hobbes seeks to grind is that many "learned" men are actually "*dogmatici*," who "take up maxims from their education, and from the authority of men, or of custom, and take the habitual discourse of the tongue for ratiocination." These he contrasts to "*mathematici*," men who "proceedeth evidently from humble principles," that is, truly utilize reason. The former "are imperfectly learned, and with passion press to have their opinions pass everywhere for truth, without any evident demonstration either from experience, or from places of Scripture of uncontroverted interpretation." As a result, whereas the *mathematici* pursue truth, *dogmatici* commit the "crime of breeding controversy" (*Elements*, 1.13.4). Because they deal not in "knowledge" but only "opinion," they therefore do not "teach" anything, but only try to "persuade." "The art of controversy" is "one in which there is little honour," and Hobbes accuses its practitioners of "seeking glory, and esteeming truth only afterwards" (*De Mundo*, 1.4).

Hobbes barely hides his scorn for fact that it this kind of person, the "Aristotelians," who dominate the universities. Their claims that Aristotle's writings should be taken as "truth" are unsupportable: "I know that this doctrine of mediocrity is Aristotle's, but his opinions concerning virtue and vice, are no other than those which were received then, and are still by the generality of men unstudied; and therefore not very likely to be accurate" (*Elements*, 1.17.14). Similarly, in *Leviathan* Hobbes denigrates the universities: "since the Authority of Aristotle is onely current there, that study is not properly Philosophy (the nature whereof dependeth not on Authors,) but Aristotelity. . . . for the study of Philosophy it hath no otherwise place, then as a handmaid to the Romane Religion." He then details the numerous errors that Aristotelian philosophy—combined with "Blindnesse of understanding"—has brought "to the Universities, and thence into the Church" (ch. 46, 688). And in *Behomoth*, Hobbes scorns, "the babbling philosophy of Aristotle," which "serves only to breed disaffection, dissension, and finally sedition and civil war."[64]

Yet despite his mockery of the "persuasion" these academics engage in rather than "teaching," one might argue that persuasion seems to be an important part of Hobbes's goal, as I suggested earlier. Indeed, it seems to play a significant role in what he calls education. Hobbes likens education to agriculture: "the labour bestowed on the Earth, is called *Culture*; and the education of Children a *Culture* of their mindes" (*Leviathan*, ch. 31, 399). As any suburban homeowner knows, though, once pernicious weeds like kudzu get into the soil, they are difficult to eradicate, and if left alone will destroy the crops and flowers one wishes to grow. Thus, the key task facing the sovereign "is the rooting out from the consciences of men all those opinions which seem to justify, and give pretence of right to rebellious actions" such as conscientious objection, civil disobedience, or holding the sovereign to the law, ideas that contemporary westerners associate with the freedoms granted by liberal democracy. Hobbes derides these ideas as the products of the dogmatics: they "have delivered nothing concerning morality and policy demonstratively; but being passionately addicted to popular government, have insinuated their opinions, by eloquent sophistry." The task of "unlearning" erroneous beliefs is a difficult one: "opinions which are gotten by education, and in length of time are made habitual, cannot be taken away by force, and upon the sudden: they must therefore be taken away also, by time and education." The challenge of unlearning poor education is to be met by the provision of proper education: "there is no doubt, if the true doctrine concerning the law of nature, and the properties of a body politic, and the nature of law in general, were perspicuously set down, and taught in the Universities, but that young men, who come thither void of prejudice, and whose minds are yet as white paper, capable of any instruction, would more easily receive the same, and afterward teach it to the people, both in books and otherwise, than now they do the contrary" (*Elements*, 2.9.8). In other words, they should read Hobbes's own works.

If they were to do so, however, the shape of education would be quite different. Geoffrey Vaughan argues that despite Hobbes's attention to the academy—or perhaps because of it, and what he sees as its failures—it is political education that most concerns him. According to Vaughan, the social contract does not merely involve a relinquishment of the right to harm others; it is also a relinquishment of the right of private judgment.[65] The kind of education offered in the universities can only yield the illusion that our private judgment is infallible, that we are learned, that we have knowledge, when all we have is opinion. This overestimation of our intellectual powers will inevitably lead to diversity of judgment about truth. Such judgment will not limit itself to the texts of Aristotle, of course, but threatens to spread to other areas, including politics. One might think that Hobbes's answer is thus to educate people to true knowledge and proper training in reason. Hobbes maintains that "the name 'man' is understood when this word brings to mind not only a human shape but also its reasoning-capacity," which distinguishes humans from "brute beings" (*De Mundo*, 4.1). Yet, although Hobbes believes humans are inescapably self-interested and follow a rational egoism to satisfy their interests, they are not often rational in the full sense of the term; hence the preponderance of the desire for vainglory, pursuit of which often appears irrational. Hobbes himself at times juxtaposes "prudence" to "reason," saying in chapter 46 of *Leviathan*, under the subheading "Prudence no part of Philosophy," that prudence "is not attained by Reasoning, but found as well in Brute Beasts, as in Man" (682). Because prudence is the primary motivation to self-interest and security, then it may be that reason, even in the narrow sense of self-interest, may not be as dominant as readers of Hobbes commonly believe. Indeed, Holmes goes so far as to say that Hobbes believed humans were often "stupidly indifferent to self-preservation. Human behavior is largely determined by beliefs, and most beliefs are irrational, even absurd."[66]

Yet it is difficult to ignore Hobbes's central claim that people never act to make themselves worse off, which suggests that they are indeed rational in a narrow sense that pertains to immediate, rather than long-term, self-interest. For we must recall that "self interest" for Hobbes can be defined in two ways: what will make the individual happy or satisfied, and what would keep her safe. Killing you might bring me enormous satisfaction because of the glory that I gain, but it is an extremely risky action that could very well get me killed, or at least injured. Thus, the question of whether killing you is in my interest is an open one: as I said at the beginning of the chapter, because Hobbes defines desire as highly subjective, it would seem that my interests are served by doing what I want, even if others are equally justified in trying to stop me because what I want contradicts their interests. But because Hobbes declares life and safety to be the primary goal of all humans, then my interests are served by having laws and a monarch to obey, and then obeying them, even when they run contrary to what I (think I) want.

THE CONTAINMENT OF DIFFERENCE

It is clear, however, that reason in the larger sense of philosophical ratiocination is not something that most people do or perhaps even can engage in. So Hobbes does not emphasize teaching logic to the masses but rather seeks to give people the right opinions. And it is in this giving of opinion that social constructivism plays such an important part. The major source of strife, whether in the state of nature or civil society, is the considerable variety of opinion among men. Because of differences among people, we have potentially great differences in our opinions; and because of pride and vainglory, we all assume we are right, so those opinions have considerable intensity. To reduce conflict, therefore, the source of conflict must be eliminated, and the most effective way to achieve that is by giving people similar opinions. This is done by regulating behavior through the promulgation and execution of law: "For the Actions of men proceed from their Opinions, and in the wel governing of Opinions, consisteth the well governing of mens Actions, in order to their Peace, and Concord" (*Leviathan*, ch. 18, 233). By requiring people to behave in certain ways, the law should make them start to think in certain ways, and that is the ultimate goal of the sovereign. Because diversity of judgment leads to conflict in society just as it leads to conflict in the state of nature, "it is, therefore, the exclusive right to exercise political judgment that most clearly characterizes the sovereign."[67]

Hobbes makes this message clear in *Behemoth, or the Long Parliament*, where he reviews the civil war, the mistakes that were made, the forces of human nature that led to it, and what must be done to forestall such an event from recurring. Structured as a dialogue between "A," who lived through the civil war, and "B," a younger man who seeks to learn about it, A starts the "lesson" by outlining the reasons for the conflict, the first three of which center on differences of religious opinion. The first concerned "ministers of Christ" who claimed a right "to govern every one his parish," thus challenging the absolute authority of the king. The second was papists, who would support the same kind of challenge by the pope. Third was sects such as Quakers and Anabaptists who supported religious freedom, and thus diversity.[68] All of these people were dangerous not simply because they challenged the unified authority of the monarch in practical terms by proclaiming conflicting rights of governance. Even more pernicious was the promulgation of diverse opinions not founded on reason. Diversity of opinion was a danger to the state; hence, the fourth reason for the political conflict was academics who believed in the virtues of democracy. But diversity of religious belief was a particular problem; as Holmes points out, religious belief is the number one proof that humans are irrational, because of the diversity in those beliefs. Indeed, they are founded on the antithesis of reason: the religious zealotry of people who do not understand what they are saying, and are willing to sacrifice themselves precisely because they do not understand it.

Such irrational zealotry is why the sovereign must be absolute, and why the absolute right of the sovereign to exercise political judgment is the key lesson that citizens must be taught. Thus, Vaughan argues that the purpose of political education is to produce not "the knowledge of natures, but . . . the *discipline* of citizens. To this end, according to Hobbes, the spread of knowledge by precept, of knowledge proven true by arguments, does not have a place." Rather, Vaughan maintains, "Hobbes sought to shape the thoughts, or more specifically the opinions, of citizens." Nathan Tarcov puts it even more bluntly, saying that political education for Hobbes is "concern[ed] with indoctrination rather than character formation."[69] This is particularly evident in *Leviathan*, where Hobbes argues that it is part of the sovereign's duty to be sure that citizens understand and accept the logic he has articulated in his book. The sovereign must not only preserve his own rights of dominion, but he must also educate his subjects so that they *understand* these rights, and understand why they are in their own interests. Law in and of itself is not enough to maintain the grounds of these rights; citizens must understand those grounds in order for law to work. For instance, Hobbes says, if I do not understand the logic of punishment, or of prohibitions against rebellion as necessary to my primary interest in peace and security, then I will seek to rebel and disobey whenever any opportunity presents itself. Further, I will resent punishment as an act of hostility and seek to avoid it whenever possible—not by obeying the law, but by evasion (*Leviathan*, ch. 30, 377). Such a situation is highly unstable, and such instability means the sovereign is not keeping up his end of the contract.

Accordingly, citizens are to be taught not to prefer a neighboring country's form of government, nor "to desire change" of any kind (*Leviathan*, ch. 30, 380); not to challenge or dispute the sovereign's power (*Leviathan*, ch. 30, 381); and indeed to be taught legalistic variations of the Ten Commandments that ensure that God is not portrayed as a superior power to the sovereign. In short, citizens are not really taught to think through the fundamental principles underlying the sovereign's authority, but rather simply to accept it as wisdom: as Flathman notes, "The Sovereign's success in teaching the demonstrable civil duties will not suffice to assure peace and order. She must eradicate all other beliefs that lead subjects to disobedience, replace them with beliefs that are supportive of their civil duties." Sovereign control must be "total," if not "totalizing" in the Foucaultian sense.[70] Hobbes seeks to compel all individuals to desire order above all else; but if such a desire is to dominate in the psyche of beings who are as radically free as Hobbes posits, these beings must be refashioned and shaped into the forms that Hobbes advises. Thus the task of his political philosophy is to persuade his readers to support a political form that will enable the monarch to compel the common people, who have not read his book, to do what Hobbes knows is in their best interest.

The patriarchal family, I have already suggested, is another significant way in which this construction of citizens is to be accomplished. The family is certainly an important instrument of education, and more generally of social construction; if the universities represent the "public" dimension of education, families represent the "private." And Hobbes says several times that one of the reasons that children owe obligations of gratitude to their parents is the education they received. But this education is clearly less formal than university education; rather, it is a mode of instruction through the shaping of personality and understanding. By creating the family, Hobbes's sovereign creates an institution that in turn creates individuals who want the very order that Hobbes wants citizens to desire. Indeed, the family is the only actual "institution" of any kind that Hobbes discusses in his work, besides government. Patriarchs have an interest in ruling and controlling the behavior of the family members under them; the sovereign then only has to be concerned with ruling the patriarchs, in teaching them not to rebel and so forth. Children's education, which Hobbes indicates occurs within the family, teaches children the values and ideals that they need to become "citizens": law-abiding, security-loving, domesticated individuals.

Women are similarly constructed to obey. In entering the family, women change from strong, self-sufficient individuals who have command over children to servants not even entitled to the money they earn through their labor. The fact that Hobbes eschews the naturalistic patriarchal arguments offered by James and Filmer, but nevertheless ends up in a place similar to such patriarchalists in terms of the form of the state and of marriage, suggests that he believes that such forms are good, but must be constituted manually and forcibly maintained. This can only be done, I have argued, by a sovereign authority instituted through a social contract. But what this means is that women are constructed to choose their subordination, to express their freedom in a singular act of giving up their freedom, or dominion over themselves. In this sense, women may serve as the ultimate model for Hobbes's citizen writ large.

As Wright suggests, Hobbes is "interested in families, and hence gender relations, only insofar as they reveal something important about the nature of political relationships,"[71] although her qualifying "only" may be too strong. In particular, I believe that Hobbes's defining the family without reference to women, and under a patriarchal authority, serves a purpose of eliminating, or more likely suppressing, its most dangerous and disruptive element. Children are much less of a threat to the rule of the father than wives are to the rule of husbands. This is especially so when women stop having babies; if we accept the standard feminist view, in which having babies puts women at a physical disadvantage, then when the children grow up, women are back on an equal footing with men. By that time, Hobbes reasons, they have consented to the husband's authority, but there is no clear reason why they cannot change the terms of the contract if their families are still in the state of nature. Children, on Hobbes's logic, owe a debt of gratitude to parents for "preserving" them and educating them, and once grown they presumably have things to gain from the father in the form of inheritance and succession. But women would seem to have nothing to gain by sticking to a contract of servitude unless it was backed by the sword of Leviathan.

And yet Hobbes does seem to think that contracts of servitude are binding, even in the state of nature; for

> The obligation . . . of a *servant* to his *lord*, ariseth not from a simple grant of his life; but from hence rather, that he keeps him not bound or imprisoned. For all obligation derives from contract; but where is no trust, there can be no contract. . . . There is therefor a confidence and trust which accompanies the benefit of pardoned life, whereby the *lord* affords him his corporal liberty; so that if no obligation nor bonds of contract had happened, he might not only have made his escape, but also have killed his lord who was the preserver of his life. . . . The lord therefore hath no less dominion over a servant that is not, than over one that is bound; for he hath a supreme power over both.[72]

Presumably, then, as a servant rather than slave, a woman would thereby be obliged to care for children if her husband so ordered it. Similarly, women would not be free to kill their husbands because their husbands spared their lives before marriage. But this is a rather surprising use of the notion of "trust." In the state of nature, where contracts are unenforceable, how can one trust that the servant will not escape or kill the master? Similarly, as already discussed, Hobbes never once explains why women consent to the husband's authority in the first place, in contrast to children. The implication of the above is that they are threatened with loss of life, but for patriarchy to have arisen on such a basis, as I have previously indicated, all, or at least most, women would have to have been so conquered, which contradicts the equality of strength and wit Hobbes postulates for women. The only logical conclusion is that Hobbes engages in this sleight of hand of invoking contemporary assumptions about women's subservient role at the same time that he challenges that role to suit his purpose: as Wright maintains, using gender instrumentally. But by containing women within the family and constructing their obedience as a matter of course, rather than through reasoned argumentation, Hobbes finesses the entire question and suppresses the danger that women pose to civil order.

The nature of this danger goes well beyond the mere disruption that physical conflict and competition between men and women would pose, or even the disorder caused by men's fighting over women. It relates to Hobbes's constructivism, for his entire theory of government is devoted to containment of difference. Differences in desire and judgment are what lead to conflict and the anarchic state of war. It is our profound difference from one another that prevents us from anticipating another's behavior or reaction and thus forces us into a self-defensive prisoner's dilemma. Carol Kay maintains that "we vary so much from one another that individual intentions can never be reliably understood, cannot be known with the certainty necessary to form a firm foundation for political decisions." Accordingly, she argues, "Hobbes's concern is not internal experience of feelings in themselves, but how people read one another, how motives are interpreted. Such interpretation will never amount to certain knowledge; it will always be a matter of debatable, uncertain opinion."[73] And as we have seen, diversity of opinion is a serious threat to the stability of society, because difference creates uncertainty.

Women, of course, represent the quintessential "difference" in the history of Western philosophy, and this is no less true for Hobbes, though it may be a bit subtler than is the case for some of the other Enlightenment theorists discussed in later chapters of this book. For Hobbes starts out by dismissing women's differences, saying women are just like men; even if women's strength is inferior, Hobbes says, so what? They are not so weak that they could not subdue a man. And at any rate such minor difference in strength has no relationship to their dominion over children, which proceeds not from strength but from preservation. Those who claim that women's physical weakness ensures father-right "show not, neither can I find out by what coherence, advantage of so much strength . . . should generally and universally entitle the father to a propriety in the child, and take it away from the mother" (*Elements*, 2.4.2).

Passages such as this return us to the question of why women are always subservient to men in the family and in civil society. My earlier argument, that the sovereign views women as sources of discord, and therefore commands his subjects to form patriarchal families in order to reduce such discord, suggests that Hobbes in fact fears women's difference, somewhat in keeping with Breitenberg's thesis of "anxious masculinity" in early-modern England.[74] That is, as I suggested earlier, Hobbes truly expresses "anxious humanity." But if the problem of difference is the inability to know what others are thinking, women's difference makes them even more inscrutable to men—and hence to Hobbes—than other men are. It is logical to assume that the regularized, even constant contact that the family provides allows for more informed judgments about others' thoughts and motivations than would be the case with people outside such relationships. Indeed, Hobbes does seem to believe that people can love each other, and especially their children, his popular imagery of the appetitive machine notwithstanding.[75] Such love implies a sympathy of feeling and thought that atomistic individualism would belie. But within the framework that Hobbes establishes, love is an emotion that is more likely to grow out of families than it is to found them. It would be foolish to fall in love—or at least to act on such feelings—in the state of nature, without laws to protect your dealings with an intimate. By contrast, the trust—or at least predictability—that sovereign law, including matrimonial law, fosters for Hobbesian men and women could allow such love to be expressed and even felt more freely.

In that regard, the family accomplishes a significant task for the sovereign, reducing the danger of difference through regularized contact, and at the least controlling the greatest differences, those that women display. Within the family, children and servants—including wives—are subjected and bound to their master without qualification. And it is this aspect of the family that provides the strongest model for civil society. In Elements, in the middle of discussing the family, including "covenants of cohabitation" between men and women and parental dominion over children, Hobbes notes that "the subjection of them who institute a commonwealth amongst themselves, is no less absolute, than the subjection of servants"—like wives—except that they have "greater hope" because they have voluntarily entered the contract, rather than "upon compulsion" (Elements, 2.4.9). He says this to explain that children are "freemen" rather than "servants" not by right, but only by the "natural indulgence of parents. . . . And this was the reason, that the name that signifieth children, in the Latin tongue is liberi, which also signifieth freemen" (Elements, 2.4.9). The next paragraph then offers Hobbes's definition of the family, cited earlier, that includes mothers: the only such occurrence in his major texts.

Several things are notable about his passage, most particularly the use of power relations within the family as a model for the state. Because

Hobbes here explicitly includes mothers in the family, women might seem to be included in the category of "parents" who indulge their children, suggesting women's power in the family. Yet just a few paragraphs earlier, Hobbes denies this by saying that only one person can rule in the family, "and therefore the man, to whom for the most part the woman yieldeth the government, hath for the most part, also, the sole right and dominion over the children" (*Elements* 2.4.7). With women thus denied the status of "freemen" that even their (male) children attain, their servitude eliminates them from citizenship. Yet Hobbes is also implying that women are the ultimate model of civil subordination: for what Hobbes does to women, he would like to do to all men, namely, subordinate them so thoroughly, and bind them so effectively to that subordination through their free choice, that the sovereign need make active use of force only infrequently. He seeks to define away men's resistance to the sovereign power and construct them into domesticated, peaceful subjects.

At the same time, the status of the "freedom" that women are being denied in this passage does not seem worth much: only better hope that the sovereign will favor them, like children being favored by a parent. Such favor may, doubtless, produce many good things—an extra large allowance, a trip to Disney World—but that is hardly the conception of freedom with which Hobbes starts *Leviathan*. Indeed, what is curious about this passage is that if all children are "free" in only this limited sense of equality of hope, then how is it possible to conceive of adults as "naturally free" in the sense described uniformly in all three of Hobbes's major treatises? How can Hobbes plausibly come up with his definition of natural freedom if people are fundamentally not the way they would need to be to make sense of such a definition? Hobbes nowhere argues, for instance, that children become free upon reaching adulthood, that they undergo a fundamental shift in their psychology; indeed, his positing of the family as an explicitly patriarchal one forbids such a notion. A son may conquer a woman and contract with her to be his wife, but he—and thereby she—is still subject to his own father, as are any children they may produce.

The tension between these two visions—people as innately dependent on social relations and people as atomistic individuals—threatens to make Hobbes's argument degenerate into incoherence. If we explicitly abstract adults from their families of origin, and particularly from the obedience and obligation they owe their parents, then his account of freedom becomes plausible. But such abstraction sits in active tension with what Hobbes says about women, for their absolute subjection as servants in the family seriously challenges the very possibility of abstract individualism and demonstrates clearly the masculinism of not only the Hobbesian subject, but the Hobbesian conceptualization of humanity and individuality.

CONCLUSION

The place of gender in Hobbes's theory at the very least raises important doubts about the centrality of negative liberty to his theory. Three interpretations are possible. The first is that Hobbes is an unabashed negative libertarian, concerned with external restraints, but that he thought women were simply not appropriate subjects of liberty. The fact that they needed to be constrained in order to facilitate men's negative liberty would, on this reading, be logically required, subject to the rational fiat. The association of woman with desire that has characterized the history of philosophy and literature takes on particular significance for Hobbes, for just as desire is not a matter that is appropriate to discussions of freedom—because we cannot choose our desires, only whether to act on them—so are women not appropriate subjects to consider when talking about freedom. But this reading would contradict the explicit recognition of equality between men and women in the state of nature; an equality that Hobbes did not need to include in his argument, as it contravened accepted notions of gendered identity. As Wright argues, "Before leaving women behind altogether"—which he did in making them invisible in the family and civil society—"Hobbes effectively disrupted gender norms, opening a space in which gender relations are dramatically—if briefly—reconceived."[76]

Indeed, it is precisely because women are such vital subjects of negative liberty that they must be constrained within the family. In this second interpretation, Hobbes is still a negative libertarian, but he does not think that liberty is as important to a well-ordered human society as subsequent political theorists asserted. As I suggested earlier, freedom may be the most fundamental characteristic of natural humanity for Hobbes, but it is not the most important to retain in civil society. Indeed, it is fundamentally dangerous to civil society, and so must be dispensed with. That women have more natural liberty than men, in the power of reproduction and the power of confederacy that it affords them, makes them that much greater a threat to civil order. It is such threats that result in Hobbes's efforts to construct citizens in particular ways, to have particular beliefs and ideas, that cohere with and support the sovereign's power so that people are not so aware of losing—or at least do not miss—the liberty they formerly had in the state of nature.

The social constructivism that such efforts produce, however, yields a third interpretation: that Hobbes is not strictly a negative libertarian, but rather was compelled to integrate elements Berlin later associated with positive liberty. That Hobbes himself may not designate these features as part of "liberty" does not detract from our ability to read them as such: indeed, it only begs the question of what liberty means. The fact that

Hobbes articulates the need for the sovereign to guide and shape people's desires fits the Rousseauian ideal of "forcing" individuals to be "free." In the same vein, that he does not explicitly discuss the shaping of women's desires does not forbid us from extrapolating such shaping from what he says about citizens more generally, and about women's disappearance from the family once patriarchy is established.

From the account I have given, it seems that Hobbes's theory of freedom is at least symbolically, if not politically, caught between the two different sides of the English Civil War. His emphasis on consent comes from the new age on whose brink he teeters, while his emphasis on absolute monarchy comes from his ties to the existing political order and his fear that civil war will result in anarchy, danger, chaos, and death. Hobbes admits to cowardice in his *Autobiography*,[77] but the courage of writing his in many ways radical arguments belie that self-deprecatory claim. A better description than cowardice would be anxiety. Indeed, his attitude about government goes well beyond any possible personal or psychological failings Hobbes might have had to an entire worldview that is extremely pessimistic and anxious about the outcome of individual choice, a pessimism that was more likely to have arisen from historical events than Hobbes's personality, as the *Behemoth* suggests.

It is this pessimism and anxiety that give way in the Enlightenment to the building blocks of positive liberty; specifically, to the ways in which theorists tried to shape people's choices, to make them choose very particular political forms that the theorist thought best. While the humanism of the Enlightenment and the desire to reject divine right and patriarchal theories of government led theorists to emphasize the human ability to make choices, these theorists were simultaneously afraid of what such choices would be. The tension between these two concerns is most obvious in Hobbes, who paints natural man in such colors so that all of his readers would immediately grasp the dangers; what *would* happen to humanity if such terrible creatures were allowed to express their wills uninhibited? It can readily be argued that Hobbes makes the state of nature so horrific as a means to manipulate his readers into accepting the wisdom of his own favored form of government, though many would nevertheless agree that it is the all-too-real horrors of civil war that inspired him. But this tension also exists in most other of the early-modern theories that tried to give a central place to human choice, and it guarantees that all of the early-modern theories of freedom are much more complex and nuanced than might at first glance appear.

CHAPTER TWO

John Locke

FREEDOM, REASON, AND THE EDUCATION
OF CITIZEN-SUBJECTS

As A THEORIST popularly seen at the founding moment of liberalism, John Locke's ideas have often been taken by late-modern and contemporary theorists to represent the central negative liberty ideals of radical individualism and freedom from external interference. Locke's views on political liberty as outlined in the *Two Treatises of Government* have been frequently recounted by commentators, the majority of whom see Locke as a key founding figure for the ideal of freedom as a realm protected not only *by* government from the interference of others, but *from* government as well, envisioned as a powerful but extremely dangerous force that could easily use that power to cross the line into people's private lives. Writing at the time of the Exclusion Crisis controversy, Locke wrote against the danger of absolute monarchy; for him the biggest threat to freedom was "Absolute, Arbitrary Power."[1] The social contract and rule of law were seen to protect against such power, and thus, though they limited our freedom to some extent, they enlarged it much more significantly to a more effective freedom.

Locke's views on political liberty as outlined in the *Two Treatises* have been frequently recounted, and because of the view of freedom he develops there Locke is often dubbed the virtual "father" of liberalism. Yet the meaning of freedom is not entirely straightforward in Locke's writings. Furthermore, as both Uday Mehta and Nathan Tarcov have argued, Locke's *Thoughts Concerning Education* is an even more important text than the *Second Treatise* to understanding his views of freedom and the free self. Other texts, such as *Questions Concerning the Law of Nature* and *Of the Conduct of the Understanding*, elaborate this argument to reveal Locke as not so much a state of nature theorist as a "social constructivist."[2] In particular, the primacy of reason in Locke's conception of freedom and, relatedly, the importance of natural law create certain tensions that complicate and compromise a negative liberty reading of Locke. Both of these features articulate the boundaries of individual choice and action, and thereby produce a positive direction for individual choice and a strong influence over what individuals "should" choose.

They also lead Locke from a concern with "external" matters—particularly the absence of arbitrary power—to "internal" ones concerning the creation of individuals who are oriented toward certain desires rather than others, who want to make certain choices rather than others.

THE ROLE OF REASON

In order to correctly understand the meaning of freedom in Locke's work, we must begin by recognizing its centrality to Locke's theory. Indeed, in almost circular fashion, freedom is defined in such a way as to preserve its natural state even after civil society is created. That is, unlike his predecessor Hobbes, who also posited man as naturally free but argued that the social contract was needed to curb that unbridled freedom, Locke believed that the purpose of the social contract was to "preserve and enlarge" natural freedom. The logic of the state of nature dictated that freedom would inevitably be challenged and compromised, though to a much lesser degree than Hobbes supposed; but precisely because God gave man free will, man had the ability to structure things so as to provide this freedom with a secure foundation in the form of civil government. Not only *were* men free, they *should* be free and had a natural right to be free; freedom's naturalness and centrality to humanity were not only descriptive, but prescriptive as well. Accordingly, any sort of political structure that humans constructed would have to have at its core the aim of protecting and promoting freedom.

Hence, Locke puts liberty at the very foundation of his *Second Treatise*:

> To understand Political Power right, and derive it from its Original, we must consider what State all Men are naturally in, and that is a *State of perfect Freedom* to order their Actions, and dispose of their Possessions, and Persons as they think fit, within the bounds of the Law of Nature, without asking leave, or depending upon the Will of any other Man. (*Two Treatises*, 2.4)

Although starting "men" in a natural state of freedom and equality as Hobbes did, Locke's vision of the rationality of natural man resulted in a much more peaceful state of nature where society and relationship were not only logically possible, but vital. Hence, liberty could not be absolute; Locke was quick to distinguish his concept of freedom from the "*State of Licence*," which Filmer disparagingly associated with consent theories, in response to Hobbes's work (*Two Treatises*, 2.6, also 2.22, 2.26).[3] There were limits posed by "the bounds of the laws of nature," which prevented men from "freely" making certain choices: we cannot take more than we can use and must leave enough for others; we cannot kill ourselves or sell ourselves into slavery, nor kill others except in self-defense; we must respect others' property and their ability to accrue property through labor. As Kirstie McClure has argued, natural law provided absolute limits on human freedom; it demarcated the boundaries within which individuals could make choices and pursue their interests. Rights constituted the realm of freedom and individual "convenience," whereas law defined the realm of virtue and duty.[4] This is consistent with the classic liberal vision of freedom-within-parameters: the archetypal freedom to swing my fist ends where your nose begins. For Locke, however, natural law defines those limiting points. "Freedom" is what God allows us to do.

But this does not mean that natural law "limits" us or provides barriers to satisfying our desires. For God created people so that they would not normally want to do the things that natural law forbids: the rationality and reason God gave all men caused them to see the logic behind mutual respect for rights and enabled them to see the interest to themselves in preserving others. For instance, the proviso that people should not take more than they can use before it spoils is a moral rule, necessary to the natural law that we preserve mankind. But it is also a rational one: it is against self-interest for people to want more than they can use, for spoilage represents a waste of labor and hence of property, thus contradicting the whole point of acquisition in the first place. Though Locke stacks the deck by "considering the plenty of natural Provisions there was a long time in the World, and the few spenders" (*Two Treatises*, 2.31), in his view, people in the natural state neither require nor want an unlimited amount of goods. Thus, while a moral maxim, the law against spoilage is also a principle that rational beings would naturally use to guide their actions. Even if men lack the "right reason" that allows them to see the laws of nature as the will of God, normal, everyday reason should motivate them, out of rational self-interest, to act in accordance with the laws anyway, even if they cannot see the benefit to humankind.

Reason is thus a key theme in Locke's vision of freedom, for it demarcates the limits not only of what I am permitted to do, but also of what I want to do (or should want to do if I am being reasonable; *Questions*, 107). But reason creates as much confusion and ambivalence for his theory as it does clarity. For what Locke means by reason, "how much" reason is "enough" to make one a free agent, whether everyone accesses and uses reason to the same extent, and what to do about those who do not use it, impact on one's reading of Locke's definition of freedom. Few negative libertarians would say that the attribution of basic rationality to humans, or the assumption that most people will in fact draw on this reason, in itself moves Locke into the positive liberty camp.[5] But Locke is on more slippery footing when he intimates that people who do not access their rationality are not following their true will. The possibility, which he particularly recognizes in *Questions Concerning the Law of Nature*, that some might not even have access to this basic reason, let alone "right reason," is a primary justification for the formation of the social contract. The question of precisely which people are able to display the reason that Locke asserts is essential to freedom is an important matter in defining who are the political actors, and hence free.

Locke distinguishes reason, which he defines as "that faculty of the intellect by which it articulates discourse and deduces arguments," from right reason, which constitutes "some definite practical principles from which flow the sources of all virtues and whatever might prove necessary to the proper formation of character. What is rightly deduced from these principles is properly said to conform to right reason" (*Questions*, 99). Because right reason can lead to only correct answers, it often appears as if Locke is saying that right reason is constituted by substantive principles rather than the process or "faculty of the intellect" that is reason *simpliciter*. But he also distinguishes right reason from "knowledge," which can only be obtained through inscription, tradition, or sense experience. Sense experience provides the foundation for knowledge of the law of nature, but reason must be used rightly to interpret it (*Questions*, 153). Right reason is therefore not simply a maxim that God gives us (through "inscription"); it is a faculty God gives us so that we can correctly interpret and fathom what God also gives us, namely, the law of nature.

Of course, how we can ever know for certain whether we are correct is a bit trickier, a philosophical problem of infinite regress: you cannot know your interpretation is correct unless your interpretation is correct. As McClure argues, Locke believed that there was an "architecture of order"; he had an elaborate vision of the ingenious way in which God laid out man and the world, designing us so that we could be directed in the use of the free will he gave us to choose the things he wants us to choose, and to execute his architecture properly.[6] To this end, many of Locke's writings are devoted to convincing us—or specifically, the educated elite who would read his books and also make the laws and wield power—of the eminent reason of the choices he advocates: parliamentary government, religious toleration, education, hard work. And indeed, Locke indicates in *Questions Concerning the Law of Nature* that he rejects "vox populi vox dei" because the majority do not use their reason and may agree with all sorts of evil propositions (*Questions*, 173–75). Although "reason is granted to all by nature, and I affirm that there exists a law of nature, knowable by reason" (109), not everyone accesses this reason, because some men have a "defect in nature" (111) or are "nurtured in vices" and "love the darkness" (109). Although he says that "man, should he make right use of his reason, and the native faculties with which he is provided by nature, can arrive at a knowledge of this law [of nature] without a teacher to instruct him" (124), the phrase "should he make right use" is a large qualifier. In *Of the Conduct of the Understanding*, Locke maintains that right reason requires careful development through scholarship, particularly Latin, Greek, philosophy, and mathematics. Moreover, it requires very broad reading and exposure to a wide variety of different kinds of ideas and interpretations: "Let not men think there is no truth but in the sciences that they study, or the books that they read. . . . He that will enquire out the best books in every science, and inform himself of the most material authors of the several sects of philosophy and religion, will not find it an infinite work to acquaint himself with the sentiments of mankind concerning the most weighty and comprehensive subjects" (*Conduct*, sec. 3, 171, 173).

Though perhaps not "an infinite work," this kind of learning meant that right reason was something that only the educated—which in Locke's day meant a relative minority of people, including most obviously the wealthy but also members of the emerging bourgeois middle class and the clergy—could achieve. True, some wealthy (and therefore, presumably, educated) people do not seem to behave very rationally, according to Locke, particularly those who take their inherited wealth as a reason for idleness.[7] But for the most part, wealth was taken by Locke as a sign of rationality, or more specifically of an individual's ability to access, develop, and use the reason that God gives all (or most). For Locke, industry—the use of property in your person (labor) to acquire property in the form of land or goods—was evidence of rationality, and a lack of property was evidence of a lack of rationality. Though "God gave the World to Men in Common," he specifically "gave it to the use of the Industrious and Rational . . . not to the Fancy or Covetousness of the Quarrelsome and Contentious" (*Two Treatises*, 2.34). After all, land in its uncultivated state was useless; thus "God, when he gave the World in common to all Mankind, commanded Man also to labour, and the penury of his Condition required it of him" (*Two Treatises*, 2.32). God set things up in such a way that we were compelled to industry, as "*Labour* was to be his [man's] *Title* to" property (2.34) and we needed property to stay alive. Hence "God and his [i.e., man's] Reason commanded him to subdue the Earth" (2.32), as once again we see that human reason coheres with God's will (or "architecture"). God has ordered things so that I must work: it is necessary and desirable that I be industrious, not just because God wants me to, but because God has made me rational enough to see its necessity and desirability.

But conversely (in keeping with the Protestant ethos, as Kramnick argues),[8] this indicates that having property is a sign of industry and thereby reason. It was not the case that all people in the upper classes necessarily were fully rational. Indeed, Locke says, "a country gentleman, who, leaving Latin and learning in the University, removes thence to his mansion house, and associates with neighbors . . . who relish nothing but hunting and a bottle" may become a judge or magistrate owing to "the strength of his purse and party." But he is still inferior in reason to "an ordinary coffee-house gleaner of the City." And even within the working classes, there is gradation: "The day laborer in a country village has commonly but a small pittance of knowledge, because his ideas and notions have been confined to the narrow bounds of a poor conversation and employment; the low mechanic of a country town does somewhat outdo him; porters and cobblers of great cities surpass them" (*Conduct*, sec. 3, 171–72). On the bottom were the unemployed, beggars, and those on parish relief.

Yet on the whole, men of the upper classes were more likely to be more rational than most laborers and artisans. As C. B. Macpherson argues, Locke links rationality and class quite clearly: "the labouring class, beyond all others, is incapable of living a rational life."[9] Macpherson's thesis of "differential rationality" maintains that Locke believed that the poor were less rational than the wealthy, that Locke attributed different natural abilities to people by virtue of their class, and that their poverty was a sign of a natural inequality. Although Macpherson is clearly correct to note differential rationality, however, he is somewhat ambiguous about its genesis. Specifically, he notes that "the difference in rationality was not inherent in men, not implanted in them by God or Nature; on the contrary, it was socially acquired by virtue of different economic positions." "But," he goes on, "it was acquired in the state of nature," and "once acquired . . . it was permanent."[10] Macpherson therefore runs together the natural and the social, suggesting that economic differences, which he considers social, in turn stem for Locke from natural differences in foresight, motivation, and laziness—all of which are expressions of (ir)rationality. But I maintain that Locke was considerably clearer on this issue and that he attributes this differential not to nature, but to practical aspects of class experience that cohere more closely to civil society than to the state of nature. This is clearest in *Of the Conduct of the Understanding*, where Locke explicitly says that "defects and weaknesses in men's understandings, as well as other faculties, come from want of a right use of their own minds[.] I am apt to think the faculty is generally mislaid upon nature, and there is often a complaint of want of parts, when the fault lies in want of a due improvement of them" (sec. 4, 175). And again: "We are born to be, if we please, rational creatures, but it is use and exercise only that makes us so, and we are indeed so no farther than industry and application has carried us" (sec. 6, 178). Even in the *Second Treatise*, where he seems to make the strongest case for the naturalness of freedom and rationality, Locke acknowledges the constructed quality of reason. Though he declares, "we are *born Free*, as we are born Rational," he also says, immediately following, "not that we have actually the Exercise of either: Age that brings one, brings with it the other too" (2.61). Of course, in this passage, reason could still be natural, something that develops with age, like secondary sexual characteristics. But Locke links "Age" with "Education" as the things that "brought him [man] Reason and Ability to govern himself, and others" (2.61). In other words, differential rationality is not natural, but socially constructed.

The distinction Locke employs is subtle. As he argues in the *Conduct*, "We are born with faculties and powers capable almost of anything, such at least as would carry us farther than can easily be imagined: but it is only the exercise of those powers which gives us ability and skill in anything, and leads us toward perfection" (sec. 4, 173). In other words, we must distinguish between *capacities*, defined as the natural potential to think rationally if people receive adequate education, and *abilities*, that is, what one actually can do given the education one has received and the cultural milieu in which one lives. "Natural disposition may often give first rise" to reason, but "it is practice alone that brings the powers of the mind as well as those of the body to their perfection" (sec. 4, 174). Hence, Locke says, "Every man carries about him a touchstone, if he will make use of it, to distinguish substantial gold from superficial glitterings, truth from appearances. And indeed the use and benefit of this touchstone, which is natural reason, is spoiled and lost only by assumed prejudices, overweening presumptions, and narrowing our minds. The want of exercising it in the full extent of things intelligible, is that which weakens and extinguishes this noble faculty in us" (*Conduct*, sec. 3, 171).

This distinction between natural capacity and learned ability is key to making sense of Locke's views of reason. It enables us to reconcile his claims about the state of nature with the considerable difference and inequality that develops in civil society. Hence, the poor do not have a diminished capacity for reason. Rather, they have less ability, and Locke clearly explains that this differential reason is a practical matter, not one of nature: "What then, can grown men never be improved or enlarged in their understandings? I say not so. But this I think I may say, that it will not be done without industry and application, which will require more time and pains than grown men, settled in their course of life, will allow to it" (*Conduct* sec. 6, 179). In other words, although Macpherson overstates the permanence of differential rationality, the development of full reason requires learning a wide range of scholarship such as philosophy, theology, Latin, and particularly mathematics, all of which require time and resources that the laboring classes do not usually have.[11] Thus, most laborers would never have the opportunity and means to develop their reason to the same level as a gentleman; as Locke argues in the *Conduct*, the "constant drudgery to their backs and their bellies" (sec. 7, 181) ensures that laborers have insufficient time and energy to develop reason. Moreover, because laborers have not been trained in the higher use of reason, they will be unlikely to seek to train themselves. Hence "knowledge and science in general is the business only of those who are at ease and leisure" (sec. 7, 182).

That does not mean laborers are entirely deprived of reason, however; they can, if they choose, develop their capacity into an ability to a limited extent. After all, Locke notes, even laborers have Sundays off and can apply themselves to the attainment of knowledge, at least of religion. For theology is "one science . . . incomparably above the rest" (*Conduct*, sec. 23, 195). Such efforts, however, are probably insufficient for laborers to develop "right reason" and the full reasoning capacity with which God endows (most) humans. Moreover, it is not necessary that they develop it, Locke believes; through their labor—and possibly the study of theology on Sundays—laborers will develop reason sufficiently to know that working hard is the right thing to do, that work is key to achieving as much contentment out of life as their lot will allow, and perhaps eventually to the actual attainment of property, though I agree with Macpherson that Locke seems less than sanguine about that possibility.

Because of their lesser reason, the poor were more prone to vice, though they did not have an exclusive hold on it by any means. And vice in turn further corrupted reason. In *Some Thoughts Concerning Education* Locke repeatedly warns against the corrupting influences of servants on the morals, discipline, and character of children; and in his "Essay on the Poor Law" he castigates those on parish relief as the most debased and corrupt, lazy at best, fraudulent cheats at worst. Given that industry was a sign of rationality, the way to overcome the vice of irrationality was to make people industrious. Hence, Locke's recommendations for strengthening the parish relief system involved strict work requirements: beggars were to be punished by forced labor aboard a ship for several years, and those who requested parish relief were to be put to work by members of the parish at "a lower rate than is usually given" ("Poor Law," 188). Even children were to be put in working schools—basically wool factories—to free up mothers from child-care responsibilities so that they could themselves work, to ensure that children were fed, and to make the children contribute to their own upkeep. Most of these measures originated under the Elizabethan poor law of the previous century, the original motivation for which was to reduce the costs of supporting and managing the poor.[12] A century later, Locke certainly shared the concern for cost, but for him the most important gain to be gathered from these measures was the creation of new habits of industry.

The true evil that needed to be rooted out, according to Locke, was not poverty per se, but irrationality, which leads to poverty.[13] For poverty and irrationality were incompatible with liberty.

NATURE VERSUS NURTURE: THE ROLE OF EDUCATION

Thus, it was not that the poor *could* not reason, but rather that they *would* not, owing to their lack of practice and the corrupting influence of the mean material conditions in which they lived: "Try in men of low and mean education, who have never elevated their thoughts above the spade and the plough, nor looked beyond the drudgery of a day labourer. Take the thoughts of such an one, used for many years to one track, out of that narrow compass he has been all his life confined to, you will find him no more capable of reasoning than almost a perfect natural" (*Conduct*, sec. 6, 178).[14] Nature had little to do with this. Rather, reasoning ability depended to a significant degree on what one did within the contingencies of life into which God placed one. Hence, "A middle-aged ploughman will scarce ever be brought to the carriage and language of a gentleman, though his body be as well proportioned, and his joints as supple, and his natural parts not any way inferior" (*Conduct*, sec. 4, 173). The irrationality of the poor was the product of habits acquired through poor living, which must be corrected for their own good, as well as the good of society. Thus, although the children in working schools may learn only a low-grade skill, the more important lesson they learn is industry and productivity: they learn how to work, and how to value work.

Obviously, there is a certain circularity to Locke's argument: if the poor do not innately lack reasoning capacity, but only lack the time and means to develop it, the logical response might seem to be to provide the resources to enable them to do so. But Locke seems to assume that there would be no point in this. Yes, it was important to change habits in the poor to enhance their industry and rationality, but there were limits to how far it was worthwhile going in this endeavor. Seventeenth-century society demanded a large number of laborers, and laboring required great expenditures of time and energy. Locke, though clearly involved in a movement to make radical changes in politics and economics, was hardly a Leveller, and was not interested in eliminating the class system. He was, rather, interested in making everyone fill his place in what reason revealed to him as God's divine order more efficiently, and thereby make everyone better off. Through their labor, laborers would become "reasonable" beings, sufficiently rational to know to follow their leaders and obey the law, even if they were not rational enough to be active parties to the social contract.

Those express consenters, by contrast, the leaders of civil society and presumed descendants of the parties to the original contract, needed to have right reason developed in its full capacity, and that required a carefully developed and executed education. Indeed, the education required to attain right reason involved more than academic study; it involved the building of character. The point of education is to habituate children to the correct behaviors, values, and attitudes: "The great thing to be minded in Education is, what *Habits* you settle" (*Education*, sec. 18). The fact that reason is a natural capacity is what makes the "white paper" theory of education possible; but as with all great paintings, the canvass must be primed. Locke asserts that "great Care is to be had of the forming of Children's *Minds*, and giving them that seasoning early, which shall influence their Lives always after" (sec. 32). Hence, long before teaching children philosophy, mathematics, Latin, and Greek, Locke is concerned with building "character" in the pupil, and most of his recommendations aim to the end of establishing a strong foundation for the acquisition of civic moral talents. The *Education* is accordingly concerned less with substantive subjects that students should learn and more with eating habits, "costiveness" (constipation) and regularity, health and hygiene, guidelines for recreation, methods and philosophy of punishment, temperament, and breeding. He seemed to have a particular passion for the strengthening benefits of cold wet feet, for he suggests that boys should wear shoes that leak, be encouraged to traipse around marshes in the rain, and have their feet washed in cold water at night (sec. 7). Girls were to follow such prescriptions as well, with some modifications; recognizing limits on girls' gallivanting, he recommended that water be put inside their shoes during the day, as well as washing their feet in cold water every night.[15]

As bizarre as such measures seem—indeed, the kind of thing that a only a childless bachelor like Locke could come up with—Locke also advocates some progressive notions, such as clothing that does not bind, for girls as well as boys, thus permitting freedom of movement; plenty of play outdoors, where boys roam fairly freely, though girls, to avoid the negative cosmetic effects of the sun, should be allowed to do this only at sunrise and sunset; few rules, because children should learn by example; and encouragement rather than force in pursuit of virtuous activities such as reading. But he does not get to "learning" and the components of what most people today associate with education per se until two-thirds of the way through the essay. His major and explicit concern in the *Education* is how to bring up a boy to be not only healthy and strong, but a "gentleman" (sec. 6). That does not preclude love and affection; it only precludes overindulgence and spoiling.

In this, Locke is concerned with the internal aspects of freedom, particularly identity and desire. A major recurring concern in the *Education* is the matter of discipline. The goal of education is the mastery over inclination, and the disciplining of desire is thus key; "contrary to the ordinary way, Children should be used to submit their Desires, and go without their Longings, even *from their very Cradles*. The first thing they should learn to know should be, that they were not to have any thing, because it pleased them, but because it was thought fit for them" (*Education*, sec. 38). Parents must teach children to "stifl[e] their Desires" and "master their Inclinations" (sec. 107).

Or more precisely, they must learn to want the right things: Locke seems to vacillate between a kind of rational, emotionless cruelty that strictly limits and forcefully pushes children in one particular direction (toward the right things) and an extremely liberal view that gently encourages and leads children down the path that they will find most rewarding (enlightened choice). He maintains that "Children have as much a Mind to shew that they are free, that their own good Actions come from themselves, that they are absolute and independent, as any of the proudest of you grown Men" (*Education*, sec. 73). Hence, "as a Consequence of this, they should seldom be put about doing even those Things you have got an Inclination in them to, but when they have a Mind and *Disposition* to it. He that loves Reading, Writing, Musick, etc. finds yet in himself certain Seasons wherein those things have no Relish to him: And if at that time he forces himself to it, he only pothers [flusters, worries] and wearies himself to no purpose. So it is with Children" (sec. 74). That is, children should not be made to do things, but rather they should have cultivated within them the desire to do those things that the parent wants them to do. Locke is concerned that children may cultivate bad desires for harmful things if they are not provided with proper guidance, and that tendency is the justification for his elaborate scheme of education. Thus, Locke's emphasis on freedom of choice sits uncomfortably with rather narrow constraints on what we should be free to choose, and which choices count as "freely made."

His views on physical punishment are relevant in this regard. Uday Mehta eloquently argues that Locke's comments on corporal punishment are consistent with a strict authoritarianism and strong parental control over the mind and will of the child.[16] In today's climate that opposes physical punishment of any kind as child abuse, these are fair views. But Locke actually is fairly limited in his recommendations for physical punishment. Although he admitted that corporal punishment was called for in dealing with "obstinate" children, he recommended that it be used only rarely, and to the end of inflicting not pain, but shame. He therefore disparaged frequent spankings, which he thought would only generate fear; and fear would not change children's habits and inclinations toward things that are bad for them, but only make them more devious about pursuing them. Instead, he advocated the use of physical punishment rarely, but thoroughly, to impress upon the child the severity of his transgression. Moreover, the punishment should never be given when the parents are in an emotional state of anger but rather when they have gained control of their anger and can demonstrate their reasoning and rationality in inflicting punishment (*Education*, secs. 43–52, 83–84).

Certainly, however, Mehta is correct to note the double edge of Locke's reasoning; though the focus on shame rather than pain at least indicates Locke was by no means heartless, it also supports the themes I have identified in the *Education* of Locke's belief in the need to gain control over the mind and will of children to develop their reason rightly. The key building block to education is thus to make children submissive to the parents' will; though the goal of education is self-discipline or self-mastery, this can only be achieved via submission to the parent. In contrast to the peaceful and rational creatures with which Locke populates the state of nature in the *Second Treatise*, Locke here suggests that children (and other human beings in the "natural" state) seek primarily to satisfy their desires. Hence, if self-mastery involves the mastery of one's desires, such beings must learn the benefits as well as the means of self-control. Locke's theory of education suggests a complicated notion of individuality and freedom that does not, indeed cannot, exist naturally but must be developed through social institutions and processes. Through education, a child should develop the best of "Habits woven into the very Principles of his nature" (*Education*, sec. 42). What is "within" us is made so by education and the outer forces of our parents and tutors. As Mehta points out, Locke is extremely concerned with charting the inner landscape of individuality: the minds, thoughts, feelings, and preferences, in short, the basic elements that make up the supposedly free, liberal individual. Because of the "malleability of the mind," it can easily turn to waste and evil, but it can also be turned toward productivity and virtue by the proper education. Accordingly, education begins at an extremely young age, and children are formed in their individuality even as they learn language and before they have a well-formed sense of themselves. Focusing on the very young has the power of "making whatever is habituated *appear* natural."[17]

Accordingly, this education must be undertaken in the family, Locke says at the very start of his essay, in the "Epistle Dedicatory." Part of his reason is attributable to classically negative liberty ideals: just as the state should not involve itself in forming individuals' consciences, so should it not be involved in forming their intellect. But this is less a protection of negative liberty rights of the family than a belief that state-run education would be far less effective than the family in shaping the will to virtuous ends, in creating a right-reasoning creature who can discern the laws of nature and interpret them correctly. Indeed, even privately run "public schools" favor academic subjects at the expense of teaching virtue and character, in Locke's view; character is thus forged de facto and ad hoc through interaction with peers, who, equally unguided, simply display "rudeness and ill-turned confidence" (*Education*, sec. 70). By contrast, because the family is the locus for love and affection, parents can be expected to have greater concern for their children's welfare than hired teachers; hence, even tutors within the family must be supervised by parents. The care parents must take is stimulated as much by the difficulty of the task as by the limited competence of most tutors. (Locke implies on several occasions that because tutors belong to a lower class than the employing family, they may be more susceptible to the corruption that afflicts other household servants, though perhaps not to the same degree.) Education in the family allows for hands-on parental involvement and oversight. For who would have a greater investment in the outcome of the educational process than parents in Locke's loving but rational bourgeois family?

The Gendered Property of Freedom

The fact that education is to take place in the family raises the question of whether daughters are to be educated similarly to sons. Indeed, it would seem an open invitation to educate girls alongside boys. The "public education" tradition in England was a convenient way to segregate the sexes. Sending boys to boarding schools at an extremely early age severs the emotional links between boys and their mothers, and acculturates boys to a masculinized world wherein the personal bonds and relationships for politics and money are set. It thereby effectively excludes girls from the world of politics and money. But Locke does not propose such a system. Rather, he recommends that boys be educated in the bosom of their families, where affection and love can be expressed and experienced along with discipline and learning. So why not expect that girls can be educated alongside boys, attain the same kinds of discipline and knowledge, and the same kinds of access to reason, knowledge, and therefore liberty?

Melissa Butler argues that Locke advocated equal education for girls, with "minor" modifications. She notes that in a letter to Mrs. Clarke (Locke's *Education* originated in a series of letters to her husband, Edward Clarke, concerning the education of their son), Locke said, "Since, therefore I acknowledge no difference of sex in your mind relating . . . to truth, virtue and obedience, I think well to have no thing altered in it from what I have writ [for the son]." From this, as well as from the fact that education should take place in the home from tutors rather than in schools, hence following what Butler calls a "ladies'" model of education, she concludes that Locke believes that "men and women could be schooled in the use of reason. . . . Women had intellectual potential which could be developed to a high level." Furthermore, because gentlemen had to be educated in politics, women would receive the same education and thereby be equipped for "political activity."[18]

Certainly in a number of places, Locke can be seen as supporting girls' education. He admonishes parents when he says, "I have seen little girls exercise whole hours together and take abundance of pains to be expert at dibstones as they call it. Whilst I have been looking on, I have thought it wanted only some good contrivance to make them employ all that industry about something that might be more useful to them; and methinks 'tis only the fault and negligence of elder people that it is not so" (*Education*, sec. 152). Similarly, he notes, "Nor does any one find, or so much as suspect, that that retirement and bashfulness which their daughters are brought up in, makes them less knowing, or less able women. Conversation, when they come into the world, soon gives them a becoming assurance; and whatsoever, beyond that, there is of rough and boisterous, may in men be very well spar'd too; for courage and steadiness, as I take it, lie not in roughness and ill breeding" (*Education*, sec. 70). Though these passages are not clear endorsements of teaching girls Latin and mathematics, it might seem that Locke believes that females have rational potential that should not be wasted. He may be a bit more explicit when he notes that "there cannot be a greater spur to the attaining what you would have the eldest learn, and know himself, than to set him upon *teaching* it *his younger brothers* and sisters" (*Education*, sec. 119). This suggests that girls should learn some basic lessons, though the significance of Locke's highlighting "younger brothers" but not "sisters" is somewhat unclear.

A number of recommendations Locke makes apply more explicitly to daughters. Indeed, Locke says that "the nearer they [girls] come to the hardships of their brothers in their education, the greater advantage they will receive from it all the remaining parts of their lives" (*Education*, sec. 9). But this is said in the context of Locke's prescriptions for physical health, which occupy the entire first third to half of the *Education*. Hence, as noted earlier, he includes girls in his recommendations concerning diet, outdoor play, loose clothing, cold wet feet, and physical punishment. Similarly, his letter to Mrs. Clarke focuses on questions of "fashion," such as dance instruction, and matters of physical health, such as how to address the need for cold wet feet when "it is not fit that girls should be dabbling in water as your boys will be." His concern is motivated by the fact that

"I should rather desire in my wife a healthy constitution," so he recommends the same "meat drink and lodging and clothing" as he does for boys, as well as similarly rigorous physical activity; for "it will make them not only fresh and healthy, but good housewives too."[19] Though the connection between physical hardiness and good housewifery is not specified, he labels women as "the softer sex," and says, "I shall not think of any rougher usage than only what [her sex] requires."[20] It should also be noted that Locke begins his previous letter by discussing Mrs. Clarke's recent "lying in." He writes that since her pregnancies tend to "produce long letters as certainly as I find it does fine children," he suggests "that Master and you would get to work again as hard as you can drive that you might lie in again as soon as may be."[21] Though an obvious jest, the understanding of sexual difference and "good housewifery" that Locke reveals in these letters, combined with the absence of any explicit references to academic subjects for girls, must at least cast some doubt on what exactly Locke is recommending by way of education for women.

Furthermore, although girls seem ambiguously included in some of his educational prescriptions as I have noted, the overt point of his book, Locke admits, is the education of boys so as to turn them into gentlemen: "I have said *he* here because the principle aim of my discourse is how a young gentleman should be brought up from his infancy, which, in all things, will not so perfectly suit the education of *daughters*" (sec. 6). Hence, when he says that "when we so often see a French woman teach an English girl to speak and read French perfectly in a year or two, without any rule of grammar, or any thing else but prattling to her, I cannot but wonder how gentlemen have overseen this way for their sons, and thought them more dull or incapable than their daughters" (*Education*, sec. 165), he is not remarking on girls' education in French, but rather boys' education in Latin, which he thinks should follow a more natural mode of conversation rather than teaching the rules of grammar. Similarly, contrary to Butler's claim that Locke's recommendation for education in the home indicates his inclusion of girls, Axtell maintains that Locke was merely following rather than setting a trend, for from 1670 to 1700 schools saw a decline in enrollments, and there was an increase in private education in the home.[22] Locke's endorsement of the trend cannot then be taken as evidence of radical views on girls' education.

Thus, the *Education*, written for Mr. Clarke, is somewhat at odds with what Locke wrote in his letters to Mrs. Clarke. Perhaps in those letters he reevaluated his position; we cannot really know. But girls, laborers, and the poor are to a significant degree excluded from the *Education*'s pages. Part of the reason for this is a bowing to social custom; Locke seemed to have a particular aversion to exposing girls' skin to the sun, in keeping with social norms of the time. But part may also be the result of his uncertainty over whether females have the ability—as opposed to capacity—to access and utilize the rational faculty. As he notes in a letter to Edward Clarke, "the manner of breeding"—not, we should note, education per se—"of boys and girls, especially in their younger years, I imagine should be the same."[23]

Understandably, then, Locke's views on women's rationality is a matter of some debate in the literature. Whereas some feminists, such as Lorenne Clark and Zillah Eisenstein, have argued that Locke denied women natural rationality altogether, other scholars, such as Rogers Smith, point out that Locke never actually says that in the *Two Treatises*.[24] Butler makes a stronger case, maintaining that Locke's belief in women's reason is unequivocal. But I believe Butler is too generous to Locke, not only in the aspects of education he recommends for girls, but in the degree of rationality he grants females. For despite Locke's opening of his essay with Juvenal's "a sound mind in a sound body" (*Education*, sec. 1), and despite his progressive views on girls' physical activity, physical "health and hardiness" do not automatically translate into reason; they merely set its stage. Reason itself, to be developed in its full flower, requires the learning of substantive subjects such as Greek, Latin, and particularly mathematics: "in all sorts of reasoning, every single argument should be managed as a mathematical demonstration," though "not so much to make them mathematicians as to make them reasonable creatures" (*Conduct*, sec. 7, 180, sec. 6, 178). And although Locke clearly states that these subjects, particularly mathematics, are largely the province of the propertied classes—only "those who have the time and opportunity" to learn them (*Conduct*, sec. 6, 178)—there is no evidence in Locke's writings that girls would learn the same *academic* material as boys.

Although, as noted earlier, Locke claims that "where the Difference of Sex requires different Treatment, 'twill be no hard Matter to distinguish" (*Education*, sec. 6), given the widespread acceptability of gender inequality among Locke's contemporaries, it is not obvious how the requirements of "the Difference of Sex" will direct his readers. Indeed, considering that Locke's greatest concern for girls appeared to be protecting their complexions from sunburn, one wonders how unconventional his *Thoughts Concerning Education* really are for females. The apparent gender neutrality with which Locke presents many of his recommendations camouflage conventionally gendered assumptions. For instance, although parents must get their "children" into the "armor" of "Fortitude," which is "the guard and support of the other virtues," courage is defined in explicitly gendered terms, as "the quiet possession of a man's self and an undisturbed doing his duty, whatever evil besets or danger lies in his way. . . . Without courage a man will scarce keep steady to his duty and fill up the character of a truly worthy man" (*Education*, sec. 115). By contrast,

Locke repeatedly associates the term "effeminate" with the worst character traits, such as weakness, crying, complaining, and whining (secs. 107, 113). Even the "truth, virtue, and obedience" he mentions in his letter to Mrs. Clarke as qualities that females share are hardly the stuff of reason: as Kant later put it, they are the "beautiful" virtues of sensibility and intuition, not the "sublime" ones of reason.[25] Furthermore, although the *Two Treatises* suggests in various places a rough equality between the sexes, and may imply women's rationality through its reiteration of the fourth commandment (why would God grant both parents equal respect if they were not equally rational?), Locke's other works are less generous to women. In *The Reasonableness of Christianity*, for instance, Locke explicitly says that laborers and "those of the other sex" can only understand "simple propositions," suggesting a natural limitation on reason.[26]

Locke's ambiguity on the question makes it, I think, safe to say that he believes that women are *less* rational than men, much as laborers display less rationality than landowners. But whether this is by nature or artificial design is the more important question than "how much" rationality Locke grants women. In this respect, the parallels between class and gender are particularly significant. As noted earlier, in the *Conduct* he attributes class differences in reasoning not to nature but rather to the pragmatic realities of laboring life, raising the possibility of the same for (bourgeois) females who must run a home and manage servants in addition to bearing and raising children.

Perhaps, as I earlier suggested about laborers, Locke is distinguishing between women's *capacities* (that is, the natural potential to think rationally if people receive adequate education) and their *abilities* (what one actually can do given the current state of things; if women are not educated, they will not be able to think as rationally as educated men). This would fit his "white paper" theory of education; if we are all blank slates at birth, with no innate ideas, and girls live an experience of emotion, frivolity, and dissipation—or at least if they are taught French, music, and household management rather than mathematics and Latin—then it should not be surprising that women do not utilize their rationality, as Locke's contemporary Mary Astell argued.[27] But, as is the case for propertyless men, that does not mean that women completely lack the capacity to reason.

But Locke may actually go farther than a fatalistic recognition of the norms of the day. That is, rather than arguing that girls or women are naturally incapable of reason, Locke may actively want girls and women not to have their reason developed to the same degree as men. The "inappropriateness" for girls of many of his educational recommendations suggests that girls' role in life requires that they not be *allowed* to develop reason to the same degree as boys or men. After all, the family in which education takes place is the bourgeois patriarchal family, where gender relations are strictly structured to serve the ends of property and inheritance. Property is key to Locke's theory of freedom: it is important both to the realm of "right," within which one can do as one likes and pursue one's interests, in keeping with negative liberty, and to the realm of virtue, in that property is a sign that one has made the right choices, in keeping with positive liberty.

But women's relationship to the institution of property is never clearly articulated by Locke. He certainly comes close to granting women property rights in several passages of the *Two Treatises*. For instance, in "Of Conquest," Locke argues that if the men in one society unjustly invade another and lose, the latter have a "right of conquest" over the former. The reason for this is that the unjust attacker virtually "consented" to rule by conquest when it launched its attack. Indeed, Locke argues that this is the only possible situation in which a right of conquest exists, though it is strictly not such, for the citizens of the victorious society are not entitled to all of the conquered soldiers' property. Certainly, the conquerors are entitled to reparation for what they lost during the attack, which may well be less than what the conquered has. Indeed, Locke seems more concerned for the property of the conquered soldiers than their lives, which have been completely forfeited to the conquerors: "the state of War he put himself in, made him forfeit his Life, but gave me no Title to his Goods." This is in part because others, specifically the wives and children of the conquered soldiers, have title to the estates of their husbands and fathers, for "They made not the War, nor assisted in it." Thus, "My wife had a share in my Estate, that neither could I forfeit. And my children also, being born of me, had a right to be maintained out of my labour or Substance." Accordingly, as the victor is more likely than the conquered soldiers' wives and children to "hath, and to spare," he must "remit something of his full Satisfaction" (*Two Treatises*, 2.182–83).

This limitation on the conqueror's right to the conquered's property could be seen to derive from the law of nature requiring us to leave enough for others, for Locke says that in the case of conflicting rights between the conquered's wife and children and the conqueror's claims of reparation, the decision should turn on who can better afford the loss (though this idea would probably have to work from the notion that international relations constitute a parallel to the state of nature, which Locke intimates [2.183]). Or it could derive from the notion that fathers cannot consent for their children, thus freeing children from any obligations of reparation that their father may have incurred through his rash actions. Both of these arguments take logical precedence in Locke's argument over any specifically "feminist" concerns to assert women's property rights. But whatever the motivation, it could be argued that in this discussion, Locke is forced to recognize women's independent, individual status, and to grant them at least a semblance of property rights.

However, I do not believe that Locke is really granting women property "rights" per se in this chapter. Rather, I believe this would probably be an example of the *feme sole* principle used in seventeenth- and eighteenth-century England and the American colonies, namely, a court-ordered dispensation granting women control over property under special circumstances when husbands or other male relatives are unavailable. The situation of a society of husbands and fathers so out of touch with rationality as to wage an unjust war—one in which, to add insult to injury, they have even miscalculated their ability to win!—would clearly constitute a "special" situation rather than a normal one in the Lockean universe. But even a *feme sole* did not have the right to dispose of property entirely as she wished, as sons had inheritance rights that could not be abrogated. Women did not gain complete legal control over their own property in England until 1882, even if they sometimes did so in practice.[28] It could be argued that the fact that Locke did not challenge the status quo is no reason to assume that he agreed with it; until, that is, we remember that his views on *men's* property rights were a radical challenge to the status quo, particularly his questioning of primogeniture.

Indeed, it would be more reasonable to argue that Locke is not establishing a right for women at all, but simply reminding us of men's duties. That is, he does not say that the conqueror has no right because it is the *woman's* property, but only that she is entitled to some of her *husband's* property. Locke acknowledges that a woman may obtain property through her own labor, but he does not distinguish this property from what she gets from her husband through the responsibilities of marriage: "the wife's share, whether her own labour, or compact, gave her a title to it, it is plain, her husband could not forfeit what was her's" (*Two Treatises*, 2.183). This could indicate that what the wife gains through the marriage compact is just as much hers as if she labored for it; but it is more likely that Locke is articulating the natural law of property to delineate the limits of the conqueror's rights, not to establish the scope of women's rights. The conqueror has a duty to recognize the duties of the soldiers they have conquered. As Lorenne Clark argues, Locke's motivation is not to delineate rights women have, but rather rights that states do not have: again, given the dominant theme of protecting property from state intervention and confiscation, this is a more likely motivation for his argument. The point, Clark argues, is "to ensure that no . . . victor in conquest or usurpation could alienate the male's property from his legitimate heirs. . . . regardless even of the father's transgressions."[29] This is particularly important, because Nathan Tarcov points out that this chapter represents the only other time in the entire *Two Treatises* that Locke argues against a hypothesis for state legitimacy other than Filmer's.[30] Just as he found it helpful in the *First Treatise* to invoke the image of woman in order to rebut Filmer's arguments, he here finds it helpful again; but his purpose is decidedly to defeat contrary arguments for state legitimacy and authority, and not to establish women's rights.[31]

Moreover, women's exclusion from property would cohere more logically with the way the institution of property is organized in Locke's theory. Protection of property is the main reason the social contract is formed, and it is the primary task of the legislature. But the centrality of property is also why the institution of inheritance is so important; men want to pursue their interests and develop their property, but if they cannot pass on that property to offspring, a serious motivation for continued productivity is removed. Because property as estate is linked to political power, however, as an important qualification for voting and holding political office, then inheritance is the institution by which men pass on political power to other men. (Indeed, this would also suggest why property in the person is not sufficient to establish the right to political participation, for it cannot be "inherited"; it exists "naturally" within each person.) Given that "property passed through blood lines, and blood lines were determined by the father," this system of inheritance would be severely compromised without the patriarchal nuclear family, for there would be no way for a man to know who his children are.[32] If women could hold property and be economically independent, their subservient role in the patriarchal nuclear family would be jeopardized, and along with it the "bloodlines" that determine property, power, and citizenship. This is why the right to divorce is allowed to women only *after* they have fulfilled the duties of the marriage contract, namely, raising children (*Two Treatises*, 2.78–83); the rather passionless and utilitarian view of marriage Locke takes clearly makes the propagation of the species and the production of offspring the primary and overwhelming purpose of marriage. Presumably Locke would have the court arrange some sort of income for the wife before approving a divorce and granting her limited powers to dispose of it through a *feme sole* status, but this economic independence would no longer pose a threat to the institution of property. Women's exclusion from the rights of property is one of the elements that makes Locke's family, as Tarcov puts it, "a family that is safe for liberalism."[33]

Because property is one of the key freedoms of the *Two Treatises*, the very core of the rationale for the social contract and the essence of human agency, then women's lack of property suggests a similar lack of freedom. Indeed, women are arguably even excluded from property in the person, as everything that they worked on in household production was already owned by men, and the only things they could be said to produce through nature, namely, children, are explicitly demarcated by Locke not as the property of either parent, but of God. Of course, this may be less significant, for even among men property in the person was not enough to establish political rights of participation. And because property is related to rationality, being a sign of industriousness and the right use of reason, property in the person was not sufficient to establish rationality, either. So women, not having property of any sort, must also be uniformly irrational as well as politically disempowered.

CONSENT, CHOICE, AND A TWO-TIERED CONCEPTION OF FREEDOM

Whether it is a result of nature or practice—and I have argued that it is the latter—this differential rationality for the poor and women impacts on Locke's vision of freedom, for the realm of the internal demarcated by his attention to right reason and intellectual development is what sets the foundation for the achievement of the external realm of political liberty. Even if women were not completely irrational, they were not considered by Locke to be rational enough to handle the political power of express consent. Indeed, ownership of property in the form of "estates" was the strongest case for consent of either the express or tacit kind: if the whole point of the social contract was the protection of property, if that good was at its heart, then it would be completely irrational for someone who owned property not to consent to the social contract, for one would be rejecting protection of one's property.

But imperfect rationality in nonlandowning males is certainly sufficient to establish tacit consent for them, so there is little reason to think otherwise for women. In this, it is worth noting that the Whigs explicitly excluded women from suffrage.[34] But of course women were expected to obey the law fully, which is completely consistent with tacitly consenting "imperfect members." Reason is particularly important to consent, which lies at the heart of political freedom for Locke: consent is the only way for people to have an established government and yet retain their natural freedom, because the restrictions that government and law inevitably produce are the result of their own free choice. But if reason—or more specifically, people's use of it—is unreliable, then the divine order is disrupted. Whether we agree with Macpherson that the invention of money produces scarce resources over which we must fight or with Dunn that the lack of a known judge makes conflict inevitable even for peaceful, rational beings, the social contract was created to address the "inconveniences" of conflict that exist in the state of nature.[35] But whereas Hobbes hung the sword of Leviathan over citizens' heads to prevent them from their naturally conflicting behavior, for Locke the point of forming a contract with government was to protect individuals from abuses of governmental power, and not just from their fellow citizens. As different in legitimation as were the patriarchal monarch Filmer defended and Hobbes's contractual monarch, both wielded a power that could abrogate the natural rights of individuals provided by the laws of nature. This was anathema to Locke, who declared that "The *Liberty of Man, in Society*, is to be under no other Legislative Power, but that established by consent, in the Commonwealth, nor under the Dominion of any Will, or Restraint of any Law, but what the Legislative shall inact, according to the Trust put in it" (*Two Treatises*, 2.22).

Like Hobbes, Locke addresses this tension through consent, the point of which is that all limitations of freedom are simultaneously expressions of it: laws made by human legislators within the framework of a representative government formed by a social contract are ipso facto laws that have been consented to by members of the civil society. Consent was the only possible basis for the legitimate exercise of governmental authority; accordingly, consent had to be given to any constraint, including one of law, on an individual's freedom to pursue his interests. In his discussion of free will in the *Essay Concerning Human Understanding*, Locke notes this apparent paradox: "That *Willing*, or *Volition* being an Action, and Freedom consisting in a power of acting, or not acting, *a Man in respect of willing, or the Act of Volition, when any Action in his power is once proposed to his Thoughts, as presently to be done, cannot be free.*"[36] That is, if I will something, then I have to perform the action to bring it about; if I will X, I am not free to avoid the action that is required to bring X about, unless I decide to no longer will X. For instance, if I decide that I want to eat, I have to obtain some food, put it in my mouth, chew, and swallow. If I do not do this, then either my will has been frustrated—as might be the case if I have an unusual phobia or perhaps a terrible toothache that prevents me from eating even though I am hungry—or I have willed something else that supersedes my prior willing (that is, I may have changed my mind). But if I want to eat, I must actually eat in order to express my will. This "must" does not mean that I am not free if I do eat, however: that apparent determinist paradox is something Locke rejects. For him, once I will something, performing that action is the only way to express my will, and thereby to effect my freedom, which "consists . . . in our being able to act, or not to act, according as we shall chuse, or *will*." [37]

This definition of freedom relates directly to the social contract; once you will a government into existence through the social contract, you are not free to act in a way contrary to that will. Or more precisely, it is only by honoring the contract—specifically, obeying the law, recognizing the authority of government to make and execute laws—that you can be free. If the terms of the contract—and hence the rules and laws that result from the government the contract establishes—are the result of free choice, then to the degree that they "limit" freedom, they do so by an act of free will, namely, consent. Such laws therefore express rather than hinder the will.

But at the same time, as Locke goes on to develop this idea in the *Second Treatise*, the very thing that protects individual choice—consent—is precisely the thing that compromises it. For whereas I can change my will about whether to eat, I seem unable to change my mind about consenting to government. In this, Locke tracks the logic of Hobbes's argument about consent but develops it in a more elaborate fashion. Locke's well-known discussion of tacit consent glosses over the ways in which a majority of the citizenry of his envisioned polity—including landless workers and women—do not in fact consent, and indeed have no choice but to obey. Individuals would be obligated to the government by simply passing through the boundaries of a country, and certainly by living there; but only if the country through which one is passing is a good one, because consent to tyranny does not bind.[38] But as many commentators have pointed out, the essence of consent—conscious choice with viable alternatives, awareness of the meaning of your choice, and the option of withholding your agreement—thereby disappears from Locke's rendition of tacit consent.[39] Tacit consent is a theoretical maneuver that on the one hand makes the social contract politically plausible by incorporating the vast majority of people who do not in fact consent to a government, but on the other contradicts its founding principle that everyone is equal, free, and rational. Tacit consent would thus seem to undercut one of the important foundations for Locke's claim of natural and equal freedom.

When considered in tandem with his remarks about reason in the *Education*, the *Conduct*, and the *Questions* concerning the importance of habit and practice in the establishment of right reason, the challenge to the straightforward liberal account of Lockean negative liberty is particularly apparent. Locke is actually making an argument for a two-tiered theory of freedom that recognizes the desirability and even necessity of a positive conception of liberty, but also recognizes that most people cannot attain this freedom. Particularly given Locke's concern with tyranny in government and education in the family, he can be seen as deploying a positive conception of liberty that comes from the private sphere, where the development of rationality and moral virtue are key, and is exercised in the public sphere through the creation of law. But he also develops a negative conception of liberty produced in the public sphere, where freedom from arbitrary and absolute power is paramount, to enable perfect and imperfect members alike to enjoy the private liberty rights of disposing of their property (including their labor) as they see fit. In this, the dividing line is not negative and positive liberty; rather, it is one of class and gender, with positive and negative liberty cutting across them.

That is, positive liberty is exercised primarily by propertied white men, the people who will develop "right reason" through proper education and upbringing, but *over* women and landless men, whose inferior rationality may be situational rather than natural, but nevertheless fits the architecture of order that Locke sets out. The educated, landowning, elite men would determine the laws to which the rest of us tacitly consent, thereby establishing our subjection to law as freely chosen, and also ensuring that our lives are circumscribed only by laws that are rational and in keeping with the laws of nature. Consent can be inferred only because express consenters use right reason, so all civil laws they make and policies they choose will cohere with the law of nature and "the light of reason," which I would myself choose if I could, as they are part of the divine order. Thus, despite Locke's repeated emphasis on majority rule in the *Second Treatise*, in fact he believes that we should be guided not by the majority—who happened to be the laboring classes—but by "the sounder and more perceptive part" of the population, though it be a minority, and most likely wealthier (*Questions*, 111). God may not have given the majority right reason, but he has given the majority enough reason to see the superiority of their betters, and to acquiesce when others use their superior reason for the common good.

Such a reading would particularly work with McClure's argument that law is concerned with virtue and duty—important elements in positive liberty—whereas right is concerned with convenience and pursuing what you want. On my reading of Locke's two-tiered conception of freedom, the educated perfect members would take on the duty of creating virtuous laws based on right reason, whereas everyone else would reap the benefits of that reason and its application in law by living under a government that provides property rights that allow them to pursue their interests. The two aspects of liberty tacitly come together because the development of rationality and virtue for the wealthy in the private sphere would enable them to control and define the public sphere by creating good laws; these in turn will shape and produce lower-class and female citizens or subjects who will make the right choices by obeying those laws. Laws in turn define the parameters of right, and indeed become the substance of freedom: "The realm of right . . . is a realm of freedom, but it can only be understood as such in relation to the law that, by framing its boundaries, makes it possible."[40] As Locke puts it,

> *Law*, in its true Notion, is not so much the Limitation as *the direction of a free and intelligent Agent* to his proper Interest, and prescribes no farther than is for the general Good of those under that Law. Could

they be happier without it, the *Law*, as an useless thing would of it self vanish; and that ill deserves the Name of Confinement which hedges us in only from Bogs and Precipices. So that, however it may be mistaken, *the end of Law* is not to abolish or restrain but *to preserve and enlarge Freedom. . . . where there is no Law, there is no Freedom. (Two Treatises*, 2.57)

This conception of law is consistent with negative liberty—laws prevent others from encroaching on your sphere of activity, and hence enlarge the sphere of right—but it is also consistent with positive liberty, because it directs us to our "proper interests," whether or not we are rational enough to know what those are.

On this reading, negative liberty could in principle be attained by anybody, express or tacit consenter, rich or poor, male or female, as long as one operated in the law and did not desire or pursue interests that run contrary to law. Indeed, it would be the only realm of freedom that tacitly consenting landless workers could actively express, for they can pursue their private interests and "conveniences" through the invocation of their "rights" within the bounds of civil law. Positive liberty, by contrast, though it can be imposed on women and the poor, can be developed only by the educated and wealthy who are able to develop their reasoning abilities to the fullest, who are able to know what the law of nature says (and thereby translate it into civil laws the rest of us can follow), and who can know truly what the proper interest of all of us is. Furthermore, rationality and positive freedom in the private sphere would be a matter of degree—some are more rational and hence freer than others, and individuals can themselves become more rational and hence freer over time— whereas in the public sphere negative freedom is a matter of yes or no: I can either do what I want or not, depending on what the laws say, and hence what my rights are.

At the same time, of course, these two tiers result in the opposite outcome at the same time; perhaps rather than two tiers, the image of four corners would be more apt. That is, because those with superior reason already want the right things, then as long as they are negatively free to pursue those desires, they are free. By contrast, landless workers and other tacit consenters need to be forced to be free; they need to be guided to the right choices, and thus positive freedom is the appropriate model for them. For after all, if negative liberty is demarcated by the boundaries of the law, as we have already seen, those boundaries are themselves more controlled for the poor and women; if women and landless workers should be free to pursue what they want within the bounds of law, those bounds are fairly narrow and do not permit them to want very much.

This would explain why the majority of citizens, who do not receive much education and therefore cannot think rationally, must be obligated to the state via tacit consent. So when Locke talks about "strong Obligations of Necessity, Convenience, and Inclination [that] drive [man] into *Society*" (*Two Treatises*, 2.77), this will appear to be a contradiction to a contemporary theorist of obligation who reads Locke as a strict consent theorist; you cannot have "obligations of inclination," for instance, because if you want to do something, whether you also have an obligation to do it is beside the point. Obligations are conceptually relevant only in cases where I would otherwise not wish to do something. Similarly, obligations of "necessity" contradict the need to base obligations on choice and consent: the idea of obligation always presupposes that I could fail to fulfill the obligation, but doing so would be wrong; that is the whole point of basing the concept of "obligation" on choice. But even though Locke is generally seen as providing the foundation for this common understanding of obligation, in fact his theory constructs a complex order in which God has set things up so that you will do the things that you need to do.[41] Such a decision must be made *for* most people, because they have not benefited from the positive liberty of the private sphere; but we can rest assured that it is the decision that they *would* make if they were rational, for such an assumption is necessary for freedom. And because of tacit consent, we can say that they actually *have* made that decision.

My interpretation highlights, at the same time that it facilitates resolution of, the tension in Locke between reason and freedom. In his *Essay Concerning Human Understanding*, Locke argues that liberty and "understanding" are interdependent:

> Without Liberty the Understanding would be to no purpose: And without Understanding, Liberty (if it could be) would signify nothing. . . . he that is at liberty to ramble in perfect darkness, what is his liberty better than if he were driven up and down, as a bubble by the force of the wind? The being acted by a blind impulse from without, or from within, is little odds. The first therefore and great use of Liberty, is to hinder blind Precipitancy; the principal exercise of Freedom is to stand still, open the eyes, look about, and take a view of the consequence of what we are going to do, as much as the weight of the matter requires.[42]

When combined with his frank claims about the limited reasoning abilities of laborers and his more ambiguous comments about women's reason, Locke could be taken to suggest in this passage that women and the poor can never enjoy freedom at all in any form because they lack understanding. But if Locke adheres to a two-tiered understanding of liberty, as I am suggesting, then perhaps he could be taken to say that liberty and understanding do not necessarily have to coexist in *every individual*.

That is, the two parts must fit together: "understanding"—which is linked to reason, the essence of freedom in the positive sense—and "liberty," defined in negative liberty terms as the absence of external impediments and particularly of arbitrary authority. But it is conceivable that the interdependence of understanding and liberty could be seen, in positive liberty fashion, in a communal sense: if a sufficient number of well-educated property owners have adequate understanding, then all of us can be free.[43]

This resolution may work better for landless workers than it does for women, however: without education, neither women nor workers can ever be subjects of positive liberty and right reason. But whereas laboring women, like laboring men, simply do not have the resources for such education, bourgeois women have them under their very roof and are, I have suggested, explicitly denied them. Furthermore, as beings confined to the private realm, women are never subjects of negative freedom either; or more precisely, the only way in which women are negatively free to pursue their conveniences is if what they want coheres with social norms about women's role, which is actually more a prescription for positive than negative liberty. The two vicious circles of gender and class are at least overlapping, however, if not concentric. If Locke bifurcates freedom into public and private components, then the "free" individual must partake of both parts, which neither upper-class women nor laborers—not to mention their wives—could ever do.

Indeed, mention of laborers' wives is somewhat misleading, for Locke argued that women of the lower classes could and should work for wages. In his "Essay on the Poor Law" he argues that although child rearing is burdensome enough to prevent women from working out of the home full time, it is not so time-consuming that their days are completely filled. Thus, women have many "broken intervals in their time" during which they "earn nothing" and "their labour is wholly lost" ("Poor Law," 189). Given that "a man and his wife, in health, may be able by their ordinary labour to maintain themselves and two children" and because "more than two children at one time, under the age of 3 years, will seldom happen in one family" ("Poor Law," 191), Locke suggested that all poor children aged three to fourteen be sent to "working schools," which were, in effect, wool-spinning factories ("Poor Law," 182, 192). By this measure, Locke ensured not only that children would contribute to their own upkeep, but also that both parents, particularly mothers, would be able to work for wages.[44] Locke does not ask whether such women are good mothers or whether full-time mothering is good for children; families who can afford to support women in these idle, unproductive "intervals" are certainly justified in doing so (though in this essay Locke assumes that middle- and upper-class women are more likely to fill these intervals productively without external prompting; presumably having servants and a large house to manage is more time-consuming than a small cottage). And Locke seems to believe that is the preferred arrangement, all things considered equal. But for those asking for parish relief, we have seen, things are not equal. Hence, Locke seeks a solution that will enable such women to be productive, namely, to take children out of the home altogether.

Whatever one might think of Locke's efficiency, and whether it was simply an excuse for class hatred and disdain, his prescriptions suggest that poor women were more on a par with poor men than bourgeois women were with men of their class, and that class intersects significantly with gender in Locke's writings. Through paid work, Locke wanted poor women to develop the same rudimentary level of reason that poor men could develop, as that level was necessary to living an independent life: that is, independent of parish relief. It is only girls and women of the gentry who would need to have their natural capacity for reason less developed than their male peers. Indeed, because women of the gentry did not work out of the home as poor women did—as I noted in the previous chapter, paid work had become taboo for such women by the end of the seventeenth century—they might be even less rational, though one assumes that the tasks of household management might be as productive of reason as was spinning wool. Perhaps that is also why it was desirable that poor women work, but not wealthy or middle-class women. The class division in social role coheres with class division in reasoning skills, for not only do poor women need merely the same basic level of reason that poor men need, but their developing it does not threaten the social order. Neither poor men nor poor women would have sufficient reason to be political agents, only enough to see the wisdom in labor and obedience. By contrast, upper-class women were in a position to challenge their second-class status, a challenge that education and the development of right reason would have facilitated.

THE CONSTRUCTION OF INDIVIDUALITY, THE DISCIPLINE OF FREEDOM

This dual theory of freedom that I have posited highlights the need to appreciate not just the classical liberal negative liberty themes in Locke's work, but the positive liberty themes as well. In particular, the idea of self-mastery that is key to Locke's *Education*—as well as the notion that such self-mastery requires outside assistance—is clearly a key element of positive liberty. Though Locke presents a gloss of liberal toleration, natural freedom and equality, and a concept of reason consonant with individual choice, underneath this gloss would seem to lie a notion of a divided will, a higher truth, and a "true" path to reason and happiness. Yet it would be mistaken to deny the classic negative liberty elements of Locke's theory, for he clearly intends these constructive elements to produce "individuals" who are appropriate subjects of negative liberty. The individuality that Locke calls a natural phenomenon in the *Second Treatise* is actually socially constructed and produced. The "naturalness" of the individual lies in the fact that we are inescapably separate from one another, with our own thoughts and desires; but without a social setting, such individuality would have little meaning because we could not get what we want. God therefore creates in us a natural need to have our individual capacities developed in social settings; he gives us the power to see the advantages of social cooperation in producing our individual development. In this sense, individuality is like reason: it is a natural capacity, but the ability to express it must be developed, constructed, and produced. Social construction, in this sense, is paradoxically natural.

This duality of negative and positive liberty is particularly evident in Locke's *Essay Concerning Human Understanding*, and especially in the chapter "Of Power" in book 2. On the one hand, Locke asserts repeatedly that freedom consists in the ability to act unconstrained by external forces: "so far as a Man has a power to think, or not to think; to move, or not to move, according to the preference or direction of his own mind, so far is a Man *Free*."[45] "Man . . . could not be *free* if his *will* were determin'd by anything, but his own *desire* guided by his own *Judgment*" (*Essay*, 2.21.71). Locke refutes Hobbes's conception of freedom as being about movement, declaring freedom to be in the realm of agency and action: "*Powers*," specifically powers to act on desire and express the will, "belong only to *Agents*" (2.21.16). Liberty and necessity are not consonant but opposed, contrary to Hobbes's assertion, for liberty requires volition and critical thinking that leads to the making of choices (2.21.8). Although such gestures away from Hobbes might lead us to think that Locke is also moving away from negative liberty, such moves in fact narrow the notion of freedom to even stricter negative liberty scrutiny. Locke goes on at considerable length to distinguish between the terms "voluntary" and "free," the former referring to the will and desire, the latter to the physical conditions that permit or prevent my acting on my will. With rather Hobbesian imagery, Locke says, "*Liberty is not an* Idea *belonging to Volition*. . . . there is want of *Freedom*, though the sitting still even of a *Paralytick*, whilst he prefers it to a removal, is truly voluntary" (2.21.11).

The divorce of volition from freedom, however, also allows Locke to permit considerable influence on the will into his definition of freedom. Particularly in "Of Power," Locke gestures toward "second-guessing." Rational deliberation of our desires is key to freedom, he maintains—not just *acting* on desires, but *evaluating* them to see if they agree with goodness, virtue, and right reason and therefore with our own happiness

(*Essay*, 2.21.52). But this deliberation, and the rationality that guides it, is very particular, ruled by morality: "*the power of Preferring should be determined by Good*" (2.21.48). Indeed, "the more steadily *determined in their choice of Good*," the freer people are (2.21.49). Given that happiness is "our greatest good," then the more we desire this good, "the more we are free from any necessary determination of our *will* to any particular action"; for "the care of our selves, that we mistake not imaginary for real happiness, is the necessary foundation of our *liberty*" (2.21.51). After all, Locke asks, "Is it worth the Name of *Freedom* to be at liberty to play the Fool, and draw Shame and Misery upon a Man's Self?" (2.21.50). People's reason and wills must be driven to the right choices: "change but a Man's view of these things; let him see that Virtue and Religion are necessary to his Happiness" (2.21.60). Such direction of the will is not constraint but liberty. In this, the fundamental difference between positive and negative liberty collapses: to repeat, "The being acted by a blind impulse from without, or from within, is little odds" (2.21.67). Locke equates external force or constraint with internal blockage or compulsion because what is essential to attaining freedom is choosing well. To be an agent, we must not only think critically about our choices, but also make the *right* choices—the path to which, Locke indicates, is clear, even if not everyone can see it.

This view of freedom and volition feeds back into Locke's account of education, for as "Men may and should correct their palates" (*Essay*, 2.21.69) to will the good, education is the most effective way to do this. Thus, a number of commentators agree with Uday Mehta that Locke seems to intertwine submission and autonomy, obedience and rationality. Where they differ from Mehta, however, is how consistent such intertwining is with a basically liberal view of the self. Nathan Tarcov, for instance, offers a largely liberal reading of Lockean individuals as "*self*-disciplining"; that is, once they are supplied with the tools to access their rationality, they must be self-directing. For him, the ability to choose, though limited by certain parameters, is still robust enough to be consistent with common notions of liberalism and negative liberty. Though education "makes" us, we also have a basic core of rationality and virtue that education pushes in particular directions.[46] Tarcov reminds us of the importance of "self-mastery" and the fact that "men desire that others should not be their masters."[47] He also argues that Lockean men "desire liberty itself more than the particular objects of their desire," which would contradict any notion of positive liberty, where the procedural elements of choice-making are subservient to the attainment of the truth.[48]

Alex Neil pushes this notion further—even criticizing Tarcov for not going far enough—by arguing for the absolute primacy of "epistemic individualism" in Locke. What is central to the *Education*, Neil contends, is not the simple imparting of particular moral beliefs that children should unthinkingly embrace as habits, but the ability to think for themselves. The reason why the character of the tutor is so important is to protect against the danger of corrupting children precisely by giving them pre-packaged ideas and thereby inhibiting their critical faculties. The tabula rasa cuts both ways, "for white paper receives any characters," bad as well as good; but it is a given that it must receive *some* characters, even simple sense data, because it is impossible to go through life with a blank slate. Given this, and given the resulting dangers of a bad education that substitutes mindless conformity for autonomous thinking, Locke's inten-tion is "not to impart knowledge, but to provide an atmosphere in which the child's understanding . . . will enable him to gain knowledge for him-self."[49] Neal Wood supports this reading by arguing that the ideal to which this education is to lead is "bourgeois man, a self-directed individ-ual with a work ethic." He maintains that "Locke's idea is the self-di-rected, autonomous individual" who recognizes the fetters of common opinion and struggles to be free of them. Self-discipline is "the only way of freedom," but it leads that way through "the path of moderation and temperance," not absolutism and authoritarianism.[50] Isaac Kramnick agrees with such readings, suggesting that although the *Education* is "a veritable diatribe against idleness" and a prescription for ensuring that children be productive, this is to the end of preparing children to be ratio-nal choosers; hence, instead of "abstract speculation and imaginative flight, children . . . should use their powers of observation and experience in examining the world close at hand." Rather than reading fairy tales and "trumpery," they were to keep account books. Such recommenda-tions were in support of a Protestantism that emphasized "activity and industry" as well as reason in the modified meaning of "the sober world of common sense."[51]

Such arguments are correct to a certain extent. In defending against Filmer's theory of patriarchy, Locke says that "*natural Freedom and Sub-jection to Parents* may consist together [as] both are founded on the same Principle. . . . The *Freedom of a Man at years of discretion*, and the *Sub-jection* of a Child *to* his *Parents*, whilst yet short of that Age, are so consis-tent, and so distinguishable, that the most blinded Contenders for Monar-chy, *by Right of Fatherhood*, cannot miss this *difference*" (*Two Treatises*, 2.61). But as Gordon Schochet maintains, "Nonetheless, Locke recog-nized that parents—and fathers in particular—effectively had great con-trol over their children and could use this control to induce their off-spring" to make certain choices about politics and other things.[52] This observation could be pushed further, however, to suggest that Tarcov, Neil, Wood, and Kramnick may miss the point that these "self-choosing" individuals have been carefully constructed through education, social institutions, and law, so that they will "want" to choose the "right" things. Thus, I rather agree with Mehta that for Locke, individuality is "disciplined" in Foucault's sense. Locke is quite concerned with the nature of desire: how I come to want what I want, how I come to be the kind of person who desires what I desire. Moreover, he is concerned that I be a very particular kind of person who desires very particular kinds of things, who sees and interprets the world in a very particular way—dictated, perhaps, by God's divine architecture, as McClure argues, but directed by Locke's all-too-human blueprint.

Locke's views on religious toleration particularly reveal this social construction of individuality. Toleration is usually taken as the quintessential liberal negative freedom, and the common reading of Locke suggests that he has encapsulated its essential principles. Locke argues that regulation of religious belief is not the business of government. The proper realm of the magistrate is specifically the "outer" realm; he has no place trying to rule people's minds, even by using his appropriate power over the external realm to do so. Being compelled to a set of beliefs cannot produce a "genuine" faith; "penalties are no way capable to produce such belief. It is only light and evidence that can work a change in men's opinions."[53] Only I can determine my beliefs for myself, Locke says. After all, if I am mistaken, I will harm only myself, whereas if the magistrate is wrong, he damns everyone. And given that the large numbers of magistrates in the world cannot agree on one true religion, the odds are that many magistrates must be wrong (*Toleration*, 19, 32). But even if a particular magistrate is correct, God requires us to discover his word by ourselves, through genuine faith and reflection. I must achieve salvation for myself: "I cannot be saved by a religion that I distrust and by a worship that I abhor. It is in vain for an unbeliever to take up the outward show of another man's profession. Faith only and inward sincerity are the things that procure acceptance with God" (34). True faith and salvation require free choice, namely, that we choose the path to God and act in accordance with belief (36–38). Thus, toleration should be practiced because repression is morally wrong and, pragmatically, does not work: "such is the nature of the understanding that it cannot be compelled to the belief of anything by outward force" (18). The magistrate cannot force people's beliefs to change simply by forcing them to behave in certain ways; such attempts will only foster discontent, which may destabilize the regime. Given this, it would be irrational for citizens to grant the magistrate the power to decide our faith; for by consenting to such authority, we place ourselves under an obligation—to believe what the magistrate tells us to believe—that we may be simply unable to fulfill.[54]

As David Wootten argues, Locke's *Letter Concerning Toleration* would thus seem to establish the fundamentals of liberal negative liberty,[55] and the relationship between the social contract and religious tolerance would seem to embody the classic liberal separation of church and state. But a deeper reading shows that Locke is not concerned with tolerance for difference as much as for one particular way of being. This is particularly evident in the exceptions he notes to toleration: we should not tolerate the intolerant (for obvious reasons) and atheists, because they cannot logically take oaths, given that belief in God is the foundation of oath-taking (*Toleration*, 52). More significantly, however, Locke says that we cannot tolerate "those who . . . *ipso facto* deliver themselves up to the protection and service of another prince." He explicitly names "Mahometans" as the target of his remarks, but implicitly, most commentators agree, he is talking about Catholics, because their allegiance to the foreign power of the pope leaves them unfree to consent to the magistrate's authority (51). Locke's emphasis on property and its placement at the heart of freedom dovetail with this concern, because Locke is highly aware that, with Catholics on the throne, such as Charles and James, property could be taxed or even confiscated for the good not of the English people, but of Rome.[56] Toleration of Catholics would thus deploy a notion of freedom that was self-defeating, if not self-contradictory.

Given his earlier argument about the inefficacy of repression stemming from the separation of belief from action, however, and his argument that the magistrate's domain is the "outer" realm of action, rather than thought, it is disturbing that here Locke seeks to purge thoughts. If action and belief were truly unrelated in the strong way suggested by his own argument, then Catholics and atheists should be allowed to believe what they want, as long as they do not act on such beliefs in a way that jeopardizes the state. That Locke seemed to believe this was a logical contradiction—that atheists and Muslims (or Catholics) threatened civil society by their very existence—relates to his fourth, and vaguest, category of what does not deserve toleration, namely, "opinions contrary to human society, or to those moral rules which are necessary to the preservation of civil society" (*Toleration*, 50). Previous to this, Locke said that "things that are prejudicial to the commonweal of a people in their ordinary use, and are therefore forbidden by laws . . . ought not to be permitted to the churches in their sacred rites." But he accompanied this with the warning that "the magistrate ought always to be very careful that he do not misuse his authority to the oppression of any church, under pretense of public good" (40). By contrast, the formulation he offers several pages later of this category of nontoleration is much broader and carries no such parallel warning to the magistrate. Furthermore, it specifically forbids opinions and beliefs, which are supposedly not the proper domain of government regulation, whereas the earlier passage, by referring to "rites," indicates *actions*, which are legitimate subjects of state regulation. The restrictions on opinion could, at least in theory, include any sort of opinion or belief that conflicts whatsoever with the principles Locke puts forth in his *Two Treatises*, putting an entirely different spin on the common reading of Locke as the father of liberalism.

These factors I have mentioned suggest a substantive political purpose behind Locke's views on toleration, rather than a liberal negative liberty defense of freedom of the mind and conscience from governmental interference; what we are to be tolerant of specifically is Protestantism, because only this faith is consonant with liberal principles, and indeed with Locke's own blueprint for government.[57] In this, Locke's partisanship over the Exclusion Crisis and his concern with the possibility of a Catholic monarch show the *Letter Concerning Toleration* to be at least as much a political pamphlet with a substantive agenda as a philosophical tract exploring general political issues. But the essay also raises some skepticism about Locke's views on the distinction between the external and internal. As we have seen in his theory of education, Locke not only believed in the ability to shape people's values and thoughts via external means, but advocated it as the only way to create beings who could realize the supposedly "natural" freedom and rationality he claims they have. Hence, the purpose of education is to turn children into rational adults, which requires them to develop "reason" into "right reason" so that they can discern and understand God's order and their place in that order.

The notion that substance supersedes process in the understanding of freedom—that we need to develop not just a "faculty of the mind" but an understanding of very particular principles and ideas that must guide our lives in order to achieve individuality—is made perhaps most strongly among Lockean commentators by Mehta. Though he is concerned more with the *Education* than the *Letter Concerning Toleration*, Mehta maintains that Locke, in overt contradiction to negative liberty, is centrally concerned with shaping the mind, the very essence of individuality, through a rigorous and authoritarian practice. What Mehta calls the "anxiety of freedom" lies at the heart of the social contract's tacit consent, for that is how the state protects against the possibility that people might consent to the wrong things if left on their own.[58] Education is crucial to this, however, because some must make the laws to which the rest of us consent. Indeed, the education theme dominates throughout Locke's political writings, according to Mehta, because "the extent and intensity of cognitive disorders Locke associates with the natural human being" justifies treating adults just like children, who need to be kept "in a condition of tutelage before they actually become free."[59] The "substitute parent" here is government, particularly a supposedly representative one that is in fact run by a small minority of propertied "gentlemen." To "free" people from the dangers of natural freedom, people must be educated; this education is not the classical liberal offering of information and competing points of view, however, but rather the unitary and relentless, even dogmatic imparting of moral values—whether through forced labor, a working school, or moral education in the family—to the end of shaping people's character in a particular way.

Formal education might be seen to challenge this shaping, for it must be conducted in the family precisely because it needs to be individually tailored to children, who are all different. But in fact the end product of such individualized education is a basic uniformity: to reason "rightly" we must reach very particular conclusions. Indeed, one could suggest that the point of individualizing education in the family is so that children can all come out the same, in direct contrast to the liberal educational ideal of providing students with the same material and helping them develop different perspectives on it. If children start out with different aptitudes and characters, strengths and weaknesses, then each one will need an individually tailored program to produce the same outcome.

But Mehta sees this process as somewhat less benign than other commentators such as Kramnick, Wood, and Neil do. He argues that, given that the end of education is to develop reason, reason itself cannot be used to make children behave. Rather, force must be deployed, usually in the form of mental and emotional manipulation and the simple brute denial of a child's desires: for example, refusing to give a child a piece of fruit (which Locke thought unhealthy). But it can also take the form of physical force in extreme cases of "stubborn" and "obstinate" children—those children who, Mehta argues, display the strongest natural individualism.[60] He suggests that in Locke's system of education, developing the intellect by providing knowledge does less to stimulate the development of reason than does forcing children to follow moral and social codes that involve the restriction and restraint of their passions and impulses.

Mehta's reading may tend to oversimplify the goal of education, for although it is true that character is a major theme of the *Education*, as I have argued throughout this chapter, standard subjects do take center stage in the last third of the book, thus suggesting that morals and character do not simply replace Latin, Greek, mathematics, and philosophy (though the former may be more important than the latter). In fact, as I have noted, in the *Conduct* Locke explicitly says that they are crucial to the development of full reason. Rather, perhaps it is that morals and character are more *difficult* to learn, because whereas mathematics does not change in response to custom and culture, child rearing does, and hence good parents need wise guidance. Furthermore, Latin, Greek, and the rest are best learned when young men reach their later teens and early twenties, which provides ample time for the "white sheet" to be sullied and ruined by that point. The character elements must be in place first; otherwise no matter how much Latin and mathematics a young man learns, he will not develop reason rightly. Because morals and character provide the foundation for putting the intellectual subjects to their proper use, Locke attends to them at twice the length—and in much greater detail—than he does academic subjects. But the latter will be equally important to the training of a gentleman and the development of right reason. In other words, though I agree with the general theme of Mehta's argument, I believe he overstates the case.

However, Mehta's reading does suggest an intriguing opening onto gender. In that discipline and building of character seem to be of greater importance to Locke's theory of education than are Latin and mathematics, there would certainly be no contradiction in providing girls with *this* kind of education. Indeed, the notion that "self-discipline requires submission not to one's own reason, but rather to the reason of others" takes on a deeper meaning. What girls need is discipline; and as this disciplinary education is to occur in the family, saying that children owe obedience to mothers as well as fathers once again serves a utilitarian purpose, for Locke has simply doubled his disciplinary force. Indeed, Mehta points out that the only illustration Locke offers of physical punishment, which as I have noted is to be reserved for a "stubborn" and "obstinate" child who displays an independent nature, is that of "A prudent and kind Mother" who is

> forced to whip her little Daughter, at her first coming home from Nurse [which would make the child at most two or possibly up to three years old] eight times successively the same Morning, before she could master her *Stubbornness*, and obtain a compliance in a very easie and indifferent matter. If she had left off sooner, and stopped at the seventh Whipping, she had spoiled the Child for ever; and, by her unprevailing Blows, only confirmed her *refractoriness*, very hardly afterwards to be cured: But wisely persisting, till she had bent her Mind, and suppled her will, the only end of Correction and Chastisement, she established her Authority throughly [sic] in the very first occasion, and had ever after a very ready Compliance and Obedience in all things from her Daughter. For as this was the first time, so, I think, it was the last too she ever struck her.[61]

Mehta comments, "One can only guess what gesture of her little body revealed her mind's refractoriness, what particular shrillness of the screech, following the eighth whip, now made clear her compliant will and her 'bent' mind."[62] Mehta's point, to show that Locke's "anxiety of freedom" is an almost incapacitating one, in response to which he builds an authoritarian edifice that will bear no breach, is particularly powerful here. In the first place, it is notable that the punishment has effected so complete a "cure" of the child's obstinacy; this suggests terror in the child's mind rather than "compliance," thus contradicting Locke's purpose for physical punishment, which is to produce shame rather than fear. Second, it is also worth noting that the mother is the parent inflicting the whipping; for Locke paints the whipping in colors of dispassionate rationality, thus suggesting that women can be equally authoritative and rational in dealing with children, rather than uselessly emotional and indulgent, as he elsewhere indicates in the *Education* (esp. sec. 7). As Locke points out in the *Two Treatises*, mothers and fathers are fairly equal within the family, at least in regard to their children (2.71, 78–84).

The purpose of granting such power to women is to the benefit of children's reason, however, not women's equality; after all, how can sons be taught discipline if their sisters are allowed to misbehave? So the dispensing of such discipline to girls does not mean that they will eventually be able to take over their own lives for themselves sufficient to the needs of citizenship and political participation, not to mention true freedom. Indeed, Mehta suggests just the opposite, pointing out "one can only wonder why, in one of the very few examples in the *Thoughts* [*Concerning Education*] of a mother and her daughter, the latter should serve as a metonomy for a form of defiant alterity in the face of which liberalism deploys the weapons of absolutism, brandished by the mother with a horrifying but precisely calibrated tenacity and certainty."[63] Indeed, physical punishment would seem particularly directed to girls, who must learn submission even more than boys, as they will have to accustom themselves to submitting to their husbands. After all, girls might naturally be more resistant to authority, because they may foresee a future of foreshortened possibilities, in contrast to their privileged brothers.

CONCLUSION

Although these arguments might suggest that the traditional reading of Locke as a classically liberal negative libertarian are simply mistaken, and that he is plainly authoritarian in the worst sense of positive liberty, I think they imply something more subtle and complicated. Locke sees himself as advocating negative liberty and classical liberal principles; again we must return to the central core value of his political writings, namely, the protection of individuals from tyrannical government, via individual rights, and particularly rights to property. The argument that Locke's theory displays the contrary forces of elitism and authoritarianism must be seen as a subtext about which he is himself unaware (or at least not fully aware); indeed, it is the "sustained denial" of such elements that "crucially jeopardizes [Locke's] political prescriptions."[64] It is not what Locke intends or wants. And yet it is there; the reading of Locke as a liberal individualist that many commentators hold on to glosses over this fact.

Instead, Locke displays a *tension between* the negative liberty view that individuals know what is best for themselves and must be able to pursue what they want and the positive liberty view that some desires are better than others, pursuit of which will produce a better, more meaningful freedom. It is this tension that results in his dual theory of freedom along class and gender lines. Reason is the foundation of natural freedom and all other freedom-related principles, especially property and consent. The problem that rationality poses for Locke in his *Second Treatise* points to a deeper problem about the role of the internal self in matters of freedom. Freedom for Locke is not simply being able to do what I want to do; it also involves some qualitative evaluation about what I want to do. Indeed, it involves a considerable amount of shaping individual desire to want certain things and not others.

In this shaping, Locke can be seen explicitly to restrict bourgeois women's liberty as well as that of the poor and laboring classes; but because, unlike Rousseau, he never articulates what precisely it is about women's freedom that fuels his anxiety, we are left on less sure footing than we are even with Hobbes. And indeed, as commentators have long noted,[65] Locke is famous for granting certain equality and freedoms to women: women are equal to men in being owed the respect of children and in exercising authority over them; they seem on a par with husbands in familial authority in general; and they should be free to divorce husbands and be given superior consideration in child custody (*Two Treatises*, 2.71, 78–84). Thus, in some ways, Locke provides the foundation for liberal feminism. But his gender politics are somewhat inconsistent, suggesting that women have at best an uncertain and incomplete relationship to liberty in his theory. This uncertainty is in some ways contingent; that is, Locke happens to deny women rights and liberty because of uncritically sexist beliefs that he could easily reject, and that indeed can be seen to contradict his fundamental theoretical claims. But in other ways, it is structural; that is, his theory of freedom is made possible only by virtue of its uneven distribution, such that freedom for propertied white men is based on the unfreedom, or at least lesser freedom, of women and unpropertied males.[66] This latter element in Locke is important because it reveals a central problem with negative liberty. As Hobbes illustrated—and as Locke recognized in his principle of equal liberty—negative liberty is conceived as zero-sum: conflicts of liberties are inevitable, and my gain must come at your loss. Locke, more explicitly than Hobbes, attributes the gains and losses to specific groups of people. The question as to whether such attribution is necessary to negative liberty or merely a contingent happenstance of a particular time and place is unsettled, but disturbingly suggestive.

Does this mean that the gender and class bias of Locke's work undermines his theory of freedom? Yes and no. His claims for universal and natural freedom are certainly unsettled by the contingent happenstances of class and gender, as the freedom of propertied men to some extent comes at the cost of the unfreedom of women and workers. But Locke does not advocate a simplistic vision of negative liberty. Although freedom from arbitrary power was the foundation of political freedom, and may have been necessary to a coherent theoretical construction of the concept, it clearly was not sufficient to Locke's notion of freedom, which was much more complexly packed than was Hobbes's. Even more than Hobbes, Locke shows that the negative/positive typology is fundamentally flawed in its reductive categories and that a coherent theory of freedom must borrow from elements of both models. But Locke also shows that the foundation for the negative/positive typology—a theorist's conception of a person—is more important to understanding his or her vision of freedom than the absence of governmental limitation. And in this, Locke has a conception of the person that is at least as much in line with positive liberty as negative liberty, if not more so.

CHAPTER THREE

Jean-Jacques Rousseau

FORCE, FREEDOM, AND FAMILY

WHETHER THE GENDER bias outlined in the previous chapter is limited explicitly to the negative liberty theory generally associated with "liberal" political theorists such as Locke is an important question, for there is an argument to be made that feminism is much more consistent with the principles of positive liberty. Its notions of community and relationship in particular suggest that positive liberty may provide a better theoretical home for feminist conceptualizations. Thus, this argument might go, if I were to consider theorists allied with positive liberty, I would have less to critique from a feminist perspective. But of course I have already challenged the common classification of both Locke and Hobbes as negative libertarians and shown that attention to gender makes this challenge particularly evident. Furthermore, in the analysis that follows of two key theorists in the modern canon who pay considerable attention to the "inner self" as the core of liberty, namely Rousseau and Kant, many of the same problems, questions, and features persist: particularly the failure to interrogate assumptions about the self that is the free subject, the gendered orientation of those assumptions and that self, and the unavoidable incorporation of elements generally attributed to the contrasting model of freedom. In this sense, though there is an overt contrast between the visions of freedom offered by these two theorists with those of the prior two chapters, there is a subtler but even more substantial continuity that reveals important insights about the concept of liberty as it has developed in the modern canon.

Rousseau's theory is a particularly significant place to start this analysis, for many of the key problems I identified in the most ostensibly negative liberty characteristics of Locke's theory are similarly recognized and confronted by Rousseau. Indeed, as Carole Pateman points out, the form of government Rousseau criticizes at the end of *The Origin of Inequality*—the duplicitous and "false" social contract that benefits the rich at the expense of the poor—is specifically a Lockean social contract.[1] This critical perspective on Locke's framework is in part the result of Rousseau's quite different conception of freedom. As Rebecca Kukla argues,

"Rousseau believed that freedom was humankind's 'noblest faculty.' "[2] And Susan Shell maintains that for Rousseau, "the essential quality of man . . . is not reason," as was the case for so many other political theorists ancient and modern, but "freedom."[3] What Rousseau actually means by freedom, however, is a complicated question. Though he is often categorized as a positive libertarian, primarily because of his concept of the general will and his infamous "*forcer d'être libre*," in fact Rousseau has an extremely complex and multilayered notion of freedom, one that goes through a number of historical transformations during the course of human development, as well as one that exists at several levels simultaneously in contemporary "man."

ROUSSEAU'S THREE KINDS OF FREEDOM

Like the other social contract theorists, Rousseau begins his theorizing by imagining man in a "state of nature," but this state, as outlined in his *Discourse on Inequality*, is very different from the one Hobbes and Locke articulated. Whereas each of them imagined a static state that humans left all at once through the implementation of the social contract, Rousseau imagined a much more developmental history in which the loss of what is "natural" and the adoption of what is "social" is gradual and often difficult to demarcate. For him, the social contract solidifies social arrangements that have already developed through other means, rather than marking a radical break with the natural past.

The most notable difference is that, for Rousseau, nature itself is a dynamic process. He posits human nature not as fully contained and defined, as do Hobbes and Locke, but as holding many different possibilities, some of which will be developed in certain social contexts and others in other contexts. Indeed, Rousseau's conjectural history can be seen as a prescient metaphor for evolution, as he traces the progression of less evolved "beasts" into "humans." Rousseau is suggesting that humans have become the creatures they currently are in part through the chance of particular world historical developments—such as the development of metallurgy and agriculture, or whatever quirk prompted "the first man who, having enclosed a piece of ground, bethought himself of saying 'This is mine,' " thereby establishing the idea and practice of private property— and in part through the "survival of the fittest," who are able to respond most effectively to such events through the development of particular aspects of their "nature."[4] Though human society is formed in response to natural events, in other words, equally important is the exercise of the human capacity of choice and will. Rousseau's belief in the "perfectibility" of man involved the idea that our reactions to external factors, the choices that we make, shape those factors and us as well. Thus, though the development of metallurgy and agriculture are social and historical forces over which no human had control, they are at the same time the indisputable products of human endeavor.

This developmental-historical representation of the state of nature is reflected in how Rousseau articulates freedom, for he postulates three different kinds. The first is natural freedom, which is based primarily on force; as for Hobbes, it is the freedom to do whatever one physically can, and is found in the first stage of the state of nature. Only "natural" limitations on freedom exist here, but these are of two kinds. The first and most obvious are constituted by the physical laws of nature such as gravity; as these are universal, they define or limit freedom for everyone in the same manner. Accordingly, the freedom within these limits can be considered absolute: if I jump off a cliff, gravity will pull me down, and no matter who I am, how large or small or strong or weak, I will fall. In this early, primitive period of the state of nature, everyone is perfectly equal.

However, natural freedom can also be limited by the superior strength of other individuals; this happens in the second stage of the state of nature, when individuals become more numerous and are forced to interact. Such interaction entails conflict over resources, and in such conflicts the strong or the smart will tend to win over the weak or stupid. Accordingly, the limits on freedom, though natural, are not universal but relative, favoring the strong over the weak, the smarter over the less intelligent.[5] This stage of the state of nature approaches Hobbes's state of war, where individuals are free to achieve whatever they want as long as they can exert superior force over others. Like Hobbes, Rousseau says that physical dependence arising from differences in strength is in itself difficult to sustain: nobody could keep anybody else in dependence for long if physical force were their sole means of doing so. Rather, there is a constant state of struggle back and forth. This struggle would seem to include women as participants; again like Hobbes, Rousseau seems to believe that in the state of nature, women are the perfect equals of men, equally perfectly free. Rousseau does not even argue that women's reproductive biology limits their freedom, for women can run easily with infants and children when hunting food or fleeing an enemy. Furthermore, women's attachment to offspring is minimal—mothers nurse to alleviate their discomfort and then out of "habit," but children leave as soon as they are able, and shortly thereafter mother and child do not even recognize each other. So women would seem to be as free as men physically, psychologically, and emotionally.

The frequent conflict that marks this stage of the state of nature leads Rousseau to postulate that people must change their patterns of interaction or perish. But rather than immediately turning over liberty to the Leviathan, Rousseau says, society develops in a more gradual fashion; people

begin associating with each other in basic and primitive nonmediated societies. These associations do not arise from a "natural" sociability, according
to Rousseau, but rather from the development of reason. Specifically, when
population increases to produce more frequent interaction, and its resul-
tant conflict, a key result is that passions intensify, thereby diminishing the
natural compatibility and compassion (*pitié*) found in savage man. After
all, if my wants are easily met, my desire for the objects of my wants will
be moderate; it is the possibility of not attaining the desired object that
increases the intensity of my desire for it in Rousseau's view. So the competition and conflict that exist in this period result not only from simple scarcity—more people competing for the same number of resources—but from
natural emotion and psychology that develop as a result of the denial of
objects desired and needed for survival. I now am forced to recognize other
people because they potentially threaten my survival.

But reason develops dialectically with the passions and fills the gap
that this new "unsociability" creates. That is, the intensified passion for
particular things stimulates the development of reason as an important
tool to facilitate the satisfaction of these passions. Rousseau seems to
suggest that as long as passions and desires are moderate, as they are in
the primitive stages of the state of nature, there is little incentive for reason
to develop. When the strong systematically satisfy their passions at the
expense of the weak, however, the reason of the weak must develop to
compensate, or they will die off. Similarly, the strong in turn must deploy
reason to use their strength in ways that will achieve the ends they seek
if they are not to lose their physical advantage. The development of such
reason does not merely facilitate conflict, however, but cooperation as
well. For cooperation provides a strategic advantage, whether it be cooperation among the weak to overcome the strong or cooperation among
men of any strength to overcome nature itself, for example, to capture a
large animal such as a deer (*Second Discourse*, 87). As Nannerl Keohane
notes, "the repeated sharing of such experiences leads to the taste for
more, and sets the stage for social life."[6] Although our passions cause
competition and antagonism, our needs cause us to enter into relations,
and even motivates the origin of language (*Second Discourse*, 89).

It is important to note that Rousseau does not posit such sociability
as natural to primitive man, but as something that is acquired through
the developmental process. Although natural feelings of *pitié* enable people to see similarities between themselves and others, and hence to see
the benefits that arise from association, cooperation is specifically a
learned ability. It derives from the natural situation in which people are
born, but it is itself not natural. It is reason, which is an intellectual
capacity that must be developed, that lies at the root of humans' so-
cialness, not natural instinct. Hence, the specific social formations that

such cooperation results in, such as the family, are not natural either; though families seem to arise in part out of natural sentiments, they also arise out of the perception of the advantages of social cooperation and the division of labor. Families are particularly developed as a result of women's manipulation of men, according to Rousseau, stemming from their own reasoned perception of the particular advantages that the family and love give them over men. The family is only the first product of such manipulation, but it is the most important, for through it women bring about the greatest shift in human development. Once the family exists, then people are born into particular social relationships; gone are the days when men and women, and even women and their offspring, fail to recognize each other. And it is during people's social life together that they learn and become accustomed to think of themselves as beings who belong to, and in, communities.

It is for these reasons that Rousseau says justice replaces instinct; reason and the ability to learn cooperation, as well as the ability to perceive and understand the need for it, replace the instinctual tendency toward cooperation found in animals. This cooperation and sociability allow humans to progress in their common endeavors of subsistence. Yet ironically, it is what cooperation allows humans to produce that brings about the means to institutionalize permanent inequality and domination, as the development of property and society begins the pernicious erosion of the possibilities of natural negative freedom. Specifically, Rousseau maintains that the development of metallurgy and agriculture allowed some to gain more economic goods than others and hence to be able to wield economic power over others (*Second Discourse*, 92). Not only were these practices the result of human endeavor, they facilitated the ability of some to act willfully to press their advantages. At this point, natural freedom undergoes a subtle change; people are free to act only insofar as another's will permits it, for this economic inequality ensures mastery and subservience as mere physical force cannot. The nature of what constitutes a "barrier" to freedom becomes more abstract, opening the door to a second kind of freedom.

For in this shift, Rousseau argues, foreshadowing Hegel and Marx, the poor are not the only ones who are unfree: "each became in some degree a slave even in becoming the master of other men; if rich, they stood in need of the services of others; if poor, of their assistance" (*Second Discourse*, 95). That is, whereas the strong could always limit the freedom of the weak and could always overcome the weak if they tried to prevent them from doing what they wanted, the nature of economic inequality is such that freedom is limited in a more complex manner. Certainly, despite his early dialectical understanding of the relationship between money and freedom, Rousseau clearly believes the unfreedom of the wealthy to be more abstract than that of the poor, but it was hardly negligible.

This inequality, forced dependence, and lack of effective freedom prompt people to seek a new kind of freedom, namely, civil or political freedom, in a social contract. Political freedom consists in having human-made laws to guide behavior. The purpose of civil law is to limit the unequal natural freedom of force and to create a new sphere where power is equalized and freedom to act is heightened. As such, civil laws enable all to pursue their desires within universal restrictions; like physical laws such as gravity, civil laws apply equally and universally, thus in principle undermining the unfair advantages that the wealthy and powerful have gained at the expense of the weak and poor. Civil freedom seeks, in one sense, to restore the freedom that could not survive in the state of nature: the freedom to do what one wants, unmolested by others. But civil freedom is also quite different from natural freedom. As Rousseau suggests early in *The Social Contract*, the conundrum is how people can submit themselves to a common authority and still remain "free as before"; Rousseau says this is "the basic problem of which the Social Contract provides the solution."[7] Locke, and particularly Hobbes, argued that people in the state of nature gave up part of their freedom in exchange for order and security, and thereby a more meaningful quality of freedom, but Rousseau argues for a more transformative vision: that we entirely give up natural freedom for a different kind of freedom altogether. For Locke and Hobbes, we always maintain some of our natural liberty; we may have less of it in civil society, but the liberty we have is of the same character. For Rousseau, however, liberty itself is transformed.

At least, it is in principle. For according to Rousseau, civil freedom can be distorted, corrupted, and even used to pervert itself, depending on the terms of the contract that establishes it. In *The Origin of Inequality*, he argued that the propertied class proposed a contract that protected their property while at the same time keeping the poor propertyless. The poor were so desperate for relief that, duped by the superficial procedural equality of the contract (it "applies to all"), they gladly accepted it. This contract did not liberate men to civil freedom at all, but rather enslaved all concerned: "All ran headlong to their chains, in hopes of securing their liberty" (*Second Discourse*, 99). Such a situation was not liberating because it merely continued, in institutionalized form, the inequality and forced dependence of the state of nature. The point of the social contract posited by Locke is to figure out a way to preserve the basic qualities of humankind while controlling for the factors that undermine them. In theory, the social contract does for natural man what the state of nature never could; it preserves humanity's essential features better than they can be preserved in nature itself. Hobbes certainly does not wish to preserve the antagonism of natural man, but he does wish to provide a more secure structure in which natural man's acquisitiveness can be expressed, and to that extent his social contract similarly makes human nature safe for humans. But the practice is a different matter for both Hobbes and Locke; as I have suggested in the foregoing chapters, their contracts do not really involve a trade of freedom for order and security, or absolute freedom for effective freedom, but rather preserve the freedom of some—landed and powerful men—at the cost of the freedom of others—women, the poor, and the powerless. It is this inequality of freedom that Rousseau critiques so scathingly at the end of the *Second Discourse*.

Nevertheless, civil freedom is a key kind of human freedom. By basing his own version of the social contract on mutuality and equality, rather than the institutionalized inequalities of the status quo, Rousseau claims to realize true freedom through civil laws and political organization. Part of the difference in his specific social contract lies in the fact that rather than alienating part of your liberty to a particular person, such as a monarch or parliamentary representative, you alienate all of your freedom to every other member of society, and every other member does likewise to you. The alienation is total, reciprocal, and impersonal. Because "each gives himself absolutely, the conditions are the same for all" (*Social Contract*, bk. 1, ch. 6). Though each alienates to the community as a whole, each is a part of that whole. The community would not exist without its members; as Andrew Levine puts it, it has "no real existence separate from that of the individuals who constitute it." That is, the contract is between people as individuals with private interests and those same people as a group or sovereign who have common interests. Hence, each person, as an individual, makes "a contract, as we may say, with himself" (*Social Contract*, bk. 1, ch. 7), as a member of the whole. As Levine explains, in contracting with "himself," each person "becomes no one's slave but his own. For Rousseau, to be one's own slave is to be no slave at all; it is to obey only oneself—to be free."[8] Or, as Rousseau says, "each man, in giving himself to all, gives himself to nobody" (*Social Contract*, bk. 1, ch. 6).

Thus, to be civilly free, individuals need only follow the law. The linkage of obedience and freedom plays a strong part in Rousseau's theory. In Rousseau's novels in particular, as well as *The Government of Poland*, the source of authority that one must obey in order to be free is at times ambiguous. But in the *Social Contract* obedience to one's own laws is the highest form of freedom, namely, "moral liberty, which alone makes him truly master of himself; for the impulse of mere appetite is slavery, while obedience to a law we prescribe to ourselves is liberty" (*Social Contract*, bk. 1, ch. 8). Rousseau believes that in order for it to have any meaning, and to avoid the slavery and dependence described in *The Origin of In-*

equality, civil freedom must also be moral freedom. Certainly, moral freedom does not also have to be political; for instance, if I resolve to lose twenty pounds before my college reunion, when I get up one night to eat a fudge brownie in secret I am at some level unfree, because while I am gratifying my immediate craving, I am not doing what I really want to do, namely, lose weight. The point of moral freedom is the control of my will: dependence on the will of another person, or even subordination to one's own passions, is slavery, but self-prescribed law expresses the will and therefore embodies self-control or autonomy. Indeed, it is control on a double level, for not only does one control one's submission to the rule, one controls—that is, one has created and can change—the rule itself. So, for instance, I can decide after reading *Fat Is a Feminist Issue* that I really do not need to lose weight after all, and that I can accept and appreciate my plump physique.[9] Such a move would be distinct from the tension between "mere impulse of appetite" and true will; it would instead involve a critically reflective reevaluation of what that true will is.

In combination with political freedom, however, moral liberty is particularly powerful, as well as more demanding; "for there is a great difference between incurring an obligation to yourself and incurring one to a whole of which you form a part" (*Social Contract*, bk. 1, ch. 7). Within the context of a political structure, if I must obey laws I prescribe to myself, then I have to make the laws I am to obey: that is, I have to be part of the legislative process. Thus, what Pateman calls "participatory democracy" is the only way to achieve freedom in Rousseau's view, for it is the only way to create laws—and thus have civil freedom—in a way that coheres with the requirements of moral freedom.[10] Such participation requires more than a superficial and formal equality among citizens; it requires a substantive equality of participation, power, and access.

POLITICS AND THE WILL

The centrality of equality to Rousseau's concept of freedom foreshadows the significance of gender and class to his theory. In order to place gender and class (in)equality in Rousseau's theoretical context, however, we must first further pursue the relationship between obedience and freedom, which centers on the relationship between desire and will. For the question of who obeys whom, and whether these relationships of obedience and authority adhere to class and gender cleavages, will tell us what Rousseau means about freedom. At first glance, the relationship between authority and obedience would seem to be remarkably egalitarian, democratic, and collective, but with a somewhat perverse twist. If moral freedom requires that I make the laws that I am to obey, it also requires that I obey the laws that I participate in making. Obedience in Rousseau's polity must be absolute if the formula of moral freedom is not to be empty. Thus, if an individual disagrees with a law and is unsuccessful at persuading other citizens to alter the law in the participatory assembly, then the society is justified in forcing obedience. But whereas Hobbes argued that such coercion was a legitimate limitation on freedom for the sake of order, Rousseau argued that such coercion was itself an enhancement of freedom, because the laws represented the individual's true will; the community was therefore only forcing the individual to be free (*Social Contract*, bk. 1, ch. 7).

The notion of *forcer d'être libre* is probably the most notorious concept in Rousseau's work, if not all of modern political theory, and it is often taken to be the heart of positive liberty as well. It derives from and depends on Rousseau's notion of the general will, which he says is the will of the society. By envisioning a society as an organic but also constructed entity, Rousseau maintains that every society has a will, one that by definition constitutes the will of its members. Yet these members are not just parts of the organic whole, but also are individuals with particular needs, desires, and preferences. Thus, as positive liberty suggests, people's wills can be divided. Accordingly, the assembly, constituted as a single legislative unit made up of members acting as sovereign lawmakers, has a "general will" that may sometimes be at odds with the "will of all," or the combined self-interest of its members who must obey those laws. Because of the "dual character" of citizens of the polity—as both creators of the law and as subjects who must obey it—Rousseau argues that both the particular and general wills are "my" will. The latter, however, is more important, for without the general will, my particular will loses most of its force and value. One cannot achieve freedom outside of the assembly; civil freedom cannot be genuine moral freedom if the participatory form of government is jeopardized, for then the laws I must obey are not those I have made for myself as part of the legislative assembly. If I advocate a law that runs contrary to the interests of the community, or if I disobey a law that the community has passed, then I jeopardize my own freedom. Disobedience does far more harm to the stability and legitimacy of the democratic polity—the only political form and process within which my own freedom is possible—than I do good in pursuing my particular will. Because both the particular and the general will are my wills, the evaluation between wills does not inhibit my liberty but enhances it, as the will that prevails under Rousseau's formulation is the will that is more important to me, my higher will, the general will.

Now, some readers will argue that I have conflated two ideas here and in the process gotten Rousseau off the hook a little too easily: it is one thing to declare that preservation of the political form is more important than any individual or legislative decision, but it is quite another to say that I therefore am wrong about my own will. After all, Rousseau says that those who disagree with the majority are *in error* about their own will, and this is why they can be forced to be free, much like an alcoholic who is restrained while her friends pour her liquor down the drain. Rousseau seems to ignore the possibility that I could believe that I am correct about what the general will is, and yet also believe that respect for majority will is even more important, and thereby agree to abide by the majority even though I believe they are wrong. Nor does Rousseau help matters by seeming to vacillate between defining the general will as "majority will" and defining it as "political right," or some objective truth. The freedom of the mind, a central tenet of the liberal version of negative liberty, is problematized in Rousseau's formulation, and the problem is located in the concept of will, as it was for Hobbes and Locke. Rousseau, however, is more explicit than they in acknowledging the will's role. For Rousseau, wills can be general and particular, long- and short-term; they can express two or more conflicting desires simultaneously. It is this dual nature of the will that leads to what Taylor calls "second-guessing," and this second-guessing is what most commentators link to the totalitarian potential of Rousseau's theory, as I discussed in the introductory chapter to this book.[11]

Although it is important to recognize this potential, however, it is also important to recognize that it is only a potential, not an unavoidable, outcome. As Keohane notes, "many of Rousseau's authoritarian passages were restatements of hoary arguments in French absolutist thought," hardly original or unique to him.[12] At the same time, many readers of Rousseau simplistically exaggerate this aspect of his theory by taking it out of the context of unanimous and express consent to the terms of the social contract itself. These terms ensure equality among members in a variety of ways and on a variety of levels, ranging from the terms of alienation (universal and reciprocal), to the requirements of law (impersonal and general), to the mode of government (a participatory legislative assembly in which everyone gets to express his or her views), to economic equality and the guarantee of equal political power this produces ("no citizens shall ever be wealthy enough to buy another, none poor enough to be forced to sell himself" [*Social Contract*, bk. 2, ch. 11]). By contrast, if *forcer d'être libre* is read in the context of a liberal democratic model of tacit consent, representation for the wealthy, and disenfranchisement of the poor, then it does indeed sound frightening. But such a liberal context is precisely what Rousseau rejects: a system of gross inequality where, under the guise of freedom, a rich minority determines the law for the poor majority, and moreover—as with Locke's tacit consent—declares that this majority has freely chosen its own situation. In such a polity, citizens are also being "forced to be free" by being forced to choose their own dependence and enslavement. This is even worse than what Rousseau proposes, in his view, not only because it is minority rule, but also because inequality guarantees that the silenced majority has never had any real opportunity to challenge the law as individuals do in Rousseau's assembly.[13]

Moreover, the "totalitarian" interpretation of Rousseau ignores the importance of central negative liberty elements in Rousseau's theory, particularly the elements of choice and agency. In *The Origin of Inequality*, Rousseau specifically cites "the human quality of free agency" and "the power of willing or rather of choosing" as the key "difference between the man and the brute." The ability to evaluate, critique, judge, agree, and disagree are not only distinctly human, but constitute the essence of humanity; "it is particularly in his [man's] consciousness of his liberty that the spirituality of his soul is displayed" (*Second Discourse*, 59–60). Ironically, Rousseau put such value on independence that he did not even allow genuine debate in the civic assembly; rather, each individual simply states his views. In this, Robert Wolker notes, "Every morally free agent . . . was required to follow rules established only within the depths of his own conscience in a self-reliant manner, free from the influence of all other persons. . . . For Rousseau, the more perfect our independence from others . . . the more likely were our deliberations to yield the common good."[14]

The apparent paradox this yields—we must be independent from each other in order to maximize our collective good—reveals a central tension in the general will. Bringing together choice and right is vital to Rousseau's vision of freedom. Thus, in *The Social Contract*, Rousseau seems to argue in various places that the general will is equivalent to the majority will, and in others that it is the objectively best answer regardless of what the majority thinks. I believe this is because he demands both conditions at once: not only must citizens choose the *right* answer and select the *best* laws: they must also *choose* the right answer and *select* the best laws. Virtue or "political right" must coexist with choice and majority rule, but both conditions must exist at once; each is useless without the other.[15] Susan Shell's equation of perfectibility with freedom is in this context illuminating; for the essence of perfectibility is not that humans will somehow "evolve" regardless of what they do, but rather that they are capable of making choices that will lead them to improvement, to progress, to virtue. But at the same time, this very ability to make choices is what leads to vice as well; "the perfectible species is also the only species intrinsically subject to depravity."[16]

For instance, imagine that ten people are trapped in a bomb shelter and that four of these people want to smoke. Objectively, even putting aside considerations of cancer and lung disease, smoking would not be a very sensible action because the ventilation system, while adequate, is limited. In this case, because six people will vote against smoking, the general will is to ban smoking; the majority's judgment coheres with the objectively best answer. But what if the numbers were reversed, and six people wanted to smoke? In this case, the majority would choose a bad law; in the objective sense, the general will would be violated. But to all practical purposes nobody can really know that for sure, and so the majority's will must be treated as the general will. Smoking is thereby permitted, and the six smokers eagerly light up.

Rousseau might suggest two sequelae to this situation of the majority passing a bad law. In the first, more optimistic scenario, the room fills with smoke faster than the ventilation system can clear it out, the available oxygen is depleted, and everyone passes out. The ventilation system will continue to work, however, and as everyone is unconscious and therefore no one can add any more smoke to the air, it eventually restores decent air quality to the shelter. The shelter residents awaken, the majority realizes that the minority was correct, that a pro-smoking policy is unworkable, and they change the law. In a more pessimistic scenario, they never regain consciousness or, even worse, they regain it but fail to change the policy. But in that case, Rousseau might say with a sneer, a people so hopelessly bound by appetite has no chance at more than animal survival anyway, so they might as well be dead. In this latter scenario, his theory allows us to see the pitfalls of democratic assembly; if a majority cannot perceive what the best answer is, then all hope for moral freedom is lost. Because it is lost, one might argue for a minority rebellion (they destroy all the cigarettes), but Rousseau would reject this: preserving the democratic procedure at least holds out the *hope* of bringing majority choice and the right answer together, so it is the course that must be pursued. A minority rebellion will never teach the majority the error of their choice and will subvert the democratic process. If we cannot be morally free, Rousseau seems to say, we might as well be dead; indeed, better to die through the only possible process that *can* yield moral freedom than to live in the slavery of a nonparticipatory system.

The interpretation of *forcer d'être libre* as totalitarian thus ignores the role that choice plays in Rousseau's theory. It assumes that the general will is static and universal, instead of temporal and dynamic, as human agents respond to changing conditions and contexts. Thus, just as my reading *Fat Is a Feminist Issue* allows me to reassess what my true will is concerning my weight, so can (and should) an assembly reevaluate its legislative decisions and hence its interpretations of its own will. On this reading, the general will is not necessarily something objective that needs to be "discovered" for all time so much as it is the creation of critical reflection on particular and changing circumstances. Thus, although there may in fact be a "right answer" to particular political problems, this answer does not need to be objectively true so much as it should be the best solution to the problem we can come up with at this time.

Furthermore, by structuring equality into the social contract, Rousseau vastly increases the chances of good laws being chosen. Equality is both economic (as I earlier noted, none should be rich enough to buy another or poor enough to have to sell himself) and political (consent to the social contract is unanimous and express, not tacit, and all citizens participate in making the laws). These two kinds of equality, economic and political, are interdependent, as Rousseau showed us in the second half of *The Origin of Inequality*, for wealth generates power. Equality of wealth and power reduces the motivation for voting for a bad law, in at least two ways. First, there is little likelihood of success for bad laws that benefit some unequally, for who would vote for them? Even if I believed in unequal benefits, I would want those benefits for myself, not for others, and thus would vote down any proposal that benefited others more than me.[17] Second, people who are genuinely equal before the law are more likely to be harmed equally by a poor one, just as smokers and nonsmokers alike are hurt by the declining air quality in the bomb shelter. As Rousseau says, because "the conditions are the same for all . . . no one has an interest in making them burdensome to others" (*Social Contract*, bk. 1, ch. 6). Such equality is not perfect, of course; insofar as the smokers suffocate too, they still enjoy their smoking. Nor does it account for "difference" that is not naturally unequal: laws making sexual harassment difficult to prosecute, for instance, produce an inequality of social power out of a difference that is not inherently unequal (sexual phenotype). One could argue that, placed against a background condition of social, economic, and political equality, sexual harassment should be less frequently encountered than it is in liberal and other patriarchal societies (despite Rousseau's sexism, to be discussed soon), because women would have greater resources for stopping such harassing behavior. But the point is that Rousseau's vision of equality does not denote sameness, and is not absolute or foolproof.

The structural parameters of the social contract such as equality, impersonality, and mutuality are therefore limited in their ability to point people in the right direction. The problem with Rousseau's social contract is that "the effect would have to become the cause; the social spirit, which should be created by these institutions, would have to preside over their very foundation; and men would have to be before the law what they should become by means of law" (*Social Contract*, bk. 2, ch. 7). That is, the political process and structure of the social contract will produce good citizens, but such good citizens are needed in order to produce the social contract. Hence, Rousseau notes, "Of itself the people always wills the good, but of itself it by no means always sees it. The general will is always upright, but the judgment which guides it is not always enlightened" (bk. 2, ch. 6). Such human fallibility is why Rousseau introduces the Legislator, who uses personal charisma and even some kinds of trickery to convince citizens to vote for the right laws.[18] The Legislator is designed to produce the citizens that the social contract needs. He is "a superior intelligence beholding all the passions of men without experiencing any of them," an "intelligence wholly unrelated to our nature, while knowing it through and through." He must "transfor[m] each individual, who is by himself a complete and solitary whole, into part of a greater whole from which he in a manner receives his life and being . . . substituting a partial and moral existence for the physical and independent existence nature has conferred on us all" (bk. 2, ch. 7).

This task might not sound very promising for freedom; Rousseau seems to want to make men dependent, which he said in the *Second Discourse* was the source of inequality and slavery. But if we are to achieve moral freedom, and if moral freedom is also to be civil, then freedom requires the formation of community, and a mutual dependence of each on all. It is the mutuality of Rousseau's social contract—we each alienate our natural liberty completely to every other member of the community, each of whom completely alienates her natural liberty to us—that demarcates the difference between dependence and *interdependence*. It is the latter that is necessary for the general will, and hence for moral freedom. If everyone alienates natural freedom completely to everyone else, then despite the fact that one alienates to other people (rather than to a thing), the resulting dependence is still impersonal: none of us is dependent on any individual or a specific group of people, but rather on the collective as a whole.

Thus, the Legislator's "transformation" of the citizens does not make them dependent on him; rather, he facilitates their dependence on each other, their interdependence. To achieve this, the Legislator must "take people out of themselves," to enable them to see past their particular will to their general will. In doing this, he prepares people for moral freedom: not only for participating as citizen-legislators in the process through which they make the laws they are to obey, but also for adhering strictly to those laws in their lives as citizen-subjects. What he really prepares them for, in the end, is virtue: to recognize it when they see it, and ultimately, presumably (otherwise we would always need a Legislator) to search it out, so that all the laws we make will adhere to it.

It is this that may prompt Judith Shklar to call the Legislator "a contrivance to give utopia a start,"[19] for the methods that Rousseau advocates that the Legislator use include the invoking of legends, mythology, and religion to get people to think in terms of the common good and to see the links between that good and their individual selfish interest (*Social Contract*, bk. 2, ch. 7). The use of such tricks obviously opens up the power of the Legislator to abuse; Rousseau's naïve response that the Legislator himself has no vote hardly undermines his ability to get others to do what he wants. But such criticisms themselves fantasize the Legislator even more than Rousseau does. For the Legislator has no official power within the polity: he cannot make laws, he cannot execute them, he cannot implement public policy. He can only propose laws and convince citizens to vote for them. And although his persuasive skill may be powerful, and the people may be gullible, his lack of substantive power, and the equality of economic and political power among citizens, means that it is up to them whether to be persuaded.

Certainly Rousseau can be saved from Shklar's and others' dismissal as utopian fantasy by calling to mind historic individuals who were able to effect great changes in human history and to attract great numbers of followers who followed their counsel (Geneva's own John Calvin would most obviously spring to mind if Rousseau did not detest Calvinism so much).[20] But the figure of the Legislator raises the question: if it is enough that we do what another superior being tells us to do, then why must we have a participatory structure at all? The answer lies in the problem of getting from here to there: from the current context of self-interested, unequal, and atomistic individuals who are at odds with the state and state power to Rousseau's vision of participatory community with a general will. In this light, the "godlike" powers of the Legislator would be needed only for the short run; eventually, one might imagine, once people are more skilled at perceiving the general will on their own and are more identified with the community, the Legislator might devolve into a role that any citizen could fulfill, on a rotating basis or through elections. Given the importance of equality that I have already discussed in fostering the ability and motivation of all citizens to think about the common good, this possibility is plausible; but Rousseau does not posit such an eventuality, perhaps because this starry-eyed dreamer was at the same time rather pessimistic about human possibility. As Shklar points out, Rousseau posited a "spontaneous march to inequality and oppression in which all men participated," and "Rousseau did not believe that . . . much could be done about it."[21] Though perfectibility is a strong theme in Rousseau's writings, the achievement of perfection was something he neither advocated nor expected. Rather, the emphasis on perfectibility was on the human capacity to improve through the exercise of choice, and this necessarily entails, as Shell pointed out, the possibility of making bad choices as well.

EDUCATION, WILL, AND THE SOCIAL CONSTRUCTION OF CITIZENS

The unpredictability of human choice was what led Rousseau to advocate the construction of social arrangements to maximize the ability to choose the right things. The particular structure of the democratic assembly is, of course, the main element. But education was another key social arrangement. As Rousseau says in *Political Economy*, "there can be no patriotism without liberty, no liberty without virtue, no virtue without citizens; create citizens, and you have everything you need." But at the same time, "To form citizens is not the work of a day; and in order to have men it is necessary to educate them when they are children."[22] It may be those difficulties to which he alludes here that cause Rousseau to devote a lengthy book to education, but only an unsatisfyingly brief chapter in *The Social Contract* to the Legislator. As problematic as the figure of the Legislator is, more significant for the theme of freedom in Rousseau's polity is the tutor, for he demonstrates the clearest evidence of the importance of social constructivism to Rousseau's theory. The two figures of Legislator and tutor are highly complementary, for both seek to undercut people's tendencies toward individualism and make them think of social unities. Both also seek to teach people to want the "right" things. The tutor's task is to educate Emile to become a virtuous man, and thereby a potential citizen. In this, like the Legislator, the tutor's task is to "transform human nature" and "transport the *I* into the common unity, with the result that each individual believes himself no longer one but a part of the unity and no longer feels except within the whole."[23]

Emile, which was written at the same time as *The Social Contract*, is Rousseau's effort to show how this should be done. By leading men to virtue, education gives men the necessary foundation on which to build virtuous political institutions and pass virtuous laws that are in conformity with the general will. Even more strongly than Locke did in his theory of education, Rousseau emphasizes character over academic subjects; although for Rousseau, character specifically refers to the quality of communalism. The good citizen must not be limited by self-interest; the central passion of self-love that Rousseau described in *The Origin of Inequality* must be tempered by the love of others and identity with community he outlines in *The Social Contract*. Hence, it is significant that it is in *Emile*—not *The Social Contract*—that Rousseau portrays the good citizen as a Spartan man who loses an election to the Council of 300 and is delighted that there are so many others more qualified than he and as a Spartan woman who is happy to lose her sons in battle as long as they were victorious (*Emile*, 40). What is key to citizenship is the ability to subvert selfish interest and place the good of the collective at the heart of the self: not to put it above self-interest, but rather to see that self-interest is identified with collective interest. As Keohane puts it, we are to abandon *amour propre* not for the simple *amour de soi* that characterized the earliest stages of the state of nature, but for a newer incarnation of that innocent self-love: *amour de nous-mêmes*, a love of ourselves that is tied both to virtue and to a love of others.[24] In turning a young boy into a citizen, the tutor must battle the childish tendency toward egoism and self-reference, and thereby enable him to realize his social/political identity; he must learn to understand the ways in which his higher will as an individual is perfectly compatible with, indeed can be realized only through, the general will of a political society.

This requires that the variable potential of human nature be channeled to develop the desirable qualities and atrophy the bad ones. In *The Origin of Inequality*, Rousseau said that the development of reason was accompanied by the loss of *pitié* or compassion, and traced how this was both an advance for man and also a loss. In the *Emile* this theme persists, for the tutor strives to enable Emile to recover natural compassion without returning to the state of instinct-driven savage. Rousseau argues that man has no innate knowledge of the good, but he does have an innate tendency to love it when reason reveals it to him. Though reason reveals the truth, however, it also fuels self-interest, alienates us from compassion, and hence from truth. So truth cannot be established by reason alone; we must rediscover or redevelop our compassion as well. In the "Profession of Faith of the Vicar of Savoyard," Rousseau seems to be suggesting that because truth exists in things, "not in the mind that judges them," we can never know the truth through reason alone; rather, we must yield to our sentiments in order to discern the truth (*Emile*, 290–94). Faith and love are at least as important as reason to discerning the truth, particularly concerning matters of vice and virtue, for conscience is the key instrument by which humans can know such matters. Or more precisely, as "man does not have innate knowledge of [the good] . . . as soon as his reason makes him know it, his conscience leads him to love it. It is this sentiment which is innate" (290). But this apparent bifurcation between reason, which leads us to "know" the good, and conscience, which causes us to "love" it, belies the vicar's true message, which is that loving the good is a vital component of truly knowing it, for it is key to living one's life by the truth. Otherwise, "knowledge" is an empty form of observation that has no connection to how one lives.

Hence, the tutor must develop all of Emile's faculties and sentiments, particularly compassion, as well as reason. He must make him "fear nothing" and give him the "finest habits" so that he is not subject to any negative qualities or constraints. Indeed, the constraints he experiences should be those of virtue, which are not constraints per se on his true will but actually enhance freedom. And indeed, the whole point of education is to produce a "well-regulated freedom" (*Emile*, 92). Just as virtue was key to the moral freedom of the general will in *The Social Contract*, so is virtue key to moral freedom in the individual; obedience to a self-prescribed law does not produce freedom if the law itself is vicious. The laws that I prescribe for myself as an individual must be good laws, the laws that are in sync with an independent standard of the good life, standards that Rousseau goes on to define as virtuous.

This is obviously even truer for the moral freedom of citizens acting within the polity; a significant point of moral freedom for individuals is that it fosters their ability to appreciate the general will in civil society. Without virtuous individuals who immerse themselves in the whole, the whole cannot really exist, and therefore it can have no will. The general will is the will of the community, but what makes a group of people a community is their commitment to a common endeavor. Hence, Rousseau's observation, cited earlier, that "men would have to be before the law what they should become by means of law" (*Social Contract*, bk. 2, ch. 7), suggests not just the circular challenge of producing citizens, but of producing the polity and the general will itself. That is, in order for the will to be general, the association must be constituted with common interest; but in order for it to be a *will*, the individual citizens within the society must want the good.

My reading of *Emile* may in this sense differ from the common view that the tutor's aim is to make Emile a natural man. Indeed, critics might note a stark contrast between civic education and Emile's education, which would seem to undermine my argument. As Rousseau says in the early pages of the book, "raising a man for himself" is quite different than "rais[ing] him for others. . . . one must choose between making a man or a citizen, for one cannot make both at the same time" (*Emile*, 39). And in *The Government of Poland*, Rousseau recommends a quite different sort of education than he outlines in *Emile*; children are educated in groups rather than individually, in public rather than in private, and are to be taught a somewhat mindless civic pride rather than the detailed development of reason and sentiment Emile experiences.[25]

But while Rousseau seeks to recapture certain natural capacities in his pupil, he also declares that "He who in the civil order wants to preserve the primacy of the sentiments of nature does not know what he wants. Always in contradiction with himself, always floating between his inclinations and his duties, he will never be either man or citizen. He will be good neither for himself nor for others. He will be one of these men of our days: a Frenchman, an Englishman, a bourgeois. He will be nothing" (*Emile*, 40). Further, his juxtaposition between "making a man or a citi-

zen," just cited, occurs only when the "three educations" that we receive—"from nature," "from things," and "from men"—are not "related" but rather "opposed." The education that Rousseau seeks for
Emile is one that, by contrast, integrates these three types of education
seamlessly (*Emile*, 38–39). Similarly, Carol Blum relates a letter Rousseau
received from the Comte de Ste-Aldegond, who wants to raise his child
in a "state of nature, in accordance with [Rousseau's] precepts." Rousseau reacts with shock: "If you insist on wishing to carry out this extrava-
gant experiment you describe and turn your child into a brute, his tender
mother will die of grief, the child will end up being put away."[26] Blum
maintains that Rousseau's reaction demonstrates his reluctance to be a
"moral mentor," but I read the letter as showing instead that Rousseau
did not want any child to be raised in a "state of nature." In *The Origin
of Inequality*, he predicts that the reader will "wish it were in your power
to go back" to the state of nature; but while this might be desirable as "a
criticism of your contemporaries," it would be "a terror to the unfortunates who will come after you" (*Second Discourse*, 51). Rousseau does
not seek a return to the state of nature, but only to make us understand
that we could be other than we are in the eighteenth-century world.

Furthermore, we must remember that context is relevant: in *The Government of Poland*, Rousseau's educational and civic recommendations
are made within a preexisting constitutional monarchy, and so the ideal
must be mixed with the expedient. By contrast, *Emile* is a novel, in which
Rousseau can construct context as he wishes. At the same time, this novel
takes place in mideighteenth-century France, which by Rousseau's standards is corrupt, a context in which no person could possibly attain virtue
by and through political participation or public education. He seeks,
through his novel, to condemn and escape that context, but to the end,
he hopes, of transforming it. Education must therefore take place in the
family, because the family can serve as a protective retreat from the corruption of urban political life. That the family did not in fact often provide
such protection, particularly if the family lived in Paris, did not mean that
it could not; and indeed it was the only possible repository of virtue in
Rousseau's contemporary society. In such a context, "man" must be opposed to "citizen." But Rousseau is preparing Emile to be a citizen of his
ideal polity—it is a work of fiction, after all—a man who is raised *both*
"for himself" and "for others" because he is raised to virtue.

It is also important to note that Rousseau's use of "nature" is multifac-
eted. He seeks to construct a world in which Emile can develop without
the passions that corrupt social practices foist on him. Rousseau repeatedly sets up elaborate schemes to direct Emile into this supposedly "natural" setting, to produce in him the reactions that he wants him to have.
But this "natural" setting is carefully constructed: the tutor is continually

manipulating Emile so that he encounters certain experiences and not others, hears certain ideas in particular settings and not others. In this way, he carefully shapes Emile's self-understanding and character, so that he will learn to want and prefer certain things and not others, but without his being aware of how he is being constructed. What is in fact artfully manipulated by the tutor is experienced by the student as natural occurrence; what is experienced as natural desire is in fact learned, manipulated, and constructed desire.

How the tutor, himself corrupted by society, can possibly know what the appropriate "natural" response is, of course, is not well recognized by Rousseau. He says, rather vaguely, "that before daring to undertake the formation of a man, one must have made oneself a man. One must find within oneself the example the pupil ought to take for his own" (*Emile*, 95). Force of will and consultation of the inner heart, Rousseau seems to suggest, will produce virtue in the tutor. But that is easier said than done, for why else would Emile need a tutor instead of teaching himself? Furthermore, Rousseau fails to address how the tutor knows to negotiate the tension between the natural and social. For the tutor seeks to control Emile not in order to keep him primitive so much as to reconstitute history, to shape Emile's development in a different way than what Rousseau articulated in the *Second Discourse*. It is as if, in an inversion of the scientific maxim that ontogeny replicates phylogeny, Rousseau is showing, through Emile, how to produce man as Rousseau wishes he had evolved from the primitive state of nature, rather than as he in fact evolved. What those who posit "man" and "citizen" as mutually exclusive miss, I believe, is the dynamic and complex conception of nature that Rousseau develops and the resulting social construction he deploys. Because Rousseau posits human nature as containing many different possibilities, some of which will be developed in certain social contexts, and others in other contexts, and which are always battling within people for dominance, it is vital that he create the environment that favors the "good" capacities. That is why we have to work so hard to get the right social order, and why Rousseau is so absolutist about it—so that the good natural capacities are developed and the harmful ones repressed. Such construction of the proper environment is at the heart of Emile's education. Thus, I agree with Linda Zerilli that "to be a man is to be no more a product of nature than to be a citizen is to be a 'denatured' man."[27]

Freedom is highly relevant to Rousseau's construction of Emile, for on the negative-liberty, classically liberal conception of freedom, manipulation is seen as starkly opposed to freedom. Although, as I have already maintained, negative liberty tends to focus on external obstacles to doing what I want, manipulation is one of those conditions, like brainwashing, that negative liberty theorists take exception to, because it is seen as overtly external interference with the area of the self—the mind—that is normally regarded as sacrosanct and untouchable. However, Rousseau believes such manipulation is necessary to freedom, not opposed to it, for it is the only way that Emile can learn virtue. True, Rousseau acknowledges that "There is no subjection so perfect as that which keeps the appearance of freedom" (*Emile*, 120), thus suggesting that only the illusion of freedom, not freedom itself, is to be encouraged. What he means, however, is that the tutor may use the illusion of natural liberty to manipulate the student into attaining moral liberty. As Bradshaw notes, "Man by nature may be free, but he can hardly be said to have a free will. Free will comes into play only when there is a tension between natural desire and the will to achieve (either creatively or morally)."[28] It is through this tension that moral freedom is expressed; the tutor creates this tension for Emile in contexts that guarantee that the will that triumphs will be a virtuous one.

GENDER, EDUCATION, AND VIRTUE

This manipulation disguised as self-motivated nature is particularly seen in the book's final chapter, "Sophie, or The Woman." Unlike most other theorists in the Western canon, for whom gender is an unacknowledged though nonetheless important feature, Rousseau explicitly acknowledges gender as a key dimension of social and political life. In his account of the historical development of humanity in the *Origin of Inequality*, for instance, women seem to undergo some of the most dramatic changes, from beings who hardly recognize their own children to wives and mothers who "mind the hut" and devote themselves to loving care of their children and attention to their husbands within the patriarchal nuclear family. This change is neither innocent nor coincidental, according to Rousseau, for early natural woman perceives the interest to herself in enslaving an individual man to forage for their "common subsistence" (*Second Discourse*, 88). Indeed, Rousseau seems to hold women responsible for the shape and development of all human relationships; it is their passion, their jealousy, and most importantly—though this is never acknowledged in *The Origin of Inequality*, only later in *the Emile*—their sexuality that gives them superhuman powers over men and allows them to manipulate history to their desire. In his *Letter to D'Alembert*, Rousseau excoriates actresses—the theater being the only other major public forum besides the *salons* in which women participated at the time—as immoral, vicious, and responsible for the corruption of otherwise fine potential citizens. Similarly, in *Emile* Rousseau blames bad mothers for all the vice in the world and praises good mothers for promulgating human virtue. Women have incredible power to make men agents, or conversely, to enslave them. But the nature of this power is somewhat vague in Rousseau's account. For instance, he attributes a great deal of power to women's nursing; if women farm their children out to wet nurses and instead spend their days in the Paris *salons*, corruption ensues; men become weak and effeminate, enslaved to sexuality. The politics that such a people can produce, needless to say, is hardly in line with Rousseau's ideal. Wet nurses abuse their charges and turn infants into deformed beings by swaddling and other treatments that suit the nurses' convenience rather than the children's health. By contrast, "let mothers deign to nurse their children, morals will reform themselves, nature's sentiments will be awakened in every heart, the state will be repeopled. This first point, this point alone, will bring everything back together" (*Emile*, 46).

It is such views that make Rousseau one of the modern canonical political theorists that feminists most love to hate. But as blatantly sexist as these opinions seem to late-twentieth- and early-twenty-first century feminists, we should note again the context; for "the stories of neglect and abuse of children by nurses in [Rousseau's] time were numerous."[29] Contemporary feminists are politically and morally opposed to child neglect and abuse, and indeed the valorization of mothering is a key theme of much contemporary feminist writing, beginning with the "maternal thinking" feminism of the early 1980s and carrying through to welfare feminism at the turn of the twenty-first century.[30] So Rousseau is not just hysterically bad-mouthing wet nursing and unfairly criticizing mothers for abusive neglect in order to further a sexist agenda of denying women social power; he may be doing that, but he may also be expressing a humanitarian concern for the welfare of children.[31] That the solution to the problem he identifies places unfair burdens on women should not be ignored, however. For instance, although Rousseau condemns the use of wet nurses by aristocratic women, Elizabeth Fox-Genovese maintains that they were used much more heavily by "working urban mothers" whose "labor was necessary to the family economy" and whose "occupations did not permit the casual combination of familial work and domestic responsibility." As Fairchilds notes, "domesticity was an upper class luxury."[32] So Rousseau's criticism of wet nurses is not only misdirected in terms of class, but presupposes that "women" occupy a bourgeois class location. He fails to recognize class differences that require some women to work, and thereby creates a fantastic ideal of femininity that only bourgeois women could possibly attain.

Similarly, in a period where birth control had produced radicalizing possibilities for liberating women from constant pregnancy and child rearing, Rousseau's hostility to birth control in particular—it "presages the impending fate of Europe" (*Emile*, 44–45)—may be viewed as hostile to women.[33] Indeed, Rousseau may have undercut his own position; for women's ability to limit family size through birth control led "aristocratic mothers [to take] a genuine interest in their children" much along the lines Rousseau praises, in contrast to a norm of sore neglect in the first half of the century. This change was tied to a parallel change of women's status in marriage. In the first half of the century, "noble wives were poorly treated by their husbands. At worst, they were bullied and threatened by everyone in the household from spouse and mother-in-law to the lowliest servant." But "the Enlightenment revolutionized the way people viewed love and marriage" by giving women more control over their choice of partners and more respect within the family.[34] Rousseau, for all the obvious sexism that he pours into his views of marriage, certainly argued for the need to honor and respect wives and mothers; given the context in which he wrote, it is arguable that his position could be seen as friendly to feminism.[35] Similarly, his opposition to birth control is lodged in his claim that "nearly half the children who are born die before they can have others, and the two remaining ones are needed to represent the father and the mother," which leads him to say that "every woman must . . . produce nearly four children" (*Emile* 362n). But this indicates that his ideal family size is small; women should not endure annual pregnancies. As Rousseau asks, "what does it matter that this or that woman produces few children? Is woman's status any less that of motherhood, and is it not by general laws that nature and morals ought to provide for this status?" (*Emile*, 362).

Thus, Rousseau was much more ambiguous on gender issues than many feminists allow. Consider, for instance, his hostility to women in public life, for which most feminists excoriate him. Susan Conner maintains that women who involved themselves in political affairs in eighteenth-century France did so out of self-interested reasons and had a poor grasp of the larger issues of state politics; for them, "personal satisfaction was paramount" over good public policy decisions. Indeed, they were called "*intrigantes*," and Conner maintains that they were not trying to increase public knowledge of the good, but rather to increase their own visibility and thereby power—or at least perception of their power. Women could only have power if others thought they had it; they could not exercise actual influence over policy or law or the courts, but only over particular men.

Why Rousseau focused on the *salons* for his criticism of public women, rather than *intrigantes*, is curious, given Conner's assertion that the *salonnières* were interested in intellectual questions and visibility rather than political power.[36] As Dena Goodman maintains, "the salonnières were not simply ladies of leisure killing time. . . . Like the philosophes who gathered in their homes, the salonnières were practical people who worked at tasks they considered productive and useful."[37] But, Conner points out, these tasks were not connected to politics and power. And Barbara Mittman argues that women involved in the theater, the other major public spectacle of the eighteenth century, and which Rousseau condemned, were already socially powerless without Rousseau's help; excommunicated by the Catholic church, they could not marry, so they were deemed whores, and any children they had were automatically illegitimate.[38] The circularity of women's public exclusion on the basis of their immorality, and the explicit designation of them as immoral if they engaged in public interactions, is almost too obvious to point out. But it is one that Rousseau, to his discredit as a philosopher, seems to accept.

In light of Conner's argument, however, women would not have to be evil sexual predators to rationalize Rousseau's exclusion of them from politics; they could be simply ignorant, shortsighted, and selfish. And of course the ambiguous relation that women had to power and morality must be linked to the poor educations women received, which severely limited their options in society. Though French law required the education of males and females to the age of fourteen, in practice women were rarely educated, and illiteracy rates were high. Convent schools provided little by way of formal education, favoring manners and embroidery instead.[39] Although Rousseau seems very sexist in granting women, in the form of Sophie, such a poor education, dependent on the goodwill of their husbands to increase their knowledge, it must be remembered that the reality for women in France at the time was even worse. Though Rousseau says in *Emile*, in an obvious swipe at the *salonnières*, that "I would still like a simple and coarsely raised girl a hundred times better than a learned and brilliant one who would come to establish in my house a tribunal of literature over which she would preside," he also says, "it is not suitable for a man with education to take a wife who has none, or, consequently, to take a wife from a rank in which she could not have an education" (*Emile*, 409). On this account, Sophie looks comparatively better off than other women, because Rousseau explicitly tells Emile to educate her. But why Rousseau does not link better education for women with their participation in politics is, once again, a puzzle.

Here again, history provides a possible clue, for although women's literacy increased perceptibly by the end of the eighteenth century, it was precisely at this time, as Margaret Darrow has shown, that many French noblewomen *abandoned* their roles as *salonnières* to devote themselves to the role of mother and wife. Again, in Conner's view, this does not necessarily entail that the *intrigantes* followed suit; but as I previously noted, women's general status in the family improved as the eighteenth century progressed, and this improvement followed the greater control women were able to exert over their fertility through the increasing availability of birth control. Thus, as women acquired the tools and skills to empower them for public participation, they retreated from the narrow corridors of publicity in which they were heretofore allowed. Certainly, the move to maternalism and domesticity was decidedly a class affair; little changed for lower-class women until the revolution. And Harriet Applewhite and Darline Levy have argued that market women and other women of the lower classes were very politically active during the revolution. But the events they describe occur more than ten years past Rousseau's death.[40] In Rousseau's prerevolutionary era, it is precisely women of the upper classes whom one might expect to have an impact on politics.

Rousseau's ambiguity over women carries through in his *Confessions*, which vacillate between perverted, even masochistic, would-be incestuous sycophant to his patron Mme De Warens and a brutish, cold-hearted, dehumanizing cruelty to his common-law wife, Thérèse le Vasseur. In relation to Mme de Warens, Rousseau is completely in thrall; he even calls her "mamma." Thérèse is a "successor to mamma," that is, Mme de Warens, and he even calls her "aunt."[41] And yet Thérèse could not be more different from de Warens in terms of her personality and identity, and Rousseau's position in this relationship is that of dominator, not dominated. Thérèse is poorly educated, and indeed "stupid," by Rousseau's account; she cannot tell time or recite the months (he claims that he tries to teach her but fails); she reads poorly though she can write fairly well. Her apparent stupidity makes the reader question why Rousseau remained with Thérèse; after all, in *Emile* Rousseau maintains that the purpose of the virtuous woman's lack of education is so that her husband can educate her. And one obvious quality that seems to be attractive to Rousseau is that Thérèse is subservient, obedient, and devoted to her rather cruel and domineering parents and siblings, as well as to Rousseau.

In this, the intersections of class with gender are prominent. As Rebecca Kukla suggests, part of the reason Mme de Warens dominates Rousseau is that she is of higher social class than he, something Rousseau himself notes.[42] Thérèse comes from "a respectable family, her father being an official at the Orleans mint, and her mother engaged in business"; but by the time Rousseau meets her, the entire family is economically dependent on Thérèse, who works for Rousseau's landlady.[43] Her family subsequently becomes dependent on Rousseau. He is thus able to dominate Thérèse in part because of the class position of her and her family. But the only redeeming virtue that Rousseau himself recognizes in Thérèse is that she gives "good advice," suggesting a kind of wisdom that exists prior to reason. Indeed, the way that Rousseau writes about Thérèse implies that she might be the "natural woman" from the "golden age" of the state of nature, shortly after families were formed, when women's mental development had proceeded to the point of seeing the advantages to themselves of finding men to care for them. Class plays a role in this as well, for Rousseau suggests that rural peasants are closer to natural virtue than are the bourgeois, like Emile, who must assiduously work at achieving virtue. Thérèse, accordingly, seems to embody a kind of primitive natural virtue; Rousseau describes uniting with her as "that which determined my moral being."[44]

Such a claim could have a double meaning, of course, depending on what one thinks of the morality of a man who abandons to an orphanage five children though continuing to live with their mother. In forcing Thérèse to give up each of the five children she bore by him, Rousseau showed a particular inhumanity; he claimed to be concerned for her "honor," for this was "the only means of preserving" it, conveniently ignoring the fact that he could readily have saved her honor by marrying her, which he refused to do.[45] Such behavior signals a dominant theme in the *Confessions*, namely, a repudiation of agency and responsibility for the more reprehensible actions Rousseau takes; such actions are painted as involuntary reactions to external conditions or others' actions. He cites social norms and "honor" as an excuse for abandoning his children, and he blames a corrupt state for making such abandonment appear vicious when it in fact should be seen as virtuous.[46]

And of course he blames women for the uncontrollable passion he feels. For instance, in his encounter with the prostitute Zulietta, Rousseau claims to lose his will, and does what she tells him, struggle as he might to resist being "the dupe of a worthless slut." He succeeds only by finding her "secret defect," which would "render her repulsive to those who would otherwise fight for the possession of her"; he finds such a defect in a deformed nipple, a "natural imperfection" that makes her "a kind of monster" in Rousseau's eyes. In this, Rousseau attributes both his enslavement to Zulietta and his liberation from her to the woman herself: her powers to charm and her own imperfection are what cause Rousseau's bondage and his subsequent release. Class once again certainly impacts this, for he is unable to find—indeed, he does not even try to find—a similar "defect" in the upper-class women to whom he is similarly enslaved, namely, Mme de Warens or, later in his life, Mme d' Epinay or her sister-in-law, Mme d'Houdetot. Ironically, Rousseau paints himself as "lower" than Zulietta, which is what inspires him to look for her defect: why, he asks, does she "lower" herself to him if she is not fatally flawed? But in fact even Rousseau is of higher status than a prostitute in mid-eighteenth-century France; Rousseau's construction of her as "higher" than he is part of the fantasy.[47]

With all of these women, however, regardless of the inflections of class difference, Rousseau abdicates responsibility for his sexual feelings. Nor does he take responsibility for his rather inhumane insistence on perfection in women, much less for his dichotomization of women into either perfect or monstrous, angel or whore. In disavowing responsibility and continually blaming others for his behavior, Rousseau abdicates agency and becomes a figure buffeted by chance encounters, much as Locke described in his *Essay*, as I recounted in the previous chapter.[48] Perceiving himself in such a way may be what leads Rousseau to rely on the organization of social life in precise patterns that force us to do the things that are good for us. And perhaps it is because he assumes everyone is like him that he relies so heavily on external structures of law and education to shepherd people toward virtuous acts. Or more precisely, that is why he identifies such an active interdependence of external and internal, presenting a theory that self-consciously and explicitly accepts social constructivism and encourages and advocates a particular construction of men (citizens) and women (wives).

The ambiguity I am suggesting runs contrary to the standard feminist view of Rousseau. Susan Moller Okin's classic critique is that "Rousseau defines woman's nature, unlike man's, in terms of her function—that is, her sexual and procreative purpose in life." This is a serious problem for "Rousseau, the philosopher of equality and freedom," for the fact that he "has not applied these basic human values similarly to both sexes" reveals a self-contradiction, if not hypocrisy.[49] Okin's critique set the tone for most feminist criticism of Rousseau, as well as other figures in the canon, for the next decade; and her theory of functionalism as a key expression of sexism in the history of political thought identifies the aspects of Rousseau's theory that assign people different roles and places in his ideal society, which is certainly correct. But more recently, feminists have noted that these roles are more complex than a simple functionalism can account for. As Kukla maintains, "When Rousseau claims that men and women are different *by nature*, we cannot presuppose, as Okin does, that he is attributing an essential character outside of human control to either gender."[50]

In particular, some have acknowledged the social constructivist elements of Rousseau's work. The recognition actually began with Okin, who asserted that "the environment in which a man is raised . . . is bound to develop and accentuate some of his innate characteristics, at the cost of suppressing and distorting others," as I have similarly argued here. However, she presents this process as a kind of "socialization" that alienates man *from* his nature, rather than as the inevitable course of human development that I have postulated. Furthermore, Okin maintains that it is only men who are so socialized: "With regard to the natural versus the current prevailing qualities and abilities of women, however, he declines to apply his theories in anything like the same way."[51] In this, subsequent feminists who recognize the social constructivism at work in Rousseau's theory suggest that Okin could not have been more incorrect. These range from Linda Zerilli's claim that "what announces 'man' or 'woman' is not anatomical difference but instead an arbitrary system of signs that stand in permanent danger of collapsing into a frightening ambiguity of meaning," to Weiss's claim that gender differences were completely artificial, manufactured explicitly and consciously by Rousseau in a masterful feat of social engineering, to Elizabeth Wingrove's use of "performative sexuality . . . to move between the functional material and semiotic levels" of social constructivism.[52] None of these, I believe, really captures the complexity of the three layers of social construction that I identified in the introduction to this book; Zerilli operates at the third layer of social construction as a function of language, such that everything is always and everywhere constructed, whereas Weiss operates primarily at the first layer, where men deploy ideology to exert control over the construction of women, but are not themselves affected. Wingrove's attempt to utilize two contrasting vectors at once comes a bit closer to my own position; she brings social constructivism to the level of the body, which is "the site of gender's construction." For her, it is through the body that gender is performed in Rousseau's writings, "that males act like men and females act like women." Discursively interpreting, placing, and producing the most material of entities, she argues, Rousseau provides "a complex and even insightful account of the ways political agendas support, constrain, and construct sexual identities."[53]

In my treatment of social construction, however, I am less concerned than Wingrove, Zerilli, or Weiss with the construction of sexuality per se, or even of femininity per se, than of citizenship and freedom. In this sense, women and men are constructed similarly as much as they are constructed differently, and what interests me about gender and sexuality is how they feed into virtue—which in turn founds freedom—rather than how virtue justifies Rousseau's construction of gender and sexuality. Thus, perhaps more relevant to my sense of social constructivism is Rebecca Kukla, who argues that Rousseau's "central thesis [is] that freedom depends on the manipulation and reconstruction of nature." On Kukla's reading, "the natural and the created do not exclude each other for Rousseau. Human nature, far from being immutable, is characterized first and foremost by what Rousseau calls its *perfectibility*—it is always changing and progressing, undergoing further sophistication and further allowing us to fulfill our potential over time." She recognizes that human nature is malleable, that change is inevitable to humanity and human society in response to changing social forces, but that human agency inevitably plays a role in these processes: "*we* are the agents of that development; we can and do reconstruct our nature."[54] However, she may emphasize agency at the cost of recognizing what comes to people independently of human action.

That is, on my reading, the difficulty inherent in creating social institutions that reproduce humans in a particular fashion is not that some independent human nature inevitably asserts itself over such construction. Rather, the issue is that this construction is affected by larger social forces over which humans have no real control, even if they participate in them to make them possible. In the *Second Discourse*, for instance, Rousseau identified metallurgy and agriculture as the key social forces that brought about institutionalized social and economic inequality. Humans clearly discovered and developed these forces; they were the result of human choice, agency, and creation, and yet they far exceed the grasp of any individual human being. Though created by humans, they are forces beyond human control.

My approach to social construction thus draws out the tension in Rousseau's theory between the conscious, active production of virtuous men and women and the ways in which such production must be tailored to dimensions of humanity that cannot be escaped. As Rousseau's account of the general will makes clear, the good society is much greater than a conglomeration of good people; just as Emile's education requires everything to be arranged precisely in order to attain his virtue, so must everything in a good society be precisely arranged. Because the point of virtue is the attainment of the good polity, the term "virtuous" means different things for different people depending on their role in and relation to that polity. And as feminists have recognized since Okin first argued it, gender is one of the primary lines of differentiation of role, position, and function. While men occupy the public sphere and participate in the assembly, women are responsible for family life and for creating a home environment in which the corruption to which men are exposed in the political arena can be counteracted. These different locations entail an entire symbolic economy of gendered difference, and this construction of gender difference is key to the success of Rousseau's polity. As Blum and Zerilli each argue, one of Rousseau's greatest fears is blurred gender lines. It is all too easy for men to become women, as the *Confessions* reveal when Rousseau takes up lace making during an illness, thus succumbing, as Zerilli put it, to "that uncanny other woman in himself."[55] His main objection to the salons is that men become effeminate and women usurp men's roles. Such an inversion would not be a simple one, however—it is not the case that women could think of the public good and seek common subsistence while men take over child care—because women want it both ways, according to Rousseau. That is, they know that having men serve them is too good a deal to give up, but they still want the power that by rights belongs to men. The balance, then, is not simply inverted by the salons, but distorted altogether. To restore the balance, and then maintain it, the sexes must be sharply differentiated, not just by function, but by role and identity, by their placement in the symbolic order of meaning. Men and women not only have different duties, but symbolize different things within the political, social, and discursive economy. It is on this differentiation that the state is based. Without sharp gender dichotomies, Rousseau's political society would not be possible; "if the code of gender difference is not strictly adhered to . . . all is lost. There will not be any citizens because there will not be any men," seemingly defined as that which is not woman.[56]

Thus, masculine virtue entails independence, strength, and courage—qualities that are generally associated with freedom in the modern canon—while feminine virtue is marked by dependence, deference, and restraint, qualities associated with unfreedom. Just as Rousseau seems to pin the hope of virtue on women's mothering skills and roles, he attributes the ultimate threat and danger of vice to women's sexuality. For instance, when he objects to décolletage, because breasts are primarily for nursing, he thereby desexualizes the female body and reduces its power over men. The assumption Rousseau makes, that women's power over children is benign, permits him to increase women's power as mothers; but the reason that such power is benign is that mothers are located within the patriarchal family. This permits shifting the site of women's power from sex to motherhood, and its target from men to children.

In the *Second Discourse*, Rousseau maintained that women discovered power over men through their sexuality; men, unable to resist the pleasures of sex, were manipulated by women into becoming the "hunters" while women grew "sedentary" and "accustomed themselves to mind the hut and their children" (88). In *Emile*, Rousseau builds on this initial idea of woman as the center of the family but also posits woman as its greatest threat; whereas in the state of nature women's sexual power resulted in something good, namely, the family, in contemporary times it threatens that very institution, and thereby all of society. Women's sexuality, when publicly expressed, threatens the stability of monogamy, and along with that the certainty of paternity, upon which Rousseau pins so much: not the institution of property per se, as it relates to inheritance, but rather the immediate investment that a man makes in the material upkeep of his children and the emotional care and love he gives them. Whether or not a man is the biological father of his wife's children, the possibility that he is not casts the paternal relation into doubt and causes the male to withdraw psychologically and emotionally from them, as well as from his wife. Once the bonds of familial connection are loosened, the primary binding agent for society is loosened as well. The general will may pertain to the good of society beyond the private interests of fathers (and mothers), but it is within the family that the ability to discern the common good is developed and sustained. Thus, without the family, the good society is impossible to create or maintain.

Hence, Rousseau criticizes Plato's *Republic* for its inclusion of women in the guardian class not because of the sexual implications of eliminating monogamous marriage. Rather, he criticizes "the civil promiscuity which throughout confounds the two sexes in the same employments and in the same labors and which cannot fail to engender the most intolerable abuses." By "civil promiscuity" he refers, I believe, to the lack of strict differentiation of gender roles, the removal of children from their parents, and the collective rearing of children by unrelated persons. Rousseau explicitly allies child rearing with civic duty; "as though the love of one's nearest were not the principle of the love one owes the state; as though it were not by means of the small fatherland which is the family that the heart attaches itself to the large one; as though it were not the good son, the good husband, and the good father who make the good citizen!" (*Emile* 363). The social organization of families, rather than biological reproduction per se, is Rousseau's concern; but Plato is at fault because he separates the latter from the former.

This apparent tension between biological sexuality and reproduction, and the social manifestations of gender and the family, is one that threads throughout Rousseau's writings, but is particularly apparent in *Emile*. Thus, the criticism of Plato that I just cited immediately follows a discussion of the social disadvantages in which reproduction places women. He says there that women's "proper purpose is to produce" children, and rejects as counterfactual exceptions the fact that "because there are a hundred big cities in the universe where women living in license produce few children, you claim that it is proper to women's status to produce few children! And what would become of your cities if women living more simply and more chastely far away in the country did not make up for the sterility of the city ladies?" In the paragraph that follows this, Rousseau links women's reproduction to politics in specific terms that identify the citizen as a soldier, which serves as a primary basis for excluding women from citizenship:

> Even if there were intervals as long as one supposed between pregnancies, will a woman abruptly and regularly change her way of life without peril and risk? Will she be nurse today and warrior tomorrow? Will she change temperament and tastes as a chameleon does colors? Will she suddenly go from shade, enclosure, and domestic cares to the harshness of the open air, the labors, the fatigues, and the perils of war? . . . There are countries where women give birth almost without pain and nurse their children almost without effort. I admit it. But in these same countries the men go half naked at all times, vanquish ferocious beasts, carry a canoe like a knapsack, pursue the hunt for up to seven or eight

hundred leagues, sleep in the open air on the ground, bear unbelievable fatigues, and go several days without eating. When women become robust, men become still more so. When men get soft, women get even softer. When the two change equally, the difference remains the same. (*Emile*, 362)

This passage suggests a fundamental difference between men and women that disables women from citizenship by virtue of their natural biology. It would thus seem to support Okin's and others' position that Rousseau reduces women to their reproductive function. The family is key to politics, and the family, it would seem, depends on biology.

But even here, a closer reading reveals that Rousseau recognizes the contingent quality of his argument: men and women become soft or robust in response to social conditions. The fact that men are "more" robust than women, or superior in other ways, is in itself not an argument for excluding women, because those women may still be more robust than "softer" men in another social context. The fact that women in some societies are stronger than women in other societies in itself indicates the social constructedness of women's fitness for politics; men's relative strength compared with women only in their own social context is a particularistic social judgment that serves to rationalize, rather than found, gender inequality. Again, biology per se is less important to Rousseau than the choices that we make *about* biology as human beings in social contexts; women's biology needs to be controlled through the proper ordering of social relations. Otherwise, "natural" sexuality will produce the most "unnatural" of effects—in the salons, for instance, where men become effeminate. But as much as women's sexuality threatens men as individual biological beings, it is really men as members—social beings— who are endangered. In order to be a member of a whole, men must be able to play their part, which they cannot do if women do not play theirs.

Thus, despite Rousseau's repeated invocation of women's "nature," he clearly believes that women must be cultivated to the feminine virtues. It is the supposed naturalness of Sophie's behavior and demeanor that irritates feminists (because it seems so palpably artificial) and political philosophers (because, as Okin maintains, it contradicts the theme of equality that dominates his political writings). But Sophie is actually so virtuous because she has been taught to be so; as Sophie says to her mother, "O my mother, why have you made virtue too loveable for me? If I can love nothing but virtue, the fault is less mine than yours" (*Emile*, 405). Rousseau articulates in book 5 the appropriate upbringing for a "virtuous" female, not a "natural" one. Sophie's education is no less necessary than Emile's to the preservation of her own freedom as much as her future husband's.

This is not to deny that it is substantively different from his. Indeed, it should lack learning of all substantive matters so that her husband may introduce them to her, thus enforcing his influence and control over her. Rather than a simple relationship of subordination, however, Rousseau sees this as one of mutuality. Both Emile's and Sophie's freedom is realized through the general will, but they play different roles and fulfill distinct tasks in relation to it: whereas Emile must pass laws in the assembly that both men and women must obey, Sophie's job is to make sure that the laws he passes are good. Hence, Rousseau calls marriage a "partnership [that] produces a moral person of which the woman is the eye and the man is the arm, but they have such a dependence on one another that the woman learns from the man what must be seen and the man learns from the woman what must be done" (*Emile*, 377). Rousseau does not mean that Sophie listens to Emile describe legislative proposals and tells him how to vote; rather, by displaying modesty and virtue, she tacitly reminds him of the good. She sees the good, and her example helps him translate that into a correct vote. Although the public sphere is the necessary realm for the creation of laws, it also contains the constant pressures of self-interest, corruption, and vice. The home, with women at its heart, is the repository of virtue to which men retreat. The home and the polity exist in a partnership parallel to that between woman and man; each is necessary to produce true freedom for both.

This partnership, of course, often appears to be of the "separate but equal" variety, which is why feminists disparage it. And it is Rousseau's fear of women's sexuality that explains its character. This fear is explicitly referred to in *Emile*; men will be "dragged to death" by woman, whose "violence is in her charms" (358–59). But it is particularly revealed in the most important lesson that Sophie and Emile receive in their construction into their respective roles as virtuous citizens, namely, the two-year separation the tutor imposes after the couple has become engaged. For Emile, the primary purpose is to learn about politics and "the principles of political right." It is only after Emile has secured the love of a virtuous woman that it is safe to teach Emile the potentially corrupting subject of politics. Yet this part of Emile's education must be done before his animal passions have been fully unleashed via the marriage bed. There are two aspects to this requirement, which are more implied than argued. The first is that through separating from Sophie, Emile learns control, both over himself and over his future bride. But second, the fact that Emile goes on to learn about *politics* at this precise moment further suggests that, just as Sophie's virtue protects Emile from the dangers of politics, politics protects Emile from the dangers of Sophie's sexuality. Politics formally defined is decidedly men's sphere; women's citizenship and political activity are limited to the home and to influence on the husband as legislative member, but men's political membership centers on participation in the legislative assembly. Politics as necessary to the realization of freedom takes on a double sense; not only is it the sphere within which men make the laws, obedience to which constitutes moral freedom, it is also the sphere that shelters men from women's sexual influence. It is a "realm apart" from women's physical presence, a place to which men not only *can* escape, but *must*. This is why women cannot be allowed into the legislative assembly. Not only would the temptations of public power seduce women into vice and subvert their virtue, making them incapable of perceiving the general will; but their presence would disrupt men and prevent them from seeing the general will as well. When either men or women step outside their roles, the dynamic is destabilized; it is only by maintaining sexual difference that the family can be sustained, and it is only by maintaining the family that Emile can be a citizen.

And indeed, in the unfinished sequel to *Emile*, which Rousseau significantly subtitled *Les Solitaires*, we see what happens when this central social unit falters. After the death of their daughter and Sophie's parents, Emile takes Sophie and their son to Paris to help her forget her pain and sorrow. (Emile himself does not seem particularly grieved.) But the couple become alienated from one another and do not even engage in sexual relations; Emile engages in "frivolous pursuits" and "too attractive liaisons . . . that habit was beginning to turn to affection." At the least, he neglects his wife, and they begin to drift apart; "we were no longer one . . . worldly manners had divided us."[57] This separateness is their undoing. When Emile, after considerable efforts to rationalize his behavior, forces himself sexually on Sophie, she repels him by telling him that she is pregnant by another man. Whether a result of rape or a consensual (retaliatory) affair is left unclear, but this is the event that drives Emile and Sophie apart once and for all.[58] Emile's family takes Sophie's son, who subsequently dies, and soon after, Sophie dies as well.[59] No longer the head of a family, Emile is no longer a citizen and becomes a stateless wanderer until he is captured by pirates and sold into slavery. Through an exercise of reason that betrays the fatalism of depression, he excels at his work to the point of becoming a manager of other slaves, and eventually a slave of the Dey of Algiers. A sign of the depths to which isolation has driven him, perhaps, is the fact that as a slave, Emile claims to be happy. Wingrove suggests that "he has found freedom in submission" and that "it is because of, not despite, the master's domination that Emile's sense of self returns."[60] But this sense of self and freedom are at best the enslaved animality of the middle stages of the *Second Discourse*. Emile says, "in order not to be destroyed, I need to be driven by the will of another" (*Emile and Sophie*, 225), thus indicating a total loss of self, rather than a recovered sense of self.

Here also, however, Emile would seem to have become what Rousseau structures his entire civil society to avoid, namely, a woman.[61] Just as Sophie finds her freedom in obeying her husband, so does Emile find freedom in obeying his master; and significantly, Rousseau repeatedly refers to husbands as women's "masters." The echoes between the situation of women and that of the slave are particularly poignant in *Emile and Sophie*, where Emile, who failed Sophie as a master, seems to find redemption in subjecting himself to another, much as Sophie subjected herself to him.[62] But this is not meant to portray a happy ending; Rousseau has repeatedly struggled to emphasize the importance of differentiating men from women, and freedom from slavery. Emile no longer deserves to be a man, and he loses both his natural and his moral freedom.

JULIE, OR THE WOMAN AS MODEL CITIZEN

If we were to stop with Emile and Sophie, freedom might seem to be a specifically masculine characteristic, even if many men, such as Emile, are unsuccessful in achieving it. For Rousseau appears fairly restrictive of women's freedom for the sake of enhancing men's. If Emile must rule Sophie in order to exercise his will, Sophie must restrict herself to enable this mastery to succeed. Hence, her pregnancy is the beginning of the end for both of them, for it symbolizes the female body that is unrestrained, not under masculine control.[63] The claim that the freedom that is restrained is the less valuable natural freedom rings somewhat false in the tale of Emile and Sophie, for they seem utterly to fail in achieving moral freedom; what, then, was the point of giving up natural freedom in the first place? But the source of such failure has gendered implications for freedom that Rousseau may not have intended. Marso comments that "the success of Rousseau's citizen . . . is had only in light of the demise of his wife."[64] But in dying, Sophie comes much closer to success than Emile; it is Emile who becomes a slave, after all, whereas Sophie is able to sacrifice her life for the good of the whole. If Emile had not abandoned his son, he could have gone on as the aggrieved widower, remarried, and provided a home for his son. But he chooses not to.

By contrast, Sophie's death, in Rousseau's rather perverse equation, represents the ultimate triumph of will over desire. This is a theme of her character throughout Emile's narration. Colmo says that Sophie's "wisdom exceeds" Emile's; "as strong as a man may be in body, he implies, a woman is stronger in intellect and will." She maintains that Sophie "embodies the general will," whereas Emile represents the citizen in the sovereign assembly.[65] Thus, when Sophie visits Emile in his woodworking shop, unbeknownst to him, she weeps "torrents of tears," and appears "on the verge of running into the workshop several times" but "appeared to hold herself back only by tremendous self-control" before she finally departs. Emile realizes later that "she had anticipated what would have happened had we seen each other again. I was reasonable but weak," and therefore would have forgiven her and reunited. But Sophie's "sublime and proud soul remained inflexible even in her faults. The idea of being forgiven was unbearable to Sophie."[66] This might suggest that Sophie was simply too proud for her own good, but given that paternity is the foundation of the family, she realizes that, regardless of whether she was raped or not, her pregnancy has destroyed them all. She thus embodies the struggle between desire and will, with the latter ultimately triumphing over the former. In this, Sophie echoes the Spartan female citizen, who gladly sacrifices her sons for the state; it is Sophie, not Emile, who is the true hero, and perhaps the true citizen, the dutiful wife to the last, despite her temporary aberration, to the point of conveniently dying, leaving Emile free to remake himself. That he does as poor a job in widowhood as he did in his marriage—abandoning his child, becoming a slave—does not detract from Sophie's sacrifice.

But even if one takes a less generous reading of Sophie, she is not Rousseau's only model for feminine virtue, nor is *Emile* the only novel Rousseau wrote depicting an ideal marriage. *Julie, ou la Nouvelle Heloise*, is devoted not to the question of how to educate a boy to virtue, but rather to the meaning and practice of virtue itself. An epistolary novel depicting the love affair of the title heroine and her nameless lover, S.G. (given an explicit pseudonym, Saint-Preux, in the last third of the novel, by which most commentators refer to him),[67] *Julie* is centrally about the relationship between freedom and virtue, for the conflict at its core is that between desire and will. This book thus particularly demonstrates the ways in which gender is a crucial dynamic of Rousseau's conception of freedom. Julie experiences the conflict between passionate desire and the virtuous will that prompts her to resist and dominate the passions. Passionate love is anathema to freedom in part because it prevents us from knowing our own will. Julie and Saint-Preux do not understand themselves because they are lost in one another: "Why do my eyes not shed half of your tears?" Saint-Preux asks. And he exhorts her to share her deepest feelings with him: "O Julie, conceal nothing from your own self" (82–83). "I feel you everywhere, I breathe you with the air you have breathed, you permeate my whole substance" (120). Though one might think that loss of self is conducive to communitarian morality, in fact Rousseau maintains just the opposite, because it instead gives way to partiality and corruption. Recall that in the legislative assembly, Rousseau does not even permit genuine debate, but requires each citizen to decide the general will in his heart and then simply say how he will vote. Independence is key to this.

The conflict between passion and will is, in my view, a conflict between natural and moral freedom. As long as Julie is ruled by passion and desire, the theme of restriction, as the opposite of freedom, dominates the letters, and particularly in terms of explicitly gendered power. Thus, at first, Julie is resistant to being "married off" by her father—"so my father has sold me? He is making merchandise, a slave of his daughter; he acquits his debts at my expense" (77). She declares that marrying without passion is enslaving. She bemoans the fact that girls live "under the tyranny of propriety," required "always to say something other than what one thinks; to disguise everything one feels; to be false for the sake of duty" (173). Certainly there is ample evidence of gender oppression in the d'Étange household to make Julie's attitude understandable. Her father's propensity to violence is something that Julie's mother clearly fears (123), and in a key scene he beats his daughter over her loyalty to Saint-Preux and her refusal to marry Wolmar.

Yet Julie gives up her lover and marries Wolmar not out of fear of her father. Rather, she does so out of a sense of duty to both her parents, and particularly out of guilt over the death of her mother, which she attributes to shock at her affair with Saint-Preux and resulting pregnancy (which ended in miscarriage). How the "duties" of daughters are constructed, feminists point out, is itself often a function of patriarchy, and one could certainly make such a case here. Lord Edward, who earlier offered Saint-Preux one half of his estate in order to permit Julie and her lover to elope, represents such a view. He says to Julie, "your fate is in your hands," for once she is in England, a woman may "give herself away" (163). The strong Lockean notion of agency and choice that Edward deploys suggests a classically liberal, negative notion of liberty as the ability to make decisions for oneself over how one will live one's life. Duty in this view leads Julie to self-denial, to "giving up what is most important to me." The phrasing that Rousseau uses in these letters prior to Julie's marriage, and explaining her decision to her lover and others, conveys the idea that in following duty she is constrained from pursuing her desire, that duty and freedom are at odds.

But the question Rousseau poses to his readers is: what kind of freedom? It is only natural freedom that Julie can experience in her love affair, a freedom that is at odds with her will. In presenting a calm and rational approach to interest and positing the individual as self-directed, Edward's version of freedom might seem to contrast to the Hobbesian passion-driven pursuit of desire, which could be said to characterize the love affair itself. But Rousseau seems to suggest that the two are equivalent, for both assert the primacy of want over will, desire over virtue, negative liberty over positive. And of course Rousseau rejects and even disparages such freedom; he clearly favors the decision that Julie ultimately makes. The love affair may testify to passions that he acknowledges in the human breast, but he does not advise that they should be followed. For Rousseau, making the right choice—as Julie does in marrying Wolmar—is more important than making the choice you (think you) really want. As Rousseau tells it, insofar as duty prevents her from pursuing her passion, it thereby liberates Julie from herself.

Thus, once she is married to Wolmar, Julie feels "reborn." In her first letter to Saint-Preux after her marriage she says, "I seemed to be beginning another life" (292). This letter and the subsequent one constitute a key turning point in the novel, describing what Julie calls a "revolution."[68] In contrast to her earlier criticism of Claire for her passionless marriage, Julie can now see that passionate love interfered with the alignment of duty and (what she rather inaccurately calls) nature. "Love is accompanied by a continual anxiety of jealousy or deprivation," thus separating the individual from her will; such a state is "ill suited to marriage, which is a state of delectation and peace" (306). Marriage is an institution that modifies and tempers passions that rob the self of control and will, not to mention virtue. As a result, passion prevented Julie from seeing *herself* clearly, and hence from making choices that she could identify with and own. Once she has followed duty by marrying Wolmar as her father has demanded, her virtuous action "restores me to myself in spite of me" (293) and reveals a side of her character that passion had subverted: namely, virtue, which according to Rousseau's vision constitutes her true will.

It is therefore by acting virtuously that Julie can achieve autonomy and true—that is, moral—freedom. But Julie thereby preserves her lover's freedom as well. When Julie's former lover arrives at Clarens later in the novel, he experiences a similar conversion. Though at first he is overwhelmed by passion upon seeing Julie, shortly thereafter he meets her children, and there in the parlor, seeing Julie "surrounded by her Husband and children," he "felt obliged to have a new sort of respect for her" as a "materfamilias. . . . I would have kissed the hem of her dress more willingly than her cheek. From that instant, I knew that neither she nor I were the same, and I began in earnest to augur well for myself" (348). Indeed, it is only when he comes to Clarens that he is given the name Saint-Preux, having remained nameless until this point in the book, much as Julie d'Etange ceases to exist as Julie de Wolmar is "reborn"; the (re)naming of Julie and Saint-Preux symbolizes the coming to selfhood of moral freedom.

Julie's marriage to Wolmar thus frees both her and her former lover. Marriage to Saint-Preux would not, Rousseau obviously believes, have produced the same result. As Julie asks Saint-Preux, "Would we ever have made such progress through our own strength? Never, never, my good friend, it was rash even to attempt it. To flee each other was the first law of duty, which nothing would have allowed us to violate" (546). If they had eloped, they could never have achieved control over their passion; it would have controlled them.

Why should marriage to Wolmar have been so superior, however? Is he, as Shklar calls him, the "hero" of the novel, "because he is omnicompetent and perfect. He cures the ill, saves the weak, and builds a model estate"? Certainly, Rousseau suggests, Wolmar is of superior character. Indeed, he might seem to embody the ideals of citizenship, for he is portrayed as rational, calm, thoughtful, and with great foresight; he cares about the good of the whole and maintains Clarens in good order so that harmony reigns among its parts. And Wolmar's interaction with Saint-Preux, when he invites him to stay at Clarens and "cure" him of his passion, is reminiscent of Jean-Jacques's effort to manipulate Emile into learning specific lessons. Shklar indeed credits Wolmar with taking "complete charge of Saint-Preux to liberate him from his obsessions."[69]

Yet even Wolmar needs Julie to free him. Though rational, he lacks emotive ability and is several times described as dispassionate and even cold (esp. 403). As we know from *Emile*, understanding the truth of the general will requires sentiment and faith as well as reason. Julie is thus Wolmar's saving grace, just as she is Saint-Preux's, for Wolmar loves Julie, and that love helps balance the rationalistic bent of his character. Hence, Julie notes to Saint-Preux that "As for Monsieur Wolmar, no illusion prepossesses us for each other; we see each other such as we are; the sentiment that joins us is not the blind transport of passionate hearts, but the immutable and constant attachment of two honest and reasonable persons who, destined to spend the rest of their lives together, are content with their lot and try to make it pleasurable for each other. . . . Each of us is precisely what the other requires. . . . it seems we are destined to constitute but a single soul between us, of which he is the intellect and I the will" (307).

This passage suggests that feminists who claim that Julie's marriage to Wolmar is a sign of her oppression are mistaken. Both Shklar and Marso, for instance, maintain that Julie is unhappy and even that she kills herself at the end of the novel, a view shared by Disch and Morgenstern.[70] These analyses forget that Rousseau's prescription for excising passionate love from marriage was also advocated by his feminist contemporary—and critic—Mary Wollstonecraft. Like Mary Astell a century before, Wollstonecraft argued that passionate love inevitably cooled, leaving women in a dependent relationship in which they were not respected. By contrast, friendship between equals provided the best foundation for a marriage that would not exploit women and that would protect them within societies that were socially and legally stacked against them. Julie and Wolmar would seem to have the kind of marriage that such feminists advocate, even though Wollstonecraft herself was extremely critical of Rousseau.[71]

Such a marriage is a necessary condition to the achievement of virtue for both men and women, and hence control over the will. It is thereby one of the necessary conditions of the good state, for it constructs passionate individuals into calmer ones who can control their passions. The connection between marriage and civil life is notable in both novels. In *Emile*, marriage was an essential element of citizenship, which is why Emile engages in his two-year sojourn to learn about politics and the state after his engagement but before he is married. In *Julie* it is explicitly noted that "one does not marry in order to think solely about each other, but in order to fulfill conjointly the duties of civil life" (306). By this Rousseau does not mean that husbands and wives will discuss political issues. Rather, "the duties of civil life" entail the production of children, as well as the creation and maintenance of a civil life at Clarens. Clarens is a small society that mirrors—or models—the virtues of civic life, a well regulated ordering of work and leisure that sustains and re-creates honesty, loyalty, truth, and the other qualities that members of Rousseau's ideal polity must have.

Thus, it is no coincidence that Julie's and Saint-Preux's conversions resonate with images of the citizen. Saint-Preux's echoes the imagery in *Emile* of the citizen who comes home from the assembly, battered by the corruption of particular interests, sees his wife and children at the hearth, and knows what the general will is. Julie's account of her own conversion reads much like the male citizen who is able to follow the general will rather than his particular will, which is ruled by passions. In a sense, Julie is the most free, the most herself, when she follows duty and virtue, for these shield her from the effects of passion, which drives individuals to do things without their own control. And that is true of Rousseau's ideal citizen as well.[72]

Indeed, I believe that Julie *is* Rousseau's ideal citizen. This might seem counterintuitive, given that women are excluded from the legislative assembly. But if Shklar is correct in likening Wolmar to the Legislator, then he cannot be the ideal citizen, for the Legislator has no vote in the assembly and thus is not really a citizen at all. Julie is the true regulator of "the admirable order" at Clarens. She is the ultimate word on the hiring and firing of servants; she regulates the interactions between men and women, keeping them separate through the assignment of vastly different duties; she supervises the realm of domesticity; she oversees the welfare of everybody on the estate (*Julie* 368–70). I distinguish this from Joel Schwartz's claim that Julie rules *over* Clarens; Wolmar clearly does that. Rather, she is "the glue that holds Clarens together."[73] Schwartz is similarly mistaken that Julie's authority comes from her sexuality; on the contrary, it comes from the virtuous ability to *resist* sexual passion. She, not Wolmar, is Saint-Preux's true teacher and savior, but not, by any means, because she "use[s] her authority to fashion men according to . . . feminine desire."[74] Rather, Julie guides by example and shows Saint-Preux the way to moral freedom. She does this not as a leader who manipulates him as Wolmar does, or like the tutor does Emile, but as a friend who suggests and gently guides: a peer rather than a parent. If Wolmar provides the opportunity for such liberation by bringing Saint-Preux to Clarens, Julie is the agent who makes it happen.

This is not to deny that even after Saint-Preux comes to live at Clarens, the two former lovers are still tied to one another; the passion between them has not diminished. But it is capable of being transformed and, indeed, undergoes transformation in the novel. Wolmar himself believes that Julie and Saint-Preux "are more in love than ever," even as he simultaneously believes that they are "perfectly cured" (417). I believe Rousseau is saying that virtue, and thereby freedom, is not obtained by *expunging* passion, but by *controlling* it while it is still felt. If one were able to expunge passion completely, then being virtuous would be simple, and hardly worthy of the label "moral freedom." Rather, it is in responding to the challenge of temptation, and winning that challenge over and over, that Rousseau believes freedom lies; such control over the self is the mark of the truly virtuous person. If one feels the passion but resists it, one is truly exercising control over the self; one exerts will over desire, and therefore one is truly free, as one is also virtuous. Hence, Julie says, "the cause that puts an end to love may be a vice, that which turns a tender love into a friendship no less fervent can hardly be equivocal" (546). The love she feels for Saint-Preux is not diminished, but rather consciously channeled into a different form. She even says, shortly after her marriage, that Saint-Preux should be "the lover of my soul." This does not mean that Julie's sexuality is *dis*empowered; she, after all, must be the one who controls it. Such "natural" freedom, however—for that is the only kind of freedom such animal passions can serve, "the impulse of mere appetite"—is inevitably enslaving (*Social Contract* bk. 1, ch. 8).

It is the denial of passion and natural freedom that prompts many feminists to declare that Julie is oppressed and unhappy, deprived of her true love. But I think it is fairer and more accurate to read this as Julie's claim that she "owns" the duty to reject passion; she sees in it her salvation and liberation, and she is very glad that she made that choice. "There are plants that poison us, animals that devour us, talents that are pernicious to us," Julie observes—and passions that ruin us. The fact that we resist them does not negate their existence; it is the presence of these natural possibilities within us that requires us to continue to exercise control, and Julie is conscious of the forces that she must resist until the very end of the novel. This does not mean that Julie, like Wolmar, must become cold and unemotional. On the contrary, as Marso suggests, Julie's loving quality is what makes her an ideal in Rousseau's eyes. I strongly disagree with Marso's conclusion, however, that "allowing and encouraging Rousseau's women to speak clearly and forcefully in the words of their own desire would constitute a more active and participatory (and dare I say, *unruly*) politics," for desire in any form, male or female, is anathema to politics according to Rousseau. The general will is about will, not desire; and though I agree with Marso that Julie "actually could become Rousseau's exemplary . . . citizen," this is because Julie would seem to be the ideal master of the will, not because of her desires.[75]

Thus, in my view, Julie is actually the freest of all characters in the novel by Rousseau's reckoning, because she is the most able to exercise control over herself without nevertheless losing connection with the feelings she must control. Saint-Preux learns this lesson less reliably than Julie, and we are left to conclude that the reason that both Julie and Saint-Preux are "perfectly cured," as Wolmar puts it, is owing to the incorruptible virtue of Julie. After all, it takes two to commit adultery, and if Julie can be trusted not to engage in it, Saint-Preux is thereby saved from himself.

Even Julie's death symbolizes her ideal status. The fact that it is she, not Wolmar, who sacrifices herself to save her child shows that it is she who can give up the immediate pleasures of the present life for the future welfare of the society, represented by the child. As I have indicated, several feminist analysts of *Nouvelle Heloise*—and some nonfeminists, such as Judith Shklar—suggest that Julie does this in order to "kill herself," because she is "unhappy" in her life at Clarens.[76] But I do not see the evidence to support such a reading; she has the same reaction—whether natural or the product of socialization—that many twenty-first-century mothers would have to their child's being in mortal danger. It is because Julie is able to put virtue before self-interest, because she identifies her "self-interest" so closely with her duties, including those of mother, that she is able to fling herself into the water without hesitation to save her drowning son.[77] And on her deathbed, she continues to express concern for those she is about to leave behind, encouraging them to eat (584) and providing instructions for her children's—especially her daughter's—education (578). In dying for her son, Rousseau seems to be saying, she dies for Clarens; and in dying for Clarens, she metaphorically dies for the state.

Julie's death, indeed, brings everybody at Clarens closer together and even reunites those who have strayed. For instance, Claude Anet returns because he has heard of Julie's impending death. Claude is the husband of Julie's loyal maid Fanchon; he abandoned her and their child (who subsequently died) to escape the debts he accumulated by lax behavior

(369). A selfish character who obviously put himself before his wife and Clarens, Claude is resurrected and restored upon his return; not only does Fanchon take him back most happily, displaying a peasant version of wifely virtue, but indeed all of Clarens is delighted (592–93). Julie's death was the obvious catalyst for this redemption and the restoration of ruptured community.

Julie's death saves Wolmar as well. Certainly, marrying him provided him much greater access to the emotional side of virtue and truth than he was capable of achieving on his own. But by the time he invites Saint-Preux to live with them at Clarens, Wolmar is still allowing reason to dominate passion, rather than permitting himself to feel and yet resist his passions, as Julie does. It is Julie's dying that forces Wolmar to come to grips with his love for her and to allow repressed emotions to come to the surface. On her last day, in a private conversation with Wolmar, "she wrote her testament in my heart" (*Julie*, 581). At her death, he feels deep and transforming pain and sorrow. And of course Saint-Preux is able to pass through the final stage of his salvation when Julie dies; he is freed of the daily temptation and allowed to treasure her memory, and the lessons she has taught him, in pristine form.

Many readers might think that death is a rather high price to pay for freedom, if not contradicting it outright. However, what Julie's death shows is Rousseau's greater level of expectation from women and his confidence that they will perform their roles more reliably than men. For instance, recall that while the Spartan male citizen loses an election, the female citizen loses five sons to battle. Both of them exemplify the sacrifice of selfish interest for the good of the whole, but which of these two has made the greater sacrifice? The answer is, I think, rather obvious.[78] The fact that Rousseau makes these two equivalent as examples of self-sacrifice and the placing of the good of the state above their own concerns suggests that he expects much more of women than of men. Accordingly, it is Julie, not Wolmar, who jumps into the water to save their son, the future of Clarens.

This is not a simple antifeminism, however, because Rousseau's conception of the ideal citizen follows the general will, attainment of which involves the submersion of ego without the complete loss of self. Julie is able to achieve this more than any other character in Rousseau's corpus. The "self" that is retained in the loss of ego is the social self, the self that identifies with others, with community. A reason that Julie's submersion of the self appears to be a problem to twenty-first-century feminists is that she is the only one who does this. That is why she ends up having to sacrifice her life. But what makes Rousseau's *Social Contract* possible is the mutual alienation of individual will to all the other members of the assembly, who similarly alienate their wills to you. That is the key to the success of the social self: if I submerge my ego, others must do the same. If I do so but you do not, I will give you more than you give me, and mutuality is destroyed. That is why, on the liberal individualist model, I never want to submerge my ego, because I can never trust others to do the same. The logical extreme of this is the Hobbesian state of war and its strike-first mentality. If we both submerge our egos, however, we each give to the other what we get in return. In *Julie*, we see the model of how one might submerge the ego; but Rousseau shows us that as long as others do not reciprocate, one hero (or heroine) pays a heavy price. But of course, by definition, it is not too high a price for a hero to pay (that is what makes it heroic) and the genuineness of Julie's submersion of ego is evidenced by the fact that she never says, "I'm doing all the giving here, what's in it for me?" If she were to ask such a question, after all, the ego would not have truly been submerged.

The typical feminist objection to this is that women are expected to sacrifice themselves for children and men, and women thereby lose. Rousseau is not, I believe, quite saying that. This is not a *feminine* ideal per se. He is saying instead that *all* individuals must sacrifice themselves for each other in an ongoing mutuality. If we each sacrifice for the other, the level of sacrifice will be much less than if such sacrifice is unevenly made, and in fact we will all be much better off. By the death of Julie, and to a lesser extent, Sophie, Rousseau is saying that this sort of tragedy is what happens when all members of community fail to reciprocate the submersion of ego. He may also be saying, however, that women are more likely to be able to make these sacrifices. That is where the feminist critique may have more bite: for the reason that they can achieve this human ideal is their socialization to a feminine ethic of self-sacrifice. But as contemporary feminists such as Carol Gilligan and Eva Kittay have shown, that ethic is not a pathology; the pathology is the individualism that refuses to reciprocate. The result of that refusal is a distorted understanding of freedom.[79] Rousseau, too, despite his emphasis on gender difference, in this case is suggesting that men would do well to emulate women.

GENDER, PASSION, AND POLITICS

If I am correct, though, then why are women not recognized as active participants in the assembly? If, as Rousseau suggests, fathers become good citizens by being good fathers, would not good mothers make even better citizens? For Aristotle, women are never as good mothers as men can be good fathers, because they are simply inferior in all ways. But Rousseau extols the virtues and importance of motherhood and lauds the women who fulfill its role as the foundation of the state. Why the role and function of "mother" excludes her from other functions is not addressed by Rousseau, at least not directly; as I argued earlier, even his strongest statement in *Emile* about women's pregnancy disabling them from politics involves the social construction of social relations rather than biology. But women's exclusion centrally affects women's freedom, for the assembly is the key to moral freedom.

One answer sympathetic to Rousseau is that the family's centrality to the state, and women's to the general will, makes both the family and women's activities intensely political. Women, like men, are citizens, but they play different roles within the state from men. Women provide the uncorrupted moral guidance that is essential to the success of the democratic assembly's search for the general will; but they can do that only if they stay away from the assembly and its potential for corruption.

A less sympathetic answer, indeed the standard feminist one, is that fear of women's sexual power motivates him to exclude women. In the *Second Discourse* Rousseau shows how inequality corrupts men; the superior press their advantages to exploit the inferior, the inferior become craven and dependent, and all think in terms of self and never of other. This is what he fears will happen if women are given public power; because women have powers of biology and sexuality, when coupled with political power they will gain superiority over men. Certainly in *Emile* Rousseau paints women's sexuality as extremely powerful, enabling women to "drag men to their deaths." But even in *Julie*, women's sexuality is equally potent, for Saint-Preux is overcome by his desire for Julie, forcing her to be the voice of moderation and restraint. And as I have indicated, in his *Confessions* Rousseau repeatedly casts himself as enslaved to various women with whom he has affairs.

I would suggest that sexuality is only part of Rousseau's larger fear, however, which is of passion. The general will involves the battle between desire and will, and hence passion would logically threaten our ability to perceive the general will. Zerilli describes the general will as "the unified inner voice of reason in every man's heart," and maintains that woman must be excluded because her sexuality presents the constant threat to reason and will blind men to the truth.[80] But this is not quite right. It is not just sexuality that women embody, but emotion and love, which are far stronger. Truth, as the Savoyard Vicar tells us, requires faith and love as well as reason; emotion and love are thereby necessary to truth. But they also contain a severe threat to truth, because they do not wish to reside in equitable harmony with reason but seek to overtake reason altogether, thereby perverting truth. Reason seems spontaneously contained by its nature; except for the rare intellect, mathematician, or philosopher, for most men there are many temptations everywhere not to think too much, too long, too hard, or too well. The temptations to lose oneself in passion, by contrast, are omnipresent and powerful, and strong measures must be enacted to ensure its containment. What is necessary to the general will, therefore, is the cordoning off of emotion and love in a separate sphere that can contain and control it, like a tethered beast, so that it can produce truth without perverting it. Truth objectively exists, but the human ability to discern it, and to hold on to it once discerned, is extremely tentative, much as Rousseau says about the general will.

Containing women in the private sphere is how Rousseau achieves control over passion; if women represent emotion and love, if they are educated and socially constructed to embody these aspects of truth, and if they are physically, socially, and psychically contained and limited to a private sphere controlled by men as the patriarchal rulers, Rousseau has achieved his equilibrium. Woman, and particularly her sexuality, may be the ultimate threat to this balance, and thus the ultimate threat to the general will; but she is simultaneously necessary for it, to balance reason. Women cannot simply be locked away, for such a crude "solution" would disable women from their useful contribution. Rather, the home must be recognized as an entire realm, a private "sphere," in which women can reign de facto, but where men rule de jure. Moreover, they must be constructed in the arts of self-control and self-containment, to disable their desire to transgress the boundary into public space, and thereby sustain the impression that men are in control. The home is, as Rousseau ironically describes the *salons* for men, a "voluntary prison" for women. As long as women remain in the home under these conditions, men can traverse the boundary between public and private, carrying reason from the political sphere to the home, and love from the home to the assembly.

Thus, it is not simplistically that Rousseau is afraid of women, but rather that he is afraid of men's inability to rule themselves. Nor is it strictly sexuality that he fears, but what sexuality represents, namely, emotion and love. Women emblemize the aspect of himself, indeed of all men, he most fears and yet most needs. By assigning men the duties of civic life and confining women to the home, Rousseau sees himself as balancing the scales between male and female power; the fear of women's power leads to the construction of institutional configurations that limit and regulate it. His construction of freedom is central to this; for women to be truly free, they must rein in the one natural power that they have over men, their sexuality, through the exercise of will. Their restraint must be self-restraint. Virtuous women "must first be exercised in constraint, so that it never costs them anything to tame all their caprices in order to submit them to the wills of others" (*Emile*, 369). On one level, this is no more paradoxical than male citizens having to choose the laws they must obey. Sophie has chosen her "master," whom she must obey. Similarly, Claire says, "in our sex, we purchase freedom only through slavery, and we must first be servants in order one day to become our own mistresses" (*Julie*, 334). Rousseau indicates that women must make such a choice—they must have "masters"—if they are to be free; but he similarly says that citizens must follow the general will and embody it in their laws if they are to be free. The demands of moral freedom are not easy, he suggests, but extreme, and require not only careful crafting of both the social structures and the individuals who make them up, but constant vigilance as well.

On another level, however, Rousseau's prescriptions for Sophie and Julie are much more problematic, and women are less free than men, for gender plays a decidedly unbalanced role in this construction of the citizen. The most important issue is that the male citizen's dependence on law is "impersonal" and thus does not contradict freedom, for Rousseau explicitly rejects "personal" dependence—dependence on another *person*—as inherently contradictory to freedom. Yet women are defined as beings who not only are, but should be dependent on particular individuals, namely, husbands and fathers. For Sophie, the law is "self-prescribed" only in the sense that she has directed her husband to virtue. That she directs her husband by being obedient and subservient to him is a paradox for which many feminists have rightly chastised Rousseau. But what they frequently fail to acknowledge is that women are constructed to choose such a situation, and that such choices are seen as liberating women from the natural freedom of their passions—or more precisely, their enslavement by them—to the moral freedom of obedience to law.

What may save them from personal dependence is Rousseau's emphasis on self-restraint. His arguments that women must control themselves often seem to be the worst of his many sexist claims, making them seem dishonest, deceptive, and manipulative. But control of the self is what preserves them from personal dependence on their husbands. It is in this regard in particular that Julie is a better model of the citizen than Sophie. Whereas Sophie loses her way once Emile retreats from his duty to his wife, Julie is less dependent on Wolmar than she is on principles of virtue that she has chosen, and rules that encode duty and obligation, even if they are religious ones. "Eternal Providence," she says in her first letter to Saint-Preux after her marriage, "Thou recallest to me the good thou hadst made me love. . . . place my heart under thy protection and my desires in thy hand. Make all my acts conform to my constant will which is thine" (*Julie*, 294). This reliance on God potentially problematizes her freedom, for like Emile's slavery, it would seem to undermine the autonomy and independence that Rousseau elsewhere emphasizes. Indeed, not long before her death, Julie and Saint-Preux debate the compatibility of religion and free will, and Julie says, "What do these idle questions about freedom matter to me! Whether I am free to will the good on my own, or obtain that will through prayer, if I ultimately find the means to do good, does not all that amount to the same thing?" (574).

Within the moral economy of Clarens, her question is well taken; perhaps it is God, not Wolmar, who should be seen as the Legislator. But according to *The Social Contract*, it matters quite a bit: moral freedom demands that we make the laws that we are to obey, not simply follow the laws that come to us from above. The ideals of negative liberty, particularly my own choice, must coexist with those of positive liberty, namely, the right choice. So it is the exclusion of women from public lawmaking that confirms women's ultimate unfreedom in Rousseau's formula. As Landes notes, both men and women are subject to the "sublimation of particular interests on behalf of a desire for the public good," as I have argued; but "woman is barred completely from active participation in the very sphere that gives purpose to all her actions."[81] Despite his account of Clarens as a state of idealistic perfection, Rousseau does not in fact believe that the private sphere is a realm of freedom; as in ancient theory, for Rousseau only the public sphere is the arena where moral freedom can be fully achieved and exercised. The home, instead, is a *precondition for* public freedom, and hence of true moral autonomy.

If the home is freedom's necessary background condition, but not its actual embodiment, then women's "imprisonment" in the home, no matter how "voluntary," poses problems for their moral freedom. Although obedience to self-prescribed law—the following of duty, the control of passion through self-restraint—is a guiding precept in both *Emile* and *Julie*, participation in the formal mechanisms of politics is the most important element of freedom in Rousseau's corpus, as Landes notes. As Rousseau said in *The Social Contract*, there is a difference between the law I make for myself alone and one that I make as a collective of which I am a part. The former is the precondition for the ability to enact the latter. Hence, the fact that Emile lives in a world without a participatory assembly means that he will never achieve true moral freedom; the elements are in place for the good citizen to come into being, but without the context of a civil society in which he can act in concert with others, the state of readiness is fragile and eventually falls apart. The manufacture of a surrogate civil society at Clarens means that Julie's friends and family have somewhat greater hope than Emile, but they, too, are in a fragile state, and the lack of actual civil society is what requires the sacrifice of its central character to hold everyone together. Though we do not know if Clarens will survive Julie's death, that is its only hope.[82] In Rousseau's worldview, death is not too heavy a price to pay for virtue.

It is here, however, that the final ambiguity of Rousseau's theory of freedom is confronted. If, as I argued earlier, the totalitarian reading of *forcer d'être libre* can be defended against by highlighting both the role of choice and agency, and the location of such choice in specific contexts of community based on mutuality, reciprocity, and strict equality, it must also be noted that women fall short on both counts. The area in which women can express their agency is exclusively the realm of the home, a realm formally governed by men regardless of the informal and indirect power that women manage to wield. Rousseau does in complex ways attend to women's power, but simultaneously disempowers them in the most critical arenas. Such disempowerment obviously compromises women's equality. Indeed, their only hope for equality—namely, by receiving men's respect and goodwill in the family—is to subvert themselves to their husbands, to make themselves unequal by denying their natural powers and giving up all claims on participation in public space. The elements that make Rousseau's notion of moral freedom palatable and plausible— democratic assembly where everyone has a voice, political equality, and unanimous consent—are absent from women's realm and experience. The criteria of freedom are thus defined in such a way as to catch women in a double bind: if women violate Rousseau's prescription, they are morally unfree because the general will cannot be realized; but if they follow his prescription, they are morally unfree because they are unable to participate in determining that will.

Conclusion

This does not mean that Rousseau is self-contradictory, however. Indeed, Rousseau is theoretically consistent within his framework. But that fact simply shows that his sexism is overtly political, not theoretical. It might seem ironic that, despite his apparent basing of men's freedom on women's restriction, his theory could be reconstructed to accommodate women without sacrificing theoretical consistency. But I believe that is the case. The necessity of the home as a complementary sphere to politics does not require gender stratification; Emile may have been a failure, but Wolmar is clearly capable of looking after and taking care of the servants and children. And particularly after Julie's death we must presume that his capabilities will extend into the emotional realm as well as the intellectual and practical. Indeed, the ease and facility with which men can occupy the domestic realm may be why Rousseau states that at Clarens, the men and women are almost completely segregated; men and women are kept from mixing not by prohibition and rules, but "by assigning to them entirely different occupations, habits, tastes, pleasures. . . . they sense that in a well-run house men and women should have little communication with each other" (370). As in his *Letter to D'Alembert*, Rousseau prescribes particular "public spectacles" such as supervised dances as the place for the sexes to meet.

That Rousseau holds so fiercely to gender differentiation reflects his own personal biases and fears, to which he admits quite openly in his *Confessions* and the *Reveries*. What this transparency about Rousseau's views of gender suggests, however, is that his theory of freedom recognizes that we are all, male and female, rich and poor, inevitably subject to social construction: the question only becomes how to engage it in a proactive and self-conscious manner to reflect a particular political configuration for virtue and moral freedom. The merging of positive and negative liberty themes that this entails is a function of this constructivist vision: virtue is obviously key to Rousseau, for without it we wallow in an unvaluable natural freedom. But choice is also vital, because we are the ones who have to create the right social institutions and practices that will encourage us and others to make the right choices. In the move from savage to civilized human in *The Origin of Inequality*, what demarcates human from animal is the ability to shape our lives in a way that leads to progress. That may not make the sexism less compelling in his theory of freedom; only, perhaps, less essential.

CHAPTER FOUR

Immanuel Kant

THE INNER WORLD OF FREEDOM

THE KIND OF COMPLICATION that I noted at the end of my discussion of Rousseau characterizes Kant's theory of freedom as well. Although the other theorists considered in the previous and following chapters would seem to be unequivocally concerned with concepts of political freedom, and while they are unquestionably part of the "canon" of modern political theory, the selection of Kant for inclusion here may seem less obvious. Although many political theorists do teach and read Kant, his discourse is moral philosophy, not political theory strictly defined, and the concerns and questions he raises are different from those Hobbes, Locke, Mill, and Rousseau raise, although they are related to them. Hans Reiss may state the case too strongly when he observes that "Kant, at least in English-speaking countries, is not generally considered to be a political philosopher of note," and is read as "merely a forerunner of Hegel."[1] But even renowned Kant scholar Allen Wood suggests that many find Kant "too far-fetched and metaphysical."[2] Jonathan Bennett declares Kant's theory of freedom in particular as "worthless" and even unintelligible, with Kant "giving in one phrase what he takes away in the next."[3] Onora O'Neill notes that "Kant is . . . reviled for giving a metaphysically preposterous account of the basis for freedom." And noted Kant scholar Lewis White Beck says about Kant's second *Critique*, in which freedom is a central theme, that "Kant's statements are so cryptic that it is hard to know whether he is entirely consistent or not."[4] Herta Nagl-Docekal merely observes that "the concept of the social contract, albeit one of the foundations of Kant's political philosophy, is not a defining element of Kant's understanding of morality,"[5] but this criticism may be even more damning; for if the social contract is unrelated to morality—indeed, if politics more generally is unrelated to morality for Kant—then his theory is practically useless to contemporary political theorists. Indeed, it might seem that Kant, with his multilayered and almost mystical vocabulary of "pure reason," the "holy will," and the "noumenal realm," is more relevant to philosophers concerned with fitting angels on pinheads than to political theorists grappling with down-to-earth questions of the state or everyday political concepts like freedom.

Yet as Reiss also points out, Kant should be taken seriously by political theorists, for in him "many of the intellectual strands of the Enlightenment converge."[6] In terms of freedom theory, Kant introduces many important ideas and raises vital questions, as "the idea of freedom occupies a privileged place in Kant's philosophy."[7] Indeed, it is to Kant that we can attribute the terminological invention of "positive" and "negative" liberty.[8] Kant was considerably influenced by Rousseau and displays many significant similarities in his theory of freedom, suggesting that Kant is another major proponent of positive liberty.[9] In the move from Kant to Rousseau, however, there are some important differences, even what we might call "shifts," in the concept of freedom. In his conceptualization of freedom Kant seems to emphasize the role of the individual much more than Rousseau does; yet at the same time, he can be seen to outdo Rousseau in linking freedom to law and morality.

TRANSCENDENCE AND PHENOMENA

Kant's treatment of liberty is, as Wood suggests, highly "metaphysical," and this aspect of his theory derives from his belief that humans occupy two realms of being, the "noumenal realm" and the "phenomenal realm." The noumenal realm involves the world of things in themselves, things as they are in their essences. These essences cannot be observed or experienced, but only known a priori, Kant says. The noumenal realm is the "intelligible" realm, the realm of ideas, and exists only in and through reason. The phenomenal realm is the "sensible" world, the world of sense objects, in which we physically live. In the phenomenal realm, our knowledge is grossly incomplete, for we can know things only as they affect us: "we must resign ourselves to the fact that we can never get any nearer to them and can never know what they are in themselves."[10] Thus, the phenomenal world is only the world of appearance; we cannot perceive things in their reality, but can only experience things "out there" as they are filtered and mediated through our consciousness and mind. But "behind appearances we must admit and assume something else which is not appearance—namely, things-in-themselves," Kant says, that is, the noumenal realm (*Groundwork*, 451). The noumenal realm entails the world of ideas that come from me alone, and not in response to objects in the sensible world. The noumenal realm thus is the realm of reason, and of "whatever comes into consciousness, not through affection of the senses, but immediately" (*Groundwork*, 451).

Though these are often interpreted as two "worlds," however—a language I persist in here because of its common usage in the Kant literature—the noumenal and phenomenal are actually different aspects of a single world, as if flip sides of the same coin.[11] Kant periodically talks about the two realms as "perspectives" and "standpoints." He certainly does not use the latter term in the epistemological sense meant by Marx and later Marxist feminists such as Nancy Hartsock;[12] but he does say that the noumenal and phenomenal are different aspects of human knowledge and experience. As phenomenal beings, we must operate in both realms, or utilize both kinds of knowledge, at one and the same time, and human beings must be marked by both aspects. We are physical beings who can reason, and these two features of human existence entail the philosophical ramifications of those states that Kant articulates. The ramifications entail, in turn, both a mutual exclusivity between the two, conceptually or intellectually, and an interdependence between them in that they both operate in each human individual. Human bodies would cease to work if we simply deployed a priori reason all day and forgot to eat and bathe. But we must use reason in order to live in society with others. Thus, Kant explicitly says that the two standpoints are compatible: "both characteristics not merely *can* get on perfectly well together, but must be conceived as *necessarily combined* in the same subject" (*Groundwork*, 456). As O'Neill puts it, "human agents . . . not only may but must adopt both standpoints, and must shift between them."[13]

The interdependence of the two realms is in large part a function of Kant's theory of knowledge. Robert Pippin argues that "Kant's position is not only that the mind has no independent access to things as they are in themselves, and can thus only know nature as subject to our forms of intuition and thought, as phenomena, but also that we are *nonetheless* 'required' to think about such things in themselves in various way[s], for various reasons, just in order to be able to have coherent, systematic, phenomenal knowledge."[14] For instance, when I refer to the two hundred-year-old white oak tree in my front yard, I have a very specific phenomenon in mind, an object of nature, which I perceive through my senses. But my ability to call it a "tree" involves an abstraction of the concept "tree," an abstract idea of "treeness" I am unable to define precisely, as particular trees have such a wide variety of features: deciduous or evergreen, different kinds of bark, leaves, needles, berries, growth patterns, and so forth. Indeed, the diversity of trees makes one wonder how the concept of "tree" ever came to be in our language. Kant would, I believe, explain it as a function of our intelligibility, our ability to think of things in themselves. The idea-in-itself of a tree, of course, must cohere with identifiable phenomenal features of sensible objects; there must be actual objects to which we can point and claim "that is a tree." But at the same time the idea-in-itself is independent, a standard against which we measure particular objects; that is, in order to call something a tree, the phenomenon to which we refer must cohere with the abstract idea as well. In other words, the specific, concrete tree and the abstract idea of a tree are mutually constitutive. But they are also two different things operating on two different levels of the understanding.

Pippin maintains that "Prima facie, this position seems inconsistent. The latter requirement [that the idea-in-itself be independent] seems to demand that reason, unaided by sensibility, be able in some nonarbitrary, well-grounded way to think about nature as it is in itself, not as it is known through sensibility, nor, theoretically, as it is a priori subject to necessary conditions for experience." But he goes on to explain that it is not inconsistent at all, for "while experience of outer objects certainly is intelligible only in terms of sensory receptivity, such experience immediately involves something more than just sense data themselves . . . a full explanation of what it means to interpret claims about objects as claims about experience of objects must involve a priori elements essential to any experience."[15] We have to interpret sense data; the nature of the difference between the physical world of sense-objects and the intelligible "world" that operates in the human brain means that there is and must be a gap between our perception of a thing and the thing in itself. Thus, "the notion of a thing in itself has a wholly negative use—where it merely restates our ignorance of the transcendent realm."[16] Thus, when I point to the white oak in my yard and say, "That's such a majestic tree," the abstract notion of treeness, the in-itself quality of the tree, can never really be known. Objects, once perceived, must be translated or interpreted in our minds into categories and concepts: that is, into language. But that interpretation is limited by what is perceived, which will be constant (we assume) for all (or most, barring visual and other sensory disabilities) observers. So there is a material reality out there, but we have to engage in the act of interpretation in order to perceive it. And that interpretive act requires us to draw on abstractions that we can never fully understand or know. The two realms, then, though interactive, do designate two distinct but related aspects of knowledge.

They also correspond to different relations of the self to freedom, if not two conceptions of freedom altogether. Part of this difference involves a divergent emphasis in the dynamic between the realms within the process of knowing. Specifically, in the phenomenal realm, the sense objects of the natural world cause us to think, act, feel, and desire in certain ways, by virtue of natural laws of the physical world: according to Kant, our actions, feelings, and desires are merely effects of nature, which causes them. Kant asserts that in the phenomenal world, we are determined. Indeed, Bernard Williams argues that for Kant "all actions except those of moral principle were to be explained not only deterministically but in terms of egoistic hedonism. Only in acting from moral principle could we escape from being causally determined by the drive for pleasure."[17] By contrast, then, the noumenal realm is the realm of freedom; or rather, freedom is possible only in and through the noumenal realm, through a priori knowledge and the use of reason to understand things-in-themselves. If, in the world of appearance, we are caught in causal chains that determine us and our behavior, then in order to break free of such determination we must occupy the realm that enables us not to be determined by previous events: "if appearances are things in themselves," Kant notes, then "freedom cannot be upheld" because "Nature will then be the complete and sufficient determining cause of every event."[18] Through a priori reasoning about the essence of things, we are radically free of all predetermined and predetermining phenomena: the mind, and specifically the reasoning mind, is the way in which this freedom is achieved.

But if we follow Pippin's insight about the interaction between the two realms through the process of apprehension and interpretation, then in fact freedom does not and cannot merely consist in knowing things in themselves; or rather, this kind of knowledge is only the first foundation of freedom, not its entire condition. Though Kant is often read, particularly by feminists, as positing the self exclusively in the mind, regarding the body as inessential to the self and hence to freedom, I agree with Henry Allison that Kant's recognition that humans simultaneously occupy "two realms" results in an understanding of freedom that accommodates this recognition, even if he does not always make this accommodation clearly or consistently.

As for Hobbes, Locke, Mill, and Rousseau, what constitutes "freedom" for Kant depends on what an "individual" is. For Kant, individuals are essentially located in the will. Desire is external or alien to the essential self, determined by external causes, as when the smell of your cigarette causes me to want one. In this regard, Kant oddly echoes Hobbes, for whom we will recall desires are not things over which we can exercise control: they simply come to us, unbidden. As determined by external causes, Kant says, desire is heteronomous; it does not come from within my essential or true self. However, as was the case for Hobbes, we *are* responsible for deciding whether to act on our desires; I can smoke a cigarette, or I can decide to stick to my resolve to quit. Whereas Hobbes declared that the desire for the cigarette is simply conquered by a stronger desire to quit, and that this triumph of one desire over the other was itself the exercise of will, Kant instead posits a stark contrast between will and desire. That is, the desire to smoke is still there, but it is superseded by an exercise of will to act in a way that "frees" me from that determination of my behavior. In this, fulfillment of desires does not seem relevant to freedom at all. As Allison argues, fulfilling desire may be *consistent with* freedom, but "inclination of desire does not *of itself* constitute a reason for acting. It can become one only with reference to a rule or principle of action, which dictates that we ought to pursue the satisfaction of that inclination or desire."[19] If I am to be free, the will, rather than desire, must determine my action.

Maxims are the way in which the will can exercise its rule. In an echo of Rousseau's moral freedom, Kant maintains that the will must be guided by self-proclaimed rules. But Kant develops a more complicated formula than Rousseau's simple (though as we saw, not always clear) formula of obedience to a law I prescribe to myself. He constructs a typology of different kinds of rules or principles that accomplish different things for human life and that contribute to freedom in different ways or to different degrees. Maxims are rules that I lay down for myself. They provide guideposts, principles, reminders, and boundaries that can contain and limit my sensible tendencies to act on my desires, and to be heteronomous. In order to be autonomous, I must follow these maxims; but even more important , I must make the rules that I follow. If I simply followed the rules that others set down for me, I would be acting heteronomously. If I make the maxims I follow, however, then I am following my own will and acting autonomously. These rules or maxims must occur "spontaneously" through the use of reason; "Autonomy of the will" is constituted in "being a law to itself" (*Groundwork*, 440). Reason is what provides the spontaneity in Kant's theory, not desire (as for Hobbes), because reason is the only thing not anchored to the world of determinism, the phenomenal realm. Reason is the feature of human will and action that is totally self-determined.

This notion of spontaneity thus means that freedom has a transcendental quality. Although Kantian subjects cannot be divorced from the physical and empirical world, they are not wholly bound by it because they have the ability to reason. Indeed, they must transcend the physical world if they are to achieve freedom, according to Kant, and creating and following maxims helps them accomplish this. But maxims cannot in and of themselves guarantee freedom, for they are still consistent with the conditional behavior that seeks the end of satisfying sensible desires. That is, I could make all sorts of maxims that are consistent with phenomenal desire, such as "don't drink caffeine after four in the afternoon" or "exercise for forty minutes three times per week." These maxims might help me lead a better life, but they are not the result of a priori reason; rather, they are logical inferences from physical experience, and they feed phenomenal desire (to sleep more soundly or maintain good cardiovascular health). Furthermore, there is no guarantee that I will follow these maxims consistently. So the fact that they are maxims in and of itself is not sufficient to make me free when I follow them: "the principles one makes for oneself are not yet laws to which one is unavoidably subject, because reason, in the practical, has to do with the subject, namely with his faculty of desire" (*Critique of Practical Reason*, 5:20).

What is needed for true freedom, Kant says, are imperatives. The idea of an imperative carries the idea of a maxim further, to a universal law. Whereas a maxim may apply to me alone, an imperative goes beyond my individual circumstances and experience. As Kant says in the second *Critique*:

> for a being in whom reason quite alone is not the determining ground of the will, this rule is an *imperative*, that is, a rule indicated by an "ought," which expresses objective necessitation to the action and signifies if reason completely determined the will the action would without fail take place in accordance with this rule. Imperatives, therefore, hold objectively and are quite distinct from maxims, which are subjective principles. (*Critique of Practical Reason*, 5:20)

A maxim allows me to treat myself as an end, rather than a means to an end—namely, the end of satisfying a heteronomous desire—because I am governed in my act by my will, not my wants. An imperative extends this treatment as-ends-not-means to other people as well. But moreover, and indeed because of this "universalizing" character of an imperative, imperatives carry more moral force than maxims for the individual himself. That is, although I can declare as a maxim "do not drink coffee after four in the afternoon," that is not a maxim that need apply to everyone; my husband, for instance, can drink coffee in the evening, and it will not affect his sleep. Furthermore, if I am tempted one evening by the aroma of a particularly rich blend of coffee being served in the restaurant in which we are dining to join my husband in drinking coffee, there is nobody to stop me, for nobody will suffer except me (or at most him, if I keep him awake). Furthermore, there might be circumstances in which breaking the maxim makes sense, such as when I need to drive a long distance after dinner. So the rule is entirely subjective. By contrast, the rule "do not kill others" is a rule that applies to everyone, under all circumstances. Maxims can be corrupted by desire and phenomenal circumstance; thus "maxims are indeed *principles* but not *imperatives*" (*Critique of Practical Reason*, 5:20). By contrast, imperatives provide objective guidance to the will through a priori reason, and hence a clearer path to freedom.

The importance of imperatives, and why they are so much more important to freedom than even maxims are, pertains to the phenomenal or sensible nature of human beings. That is, although we may recognize the logic of what Kant says, we may not always be able to follow it:

if . . . the will is not *in itself* completely in accord with reason (as actually happens in the case of men); then actions which are recognized to be objectively necessary are subjectively contingent, and the determining of such a will in accordance with objective laws is *necessitation*. That is to say, the relation of objective laws to a will not good through and through is conceived as one in which the will of a rational being, although it is determined by principles of reason, does not necessarily follow these principles in virtue of its own nature. (*Groundwork*, 412–13)

Kant thus posits an unavoidable tension: true freedom exists in the noumenal realm, but humans cannot perfectly reside there. As humans, with bodies that have physical needs that determine us, we are located in the phenomenal realm. Freedom thus involves the struggle to get beyond our phenomenal desire and attain the "holy will" (or "such a will as would not be capable of any maxim conflicting with the moral law"), in which we are guided only by reason to do only that which is good and true. However, as humans, we can never really or fully achieve a "holy will"; we are always drawn to desire things that are not in themselves good, "insofar as [humans] are beings affected by needs and sensible motives" (*Critique of Practical Reason*, 5:32). The holy will, in fact, can be embodied in its perfection only by God.

As rational beings, however, though we may not be able to attain a perfect will, "one can presuppose a *pure* will," which can recognize and choose to exercise restraint over phenomenal need and to follow moral law:

Accordingly the moral law is for them an *imperative* that commands categorically because the law is unconditional; the relation of such a will to this law is *dependence* under the name of obligation, which signifies a *necessitation*, though only by reason and its objective law, to an action which is called *duty* because a choice that is pathologically affected (though not thereby determined, hence still free) brings with it a wish arising from *subjective* causes, because of which it can often be opposed to the pure objective determining ground and thus needs a resistance of practical reason which, as moral necessitation, may be called an internal but intellectual constraint. (*Critique of Practical Reason*, 5:32)

What should be noted here is Kant's recognition that constraints on freedom can be internal, and not just external. If true freedom lies in the noumenal realm, then external matters should not be relevant to freedom at all, for they should have little if any effect on a priori reason. But internal restraints that are intellectual are different from those that are emotional; the constraints of reason are qualitatively different from those of fear or desire, because the former represents the true self, whereas the latter distorts or interferes with true self-realization. As I noted previously, because they belong to the sensible realm, according to Kant, they are "alien." Indeed, true freedom "restricts all inclinations . . . to the condition of compliance with its pure law" (*Critique of Practical Reason*, 5:78). That is, because inclinations, desires, and emotions restrict or interfere with the will, which is the crux of freedom, the will may restrict emotions without compromising freedom; indeed, doing so enhances freedom. We are free only if we escape desire, and we can force ourselves to get free of desire by acting on law. As we saw with Rousseau's distinction between obedience to law and the compulsion of appetite, the constraints of reason do not "constrain" individuals per se, but only guide them to their true wills. Desires, by contrast, impede our ability to follow a priori reason, and thus compromise our freedom. Whereas Rousseau distinguished between good desires and bad, however—even sexual desires could be either morally virtuous and therefore liberating, or morally vicious and thereby enslaving—Kant juxtaposes reason to desires of all kinds.

The fact that the will is "pure," even if it is not perfect or "holy," means that maxims must be translated into imperatives. The purpose of imperatives is to help keep us as close as possible to the holy will, and hence as free as humanly possible, given our inevitable limits as phenomenal beings. Imperatives provide us with moral "oughts," when rational inclination (what I "would" do if I were acting rationally) is not sufficient. Imperatives "say that something would be good to do or to leave undone; only they say it to a will which does not always do a thing [simply] because it has been informed that this is a good thing to do." And it does this by "determin[ing] the will by concepts of reason, and therefore not by subjective causes, but objectively—that is, on grounds valid for every rational being as such" (*Groundwork*, 413).

But even this idea of an imperative is not always enough to determine the will reliably, for there are two kinds of imperatives. The first is the "hypothetical" imperative, which is conditional, that is, action that "would be good solely as a means *to something else*" (*Groundwork*, 414). This kind of imperative is too closely linked to the natural world to provide guidance to the holy will and freedom. The other kind of imperative is "categorical," in which an "action is represented as good *in itself* and therefore as necessary, in virtue of its principle, for a will which of itself accords with reason." This imperative "may be called the imperative of morality," and is the essence of freedom (*Groundwork*, 414, 416).

The categorical imperative is one of Kant's most famous legacies. It is "the supreme principle of practical reason" and is "central not just to [Kant's] ethics but to his whole philosophy," including most particularly freedom.[20] The categorical imperative (in its clearest and most basic formulation) states: "*Act only on that maxim through which you can at the same time will that it should become a universal law*" (*Groundwork*, 421). The importance of this universalization is that it cannot by definition be instrumental or hypothetical, because anything that meets the standard of universal law, Kant asserts, must be good in itself. Thus, the categorical imperative is the surest guide to moral action and the free will; if I measure what I will against the categorical imperative, I can assess whether what I will is good in itself, and hence whether it is really what I will.

Like Rousseau, Kant locates freedom in law and morality, and specifically in the categorical imperative. Freedom is defined by the will, which in turn is defined as the power "of a rational being . . . to act *in accordance with his idea* of laws" (*Groundwork*, 412). Reason is necessary to this process, for only a rational agent can have this power; only a "rational being" can perceive what the law should be and establish it. It is only by following the will that we can achieve "freedom from dependence on interested motives" that would make a person "subject only to the law of nature—the law of his own needs," that is, to sensible necessity (*Groundwork*, 439). Freedom consists in rational action, which is the true expression of the will. But more than that, what constitutes "rational action" must be what conforms to moral law: a central feature of Kant's theory "is the virtual identity of rational agency with action on the basis of an ought."[21] That is, we act rationally when we conform to our duty, and hence we can be free only by doing our duty. Thus, "the will is nothing but practical reason," which is the faculty that enables individuals to determine what principles and laws are the best, and then also provides the motivational force for following them (*Groundwork*, 412).

Choice thus enters Kant's theory of freedom in two ways. The first involves following the law—or more specifically, choosing and deciding to act in a way that coheres with the behavior that the law requires of you. This is "*objective* accord with the law." But this behavior, and this choice, must arise out of "*subjective* respect for the law" (*Critique of Practical Reason*, 5:81). That is, the fact that this behavior is *required* by the law does not mean that choice is irrelevant because I am coerced; rather, the fact that law requires you to do something must be the reason motivating your choice to do it. If I offer to share my ice cream cone with you because I know that it is a good thing to share, then I am acting morally, and of my own free will. But if I do it only because I am already full, or feeling anxious about how I am going to fit into the new dress I bought, then I am not acting morally, even though the end result is the same. Nor am I acting freely, because I am driven by my phenomenal fullness or anxiety, not by the fact that it is a good thing to do.

Choice enters in a second way, though, in that I have to be able to decipher what the law is through my *own* independent reasoning. If you tell me what the law is, and I accept that without thinking, or because I am used to obeying you, that behavior is not sufficient for freedom; rather, I must make the choice to follow the law because I have used a priori reasoning to determine for and by myself what the good action and the law that guides it are. It is not even enough for me to follow the maxim "I know that you are always right, and therefore I must always do what you tell me to do," for such knowledge is based on sensible experience, even if reason is utilized in the mix (I know you have been right in the past, so reason tells me that you are likely to be right this time as well). Nor can I even say "sharing is good" without thinking about why it is good, or about the steps that lead me to that conclusion, because otherwise I am simply accepting a principle that someone else has told me to accept—even if I cannot tell you who that "someone" is, because it is simply "accepted wisdom" or customary practice. I must engage in a priori reasoning for myself, and make my choices based on that reasoning, if I am to be declared free.

Ethics and Politics

The positive liberty aspects of Kant's account are obvious: the duty to develop one's potential, the equation of freedom with morality, the necessity of acting according to the categorical imperative if one is to be free are all notions identifiable with positive liberty. The will is good only if it is universalizable, and I am free only if my will is good (*Groundwork*, 437). As does Rousseau, Kant links freedom and morality; freedom lies in treating myself as an end, rather than a means, and, by virtue of the categorical imperative, therefore treating all others or "every rational agent *as an end in itself*" (*Groundwork*, 430). But in slight contrast to Rousseau, I must do this because I will it as an independent and separate thinking being (the criteria for autonomy) and not because others do (which would be heteronomy); for example, not because of habit, or custom, or even a law externally generated by a democratic political authority that I have not reconciled with or determined by my own will. For instance, Rousseau's minority, which must not only obey laws that it does not vote for, but also accept the majority's determination of the general will as its own will, would not be considered free on Kant's account. Kant thus makes the linkage between morality and freedom more individualistically—and perhaps less politically—than does Rousseau. The latter, recognizing the difference between a law I lay down for myself alone and the law created by a collective of which I am a part, held a more communitarian view of liberty: true moral freedom needed to be connected to civil freedom, and was therefore possible only in a particular kind of democratic society. To make this society work, minorities would have to accept majority decisions as their own, for it was only in this society that each citizen could potentially achieve moral freedom both negatively (by having a voice, and therefore choice, in determining the laws that she is to obey), and positively (conditions of equality and active participation produce a context in which the chances of people's ability to choose good laws increases). For Kant, by contrast, freedom is located completely in individuals and their wills: the nature of the categorical imperative is that I should act in ways that are conformable to the universality requirement, but my determination of the law comes from myself.

At the same time, however, this strong individualism might link Kant with negative liberty as well. Particularly the notions that the will must follow the categorical imperative on its own, and from itself, that morality and hence freedom cannot come from an outside source but must work from the inside out, that individuals must activate and draw on their own reason to determine the actions that will properly make them free agents are all consistent with negative liberty ideals of strong individualism and self-determination. This may be even more the case in Kant's political writings. Reiss argues that Kant is essentially a "liberal" and that "his conception of political freedom is not positive, but negative. It is concerned with those restraints which the individual must accept in order to avoid conflict with others so that he may enjoy the freedom of moral action."[22] Making Kant sound almost like Hobbes, Reiss argues that for Kant, "Freedom implies that we have a hypothetical right to acquire anything in the world of a nature which we are potentially capable of acquiring." This, of course, creates conflict, which laws are necessary to settle: the "freedom of each individual has consequently to be regulated in a universally binding manner. Thus, external freedom is freedom from any constraint except coercion by law, a freedom which allows each individual to pursue his own ends, whatever they may be, provided that this pursuit leaves the same kind of freedom to all others."[23] The exception of "coercion by law," as I have suggested in previous chapters, does pose a conflict with negative liberty ideals; but I also showed that even Hobbes could be interpreted to argue for the necessity of law to the effective preservation, if not enlargement, of people's freedom: law simply provides people with a different set of choices than the state of nature provides. The fact that most people would not want to risk going to jail, and therefore choose to obey the law, is arguably both the result of coercion and the result of choice. The same paradoxical idea was found in Locke as well, I have argued.

The critical emphasis Kant repeatedly places on individualism in his understanding of "autonomy" might also seem to support Reiss's view that Kant is a negative libertarian. Kant repeatedly extols the ability "to use one's understanding without guidance from another." The strong individualism in Kant's approach to reason must be acknowledged. His cry in "What Is Enlightenment" to "have courage to use your *own* understanding"[24] emphasizes the kind of argument that I made about Rousseau: freedom is obtained through constructing and following the *good* laws, but we must *choose* those good laws. For Kant, such choosing is not the simple acceptance of the lessons of virtue, however, as it tends to be for Rousseau, but the deployment of the individual's reason to work out the laws for himself a priori. This idea is echoed in "What Is Orientation in Thinking" where "*to think for oneself* means to look within oneself (i.e., in one's own reason) for the supreme touchstone of truth: and the maxim of thinking for oneself at all times is enlightenment."[25] As Pauline Johnson argues, "the vocation for independent thinking" emphasized by Kant highlights his desire for a "radical emancipation from the dogmas of the past."[26] Accordingly, Kant says, the "*public* use of one's reason must always be free," while the "private use of reason" must be regulated. Somewhat eccentrically, of course, by "private" Kant refers to people in civic posts, not people in their homes, whereas "public" refers primarily to public speech, and particularly public speech that critiques civic requirements. So, for instance, in exemplifying the private, Kant says, "it would be disastrous if an officer on duty" challenged his orders or if a citizen refused to pay taxes. And yet either of these same people could, "as a scholar," publicly criticize these very same governmental actions.[27] Here, as Onora O'Neill points out, Kant's apparently eccentric use of the public/ private distinction turns on the use of reason: what is "public" pertains to "not 'the world at large,' but an audience that has been restricted and defined by some authority. . . . other than reason." Claims founded on reason alone are "in principle accessible to the world at large and can be debated without invoking authority" and are therefore "public."[28]

As O'Neill also notes, Kant hardly thinks that all, or even most, people actually *will* understand such claims founded on reason; as she says, "publicizability is more fundamental than publicity." That is, for Kant it is a more important criterion for calling something public that it be founded on reason than that large segments of the population understand or agree to it. In this sense, one could argue that obedience to law is a private act, not a public one, because it depends on acceptance of an external authority. Such a claim might appear to be incoherent, but again we must remember the very particular usage of the term "private" that Kant deploys. His dubbing all citizens "scholars" in this capacity of critique and reason refers to our dual character as people who must obey the law, and yet who also maintain the ability to occupy the noumenal realm to reason *about* the laws.

Because it is people's capacity to reason that holds the key to their freedom, people's ability to critique government and public policy are vital to Kant's vision of politics. As he argues in the first *Critique*, "Reason depends on this freedom for its very existence. For reason has no dictatorial authority; its verdict is always simply the agreement of free citizens, of whom each one must be permitted to express, without let or hindrance, his objections or even his veto."[29] Thus, although reason is key to freedom, the reverse is true as well. In "Conflict of the Faculties," Kant flatly states that governmental regulation of philosophy is never justified: as opposed to medicine, for instance, philosophy must be able to proceed without external restriction or regulation imposed by governmental authority. The will must determine right action introspectively through the use of reason; hence the branch of scholarship dedicated to the development of reason—that is, philosophy—must draw on its own resources to determine the truth. External influence in this case is unjustified and dangerous interference. The extreme requirement that moral laws must come spontaneously from the self, a self abstracted—even more, actively "protected"—from social context and contact, relationships, and emotions suggests an extremely radical notion of autonomy, reflected in a self that exists solely in the independent, individualistic, even atomistic mind. This emphasis on the will expresses not merely agency, but "consciousness of myself as an agent" as well.[30]

To this end, Kant supports "republican" government, because that is the only form that "follows from the idea of an original contract."[31] The confusion over public and private, however, bleeds into Kant's arguments about the role of government in freedom as well. If free will requires autonomy (following my own laws), not heteronomy (following alien impulses, or others' laws), then it might seem to follow that laws must be authorized by citizens, not simply handed down by an independent authority to subjects who must follow them blindly. So key to this republican form of government is a notion of consent, of popular democratic legitimation and authorization. The consent that Kant deploys, however, does not entail a democratic form, which Kant rejects as "despotism."[32] He says this in part because the executive and legislative are not separated in a democratic government, and separation of powers is crucial: the "sovereign" legislature, which embodies the will of the people, must be separate from the "Ruler" executive, who carries out that will. But Kant also seems to mistrust democracy because centralization is to him the safest path to good laws. Republican government must engage in a form of representation; the sovereign legislature must be a representative body. But as we have seen in previous chapters of this book, representation can take many forms. Kant's idea of representation may be somewhat akin to the elitism of Locke's, though perhaps with even greater antidemocratic potential, for Kant says that "the smaller the number of persons who exercise the power of the nation . . . the more they represent and the closer the political constitution approximates the possibility of republicanism." This is "more difficult in an aristocracy than in a monarchy," and impossible in a democracy, thus suggesting that monarchy may in fact be the best and "most representative" form of "republican" government.[33] Thus, we may end up with a Hobbessian form, though on a Lockean rationale, because for Hobbes the point of an absolute sovereign was never representation, but order.

This monarchy might violate Kant's requirement that powers of the legislative and executive be separated, however, because in a monarchy, as Hobbes showed—and Locke too, in his rejection of its stronger, unmixed forms[34]—the monarch is "sovereign," not the people, in which case the sovereign and the ruler would be one. Even so, Kant wants to distance his argument from advocating an absolute monarch, for Kant's monarchy must still be a "republican" one; in particular it must have a constitution, which embodies a set of fundamental laws and principles even the sovereign cannot violate. This constitution is the "general will" for the society. A constitutional monarchy would provide a unified, well-ordered governing body that could then express its will to other nations. In *Perpetual Peace* Kant argues that nations must follow the categorical imperative just like individuals, and individual sovereigns facilitate this most easily.[35] But the slippages here are obvious. To begin with, his rejection of democratic ideals conflicts with the need for individuals to determine the categorical imperative for themselves. As Rousseau argued, if freedom consists in obedience to a law I prescribe to myself, then I must participate in making the laws I am to obey. This would seem to be even more important for Kant, who insists on this lawmaking in a radically individualist sense. That is, whereas Rousseau explains the apparent paradox of the general will and moral freedom by differentiating between a law I make for myself and one made by a community of which I am a member, Kant makes no such distinction. Indeed, in his view the latter situation would be one of heteronomy, not autonomy. Yet Kant insists that representation is the necessary governmental form and, indeed, advocates government that has a very small number of representatives.

The way in which Kant tries to resolve this apparent contradiction is to postulate a division between two types of freedom, namely, "transcendental freedom" (or "rational freedom") on the one hand and "practical freedom" (or "civil freedom") on the other. Thus, as it is for other theorists discussed in previous chapters, freedom is dualistically structured for Kant, though not in quite the same way. Transcendental or rational freedom is freedom of the will, whereas practical freedom relates to the empirical conditions that allow one to enact that will. Those conditions are often, though not exclusively, determined or at least shaped by the parameters the state sets to individual action. Kant maintains that in the phenomenal world, including politics, we must be free from external restriction so that we can allow our wills to spontaneously occupy the noumenal realm; that is, the state must help create the conditions that will facilitate a priori reason's leading me to the categorical imperative. For instance, let us say that my will tells me that the categorical imperative requires me to do X, but external circumstances ranging from lack of economic resources to physical force prevent me from doing X. In such a situation, I may be transcendentally free, because my intention and will are to follow the categorical imperative, but practically unfree because I am physically or materially unable to follow it. This latter, practical, freedom is thus not the passion-driven behavior of Hobbessian beings to do whatever they want at any given moment. Rather, it is reasoned action, though centered on sensible desire and the empirical world, not a priori reason. This formulation of freedom as dually conceived involves a contrast between the will that creates the categorical imperative and the will that chooses how to fulfill it in a sensible world of limited options, and in the context of the need to meet physical needs. This would recognize and sustain the dual location of humans in both realms and acknowledge that the noumenal self is logically dependent on the phenomenal; it cannot exist unless the phenomenal body stays alive. On this reading, the phenomenal self is clearly insufficient to attaining the noumenal realm, but it is necessary. The essential liberty is thus positive, based on self-prescribed law, morality, and a priori reason, but it comes out of, or works off the base of, negative liberty, delineated by the conditions that prevent me from doing something or permit me to do it.

Henry Allison defines Kant's distinction somewhat more strongly. In his view, the condition of practical freedom would involve being affected but not determined by the sensible world. By contrast, transcendental freedom would entail not being affected by the phenomenal world at all.[36] This might make the idea of transcendental freedom appear unattainable, if not preposterous, for how can we be entirely unaffected by the phenomenal world? We are phenomenal creatures; we have certain biological needs for food, water, and elimination that cannot be escaped. Yet Kant's idea of pure reason reveals that he believed such transcendence was not only possible to sustain, but necessary for morality, and hence for freedom. Indeed, in the second *Critique* he maintains that "*freedom* in its strictest, that is, in the transcendental, sense" requires that "no determining ground of the will other than that universal lawgiving form can serve as a law for it[;] such a will must be thought as altogether independent of the natural law of appearances in their relations to one another, namely the law of causality" (*Critique of Practical Reason*, 5:29). Furthermore, given that Kant locates morality solely in intention, "let the consequences be what they may," then so must freedom lie in intention (*Groundwork*, 416). The empirical failure to realize the will, or to have the intended consequences—whether owing to external obstacles or my own miscalculation or incompetence—does not alter this, and hence would not affect freedom.

If we could accept such a duality as I am positing and as Allison offers, we might think of transcendental freedom as "moments" in existence, times when we are faced with moral questions and employ a priori reason to solve them, much like a meditation. Such freedom would require that the free individual be left alone to meditate, which would allow Kant to then cast government as a liberal framework within which individuals have the greatest latitude to work out the categorical imperative for themselves. That is, the state would not be seen as authorized to legislate morality for individuals in a positive sense, but only in a negative sense, preventing people from interfering with other people's liberty and autonomy, necessary for their working out the categorical imperative for themselves. This is a reading with which Mary Gregor agrees; she argues that Kant envisions civil law as primarily "negative, restricting actions that would violate rightful freedom," for "the function of the state is basically to protect citizens' freedom,"[37] defined, similarly, in the negative sense. The government, then, would probably be involved in determining only hypothetical imperatives, namely, deciding what laws will facilitate the greater good of citizens' ability to follow the categorical imperative.

This protective function of the state might work with Kant's apparent assumption that "human nature" will move, if not impeded, toward the categorical imperative on its own (though if people really did have this tendency, then it is not clear why Kant must reject democratic legislation and popularly elected executive officers in the first place). But it also keeps faith with classically liberal elements of Kant's theory of politics, such as freedom of speech and expression. The sovereign's duty is to preserve "a spirit of liberty," and the ability to express one's views, and particularly to make verbal protest against the government, is critical to this: the "*freedom of the pen* is the only safeguard of the rights of the people." The constitution "should itself create a liberal attitude of mind among the subjects. To try to deny the citizen this freedom does not only mean . . . that the subject can claim no rights against the supreme ruler. It also means withholding from the ruler all knowledge of those matters which, if he knew about them, he would himself rectify."[38]

Yet O'Neill notes that there is a real ambiguity between the transcendental and practical forms of freedom, particularly in the latter's political manifestations. This ambiguity brings us back once again to the interaction between the noumenal and phenomenal realms. O'Neill critiques "Kant's distinction between civil and intellectual freedom" as "too sharp," because "intellectual freedom is from the start not merely freedom to engage in inward or solitary reflection." She notes that his remarks about the interaction of the noumenal and phenomenal in each human entails that "any use of reason involves some outward action, and so needs some civil freedom." This is why, she maintains, the public use of reason is so important to Kant and why he is adamant that government not interfere with it. But at the same time, she says, Kant falls short of his own theory, explicitly defending a form of public freedom that is surprisingly timid, given his ethics: "Kant does not provide us with an account of the material and social requirements for exercising intellectual freedom under various historical conditions," and his "celebration of the 'freedom of the pen' is quite inadequate as an account of the social arrangements and technical resources needed if we are to succeed in communicating with the world at large," namely, in public use of reason.[39]

Thus, perhaps Reiss is correct that Kant's "conception of political freedom is not positive, but negative," and that his politics embodies the fundamentals of liberalism. Though Kant's "theory of politics . . . is inevitably a part of a metaphysics of morality," its key distinguishing feature is that political duties concern others exclusively, and therefore involve actions that may be subject to force, while moral duties importantly center on duties to the self. Politics inevitably involves the possibility of coercion, which may be necessary to protect individuals' capacity to decide and act on moral matters for themselves, but at the same time unavoidably brings with it the danger of freedom's subversion. Because of this dual possibility, Reiss argues that politics for Kant is based almost entirely on rights: "Right is to be found only in external relations, which are the proper business of politics."[40] In his essay "*On the Proverb: 'That May Be True in Theory but Is of No Practical Use,'*" Kant argues that politics is concerned with the notion of rights and that "the concept of an external right in general derives entirely from the concept of *freedom* in the external relations among men." In particular, the "civil state is based *a priori*" on three intertwined and inalienable rights: on "*freedom* of every member of society as a *human being*," "*equality* of each member with every other as a *subject*," and "the *independence* of every member of the commonwealth as a *citizen*." These rights, Kant is clear, do not stem from political society, but explicitly found it: they are "natural" rights in that they exist a priori and independently of any particular political structure. Rights provide the basic protection of individuals' ability to express and follow their wills and to be free, which is the condition that "every person may seek happiness in the way that seems best to him." But this is so "if only he does not violate the freedom of others . . . under a possible universal law." Freedom and equality, or the first and second fundamental rights on which all legitimate states are founded, thus come together for Kant under a liberal principle of equal liberty. "*Right* is the limitation of each person's freedom so that it is compatible with the freedom of everyone, insofar as this is possible in accord with a universal law; and *public right* is the totality [*Inbegriff*] of *external laws* that make such a thoroughgoing compatibility possible."[41] Because of our location in the phenomenal world, we will be driven to pursue desires that will inevitably bring us into conflict with others; laws regulate such conflict and ensure that each of us has the same degree of (practical) freedom to pursue those desires. And our belonging to the noumenal world allows us to step back from the particularity and determinism of our desires to see that laws and rights in fact enlarge and protect our (transcendental) freedom, though they seem paradoxically to limit it (practically).

This is, of course, the paradox of the social contract we have earlier encountered in Hobbes, Locke, and Rousseau, and it is no coincidence that Kant, too, emphasizes the importance of a social contract in talking of government. Indeed, contemporary theorists' ability to formulate the tension found in Hobbes, Locke, and Rousseau in the terms of a "paradox of promising," as Carole Pateman phrased it, is to a large degree the result of the conceptual vocabulary that Kant bequeathed us.[42] It is Kant who clearly articulates the idea that by making commitments to the moral law we express our freedom, even as we seem to limit it. As he notes in *The Metaphysics of Morals* about the act of putting oneself under an obligation, though it "contains (at first glance) a contradiction," this antinomy is resolved by recalling the dual perspective of each individual in both the noumenal realm (through which she makes the law that creates the obligation) and phenomenal realm (in which she is practically bound to act in a way that fulfills the obligation).[43] It is this dual relationship to duty and obligation that makes freedom so complex for Kant, and this complexity relates to his location of freedom in reason and the noumenal realm. In contrast to these other theorists, however—who, despite acknowledging the contract's hypothetical quality, still talk about it as if it were a historical actuality—Kant says unequivocally that the "*original contract* . . . is by no means assumed as a *fact* (and indeed, it is utterly impossible). . . . Instead, it is a *mere idea* of reason, one, however, that has indubitable (practical) reality." Its practical reality pertains to the determination of just laws, which can be achieved "if *only* it is *possible* that a people could agree to it . . . even if the people are presently in such a position or disposition of mind [*Denkungsarf*] that if asked it would probably withhold its consent."[44]

Such "hypothetical consent" sounds like the second-guessing of Hobbes's, Locke's, and Rousseau's theories; even if people will probably say no because in their current situation they are blinded by self-interest or otherwise corrupted, as long as they would have said yes if they were perfectly rational, then consent can be assumed. Kant's strong emphasis on reason as the embodiment of autonomy is what allows him to hold his views. Whereas Hobbes and Locke in particular talk in terms of interest, which leads directly to the notion of second-guessing (that is, the sovereign decides what it is you truly want), Kant's ruler is not concerned with the interests or happiness of his subjects, but with their rights, with the goal of ensuring that citizens are treated as ends and not means, so that they can determine for themselves what they want: or, more precisely, what they *will*. The sovereign "duty," as a function of pure practical reason, is objectively clear and will broach no error. Because of this, as Reiss suggests, Kant insists that the sovereign must also obey the laws that he promulgates. That is, this government provides the second right of political equality: all are equal before the law, including the sovereign.[45] This equality is what ensures our freedom. Although the right to own property is supported by Kant, the essential equality among citizens is a political equality—that is, equality of rights—not economic equality. This equality of rights in turn lends itself to the third right of self-dependence, namely, the notion that people must retain the ability to participate in politics. Accordingly, suffrage is vital, for it is the practical expression of the right to participate in government: "The only qualification for being a citizen, is being fit to vote" (*Metaphysics of Morals*, 6:314).

Yet this is precisely where problems begin to emerge in terms of characterizing Kant as a liberal defender of negative liberty, for the three rights of freedom, equality, and independence actually fail to measure up to negative liberty ideals. For instance, a reason that free speech is important is that rebellion is forbidden, for rebellion would destroy law, which is of central importance to freedom. But even free speech "must not transcend the bounds of respect and devotion towards the existing constitution," which is why O'Neill, as cited earlier, thinks Kant's "freedom of the pen" is "inadequate."[46] Respect for law must be absolute, and rebellion is "evil" because it involves breaking or disregarding law. In theory, this could be gotten around by writing a "right" to rebel into the constitution; this would then make rebellion consistent with obedience to law. But it would also be self-contradictory, by setting up two sovereigns simultaneously: that is, the people as embodied in the king or representative assembly and the people as an unrepresented mass who can decide whether or not to overthrow the king or assembly (*Metaphysics of Morals*, 6:319–20).

At the same time, if a rebellion were to occur, as wrong as that would be, it would be equally wrong to fight to restore the original government: like Hume, Kant seems to suggest that we must obey whatever government is in power. But whereas Hume said this because order and security were of paramount importance, it is difficult to reconcile Kant's position with his concern for freedom and his insistence on a "republican" form of government.[47]

Kant seems to be suggesting—or at least assuming—that the monarch has a "holy will:" that it is impossible that he do anything contrary to the categorical imperative and moral goodness. But this would be putting it too strongly. After all, in his discussion of rebellion, Kant allows that "the people can legally *resist* the executive authority," but not directly, and not actively. That is, the people can resist only "by means of its representatives (in parliament)" and can offer only "*negative* resistance, that is, a *refusal* of the people (in parliament) to accede to every demand the government puts forth as necessary for administering the state." He even goes on to indicate that such periodic resistance is a sign of the health of the republic (*Metaphysics of Morals*, 6:322). But on the whole, Kant's assertions about "republicanism" seem to be based on the assumption that government will produce good laws, laws that embody the categorical imperative. If that is the case, then people are fundamentally unfree if they disobey the monarch. However, in the *Education*, Kant says that "Sovereigns look upon their subjects merely as *tools* for their own purposes;"[48] and at any rate, the "despotic" possibilities here are obvious. For on this reading, if I follow the categorical imperative, it does not matter whether I have thought of it myself or been told what it is: the imperative means I must do it, and categorically everyone must do it, full stop. This contrary indication to Kant's strong individualism and emphasis on spontaneous, a priori reasoning should give us pause, for it is easy to see how such a schema could be adopted and used to the totalitarian ends of which positive liberty is often accused.

CLASS, EDUCATION, AND SOCIAL CONSTRUCTION

Kant may be particularly vulnerable to such charges. To a perhaps even greater extent than the other theorists considered here, what Kant gives with one hand, in proclaiming the universality of reason and the need for individuals to determine the categorical imperative for themselves, he takes away with the other, in strictly limiting political participation to the same elite group of propertied white men. Although Kant seems, in his emphasis on the rights of political participation and voting, to be advocating a conception of "republicanism" that coheres with its participatory basis, he is in fact quite exclusive. For instance, though voting is an important political activity, only "active" citizens are deemed "fit" to vote. "Passive" citizens secure their equality through obedience to laws, but active citizens further express their rights by helping to form the laws.

The terminology of active and passive might make Kant's position intuitively appealing for contemporary democracies such as the United States, where apathetic nonparticipation is rampant (and might be cured with a public threat to strip such citizens of their rights to participate in the future). But in fact Kant describes the difference between active and passive citizens as a function of independence, the criteria for which do not arise out of politics but instead predetermine the right to participate. Specifically, passive citizens are people of inferior social position or personal and economic dependence, such as "an apprentice in the services of a merchant or artisan; a domestic servant (as distinct from a civil servant); a minor; all women, and in general, anyone whose preservation in existence (his being fed and protected) depends not on his management of his own business but on arrangements made by another (except the state). All these people lack civil personality" (*Metaphysics of Morals*, 6:314).

The justification for Kant's position is that such people are not their own masters economically, which means that they cannot be their own masters intellectually. This in turn means they may not be allowed to participate politically. But the way in which Kant delineates his distinction is noteworthy. For although dependence on the state for one's livelihood is excused—thus allowing all civil servants a particularly privileged status—most service economy labor is denigrated. And within the service economy, further distinctions are made. For instance, he labels barbers as passive, but not wigmakers, for the latter sells a commodity while the former relies solely on his labor. Similarly, he dismisses blacksmiths in India as passive, because they sell only their labor, but not smiths in England, who sell the products of their labor. In this, Kant diverges from the Lockean position that labor produces property; instead Kant seems to be drawing on pre-Marxist ideas of commodities rather than labor per se as a source of independence, which would be consistent with his assertion of the right to property. After all, if I do not like the wig you make for me (even, Kant says, if I have given you my own hair out of which to make it) and refuse to pay, you can sell the wig to someone else; but if I get similarly angry about my haircut and refuse to pay, you can never get the value of your labor back.[49] Kant thus "assumes a sharp distinction between one's labour and the product of one's labour."[50]

Kant does not advocate economic equality, however, despite his assertion that "economic independence" is an important criterion "for active participation in political affairs." The criterion of economic independence, rather, serves as a reason for excluding unpropertied persons from politics altogether. Like Locke, Kant seems to posit a strong connection between property and rationality; obviously, not the self-interested and independent rationality that superficially undergirds Locke's and Hobbes's emphasis on government as the umpire of competing interests and views, but rather the strong rationality of the categorical imperative, even stronger than what we see in Locke's right reason. Because economically dependent individuals are not fully rational, they must be excluded from politics. Such differentiation is not simply reducible to class bias, for the smiths in England and India most likely belong to relatively similar economic strata in relation to their societies. But the notion of economic dependence per se does make it more difficult for poor and lower-class people to achieve the status of active citizen.

Such implications of class bias in Kant's theory may, of course, be averted by asserting that all passive citizens must be given the opportunity to ascend to the status of active citizens, presumably by gaining their economic independence, in typical liberal equality-of-opportunity fashion: the apprentice may eventually establish his own business, the minor will eventually come of age, the barber may develop a line of hair-care products. That is, it could be argued that their irrationality is situational rather than natural or inevitable.

This is particularly true of children, whose irrationality is situational by virtue of their youth. However, as we have seen particularly in Locke and Rousseau, the relationship between ability and capacity to reason, and between capacity and use of reason, means that it may not be enough for children simply to come of age; after all, some children grow up to be barbers, apprentices, domestic servants, and, of course, women. Children's situation of unreason can only be assuredly changed through education; for indeed, it is true of all human beings that "virtue . . . is not innate" and so "can and must be *taught*" (*Metaphysics of Morals*, 6:477). Education is vital to the categorical imperative, and hence to freedom, for it helps "develop [man's] tendency towards *the good*" (*Education*, sec. 11). Thus, Kant says that "Man can only become man by education" (sec. 7), in an echo of Rousseau. But Kant also echoes Locke: because "the first endeavor in moral education is the formation of character" (sec. 78), this process is best begun in childhood. One can learn "facts" later in life, but character, or the ability to act in accordance with maxims must be established at a young age; "moral training" of children is thus of utmost importance, for it "aims at freedom" (sec. 63). Indeed, there are quite a few similarities between Kant's and Locke's prescriptions, such as cold baths, not dressing too warmly, nonbinding clothing, a "cool and hard bed" (sec. 38), and avoiding "too warm foods and drinks" (sec. 37). Kant cautions against "*playing with* and *caressing* the child," which is something that working-class parents particularly tend to do, because it makes the child "self-willed and deceitful" (secs. 50–51). He cautions nursing mothers against "a vegetable diet" because it will make their breast milk curdle (sec. 36). And though he rejects swaddling, he recommends that babies be kept "in a kind of box covered with leather straps, such as the Italians use. . . . The child is never taken out of this box, even when nursed by its mother" (sec. 39). As surprising as it may seem for a philosopher so closely associated with the mind/body dualism, Kant *links* the body with the mind here, not only making numerous recommendations for care of the body, such as unrestrictive clothing, but also insisting that "physical education of the mind" must complement "moral training," even if the two are distinct (sec. 63). The goal for Kant in this is to produce the ability to control the body; though the phenomenal self is an unavoidable fact of human life, the effects of sensible desire on the intelligible self can nevertheless be modified and to a considerable measure even controlled. Reason is aided by a strong body, as Locke similarly held. As Hobbes noted, we have no choice over whether to feel hungry, but we can exercise choice over whether to eat. Kant, too, does not deny phenomenal desire but believes that reason can control it and therefore that through the use of reason we can control ourselves: hence, Allison's claim, mentioned earlier, that transcendental freedom involves not being affected by the phenomenal world at all. Thus, the focus on "physical education *of the mind*" suggests that Kant is not interested in keeping children physically fit for its own sake, but to the end of learning how to discipline and control the body and its sometimes inconvenient, and almost always contrary, sensible desires.

Reason, of course, is the ultimate tool for a child's pursuit of morality and freedom, so Kant advocates teaching children how to think rather than "breaking" them like a horse or demanding rote learning; children must do right on account of developing their own maxims about right and wrong, and not merely from habit, any more than from fear of punishment (secs. 19, 47, 54). At the same time, however, it is essential that children be governed by rules, for only this will develop their character and their ability to follow their own maxims in the first place; obedience "to his master's commands" prepares him for obedience "to what he feels to be a good and reasonable will" (sec. 80); the former lesson of obedience prepares him to be a citizen who must obey laws that are inconvenient, such as paying taxes, and the latter prepares him to exercise a moral will. These lessons must be taught through the use of discipline and "natural opposition" (sec. 56), which most effectively takes the form of disapproval, as both Locke and Rousseau also maintained; rather than punishing children, parents and teachers should show "contempt" and "humiliate the child by treating him coldly and distantly" (sec. 83).

Such an education would seem to prepare children to think for themselves; but in fact the rules that they are socialized to follow are surprisingly conventional, such as Kant's declaration that children should learn that paying debts is more important than giving to those in need (*Education*, sec. 97), not to mention his remarks about sex. Kant is particularly concerned in this essay with preventing adolescent boys from masturbating, as "nothing weakens the mind as well as the body so much as the kind of lust which is directed towards themselves. . . . We must place it before him in all its horribleness, telling him that in this way he will become useless for the propagation of the race, that his bodily strength will be ruined by this vice more than by anything else, that he will bring on himself premature old age, and that his intellect will be very much weakened, and so on" (sec. 111). Again, control over the body is Kant's key to morality, which in his view is compromised in the worst way by masturbation. He thus recommends "constant occupation, and . . . devoting no more time to bed and sleep than is necessary" as remedies to adolescent sexual urges; but he goes so far as to recommend "relations with the other sex" as "certainly better than the other" alternative. Although Kant argues that "it is the duty of the young man—to wait till he is in a condition to marry" before having sex, given that the age at which "the feeling of sex develops itself in the youth" is about thirteen or fourteen, his recommendation logically implies that teenage premarital sex is preferable to masturbation (sec. 111).

Kant's assertions may appear irrational to twenty-first-century readers whose attitudes to sexuality have been enlightened by scientific research and a wide variety of popular and academic writings. But the point for my purposes is that Kant, like Locke and Rousseau in their educational treatises, uses education to "socially construct" the people who should populate his state, to create people who are appropriate "subjects" of freedom and of authority. Though a number of commentators talk about "Kantian constructivism" in his theory of knowledge, few discuss the broader implication of social constructivism in his work more generally. Onora O'Neill, for instance, talks about "constructivism" as the fundamental process by which humans apprehend the empirical world and translate that into language and meaning. For her, "construction" simply means that Kant defines reason in particular ways, that he produces our understanding of ourselves. Reason is thus not "given or posited" but rather "named or constructed,"[51] and this is how he builds his argument. Similarly, Robert Pippin argues that claims about empirical objects are "empirical claims about inner states of the subject and are quite different from, not at all equivalent to, claims about objects of outer sense."[52] We have to interpret sense data, and we do that via some other capacity of our minds than the sensory perception itself (sight, hearing, touch, and so forth); but that interpretation is limited by what is perceived, which will be constant for all observers. So there is an objective reality "out there," but we have to engage in the act of interpretation in order to perceive it. We thus "construct" the world through interpretation.

Certainly these accounts are important to understanding Kant's theory of knowledge, for the relation of the phenomenal to the noumenal realm is key to how knowledge is produced. That is, if we cannot perceive the truth of phenomenal appearance, if perception cannot reveal the reality of objects, then some other process, which occurs in the mind through critical reason, must be what produces such knowledge. We mediate and interpret sense data; we translate them into meaning. As Reiss suggests, even "the laws of nature were not inherent in nature, but constructions of the mind used for the purpose of understanding nature."[53] The fact that they are "constructions," however, does not mean they are not "real" in Kant's view. Indeed, their "reality" has produced the appearance and the impulse to "construct" meaning.

But at the same time, these accounts seem too weak to comprehend the full significance of social constructivism in Kant's theory. That is, Kant seeks to exert a more active control over citizens' and subjects' ways of thinking and therefore understanding and interpreting. O'Neill, for instance, notes that Kant permits governmental restriction on "any private uses of reason that damage public uses of reason. For example, communications and expressions [that] denigrate or mock or bully others, or more generally fail to respect them, may make it harder or impossible for some to think for themselves, and so to follow the maxim of Enlightenment."[54] What this suggests, however, is that government restriction serves a purpose of regulating citizens so that they can deploy reason for the public good: it suggests that government should actively shape and construct citizens into the kinds of beings who can support its enterprise. For after all, assuming that the enterprise of the state is in accord with the categorical imperative, it produces the greatest freedom, reason, and autonomy in its citizens. The question, however, is who decides what restrictions are acceptable, who decides what is in violation of reason and what is conducive to it, and what evidence is accepted that one has achieved autonomy? This is where Kant's "constructivism" is, and must be, more proactive than O'Neill and Pippin grant. As Marcia Moen observes, "Kant promoted the insight that knowledge is constructed. This is not yet the idea of social construction of reality; for the most part, Kant thought the 'mind' did the constructing," although she argues that in the third *Critique*, in Kant's consideration of aesthetics, "his thought opens in the *direction* of social construction."[55] I believe, however, that social constructivism is evident throughout his moral theory, and particularly in his conception of freedom.

Where this constructivism has its most significant impact is in the very close links between freedom and Kant's narrow understanding of rationality. This is an insight that O'Neill notes: "*If* we are rational in the required sense, then we are also free and so capable of autonomy and bound by morality. If we are not rational in the required sense, but only in some other (e.g., purely instrumental) sense, then there will be a gap between our rationality and our freedom, and the Kantian conception of autonomy will be irrelevant to us." But, she asks, if Kant posits such a strict notion of rationality, such that it involves adherence to certain conclusions rather than to certain forms of thinking, then "why is not conformity to reason, even to a supposed supreme principle of practical reason, just another mode of heteronomy? Why does Kant take conformity to desires for heteronomy, and conformity to reason for autonomy? Why are desires but not reason to be seen as 'alien'?" The answer, she maintains, lies in the link between reason and autonomy, and the ties between autonomy and (positive) freedom: "Only autonomous, self-disciplining beings can act on principles that we have grounds to call principles of reason. . . . [Kant] argues not from reason to autonomy but from autonomy to reason."[56] That is, it is not reason that makes us autonomous; rather, autonomy is what makes reason possible. But what is the measure of autonomy if it is not the ability to reason a priori to the categorical imperative? It would seem that the measure is independence, in the economic sense, and presumably, the emotional and intellectual senses that go with it. But this would seem to indicate that Kant is socially producing an understanding of reason that coheres with the social characteristics that he finds desirable: and they, not coincidentally perhaps, are the social characteristics of a particular gender, race, and class in a historically specific locale.

In the *Education*, this more active constructivism is particularly visible, and we see the positive production of future citizens who are capable of reasoning to the categorical imperative. Like Locke, Kant seeks to "prime the canvas" by introducing physical rigors and discipline to children's regimens, to the end of building a rather vaguely conceptualized "character" (or "virtue" for Rousseau). It is here that the tensions in Kant's work between making our own choices and making the right choices are called explicitly into view. So many of Kant's recommendations seem at odds with late-twentieth- and early-twenty-first century norms of child rearing and education, particularly concerning nutrition, physical affection, and shame, that it is difficult to see them outside of Kant's particular time and culture. They seem more the result of Kant's peculiar vision than of a priori reasoning. However, it is the arena of gender in which the link between constructivism and freedom is most explicit. As in Locke's and Rousseau's treatises, girls are nowhere mentioned in Kant's *Education*;

and despite references to "parents" participating in their children's education (about which Kant seems rather dubious, preferring public education [secs. 22–24]), women are mentioned only twice in passing, once to declare that fathers must be responsible for shaming children when they lie because mothers tend to view lying as a sign of cleverness (sec. 91), and once when Kant suggests that the best way to prevent boys from masturbating is to channel their sexual interest toward women (sec. 111). He indirectly refers to women as well when he says that education should prevent boys from becoming "effeminate," which is the opposite of hardiness (sec. 44). One is left to assume that girls' education is not important because females are not rational; they are incapable of independence and therefore are eternally passive citizens.

SEXUAL CONSTRUCTIONS

Kant's categorical exclusion of women from active citizenship suggests significant insights into his conception of freedom. Certainly, because "all women" are categorically designated by Kant as passive citizens, questions about the situational character of independence, which education supposedly cures for (male) children and which economic enterprise cures for the apprentice, would have to be resolved in the negative for women. For they will never change their gender and therefore cannot attain such status as "active" citizens. As Annette Baier notes, Kant "makes it quite clear that he does not expect women to 'work their way up' to civil personality."[57] Women are naturally dependent, according to the dominant feminist reading of Kant. Perhaps, however, women's dependency is situational in a different sense: that is, rather than claiming that women are dependent by nature, he believes that they *should* be dependent for their own good as well as the good of society and of men in particular. And in order to make them dependent, Kant must make them irrational. If true freedom, or noumenal freedom, requires adherence to duty and morality through the categorical imperative, and if such adherence requires the use of reason, then in order for women to be free in Kant's schema, they must be able to use reason. Indeed, they must not only be *able* to use it, but they must *use* it. The question is, can they?

Whereas feminists are divided on whether Kant is radically individualist or instead gives an important place to relationship,[58] most feminists agree that Kant is fairly negative on women's rationality. Sally Sedgewick, for instance, maintains that "women are excluded from Kant's moral theory because he finds them lacking in that quality which constitutes human dignity," namely, reason; they are thus on his view "imperfect members of humanity, or only imperfectly human."[59] Herta Nagl-Docekal similarly maintains that "Kant was convinced women were incapable of acting in accordance with what he described as the ideal type of morality. Only men, in his view, could act out of respect for the moral law; only men could do good out of a sense of duty," because only they could reason.[60] Jean P. Rumsey goes further to claim that Kant's "gendered perception of human nature . . . infects his entire theory. . . . Kant's conception of the moral agent is flawed, because, excluding women from full moral agency, Kant then takes the pattern for 'normal agency' to be that of the man of his place and time."[61] And Robin Schott claims that the "contradiction between women and scholarship" that Kant posits "is rooted in a natural condition, not a social one."[62]

Although I agree with these feminists that Kant is solidly misogynist on the question of reason, I believe that the particulars of his position, and the foundation of his views, are somewhat inconsistent. Kant indicates in some places that women are naturally rational, in others that they are naturally irrational, in others that they have the natural capacity for rationality but should not develop it. It is this last argument, I believe, that holds the key to Kant's theory; my position is that Kant not only recognizes women's natural reasoning abilities, but fears them, and wishes to curtail them. He thus develops an account of gender that does not describe but rather *prescribes* women's irrationality. He constructs women as irrational both conceptually and practically. That is, not only does Kant define reason and gender to exclude what he defines as rational, but he also makes specific recommendations for women's empirical treatment and experience that ensure they do not acquire the skills of reason.

This construction of women and women's reason, I maintain, indicates that Kant's theory of freedom is specifically gendered even more strongly than Hobbes's, Locke's, or Rousseau's. Even his supposed "transcendental" freedom is a function of culture, period, and convention, encoding sexist beliefs and values. In my account of Rousseau, for instance, where I argued that men's freedom in important ways depended on the unfreedom of women, women's unfreedom was situational, determined by social customs and practices that Rousseau advocated. Moral freedom could be attained by both men and women; they just had to fill different roles and engage in different sorts of behavior to achieve it. It was thus a contingent function of a particular way of structuring the family and relations between men and women. Gender was socially constructed, as was the way freedom was achieved, but not the meaning of freedom itself. By contrast, Kant defines freedom in gendered terms; gender is built into the structure of meaning that he deploys in defining freedom in the way he does. Freedom itself is socially constructed. But this structure is dependent on factors that, despite Kant's treating them as natural or even a priori, we can see as contingent. That contingency is what permits the feminist critique to gain purchase.

We start by noting Kant's inconsistency on women's capacity for rationality. Kant notes that women are "rational beings" in several places, particularly in his remarks about sex in his *Anthropology*. Sex is clearly a problem for Kant—"worse than suicide," which he condemns in the *Groundwork*—because, as he also notes in the *Lectures on Ethics*, sex involves treating people as means, not ends. Even worse, sex entails treating others as a means to the basest animal desires and pleasures. "As soon as the person is possessed, and the appetite sated, they are thrown away, as one throws away a lemon after sucking the juice from it. . . . Humanity here is set aside. . . . [and] sacrificed to sex."[63] The deployment of a "lemon" rather than a sweet fruit in his metaphor entails its own negative connotations about the pleasure involved in sex, but the message is clear: sex embodies the worst of the phenomenal realm. It thereby compromises free will and reason, because it violates most of the conditions for autonomy and the categorical imperative. At the same time, Kant recognizes that sex is necessary for procreation, which helps fulfill our duty to "the preservation of the species" (*Metaphysics of Morals*, 6:420). Again, we are phenomenal beings, and the two conflicting aspects of our humanity must work together. However, procreation is distinct from sexual pleasure; to engage in sex for purposes other than procreation is "an unnatural use of [one's] *sexual inclination*" (*Metaphysics of Morals*, 6:420). For "by it man surrenders his personality (throwing it away) since he uses himself merely as a means to satisfy an animal impulse" (6:425), which would constitute "a *defiling* (not merely a debasing) of the humanity in his own person" (6:424). The notion that the sexual impulse is "mine" is something that Kant is able to deny through his distinction between the intelligible and phenomenal aspects of our being, for sexual impulses belong to the latter. They are thus alien to my true self and thereby impede my freedom and autonomy. But at the same time, as discussed earlier, I can choose to resist such impulses, and so failure to do so violates the "duty to oneself."

Such a duty would clearly forbid masturbation and homosexuality, because neither can result in pregnancy. It is less clear whether it would eliminate sex within marriage without the consideration of procreation, "if, for example, the wife is pregnant or sterile" (*Metaphysics of Morals*, 6:426). (Note that the husband's sterility is not considered, as Kant perhaps collapses sterility and impotence.) Kant poses the question of sex in marriage without the intention of procreation as a "casuistical question" (6:426). It is not entirely clear, however, whether he means casuistry in the sense of specious reasoning for the purpose of rationalization—which would suggest that he thinks sex in marriage simply for pleasure is not permitted—or in the sense of evaluating right conduct through the use of cases that illustrate the relevant rules—which would suggest that it might be permissible. He does say in the following paragraph that sex in marriage, regardless of its intent, does embody a kind of "love"; though it is not "moral love properly speaking" (such as is "love of benevolence"), it nevertheless "can enter into close union with it [i.e., moral love] under the limiting conditions of practical reason" (*Metaphysics of Morals*, 6:426). He also allows that "it is not requisite for human beings who marry to make [procreation] their end in order for their union to be compatible with rights, for otherwise marriage would be dissolved when procreation ceases" (6:277).

Thus, men and women both, though driven by their physical desires, "are still *rational* beings." This rationality can enable them to see that, within the context of their need for sex both as individuals and members of the species, they must contain and order this desire in the least harmful way possible.[64] Monogamous marriage provides this way, for it introduces a "reciprocity" into the use of others as means, as well as a constancy that requires sex to be located in a larger context of reason and emotion; "for in this way each reclaims itself and restores its personality." In phrasing that oddly echoes Rousseau's description of the mutual alienation that takes place in the social contract, Kant says that "*Matrimonium* signifies a contract between two persons, in which they mutually accord equal rights to one another, and submit to the condition that each transfers his whole person entirely to the other, so that each has a complete right to the other's whole person," that is, not simply to her or his body or sexual organs. Kant goes so far as to say that sex is *only* permissible in marriage; any sex outside of wedlock is "*crimen carnis*," as are masturbation, homosexuality, and bestiality.[65] So unless you are celibate, you must marry, or else abandon your humanity. The reciprocity that marriage permits is the only saving grace, even if an imperfect one, from the descent into animality.

The reciprocity Kant posits in marriage might suggest a kind of equality within the family. But Kant maintains that this reciprocity stems not from equality; indeed, he claims that "respect rules out equality."[66] The primacy of respect in marriage means that reciprocity stems from the notion that men and women are each superior to the other in different ways; man "through his physical power and courage," the woman "through her natural talent for mastering his desire for her." Thus, perhaps complementarity, rather than reciprocity, is what Kant is really talking about. Like Rousseau, he believed that women had a natural talent for dominating men; though whereas Rousseau believed this power lay in raw sex, Kant locates it in love and women's shrewd manipulation of men's emotions. "Loquacity and eloquence full of affect, which disarms the man" are women's tools of "*domestic warfare.*"[67]

Yet we must wonder what kind of "respect" women are entitled to, because for Kant, as was the case for Rousseau, women's apparent power and equality mask a gross inferiority. Or perhaps it is because of women's power that they must be made to be inferior. Despite his claim that "marriage is a relation of equality of possession . . . of each other's persons . . . and also equality in their possession of material goods" (*Metaphysics of Morals*, 6:278), Kant also claims that "Two persons convening at random is insufficient for the unity and indissolubility of a union; one partner must *yield* to the other and, in turn, one must be *superior* to the other in some way, in order to be able to rule over or govern him."[68] Again, Kant really is talking about complementarity rather than reciprocity. Much as Locke and Hobbes seemed to suggest that, despite possible equality between men and women, one of them had to have ultimate rule (or the final say) if the family was to avoid discord, Kant says "there certainly can be only one who coordinates all transactions in accordance with one end, which is his." The "his" is significant, for this ruler must be the man; "the woman should *dominate* and the man should *govern*; for inclination dominates, and understanding governs," or "reason rules." He compares the relationship between husband and wife to that of "a minister to his monarch who is mindful only of enjoyment . . . so that the most high and mighty master can do all that he wills, but under the condition that his minister suggests to him what his will is."[69]

In *The Metaphysics of Morals*, Kant rejects "morganatic marriage, which takes advantage of the inequality of estate of the two parties to give one of them dominion over the other" as "not different, in terms of natural rights only, from concubinage, and is no true marriage." But in the very next sentence, Kant then asks whether the law's granting the husband superiority conflicts with the equality he insists on in marriage. He answers that "this cannot be regarded as conflicting with the natural equality of a couple if this dominance is based only on the natural superiority of the husband to the wife in his capacity to promote the common interest of the household" (6:279). He is here suggesting that the wife's "equality" is completely dependent on the husband's ability to discern the categorical imperative and protect the rights and welfare of the wife, if indeed it can even be plausibly claimed at this point that she has any rights at all. This condition of inequality leads Hannelore Schroder to maintain that "there is no mutuality to be found in [Kant's] concept of marriage. The law is that men have the 'right' to use women for any purpose, including sex."[70] That this contradicts Kant's overt writings on sex, Schroder implies, simply indicates that women are not considered by Kant to be full human beings.

Women would thus seem not to qualify for the duty of "equal mutual love and respect" that Kant calls "friendship," for "even the best of friends should not make themselves too familiar with each other," a requirement that would seem rather difficult to fulfill with someone with whom one engages in sexual relations. Though "the human being is a being meant for society . . . he is also an unsociable one" because "he cannot risk" sharing his innermost thoughts with others for fear that they "might use this to harm him" or that they will not reciprocate in candor and thus jeopardize equality of respect. The possibility of a truly mutual friendship holds a key to freedom, however, for then "he is not completely alone with his thoughts, as in a prison, but enjoys a freedom he cannot have with the masses, among whom he must shut himself up in himself" (*Metaphysics of Morals*, 6:470–72).

Such intimate relation is thus crucial to freedom. And yet, as a function of the expression of ideas, rather than feelings, and given that "every human being has his secrets and dare not confide blindly in others," these relationships must always involve a holding back. Such holding back clearly coheres with traditional (or stereotypical) masculine behavior in heterosexual intimate relationships, but it also depends on and derives from the dominance of reason over feeling, and the intelligible over the sensible. Hence, Kant says that "the love in friendship cannot be an affect; for emotion is blind in its choice, and after a while it goes up in smoke" (*Metaphysics of Morals*, 6:471). Rather, friendship must be "moral friendship," which is based in "a duty set by reason" (6:469). And whereas "the principle of love bids friends to draw closer, the principle of respect requires them to stay at a proper distance from each other" (6:470).

The true sharing of the self, then, cannot occur within marriage, but can be found only outside of marriage. And presumably, it can only be found by men, with other men, insofar as women lack the intellectual status to share the kinds of thoughts that characterize the true inner self, and insofar as heterosexual relations are supposedly founded on love and affect. If women cannot use reason, then they cannot participate in such relations of equal respect. They therefore must be denied one of the key conditions of freedom. Marriage, certainly, cannot serve as such a friendship, for none of these descriptions of moral friendship seem applicable to Kant's depiction of marriage. Indeed, Kant explicitly says that "the relation of a protector, as a benefactor, to the one he protects, who owes him gratitude"—a description that clearly characterizes Kant's view of marriage, in which the husband protects and supervises the wife's conduct and welfare—"is indeed a relation of mutual love, but not of friendship, since the respect owed by each is not equal" (*Metaphysics of Morals*, 6:473). Husbands and wives cannot also be friends, in direct contrast to most feminist writings on marriage in the seventeenth and eighteenth centuries, such as those by Mary Astell and Mary Wollstonecraft.[71]

Thus, despite Kant's earlier claim that men and women both are "rational beings," the reason for men's control seems to come back to their superior reason. In *Observations on the Feeling of the Beautiful and Sublime*, Kant says that men and women both have "understanding." But women have "a *beautiful understanding*," whereas men's "should be a *deeper understanding*, which is an expression that means the same thing as the sublime," or reason. Given that reason is necessary to morality, this might not bode well for women's virtue, but Kant insists that women have a "beautiful" virtue; "women will avoid evil not because it is unjust but because it is hateful, and for them virtuous actions mean those that are ethically beautiful." The notion of "ethical" beauty might indicate that women are not simply phenomenal creatures. But women are attracted to the good and repulsed by vice not because of duty, but because of their *inclinations* toward beauty: "women have a stronger innate feeling for everthing that is beautiful.[72] The relevant question is obviously whether the beautiful understanding "counts" to establish women's humanity, if humanity is measured by morality. In the *Groundwork*, Kant refers to "spirits of so sympathetic a temper that, without any further motive of vanity or self-interest, they find an inner pleasure in spreading happiness around them and can take delight in the contentment of others as their own work." Such virtues, however, are inferior to reason-based morality, for Kant continues, "Yet I maintain that in such a case an action of this kind, however right and however amiable it may be, has still no genuinely moral worth. It stands on the same footing as other inclinations" (398).

This does not bode well for women's reason, because as Kant says in the third *Critique*, "Sense has not the least capacity for expressing universal rules." He recognizes that women have some capacities for knowledge, for "no representation of truth, fitness, beauty, or justice, and so forth, could come into our thoughts if we could not rise beyond Sense to higher faculties of cognition." At the same time, however, his recognition of women's cognitive capacities and their ethical relationship to beauty is ambivalent, for although Kant states that "charm" and "beauty" are distinct things, what Kant describes as the "beautiful" attributes of women would seem to be "charming," fitting the conventional forms of femininity.[73] In contrast to men who follow the categorical imperative because reason tells them they must follow the universal law, appealing to their sense of duty and their will to follow such duty, women are naturally inclined to the good because it sensibly, or phenomenally, pleases them: "Nothing of ought, nothing of must, nothing of obligation" sways women to the good, but only their inclinations to beauty.[74]

Thus, it might seem that women *are* constitutionally incapable of the reason that directs men to the categorical imperative, and hence to freedom, as most feminists maintain: "It is difficult for me to believe that the fair sex is capable of principles," Kant notes. But "providence has implanted goodly and benevolent sentiments in their bosoms, a fine feeling for uprightness and a complaisant soul." Thus, "Her philosophical wisdom is not reasoning, but sentiment."[75] Hence, Kant derides "scholarly women" who "use their *books* somewhat like their *watch*, that is, they carry one so that it will be seen that they have one, though it is usually not running or not set by the sun."[76] The fact that such pronouncements seem to contradict his earlier ones about women's capacity for reason, however, should give us pause: How to explain this confusing ambiguity?

We may get some hints in his remarks on non-European women and men, where the ambiguity is even more pronounced. In the *Anthropology*, Kant says his remarks about reciprocity pertain only to "civilized" cultures; in "uncivilized conditions superiority is simply on the side of the man."[77] And in the *Beautiful and the Sublime*, Kant spends several pages talking about African, Asian (under which he includes "Arabs," "Persians," Japanese, and Indians), and Canadian Indian cultures, saying that none have a genuine appreciation for beauty. Though some, such as "the savages . . . of North America," have a "sublime character" with a "strong feeling for honor," and the "Canadian savage" is "truthful and honest . . . proud, sensitive to the entire value of freedom," Kant insists that "all of these savages have little feeling for the beautiful in the moral sense." Hence, in "the Orient," women are "always in a prison." Similarly, Kant asks, "In the lands of the blacks, can one expect anything better than what is always found there, namely the female sex in the deepest slavery?"[78] Thus, it would seem that nonwhite women's irrationality is compounded by the natural inferiority of their race.

Yet Kant notes that indigenous Canadian men give women respect and authority; women "meet and take council about the most important affairs of the nation, about war and peace. They send their delegates to the masculine council, and commonly it is their vote that decides," suggesting that they are equally capable of reason with men. But, Kant cautions, "they pay dearly enough for this preference. They have all the domestic concerns on their shoulders and share all of the hardships with the men." Here Kant seems to be saying that women do have the capacity for reason, but it is not in their interest to use it. Because they *are* non-Europeans, this conclusion is particularly surprising: Kant relates the story of "a Negro carpenter" who called whites " 'fools, for first you concede so much to your wives, and then you complain when they drive you crazy.' There might be something here worth considering, except for the fact that this scoundrel was completely black from head to foot, a distinct proof that what he said was stupid."[79] Given that skin color is "a distinct proof" of irrationality, his remarks about the Canadian "savages" is puzzling. If non-European men cannot reason, one would assume that non-European women cannot either, and yet Kant here apparently thinks they can. He may be pointing out this "inversion" of the "natural" hierarchy of gender to bolster his claims that other races and cultures are inferior, but that hardly ameliorates his sexism.

In terms of the question of women's rationality, this passage provides insight into white women's reason as well; namely, they may indeed have a natural ability to reason, but they should nevertheless forsake or repress it. Like Locke and Rousseau, Kant suggests that a natural ability to reason does not guarantee the natural use of that reason; this use must be learned and developed. In the *Education*, Kant says that the purpose is to teach the child to formulate and follow maxims, as well as the reason that will allow "him" to judge their rightness and conformity with the categorical imperative. However, in women this learning is contrary not only to their own interest, but to the interests of mankind in general. "Women, although potentially capable of moral agency, are . . . to be educated in such a way that they will be unable to actually achieve it."[80] For "what is most important is that the husband become more perfect as a man and the wife as a woman." The "becoming" suggests that nature cannot be left to its own devices; even the "beautiful virtues" to which women are supposedly drawn by inclination cannot be guaranteed, but must be taught. If women "do something only because they love to," then "the art lies in making sure that they love only what is good."[81] In other words, if women are left to their own devices and inclinations, there is no guarantee that the beautiful will be realized. Instead, women must be "constructed" in the most active sense of manipulation to be inclined toward it; they must be taught what it is that they should like.

Yet although the struggle to follow duty is very difficult for most phenomenal creatures who strive to live in the noumenal realm (i.e., men), Kant indicates that women have an easy path in following their natural inclinations to beauty. But woman's beautiful understanding is far from being spontaneous or an end in itself. Rather, it is socially produced to serve the greater end of man's perfection as an end in *him*self. If women abandon that understanding for reason and scholarship, they will hurt themselves by hurting their husbands. Accordingly, "Laborious learning or painful grubbing, *even if a woman can bring it off*, destroy the merits that are proper to her sex" and particularly "weaken her charms, by means of which she exercises her great power over the opposite sex." Such a woman "might as well also wear a beard." Because "the beautiful understanding chooses for its object everything that is closely related to the finer feeling . . . [w]oman should accordingly not learn geometry. . . . The beauties can leave Descartes's vortices rotating forever without worrying about them."[82] As Kim Hall notes, "In all cases, it is clear that men should not discuss any 'serious' matters with women. Rather, women should concern themselves with such matters that would make them pleasant hostesses at parties or the 'pleasant object[s] of a well-mannered conversation.' In addition, Kant declares that women are not to be told things that would require rigorous thinking on their part."[83] But is this because women cannot engage in such thinking, or rather because they might?

The passages I have cited suggest that Kant seems to be arguing that rather than being *unable* to reason, women *should not* reason, indeed that they should not even develop their natural capacity to reason, for it will corrupt and compromise the "beautiful" understanding needed to complement men's "deep" understanding of reason.[84] In other words, his ambiguity on the question of women's reason is a function of Kant's prescriptive vision, which is one of gender hierarchy, male privilege, and male freedom, all of which are made possible by female unfreedom. If women should not develop their reason, then Kant is saying that women should never be independent, and they can thus never be free. This similarly coheres with Kant's overall schema for the family, which is formed importantly on the basis of women's need for men's protection. Not only does reproduction seem to put women at a disadvantage, but women's awareness of this disadvantage makes them "timid" and fearful so that they seek and demand men's protection; "Nature was frightened so to speak about the preservation of the species and so implanted this *fear*—namely fear of *physical* injury and *timidity* before similar dangers—in woman's nature; through which weakness, this sex rightfully demands male protection." Not only does this clearly demonstrate that Kant believes that all women are locked into the phenomenal realm, because they cannot transcend the body; but this fear is seen as a weakness, something that makes women timid, rather than, as might be the case for Hobbes, a source of hostility and aggression. Women obtain protection from men, moreover, by emotional manipulation of men's "generosity" to get them to care for their children, thereby attaching themselves to a nuclear family unit. To this end nature gave women "modesty" and "eloquence," and made them "clever while still young in claiming gentle and courteous treatment by the male," so that he would find himself imperceptibly fettered by a child through his own magnanimity." The husband is the woman's "natural curator"; she is under his "civil tutelage." Indeed, though "woman, by the nature of her sex has enough of a mouth to represent both herself and her husband, even in court. . . . just as it does not belong to women to go to war, so women cannot personally defend their rights and pursue civil affairs for themselves, but only by means of a representative."[85]

Although this "legal immaturity with respect to public transactions" supposedly gives women more power in the domestic realm—for reasoning men will "respect and defend" the "*right of the weaker*"[86]—it would seem clear from this account that women are not only passive citizens, but unlike the apprentice or (male) servant, can *never* rise to the level of active citizenship. Indeed, for all Kant's talk of "beautiful virtue," this phrase would seem to be an oxymoron in the Kantian vocabulary, for true virtue can never be the result of inclination; in order to be truly moral or virtuous, actions must be done on the basis of duty. It is precisely because women act out of inclination that they must be subject to their husbands, who can act out of duty rather than inclination.

Moreover, because the family is the foundation for morality—as the basic building block for children's education—then women's subservient position in the family is a necessary foundation for morality. And because morality and reason are inextricably linked to Kant's conception of freedom, women's subservience is a necessary condition for men's reason, and hence for their freedom. Thus, once again, not only are women not deemed free creatures in and of themselves—that is, not deemed worthy of freedom, or able to handle it without destroying themselves and everyone else—but this state of unfreedom for women is necessary to the freedom of men. It is only because women safeguard the beautiful that men can occupy the realm of the sublime; it is only because of women's subservience that the family can impart morality and reason to children. The duality of Kant's theory—between the phenomenal and the noumenal, the sensible and the reasonable—would thus seem to cohere with the duality between body and mind, emotion and reason, woman and man. As a number of feminists have argued, the general ontology and epistemology of Kant's work would seem to require women's subordination, if not invisibility.[87] But this takes on a particular significance within the context of freedom, which is for Kant a central ideal of humanity, given its close linkage with autonomy, morality, and reason.

Although the notion that men's freedom is structurally premised on women's unfreedom is significant enough in and of itself from a feminist perspective, it is even more problematic for Kant in particular, for it presents several problems for his own theory. As Sally Sedgewick notes, "Kant's judgments about women reflect not just his failure to properly apply the categorical imperative, but also a bias in the categorical imperative itself or in the model of agency upon which it is based." Nancy Tuana points out that Kant's treatment of women is in strictly functionalist terms; that is, by arguing that women serve the species (through reproduction), society (through its enculturation), and men's perfection (by being good wives). Because functionalism by definition involves the treatment of women as means, not ends, as Susan Okin demonstrated in *Women in Western Political Thought*, Kant violates his own moral imperative.[88] He tries to get around this by arguing that *nature* has made woman as she is; and the idea that nature is immoral—or perhaps amoral—because it treats women as means, not as ends in themselves, would be perfectly consistent with Kant's theoretical framework, as nature is the core of the phenomenal world and hence the fulcrum of determinism. If women's nature puts them in this unfortunate position, there is not much to be done about it. But if, as I have suggested, it is not women's "nature" per se but rather Kant's beliefs about what women should be and need to be for the ends of society and men's perfection, then it is not nature but Kant himself who violates his own imperative. He not only treats women as means rather than ends, but prescribes such treatment of them to men for the sake of their own reason and thereby freedom.

Kant does this, moreover, as Tuana, Hall, and Mendus each separately argue, by replicating the prejudices of his day and passing them off as objective truth. Though in the *Anthropology* Kant dismissively chides women for their conventionalism—" 'what the world says is *true*, and what it does, *good*,' is a feminine principle that is hard to unite with *character* in the narrow sense of the term"[89]—Kant himself does exactly what he disparages women for doing. Thus, Mendus argues that "Kant simply appears to indulge in an unthinking endorsement of the prejudices of his day and an uncritical acceptance of the dogma of others—notably Rousseau."[90] Though unlike Rousseau, Kant sees sex as a major stumbling block for both men and women, as I have earlier discussed, he does seem to echo Rousseau's contradictory position on women as naturally subservient and yet dangerously powerful. However, whereas Rousseau at least had personal experiences of sexual relations with women on which to base his neuroses, "Kant's mind [is] almost wholly uncluttered by any actual experience,"[91] and so he draws on every standard sexist cliché. He attributes to women the standard sexist dogma of jealousy of other women and the inability to form deep relationships with each other because of competition for men's attention; Mendus notes that he claims "women are loquacious, quarrelsome, jealous and possessed of an overpowering inclination to dominate," particularly to dominate men.[92] Yet the obedience of wives to husbands is seen as a natural subordination. Kant takes his own prejudices, and common custom that suits these prejudices, as not merely empirical fact, but as the even higher dictates of objective reason.

This is particularly the case in *The Beautiful and Sublime*. Although Kant makes a great deal of women's "beautiful understanding" as a necessary complement to men's "deeper" and "sublime" one, his account of women's beauty is limited to the conventional, and even banal. Women "have a stronger innate feeling for everything that is beautiful, decorative, and adorned." They are "delicate . . . cheerful and laughing," and "can be entertained with trivialities." Beautiful women have "regular features" with "colors of eyes and face which contrast prettily," a "pretty appearance" and a "fine figure, merry naivete, and charming friendliness." They are "agreeable" but display "roguish coyness." They are "very delicate with respect to everything that causes disgust." These qualities that mark women's beauty are hardly what one might expect from a vision of the beautiful that is to complement the sublimity of reason. Kant even goes so far as to argue that "vanity"—a terrible failing in men—should not be condemned in a woman because it "enlivens her charms."[93] Such standards of beauty are entirely historically located; yet Kant tries to pass them off as objective truth. Thus, "Kant fails to distinguish between what is merely conventional . . . and what is a command of reason," as his "prejudice and bigotry"—not to mention petty conventionalism—"are revealed."[94]

CONCLUSION

Such obvious tensions pose problems not only for Kant specifically, but for the kind of freedom he endorses, namely, the positive liberty of the "true" will. By locating freedom in the noumenal realm and identifying the phenomenal realm as the realm of sensible determinism, Kant does not rule out negative liberty altogether, however: we have seen that it is an important basis on which the noumenal realm is built. In Kant's construction, positive liberty comes out of negative liberty; the former does not entirely reject the premises of the latter (though it may object to certain of its conclusions) but rather begins on that platform and carries it further. In this regard, as I argued about Locke and Rousseau, Kant may deploy a dual conception of freedom, though once again the particulars of this duality are specific to his theory. That is, for Kant the public realm would be the realm of negative liberty, where government protects my rights through promulgation of civil laws, so that I can determine the categorical imperative for myself. Positive liberty, by contrast, would be developed and expressed in the private realm. The latter is so not only in the sense that the family and private association are where children learn to become the kinds of individuals who can reason to the categorical imperative; even though Kant recommends formal education be gained in schools rather than the family per se, it is the family that oversees the child's intellectual development and prepares the child's character to receive intellectual education. But positive liberty is also a function of the "private sphere" in the sense that such reasoning occurs within each separate individual's mind, which is the essence of the self for Kant, and the essence of privacy as well. As we saw in Locke's and Rousseau's theories, of course, the pairing of public and private respectively with negative and positive liberty is complicated. For morality is public in Kant's unique sense; though it may develop in the private realm, through the use of reason within individuals' minds, its target and aim is the public use of that reason and the public expression of its ideas. Similarly, although rights are produced and enacted in the public realm, their purpose is to protect individuals' private pursuit of the good, and thus are, in a sense, private.

In this light, then, the question is not whether I am free in relation to the sensible world, for obviously Kant's notion of "practical" freedom plays an important role in his theory of politics in particular. Rather, the essential question is whether such freedom has any genuine significance to my being able to consider myself "a free person." Kant believes the freedom I exercise in acting on desire is empty, or at least not worth much to me. Without rationality and the categorical imperative, the freedom I have is severely impoverished, or as Allison puts it, "thin": "only a being with freedom, positively construed as the capacity for self-determination on the basis of rational grounds (the capacity to act according to the conception of law), can be meaningfully conceived to have a corresponding capacity to deviate from the dictates of reason. . . . only a being with freedom, positively construed, can be regarded as capable of misusing that freedom. Nevertheless, deviation from the law constitutes a misuse of such freedom rather [than] the absence of it."[95] Implicit in Allison's argument is the notion that practical freedom, and concomitantly, negative freedom, may be important but never sufficient; indeed, they may not even be necessary. By contrast, transcendental, positive freedom is always necessary and may alone be sufficient.

The last line of Allison's passage, however, points to the idea that negative liberty is not at all irrelevant to Kant's vision of freedom. After all, if it were, then a classic paradox opens up for Kant. Namely, if I am free only when I follow the categorical imperative and act morally, then am I unfree when I act in violation of this imperative, and do evil? And if I am unfree when I do evil, can I be considered responsible for such action? Though the logic of Kant's argument might appear to suggest that I am not responsible for any such evil actions I perform, Kant does in fact say that I am responsible. For

a rational being can . . . rightly say of every unlawful action he performed that he could have omitted it even though as appearance it is sufficiently determined in the past and, so far, is inevitably necessary;

for this action, with all the past which determines it, belongs to a single phenomenon of his character, which he gives to himself and in accordance with which he computes to himself, as a cause independent of all sensibility, the causality of those appearances. (*Critique of Practical Reason*, 5:98)

In other words, we recognize responsibility for our choices even if we are driven by phenomenal desire; as I argued earlier, and as Hobbes maintained, I may not have any choice about whether to feel hungry, but I can exercise choice about whether, when, and what to eat. And whatever arises from one's choice—as every action intentionally performed undoubtedly does—has as its basis a free causality. As Andrews Reath notes in his introduction to the second *Critique*, "we are free in *all* exercises of agency, not just those in which we act from moral reasons. . . . immoral and evil actions are freely chosen—that is why they are evil." But as Reath also indicates, the two kinds of freedom are interdependent: "Since the moral law provides reasons for action that are independent of the content and strength of our desires . . . The ability to act from the moral law . . . reveals in us an ability to act independently of determination by empirical conditions. . . . Thus the fact of reason, in which we recognize the authority of and are aware of our ability to act from the moral law, discloses our freedom. . . . it is our recognition of the authority of the moral law that reveals our freedom, and that in the absence of such moral consciousness we would have no reason to ascribe freedom to ourselves."[96]

Thus, as we move from Rousseau to Kant, we see a greater attempt to incorporate negative liberty *into* a positive conception; to emphasize the choice or voluntarist aspects of the former more fully within the law or virtue aspects of the latter. Kant does not force people to be free, but he does evaluate their freedom as poorer or richer. This would be consistent with the greater individualism, when compared with Rousseau, that Kant incorporates into his moral methodology for defining freedom. Certainly, my own reading of Rousseau suggested that he also incorporates many of these negative and individualist elements, for natural freedom never fully dissolves; people can always misconstrue the general will by being misled by self-interest and passion. Like Kant, Rousseau thinks such freedom to be worth very little, but he does not deny its existence. But at the same time, Rousseau's own moral methodology for defining freedom is itself more communal than Kant's (or indeed, than any other theorist's discussed in this book), dependent on a particularly social political structure. This feature makes Rousseau's theory of freedom appear less individualistic, and more antagonistic to negative liberty principles, than Kant's.

Also like Rousseau, Kant is concerned that people, to be free, must make the right choices if autonomy is to be achieved: they must make the choices for themselves, but those choices must be in accord with the categorical imperative. Indeed, Kant goes farther, for Rousseau argued that when push came to shove, the choosing self had to take precedence over the right choice. Hence, he advocates participatory democracy. Kant, by contrast, though attributing such moral importance to autonomy, seems to have little faith in many people's ability to achieve or exercise autonomy. This is not only evident in his views of women, not to mention the lower classes and people of non-European races—for Rousseau can hardly be said to be any better on those matters—but in his more general attitude toward democracy. He accordingly outlines a political structure where obedience takes precedence over self-legislation, where the right answer takes precedence over choosing the answer for oneself. In this structure, the privileged reasoners have authority and power over those who have failed to prove or develop their reason (passive citizens, the lower classes, and unpropertied workers), those who are constitutionally unable to use or do not have reason (non-Europeans, minors), and, most significantly, those who should not use their reason, namely, women. Yet these very people are his undoing, for they show that Kant himself fails to live up to his ideal. As the theorist for whom universality and objectivity are of ultimate importance, Kant's failure to apply those principles to women, (many kinds of) workers, and people of color is a serious, perhaps even crippling problem if our goal is to utilize Kantian thinking for contemporary issues, rather than simply to treat him as a figure of historical interest. For Kant's thinking about these groups is clearly demarcated—or perhaps tainted—by the phenomenal realm, as the dictates of his own sensibility shape and even dominate his supposedly reasoned argumentation.

That women are the group for whom this contradiction is most visible is not coincidental, of course; as Monique David-Menard notes, Kant's morality is not only "an affair of men," but this "construction" of morality is "one founded within a structure of masculine desire."[97] Gender, however, is not the only social category that challenges Kant's theory, as I have shown. The main point of identifying such sexual, racial, and class bias, however, is not to point out how "politically incorrect" Kant is: one could hardly expect anything else. Rather, the point is that the understanding of freedom that Kant develops is not as "transcendental" as he claims it to be. Rather, it is located within specific economies of power along the vectors of gender in particular, as well as race and class. It is Kant's particular desires, indeed, within the gendered, classed, and raced economy of power that motivates his construction of reason, morality, and freedom in such a way as to eliminate from the start entire categories of human beings. Thus, to the degree that women's unfreedom is the basis for men's freedom, then that freedom—the pure freedom of the noumenal realm—is built on sand. For if it is precisely women's phenomenal status that serves as the foundation of men's noumenal freedom, Kant would seem to be involved in a paradox: the noumenal realm is independent of and superior to the phenomenal, and yet at the same time intimately and inescapably dependent on it.

The role of constructivism in Kant's theory suggests a further tension in his work. Insofar as true freedom is noumenal or transcendental freedom, it operates in a realm divorced from contingency, social arrangement (including language), and empirical phenomena. Yet the latter are key aspects of what social constructivism is about: these are things that are socially constructed, and that in turn socially construct human beings to be able, or not, to engage in certain ways of thinking and knowing. Thus, it is not merely women's location in the phenomenal realm that poses a challenge to Kant's noumenal freedom; it is the status of the phenomenal realm itself, and how humans live in it, that determines their ability to transcend it, in Kant's view. Such transcendence can never really be achieved in the terms Kant offers us, however, because it is a function of how humans are produced as reasoning subjects, and the kind of reason that is produced in them. The socially produced and located use of reason is therefore in significant ways a phenomenal ability, itself contingent on social forces that are themselves in turn contingent on other social forces, including the dominant understanding of reason and of how to produce people who can think in the terms that reason requires. One might argue that the link to the phenomenal realm does not matter, as long as the end point of existence is this transcendence; but the foregoing argument also shows that what is achieved in the noumenal is itself phenomenally located, defined, and interpreted.

Thus, as I argued about the other theorists considered so far, Kant's constructivism occurs in more than one way. That is, not only does Kant engage in social constructivism by prescribing particular practices and social arrangements, ranging from education to the state, that will increase humanity's chances of realizing the noumenal realm and transcendental freedom. He also engages constructivism through the philosophical framework he creates to portray the specific picture of the world that he wants. In supporting or promulgating a particular way of thinking about the world, social relations, "reality"—what one might call Kant's ideology, perhaps an ideology of liberalism—he produces and supports social institutions that ensure the ideology's realization and materialization. But these are not seen in their mutually constitutive framework because of the language that Kant uses to portray this picture: the third layer of social construction discussed in my introductory chapter. By dividing the world into two realms, the noumenal and phenomenal, Kant develops a structured philosophical framework that permits him to abstract his questions out of politics, and thereby obscure their political significance and meaning. Whereas the political significance of even Locke's writings on language and meaning, not to mention those on religion, is difficult to ignore, it is easy to be seduced by Kant's desire to abstract politics from knowledge, morality, and truth. If freedom is found in following the universal law, this must be true regardless of the kind of state or social relations one finds oneself in. Yet we see that this is not the case: that is why Kant also prescribes particular political forms. Whereas Hobbes posited a notion of nature that differed substantially from civil society, thus revealing fairly obviously the ways in which he expected men and women to change, Kant collapses human nature into people's civil persona in many respects, taking "man as he is" for "man in his essence," thereby making Kant's constructivism a bit more difficult to decipher.

In other words, the interactive relationship between the three layers of social construction—ideology, materialization, and discourse—is perhaps more intimately intertwined for Kant than it is for other theorists, where elements of "progression" are more obvious: ideology leading to materiality, reflecting discourse, feeding back into ideology. The various elements are thus at times more difficult to differentiate in Kant's work. By attending to gender and class, however, and analyzing the political meaning of his moral philosophy, we can see that Kant's morality hinges on a particular structure of humanity, reason, and morality that reflects a specific kind of person in a specific cultural context: namely, European men, of a minimal economic standard, in the age of Englightenment. Freedom, then, far from the abstract universal of the categorical imperative, is seen to take a specific social form that is produced through Kant's theories, which in turn constitute a particular way of seeing, interpreting, and understanding ourselves. And how we see and understand ourselves through Kant's theories supports, perpetuates, and further develops the specific social forms, encoding sexual, class, and racial privileges and inequalities, that fueled his theories in the first place. If this circularity of Kant's theory is subtler and more difficult to discern than it is in other modern theorists, it is no less troubling for freedom.

CHAPTER FIVE

John Stuart Mill

UTILITY, DEMOCRACY, EQUALITY

THE HISTORICAL TRAJECTORY we might logically follow from Rousseau and Kant could lead us to Hegel and Marx instead of to John Stuart Mill. For Hegel and Marx developed understandings of freedom that worked from complicated understandings of desire and will, and they clearly adopted positive liberty's idea of the divided self. Furthermore, truly foreshadowing, if not founding, contemporary elaborations on positive liberty, Hegel in particular lent the "fear factor" to the idea of positive liberty. By declaring that the state, as an independent entity rather than a democratic collective, was the ultimate repository of the collective will and thereby of the individual's true will, Hegel fed the interpretation of positive liberty by Berlin and others as a doctrine of totalitarianism. For his part, Marx developed the case for viewing large social forces—namely, capitalism—as socially constructed barriers to individuals' ability not only to do what they want, but to formulate desires in the first place. By seeing what was assumed to be the natural and unchangeable landscape as a function of human choice and power in historical development, Marx traced the ways in which supposedly individual and personal desires were in fact produced, if not determined, by large social forces external to the individual, so that both their artificiality and their externality were made invisible to most people. Thus, turning to these theorists would suggest a "story" about freedom that made it increasingly—or at least more overtly—associated with positive liberty ideals over time.

But that would not be historically accurate, for negative liberty has continued to dominate the modern Western understanding of liberty. Aspects of positive liberty still tend to be glossed, obscured, and denied, even if they are actively present. A better sense of that conception is to be gained by considering Marx's contemporary John Stuart Mill, who seems to return political theory to the more straightforward definition of liberty as doing what you want that was introduced by Hobbes and Locke: "pursuing our own good, in our own way."[1] And indeed, like Hobbes and Locke (despite the significant differences between those two that I have already articulated), Mill is often considered to offer the classic notion of negative liberty. He is certainly the primary canonical figure mentioned by contemporary thinkers in relation to freedom. Berlin in fact draws on Mill explicitly several times in formulating this conception, much more than he does the social contract theorists.[2] One of the key themes in *On Liberty* is the importance of people's being able to pursue their desires and act as they wish without interference from other people or government. "The struggle between Liberty and Authority" and "the nature and limits of the power which can be legitimately exercised by society over the individual" (*Liberty*, 5) constitute the central theme of his book.

Particularly by focusing on conscience, thought, and speech as the essential dimensions of human freedom, Mill seems at first to operate from a strongly individualist notion of the subject and individual desire. The essence of the individual lies in the mind, in the private realm of thought and conscience, which no other person is entitled to—or indeed, even *can*—affect or restrict.[3] This means that we are all different and have different ideas. We therefore must be allowed to explore and express those ideas, which are the essence of our difference and uniqueness. Indeed, Mill valorizes the "eccentric" simply because difference is so vital to the productive confluence and interaction of ideas, an interaction that in turn stimulates individual mental processes. Similarly, he loathes the mediocre masses who conform to common opinion and fail to think for themselves, for this gives way to the antithesis of individual liberty, namely, the tyranny of the majority. "The danger which threatens human nature," he writes, "is not the excess, but the deficiency, of personal impulses and preferences" (*Liberty*, 68). The need to be independent and different, to think for oneself, is for Mill the essence of human liberty, suggesting an extreme individualism: "The only freedom which deserves the name, is that of pursuing our own good in our own way, so long as we do not attempt to deprive others of theirs" (*Liberty*, 17). That last condition, preventing someone from harming other persons, and specifically from interfering with their liberty, Mill maintains, is the only justification for limiting anybody's liberty. Accordingly—in an example that thematically pervades *On Liberty*—one cannot prevent a man from drinking unless he regularly spends his paycheck at the pub and thereby deprives his wife and children of food or shelter, or he habitually becomes violent, or commits some other harm to others (108). As long as the activity is self-regarding, individuals should have an unbridled liberty to pursue it. Indeed, in an apparent repudiation of any hint of positive liberty, Mill baldly states that

> His own good, either physical or moral, is not a sufficient warrant. He cannot rightfully be compelled to do or forbear because it will be better for him to do so, because it will make him happier, because, in the

opinions of others, to do so would be wise, or even right. These are good reasons for remonstrating with him, or reasoning with him, or persuading him, or entreating him, but not for compelling him, or visiting him with any evil, in case he do otherwise. To justify that, the conduct from which it is desired to deter him must be calculated to produce evil to some one else. The only part of the conduct of any one, for which he is amenable to society, is that which concerns others. In the part which merely concerns himself, his independence is, of right, absolute. Over himself, over his own body and mind, the individual is sovereign. (*Liberty*, 14)

Similarly, negative liberty is an important theme, and the most apparent one, in Mill's arguments against the subjection of women. Mill maintains that women are fettered by laws that prevent them from voting, from obtaining education, and from pursuing professional careers; they lose control of their property upon marriage through coverture and are subject to violence and abuse by their husbands. Mill goes so far as to say that marriage is the only "legal" form of slavery (*Subjection*, 482–85). These restrictions make women economically dependent on men and forestall their ability to formulate life choices and act on them. Furthermore, such laws are self-contradictory: if women are indeed inferior, the market will ensure their failure, so allowing them the (negative) freedom to compete is the only justifiable course (489–90, 499). But it is not just in economic terms that women are restricted. Legal restrictions on social practices, like divorce and contraception, make women vulnerable to physical and sexual abuse by their husbands, in addition to economic exploitation. Furthermore, it is not merely restrictions on women, but privileges granted to men, particularly to beat their wives and to sexual "prerogatives," that limit women's freedom to pursue their own good in their own way. But these privileges themselves take root in the restrictions on women; restrictions on divorce and property, for instance, enable men to do what they like to their wives, who cannot get away. Thus, the only morally defensible course of action, Mill argues, is to recognize women's ability and right to make their own decisions, and that requires ending the legal restrictions on them in terms of education, employment, property, contraception, and divorce.

This reading of Mill as a negative libertarian is the one that is most familiar to most readers. Yet when read in light of his arguments on utility, political economy, education, gender, and logic, Mill's theory of liberty demonstrates at least as much sympathy with Rousseau and Kant as with Hobbes and Locke. Of course, as we have already seen, Hobbes and Locke also adopt certain positive liberty elements in their theories and deploy social understandings of humans. Whereas I argued that Hobbes and Locke deployed such elements in spite of themselves, however, Mill seems to utilize them self-consciously and explicitly. Mill particularly draws on the aspects of positive liberty that have to do with second-guessing, of pushing people to make the best and right choice for themselves, his previously quoted disclaimer notwithstanding. As with the other theorists, Mill deploys a social constructivism that, rather than simply imposing such choices and preferences onto people, seeks to produce people with those preferred desires who will make the choices that he wishes them to make.

The "Two Mills"

In this reading, I agree with those commentators who maintain that Mill's theory of freedom is more nuanced and complicated than is commonly assumed. Gertrude Himmelfarb's "two Mills thesis" is often cited (and contended with), for she maintained that the Mill who authored *On Liberty* and championed individual sovereignty differed significantly from "the other Mill" who wrote the rest of his work, presenting "a different mode of liberal thought" that gave prominence to civic responsibility and social obligation.[4] Though this latter view is consistent with some aspects of positive liberty, other commentators explicitly take up Mill's relationship to the typology, and some even argue that Mill advocates positive liberty flat out.[5]

G. W. Smith, for instance, argues that there are several aspects of Mill's theory that demonstrate affinity with positive liberty, namely, the notion of "self-mastery or self-determination," his focus on powers and abilities rather than simply the absence of impediments, the importance of self-development to individuality, and the fact that he acknowledges that barriers to liberty can be internal as well as external. Smith notes, however, that Mill is also, and perhaps more strongly, in the negative liberty camp because making your own choice is more important than making the right choice: though self-mastery is important, it is "not a condition of freedom." Lazy drunks, after all, can be free, "just so long as we could resist, if we wished."[6] Bruce Baum reads Mill as more strongly in league with positive liberty theory, particularly its emphasis on higher-order desires; Mill's emphasis on critical deliberation and education facilitate "our capacity to pursue reflectively our more important purposes."[7] But also echoing my own argument about social construction's importance to positive liberty, Baum argues that for Mill, "the issue of *why* people desire what they desire is indispensable for assessing the extent of their freedom." Like Baum, Nicholas Capaldi argues that Mill takes "freedom as autonomy, understood as self-discipline not mere self-assertion . . . as the intrinsic end" of utility. He maintains that Mill's ostensible focus on external barriers is really to the end of individuals' being able to achieve self-realization. "For Mill, the only real sense of fulfillment that a human being can achieve comes when he disciplines himself in the service of some inner intuitive conception of an ideal that gives shape and meaning to the projects of his life." Whatever that ideal might be—and it is bound to be different for different people—"what is necessary is that we grasp it voluntarily instead of having it imposed from the outside."[8] Thus, "for Mill the problem of liberty is not simply one of government control" which might threaten individual liberties, "but of social control . . . understood as the undue influence of those who have failed to become autonomous individuals" over the autonomy and freedom of those who have achieved it or are struggling to achieve it.[9]

Others reject Mill's association with negative liberty on more complicated grounds. Nadia Urbinati suggests that "there are three concepts of liberty in Mill's work," not two: "liberty as *noninterference*, liberty as *nonsubjection*, and liberty as moral *self-development*."[10] These three, taken together, incorporate and cut across the positive/negative typology, leading Urbinati to claim that Mill's conception of freedom actually demonstrates the incoherence of the typology. She locates Mill's conception not in modern liberalism, but in the ancient ideal of republicanism that involves contestation, discussion, debate: "Mill's model was Socrates, not Plato." This ideal, and that of moral self-development, commit Mill to "a notion of liberty that doesn't fit into the conventional dichotomy of the negative and positive" because it involves "decisions supported by reasons" rather than "solely . . . personal preferences."[11]

Joseph Hamburger takes an even more critical view. He does not claim that Mill actually follows positive liberty, but he argues that Mill's devotion to negative liberty is exaggerated. Mill "advocated placing quite a few limitations on liberty and many encroachments on individuality. . . . far from being libertarian and permissive, Mill advocated the introduction of inhibitions, moral restraints, and social pressures." We cannot ignore, Hamburger argues, the emphasis that Mill placed on social control as a necessary and positive force rather than a pernicious one. For "Mill's overarching purpose" was not the rights of the individual or his liberty of self-regarding action, but rather "bringing about moral reform, or, as he called it, moral regeneration." Hamburger says that Mill put less emphasis on, and trust in, the cultivation of individuals' *self-*restraint and more trust in restraints from external sources.[12] Thus, rather than inconsistency or a tension between "two Mills," one of whom advocated liberty while the other promoted utility, or one of whom favored liberty while the other sought control, Hamburger argues that there is in fact only one Mill who developed a coherent theory. Mill saw his contemporaries in "an age of transition" and tried to develop a theory that could negotiate the inevitable tension between things as they were and things as they could be: the real and the ideal. The elite individuals of that time needed a great deal of negative freedom so that they could oppose the prevailing public opinion and not be restrained in developing new and better ideas. A necessary by-product of this was that lesser-educated people would have to share in those same freedoms, though, according to Hamburger, Mill thought they would not actually make use of them. But once this new society was achieved, Hamburger maintains, people would have much less freedom, presumably because they would no longer need it, because society would have embraced the new ideas that the current elite had successfully promulgated.

Hamburger's argument follows that of Maurice Cowling, who similarly challenged the "libertarian" and "simply individualistic" reading of Millian liberalism, emphasizing instead Mill's attention to "the religion of humanity" and "moral totalitarianism."[13] Rejecting descriptions of Mill offered by such commentators as Plamenatz, Laski, and Berlin as "gentle," "patient" and "exceptionally good," Cowling instead claims that "Mill was a proselytizer of genius: the ruthless denigrator of existing positions, the systematic propagator of a new moral posture, a man of sneers and smears and pervading certainty." He argues that Mill's conception of liberty "is a sort of spiritual, moral and rational liberty more extensive than the libertarianism for which Mill's doctrine is sometimes mistaken."[14] Foreshadowing Hamburger's claim, derived from Mill's essay "The Spirit of the Age," that called the mid-nineteenth century "an age of transition,"[15] Cowling argues that Mill "feared that democracy would destroy the higher cultivation" of "good" desires because of "collective mediocrity." But this is less a condemnation of democracy per se, Cowling avers, than a fear of democracy's emergence at a particular time in history when "old opinions are dead" and the new ones are based on, as Mill put it, "the despotism of custom" rather than new and bold ideas that reflected the powerful changes that were occurring in industry and in social formations around the world (such as the struggle against slavery). Mill's project then became "to provide a body of commanding doctrine which, by stimulating the higher intelligence of all citizens, will . . . tell men what their duties are, and induce that sense of common participation, of which the great changes in European society, and the decay of old opinions, have deprived them." Criticizing the failure of Christian churches to provide this moral leadership, Cowling argues, Mill advocated a "religion of humanity" to be led by an elite "clerisy" of intellectual, educational, and moral character.[16] Liberty thus requires "a society which is morally homogeneous and intellectually healthy" because all members attain "an educational level sufficient to enable them to . . . replace customary deference to arbitrarily established authority by rational deference to elevated intellect." The purpose of free exchange articulated in *On Liberty* is not to have an ongoing debate throughout history, but to achieve truth; for "once good principles have been established as a basis for conduct, they will not need to be subjected to critical examination on every occasion." This does not eliminate the need for freedom of thought and discussion, of course; for "a free individual is more likely than an unfree one to contribute to the higher cultivation."[17] If the "clerisy" is to guide the masses to the truth, they must be free to explore new ideas.

The plethora of critical commentary on Mill (I have mentioned only a very few sources here) makes it even more daunting to attempt a new contribution than it perhaps is for any of the four theorists considered in the previous chapters of this book. So many different arguments have been made about Mill that one wonders whether anything new can be said. I will therefore admit from the start that I agree with many of the aforementioned commentators, though I have differences of interpretation on specific aspects of their arguments. For instance, I take issue with Baum's and Capaldi's deployment of a distinction between autonomy and freedom, or between freedom and liberty, to challenge Mill's negative liberty focus. In the first place, as Hamburger rather dryly notes, Mill never uses the term "autonomy," so it is a bit difficult to swallow the argument that that is what he really meant.[18] Second, the conflation of autonomy into freedom is precisely what the standard negative liberty camp rejects about positive liberty: autonomy is not freedom for them, but something distinct. Third, the distinction between freedom and liberty is strained, if not implausible. Indeed, in the early pages of *On Liberty*, Mill directly contradicts the idea that he is distinguishing freedom from liberty; after articulating the centrality of the liberties "of tastes and pursuit," Mill says, "No society in which these liberties are not, on the whole, respected, is free, whatever may be its form of government; and none is completely free in which they do not exist absolute and unqualified" (*Liberty*, 17). Here the use of "liberty" and "freedom" is determined by linguistic usage, possible only because they share meaning. So by defining "liberty" as the negative liberty ideal, such interpreters simply eliminate that ideal from Mill's definition of "freedom" and therefore can obtain the conclusion they wish to reach about the distinction between the two concepts.

Although I agree with Urbinati's rejection of the either/or choice between positive and negative liberty, why she thinks this entails the rejection and delegitimation of both is less clear; it is more plausible to maintain that Mill embraces a combination of both models in his conception of freedom. Her claim that Mill's "refusal to think dualistically suggests a viable and timely solution to the deadlock presupposed by antithetical readings of liberalism and democracy and of individual and political liberty" exaggerates the distance between Mill and the other modern freedom thinkers she implicitly critiques in comparison, all of whom, I have argued in the foregoing chapters, incorporate both positive and negative liberty ideals into their theories.[19] What Urbinati's claim about Mill does, however, is correctly identify a general error that characterizes *contemporary* arguments that allegedly base themselves on the canon, and that is an important insight with which I more or less agree. That is, despite the particular emphasis he places on eccentricity and speech, Mill is no different from any of the other theorists considered in this book; they all challenge the dualism between negative and positive liberty, and thereby reveal that what Berlin posited is actually different aspects of liberty, more or less consistent with different conceptions of the self that vary along vectors of gender, class, race, and historical context. Mill may be more firmly in the middle than the other four theorists, but the dynamic he displays is not so different.

I am the most persuaded by Cowling and Hamburger, both of whom emphasize Mill's interest in Comte's "religion of humanity" as a positive vision for a world where people think of the common good and see themselves as linked with others. At the same time, however, I believe that Cowling and Hamburger both underemphasize the importance that Mill granted to personal choice. Hamburger notes that Cowling's book was severely criticized for being an ideological apology for conservatism (not a philosophy with which my own works have much sympathy).[20] Hamburger also points out that Cowling downplays the devotion to individual liberty that Mill displayed alongside his emphasis on control, a charge with which I agree.

Yet Hamburger, too, tends to downplay the place of individual freedom in Mill's work. Ostensibly this is a product of his attempt to point out the contrary themes that other commentators have missed, instead of repeating the too-familiar passages in which liberty is championed. But the result is that his argument, though asserting the importance of liberty, does not satisfactorily explain how control and liberty are reconciled for Mill. Hamburger rightly distinguishes between legal and social restraint, arguing that even if the state cannot legally punish individuals for behavior and thoughts that harm the self, society may do so, generally through the expression of "distaste and contempt," and the censure of public disapproval.[21] But Hamburger overemphasizes Mill's use of the word "penalty," for Mill also says that "he suffers these penalties only in so far as they are the natural, and, as it were, the spontaneous consequences of the faults themselves, not because they are purposely inflicted on him for the sake of punishment" (*Liberty*, 86). Such "penalty" of censure, in other words, is less an actual "punishment" and more a mode of expression meant to persuade people that their behavior is wrong. Indeed, Mill says that "the inconveniences which are strictly inseparable from the unfavorable judgment of others, are the only ones to which a person should ever be subjected for that portion of his conduct and character which concerns his own good, but which does not affect the interests of others in their relations with him" (86–87), a much milder statement than Hamburger attributes to him. However, Hamburger's basic point, that the classic vision of self-regarding actions being sacrosanct is an inappropriate interpretation of Mill, is helpful because it points to a much broader and more inclusive conception of freedom that problematizes the notion of the free agent and the material and conceptual borders between "individual" and "society."

As I have suggested about the other four theorists, Mill is very concerned that people make the right choices. But like Smith, I believe that Mill also emphasized people's own choices, regardless of the outcome of those choices, considerably more than did Hobbes, Locke, Rousseau, and Kant. The fact that scores of scholars have read Mill as a negative libertarian and a standard bearer for classical liberalism is not the result of widespread careless reading and sloppy scholarship, as Hamburger charges;[22] rather, Mill sincerely believed it. The fact that Mill provides the strongest defense of negative liberty principles while at the same time creating a sophisticated and complex social construction of individual preference and choice to guide people to the correct ones is less a sign of a confused mind, much less a split personality, than it is of a complex set of beliefs about freedom that Mill struggled to address.

Despite the differences among these theories, however, they surely suggest that the common reading of Mill as a founder of contemporary liberalism and an ideal spokesperson for negative liberty is simplistic if not outright wrong. Yet none of these arguments (with the exception of Urbinati)[23] take on the place of gender and class in Mill's theory of freedom (indeed, Jones says that "Mill was rarely inclined to think in terms of class").[24] The result is an incomplete, rather than incorrect, understanding of Mill's conception of freedom. For gender and class enable us to see that the duality with which Mill is struggling is not between positive and negative liberty. Mill's theoretical ambivalence is not about what freedom means. Rather, Mill's ambivalence is about what kind of freedom should be attributed to what kind of person.

Many of the aforementioned commentators, as well as many others who are not particularly focused on Mill's conception of freedom, such as Terence Ball, have long acknowledged that character is one of the central themes in Mill's writing. Like Rousseau, Mill constructed a vision of the free individual as one who was intelligent and knowledgeable, creative and thoughtful, virtuous and sympathetic, forceful and strong yet civil and civic-minded, respectful of the welfare of others. He also constructed a vision of the kind of individual who needs guidance if he is to be free: one who is lazy, uneducated, unthinking, uncritical, unmotivated, unoriginal, conforming, self-centered, focused on immediate pleasure and short-term consequences. I maintain that, like the other canonical theorists discussed in the previous chapters of this book, Mill has a twofold theory of freedom that allocates one kind of freedom, marked predominantly by the values we associate with negative liberty, to the former group of people, and another kind, characterized predominantly by the themes we have come to associate with positive liberty, to the latter group.

For Mill, however, as I argued was the case for the other theorists, the divisions between these groups significantly cohere to lines of class and gender: generally propertied men, and some upper-class women, occupy the first group, while laborers, the poor, and most women occupy the latter. These divisions are not as exclusive as they were for the other theorists, for Mill seemed to allow that the boundaries between the two groups were fairly porous. Some workers and women could display a facility for creative and rational thinking and cross over into the kind of freedom enjoyed by wealthy and educated white men, just as wealth might cause some privileged white men to fall into indolence and sloth, in need of guidance. But these exceptions in part served to prove the rule; or perhaps they were theoretical possibilities that were not usually realized in practice, in keeping with Hamburger's distinction between the ideal and the real in Mill's work. Thus, the coincidence of those lines of cleavage are, I maintain, significant; though whether Mill's views on gender and class actually caused him to develop a bifurcated theory of freedom, or whether he simply found that it made sense to apply this bifurcation along class and gender lines, is not an issue to be answered directly, if at all. Hamburger argued that freedom needs to be allowed for the intelligent to develop new ideas and lead society out of its transition and into the new improved order, while control must be exerted over the mediocre masses to prevent them from hampering their superiors. In a slightly different vein, I am suggesting that negative freedom is granted predominantly to educated men and some women, who can be relied on to make the right decisions for themselves and for whom it is therefore safe to permit, and even encourage, a wide range of experimentation in eccentricities. But positive freedom is developed for the workers and most women, the people who need to be guided to their true preferences.

The duality in Mill's theory, then, is not between positive and negative liberty per se, but between the kinds of people who are the appropriate subjects of different aspects of liberty that cohere in different ways with positive and negative liberty ideals. This argument differs from Himmelfarb's claim about "two Mills," and even more from those who believe Mill is really just a positive libertarian, because I maintain that Mill wanted and needed to hold on to both threads at once, that he was aware of holding them at once, and that he did not see this as problematic. In other words, as Mill crucially deploys key aspects of what have come to be seen as negative and positive liberty, he thereby simultaneously confounds Berlin's duality. Instead, he creates his own divisions and dualities that are marked importantly by gender and class.

INTERNAL AND EXTERNAL REALMS

The basic understanding of Mill as a negative libertarian is challenged right from the beginning of *On Liberty* in what is known as Mill's "harm doctrine," which states that the only justification for limiting someone's liberty is harm to another. This simple ideal immediately gives way to the conflict between the "punitory" and "preventive" functions of law. For instance, if you drive while drunk and kill someone, you will go to jail, because society is justified in punishing you for harming another. But because driving while intoxicated may result in your killing someone, society is also justified in outlawing it regardless of whether you actually do ever harm anyone by such behavior.[25] The distinction is important because the latter category would readily involve positive liberty's "second-guessing" and could justify a wider scope of state interference for the alleged purpose of preserving others' liberty. By contrast, the former takes a narrower focus on people's actual actions, and treats individuals as different from one another, which prevents us from predicting their actions—a classic ideal of twentieth-century liberalism.[26]

Mill seems unsettled on the issue; he is opposed, for instance, to banning alcohol, or the sale of poisons, or even prostitution. Indeed, in his testimony against the Contagious Diseases Act, Mill says, "I do not think it is part of the business of the Government to provide securities beforehand against the consequences of immoralities of any kind. That is a totally different thing from remedying the consequences after they occur. That I see no objection to at all."[27] And yet, as I will discuss in greater detail below, he advocated quite intrusive measures in regulating reproduction among the poor. Such ambiguity may attest to the notion that Mill takes a contextual approach to freedom, even in terms of his central liberty of thought and expression. That is, because of the ways in which expression can lead to action, the context of speech is important. "Even opinions lose their immunity, when the circumstances in which they are expressed are such as to constitute their expression as positive instigation to some mischievous act." Expression and action are the social forms of liberty of thought and conscience; and although they are vital to giving the latter concrete meaning, they also pose more danger to others' liberty and to our ability to function as a society. Hence, "an opinion that corn-dealers are starvers of the poor, or that private property is robbery, ought to be unmolested when simply circulated through the press, but may justly incite punishment when delivered orally to an excited mob assembled before the house of a corn-dealer, or when handed about among the same mob in the form of a placard" (*Liberty*, 62).

Of course, how Mill reads context is itself an important question; his example here ignores the realities and inequalities of class power. For the corn dealer does not need to gather with his peers to protest outside the worker's house in order to get his views across. He has the power to execute his opinions every day. The "barrier" to the worker's freedom is not the "speech" of the corn dealer, but the way in which he structures the worker's reality. This latter aspect is something that Mill incorporates in other writings, however. In *Political Economy*, for instance, he notes that workers' conceptions of themselves and their perceptions of their power—or lack thereof—directly affect their productivity. Hence, national education and cooperative ownership of industries will help create workers who are more productive.[28] And of course Mill was keenly aware of the ways in which sexism restricted and distorted women's desires and self-conceptions.

Hamburger argues, in fact, that Mill was very attentive to "internal" barriers to liberty for all people, and maintained that such internal barriers meant that even self-regarding actions, indeed, even the characteristics that led to such actions, were appropriate subjects of penalties: for after Mill's assertion that an individual's "own good, either physical or moral, is not a sufficient warrant" for restricting liberty (*Liberty*, 14), Mill asserts later in that same essay that "a person may suffer very severe penalties at the hands of others, for faults which directly concern only himself" (86). And Mill even identifies "acts not in themselves condemnable" but "which, if done publicly, are a violation of good manners" and "offences against decency" as legitimate targets for state intervention (108–9). What gives the reader pause about such passages is the way Mill seems to invoke a rather uncritical acceptance of contemporary valuations and norms as "natural" or self-evident. This would seem to contradict his rejection of public opinion, his emphasis on "eccentric" views for the attainment of truth, and his argument that "harm" must pertain to material interests and not to sensibilities or emotional states, which "offences against decency" would seem to involve. But these passages suggest that, despite Mill's defense of the individual freedom of thought, he drew certain limits around that freedom and sought to push it in a particular direction: some thoughts were freer than others.

In keeping with positive liberty ideals, Mill not only allows that barriers to freedom can be "internal," but also that they can come from the very structure of society itself, which can limit *or* enhance capacities. In this aspect of his work, Mill takes an overtly social constructivist approach to understanding humanity. The social construction of freedom that Mill engages is both a material one, a production through socialization norms and education of the kind of people who make particular choices, and a discursive one, a telling of a story, particularly about women and the poor, to create an image for understanding what the correct or "free" choices are, how to interpret choice-making action, and who counts as a legitimate chooser. By placing the emphasis on what constitutes a barrier, we can also see the tension or duality between positive and negative liberty a bit differently, because barriers, in a social constructivist view, are always both internal and external: social conditions and phenomena inevitably affect the workings of the self, and the choices that the self makes inevitably impact on the external world.

This is particularly evident in his essay *The Subjection of Women*, where Mill argues that "what is now called the nature of woman is an eminently artificial thing—the result of forced repression in some directions, unnatural stimulation in others," and attributes many of women's current psychological and personal qualities not to nature but to social customs. "It may be asserted without scruple, that no other class of dependents have had their character so entirely distorted from its natural proportions by their relation with their masters" (493). At the same time that Mill asserts that women are externally fettered from pursuing their preferences, however, he also acknowledges the deeper ways in which women have become the beings they are, with the desires they have, because of the ways in which external constrictions have created internal ones. If women are beings who are not taught to think rationally but encouraged to indulge in useless activities and gossip, then it is not surprising if women develop into beings who seem to want no better than they get: women's self-sacrificing characteristics (516), their absorption in "small but multitudinous details" and trivia rather than intellectual questions (540), their "devotion of the energies to purposes who hold out no promise of private advantages to the family" (566), their reluctance to press charges against abusive husbands, and even "to beg off their tyrant from his merited chastisement" (485–86), are all a function of what society makes of women. They are a result of the attitudes, self-conceptions, beliefs, and values society requires women to adopt in order to be "women."

In making this argument, Mill seems to be not displaying but rather identifying and critiquing the first two layers of social construction, namely ideology and materialization. He recognizes that patriarchal ideology tells falsehoods about women's identity and abilities through the trope of "nature." He then notes the ways in which women actually become the kinds of individuals that the ideology wants and needs them to be: by denying them education, autonomy, and access to resources that would permit them to make contributions to society, patriarchy turns women into mindless subordinates. This dynamic is especially evident in Mill's comments on domestic violence, an area on which he particularly focused his attentions. Mill argued that the prevalence of violence and women's vulnerability to it stemmed not only from women's inferior strength but also from the way laws and legal institutions enforced men's "right" to discipline wives. This, more than anything, evidenced women's "enslavement" to men within marriage. Clearly, violence abrogated negative liberty, presenting physical barriers that prevented women from acting as they wished. But when combined with legal and social practices that made escape impossible—no divorce, little chance of conviction for abusive husbands, and no means of self-support if a woman should manage to get away—a clear message of women's lesser value as human beings communicated itself to women's minds, distorting their self-perceptions and their desires. Indeed, the practice of domestic violence perverted men's minds as well, for the power of violence over their wives gave men a distorted self-perception of their value and importance. Thus, the fact that the law excuses spousal (and parental) violence, and that judges and lawyers apply the law in biased fashion, demonstrates "a profound ignorance of the effect of moral agencies on the character . . . how deeply depraving must be the influence of such a lesson given from the seat of justice."[29]

But a woman did not need to be physically abused to be beaten down by sexist social attitudes, according to Mill. This is one way that the third layer of social construction, discourse, has some relevance. By contrast to the woman of superior abilities who can rise above the confining social strictures of opinion (such as Mill's friend, collaborator, and eventual wife, Harriet Taylor), the average, uneducated woman is virtually helpless against the vast social forces arrayed against her to support male privilege. The average woman has so internalized the tyranny of "common public opinion" as to be its "auxilliary" (*Subjection*, 568); the critical and analytical abilities that might allow her to critique and analyze such opinion are so atrociously undeveloped that she seems incapable of even questioning, let alone rejecting it. Such arguments suggest that removal of external barriers to women's equality is not enough, but that social norms and attitudes must change *within* women as well as men, in order for women's *or* men's freedom to be achieved. For of course one of the main arguments that Mill deploys in the *Subjection* for the support of women's rights is that men will be better off. Not only will they benefit at home by having wives who can converse with them intelligently and help them improve themselves, and who can raise their children better. They will also benefit as members of society, because adding women to the labor force will double the applicant pool for important jobs and thereby result in better doctors, lawyers, and producers (*Subjection*, 501, 561–62).

This notion of socially constructed barriers pervades *On Liberty* as well, in Mill's criticism of the mediocrity of public opinion. The core of his critique is not that people "choose what is customary, in preference to what suits their own inclination," but that "it does not occur to them to have any inclination, except for what is customary" (68). That is, the barriers to freedom are not simply laws that forbid women from entering professional school or managing their own property. They also include social customs that prevent women from *wanting* to do these things in the first place. Mill rails against the ways in which gender subordination conditions women to defer to men, to choose their own subordination, and even to believe that they love their subordinators. By "social customs," Mill means something more than "the usual practice of things"; he means something closer to Foucault's use of "discourse"—an entire range of mental, psychological, and emotional forces that act on individuals' understandings of themselves, of the meaning of the social order, and of the natural world. A woman who wishes to pursue a profession in Mill's day is forced to question her own desire and indeed her identity as a woman because everywhere she hears others extol the virtues and naturalness of motherhood or the "charms" of feminine incompetence. She must question her desire, and why she seems so dissatisfied with what everyone else tells her she should want. This kind of barrier to liberty is not simply internal, because her doubts come from social custom and the beliefs of others. But insofar as it is an external barrier, it does not have clearly identifiable sources, in contrast to law, for instance, or a violent husband. In Mill's view, social custom and common opinion are social forces that are much more widespread and amorphous, with multiple "agents" to promote and support them. Indeed, such widespread social norms and pressures form the contextual background that makes it possible to create and enforce gender discriminatory laws and for men to beat their wives.

Yet at the same time, Mill seems to realize, these forces also produce the capabilities that humans have for choice, illustrating the ambiguity of the third layer of social construction. Mill does not argue that society is bad per se, or that we must struggle to let some repressed natural self come out. Rather, recognizing the inevitability of social construction, he advocates for a better kind of construction. Although his claim, cited earlier, that "no other class of dependents have had their character so entirely distorted from its natural proportions by their relation with their masters" (*Subjection*, 493) implies that women do have a nature that sexism inhibits, he also problematizes the notion of nature altogether as any source of normative judgment. In his essay "Nature," Mill contends that "conformity to nature, has no connection whatever with right and wrong." Nature is a subject for scientific study, an attempt to understand facts, not judgments or values. So to hold up "the maxim of obedience to Nature, or conformity to Nature . . . not as a simply Prudential but as an ethical maxim" is "not merely . . . superfluous and unmeaning, but palpably absurd and self-contradictory" because nature produces many bad things such as illness, suffering, and death. Often, what is "unnatural" is what humans most value as "good"; for example, "the sentiment of justice is entirely of artificial origin." Indeed, "to do anything with forethought and purpose, would be a violation of that perfect order."[30]

Even more important, Mill argues, the whole point of humanity is to change nature; "the duty of man is the same in respect to his own nature as in respect to the nature of all other things, namely not to follow but to amend it." If reason, agency, and choice are the hallmarks of humanity, then it is illogical, and contrary to human nature, to elevate nature to a moral good; "If the artificial is not better than the natural, to what end are all the arts of life? To dig, to plough, to build, to wear clothes, are direct infringements of the injunction to follow nature." The creative aspects of humanity are what Mill's principle of freedom of expression is all about; what is the good in challenging common opinion, for instance, if we must assume that that opinion is natural and cannot be improved on? "All human action whatever, consists in altering, and all useful action in improving, the spontaneous course of nature."[31]

Mill repeatedly displays a belief that people are the products of their environments rather than of nature, and that a better environment will produce better people. People who are socially constructed to want better things are people who can engage in higher levels of discourse, and hence are people who have a greater chance of finding and holding "true" beliefs, values, and opinions. But this is not as easy as it sounds, Mill understands. That is, even as society can construct external barriers to exercising my preference, Mill also acknowledges that society produces in us the very powers we have to make choices. This is so both in the sense, already discussed, that social custom can pressure and socialize people to have particular preferences and in the deeper sense that any and all capacity for choice whatsoever is a product of social configuration; we could not be what we recognize as "human" without specific social relations and customs. That is why Mill attends to how society is structured, rather than simply accepting it as given or natural. He recognizes that we cannot simply, through an act of will, make ourselves who we are, and yet he also recognizes that who we are is the product of social relations. Thus, much like Rousseau, Mill is engaged in the struggle for better social relations that will construct better individuals to make choices that produce a better quality of freedom.

THE WILL TO UTILITY

Two aspects of Mill's theory help elucidate this apparent paradox between his emphasis on individuality and difference and his evident attempts to push people to make specific kinds of choices. These aspects are, first, the way in which he reconciles the tension between free will and determinism and, second, his particular brand of utilitarianism. In *On Liberty*, Mill asserts that he will consider "Civil, or Social Liberty," rather than "the so-called Liberty of the Will" (5). Yet it is precisely the chapter "Of Liberty and Necessity" in his *System of Logic* that most significantly reveals what he means by liberty. In this chapter, Mill compares "the doctrine of Necessity, as asserting human volitions and actions to be necessary and inevitable," and the doctrine of free will, which holds "that the will is not determined, like other phenomena, by antecedents, but determines itself; that our volitions are not, properly speaking, the effects of causes, or at least have no causes which they uniformly and implicitly obey."[32] Though he allies himself more with "the former of these opinions," he criticizes both schools of thought for misconstruing themselves. The free will position holds not only that we do what we want, but that the formation of our desires is itself something we can consciously control: we can will our will. Much like Hobbes, Mill dismisses this idea as illogical, because our choices are clearly caused:

> Correctly conceived, the doctrine called Philosophical Necessity is simply this: that, given the motives which are present to an individual's mind, and given likewise the character and disposition of the individual, the manner in which he will act might be unerringly inferred; that if we knew the person thoroughly, and knew all the inducements which are acting upon him, we could foretell his conduct with as much certainty as we can predict any physical event. (*Logic*, 836–37)

At the same time, however, the determinist position is flawed because it claims that all choice is meaningless, as who we are and what we do is beyond our control. Mill dismisses this as "fatalism," and attributes it to the Owenites, who sought to take a radically progressive view that criminals should not be punished because their actions were the result of poor conditioning, not of "free will." In Mill's view, that is not what true determinism claims, as the above quote indicates; it recognizes the role of choice and only asserts that we cannot change things by a *mere* act of will, that we cannot will our will into existence, out of thin air, "We cannot . . . directly will to be different from what we are" (*Logic*, 840).

Thus, Mill rejects both of these extremes as caricatures. Instead, he maintains that each holds part of the truth, and that these two aspects of freedom are linked through a central notion of character. The issue that "Liberty and Necessity" implicitly takes up, as I read it, is how the individual comes to make the choices that she does. And the answer is that her character determines her desires and causes her to act on her preferences. But if that is so, what determines our character? This is the point on which Mill wants to converge determinism and freedom. For an individual's "character is formed by his circumstances": by the experiences he has, how he was brought up, the kind of influences and education he was exposed to, and so forth. In true social constructivist fashion, Mill says that we cannot stand outside of ourselves to create ourselves as we wish ab initio, because we are who we are through the social conditions, institutions, practices, relationships, language, and social framework in which we come to be. But that a person's character is "formed for him, is not inconsistent with its being, in part, formed *by* him as one of the intermediate agents." That is, "he has, to a certain extent, a power to alter his character." So even if the Owenites are correct that our characters have been made for us, they have not been actively produced by conscious others with specific intent: for "neither did those who are supposed to have formed our characters, directly will that we should be what we are. Their will had no direct power except over their own actions" (*Logic*, 840).

But actions and choices alone are never enough. If character shapes our choices, and experience shapes our character, then the only way to change our choices is to change our characters. The only way to do that is to change our experiences. "We, when our habits are not too inveterate, can, by similarly willing the requisite means, make ourselves different. If [others] could place us under the influence of certain circumstances, we, in like manner, can place ourselves under other circumstances. We are exactly as capable of making our own character, *if we will*, as others are of making it for us" (840).

Yet this idea, that in order to change our characters we simply need to change our circumstances, is more complex than appears at first glance. As social constructivism suggests, there is something of an infinite regress: even if I desire to change my character, where does the desire to change come from? This was the view of the Owenites, who according to Mill believed that "the will to alter our own character is given us, not by any effort of ours, but by circumstances we cannot help: it comes to us from external causes, or not at all" (840). The Owenites believed that this fact led to a complete determinism that removed free will altogether: if the desire to change is itself constructed for us, what role could "volition" possibly have?

Mill swats away such questions, saying that the desire to alter our character, and thereby our circumstances, comes from the "experience of the painful consequences of the character we previously had; or by some strong feeling of admiration or aspiration, accidentally aroused" (*Logic*, 841). In other words, experience is not only backward-looking, to consider how we got to be the way we are, but forward-looking, to possibilities of what we could be.[33] We are not just the effects of causes; we have the power of rational thinking, and therefore we can also see and understand the relation of cause and effect. We can, in effect, construct ourselves. Indeed, the determinist claim that we are effects of prior and external causes testifies to our ability to discern this relationship rationally. If we can understand that relationship, then we can try to put ourselves under the influence of causes that are likely to produce the effects that we wish. Thus, "to think that we have no power of altering our character, and to think that we shall not use our power unless we desire to use it, are very different things" (*Logic*, 841). It is the latter thought that Mill endorses.

This distinction, however, is still not enough to satisfy the determinist; for where does the desire to use this power to change our characters itself come from, if not from external causes over which we have no control? Mill's answer is not entirely satisfactory; he seems to think we just have it. In his *Autobiography*, Mill says, "I saw that though our character is formed by circumstances, our own desires can do much to shape those circumstances; and that what is really inspiriting and ennobling in the doctrine of free-will, is the conviction that we have real power over the formation of our own character; that our will, by influencing some of our circumstances, can modify our future habits or capabilities of willing."[34] It would seem that there is an innate capacity to desire to change, even if such change cannot be directly enacted by the will. But such self-creation is crucial to freedom. Thus, in the *Logic* he maintains that "This feeling, of our being able to modify our own character *if we wish*, is itself the feeling of moral freedom which we are conscious of. A person feels morally free who feels that his habits or his temptations are not his masters, but he theirs" (*Logic*, 841). Mill's notion of "moral freedom" is not quite what it meant to Rousseau, obedience to a self-prescribed law, but it does share with Rousseau the notion that will, rather than simple brute desire, is key to freedom: that freedom involves not simply wanting, but having a vision of what one should want, a vision that takes virtue as its guide. Hence, Mill says that "at least, we must feel that our wish, if not strong enough to alter our character, is strong enough to conquer our character when the two are brought into conflict in any particular case of conduct. And hence it is said with truth, that none but a person of confirmed virtue is completely free" (841).

We have seen the link between freedom and virtue in other theorists considered in this book. What sets Mill apart is that "virtue" is construed not merely as the embodiment of certain qualities, but as a desire to better oneself, to contribute to the public good, to seek the truth. That desire, however, presupposes a certain kind of character that will lead us to certain kinds of choices. An alcoholic who does not want to stop drinking, for instance, will not join Alcoholics Anonymous; someone on parish relief (in Mill's view) is not likely to want to get a job. Mill wants us to choose the right things; that is key to his social constructivism, and in this he is not that different from the authors previously discussed. Like Rousseau in particular, Mill wants to construct people who will make the right choices, but, paradoxically, they can only be constructed to do so by the things they must choose. Accordingly, Mill must push them to make those choices to get the process started, until they become the kinds of people who can make those choices on their own. The myth of liberalism, which many associate with Mill, is that the self stands outside of context, and hence that it is possible to choose your own way as if divorced from context. Mill challenges that idea. He accepts the inevitability of context and its construction of individuals, but he wants a better context that will produce better people who make better choices. He may want more diversity among such people than does Rousseau, because diversity helps secure truth; but truth is still attainable in Mill's view, and diversity serves as a means to that greater end. The desire for improvement will occur only to people who already have the capacity to appreciate gradations in human refinement and intelligence. There is thus a circularity to Mill's reasoning that plagues the determinist position more generally.

This circularity affects Mill's utilitarianism as well. Utility is key to Mill's theory of liberty: "I regard utility as the ultimate appeal on all ethical questions," he says in the opening pages of *On Liberty*, "but it must be utility in the largest sense, grounded on the permanent interests of man" (15). Mill came to reject the individualist variant of utilitarianism put forth by Bentham to adopt a more social notion of utility, the version we find in Hume and that Urmson allies with "rule utilitarianism."[35] Mill distinguishes between what people *do* want, that is, what they think will make them happy, and what they *should* want, that is, what actually will make them happy. Bentham's famous axiom that "pushpin is as good as poetry" suggested that utility is a matter only of quantity; one person's enjoyment of a mindless game has the same value as another's enjoyment of the intellectually complicated task of interpreting literature.[36] But Mill sharply disagrees, arguing that utility is a matter of quality: "It is better to be a human being dissatisfied than a pig satisfied; better to be Socrates dissatisfied than a fool satisfied" (*Utilitarianism*, 140), Mill maintained, because some kinds of desires and preferences are more valuable than others. In particular, the mental pleasures are superior to the physical (138), and "a sense of dignity, which all human beings possess in one form or other" and which is vital to human happiness, is "in some, though by no means in exact, proportion to their higher faculties" (140).

Although Mill does link higher pleasures to the mental and lower to the physical as I have just noted, this mapping is not exclusive, and he repeatedly uses the terminology of higher and lower pleasures throughout his essay. Moreover, he distinguishes between higher and lower physical pleasures when he condemns the pursuit of "sensual indulgences to the injury of health," suggesting a hierarchy within physical pleasures. His scorn for popular novels similarly attests to the notion of higher and lower gradations among mental pleasures. It is fair to say, however, that most higher pleasures will include some intellectual component; drinking a 1982 Bordeaux or listening to an opera by Puccini, for instance, appeals to the senses as much as to the mind. Given the higher order utility of the higher pleasures, then presumably satisfying one person's desire to hear a Puccini opera might produce more utility than satisfying ten people's desire to hear pop music, and thus devoting resources to the opera would produce greater utility even if fewer people enjoy it.[37]

Or rather, such would clearly be the case if that one person had experienced both kinds of music and the other ten had never heard Puccini before. Mill gives to those who have experienced two potential pleasures the authority to declare which of the two has the greater utility. This condition would seem to have an egalitarian and democratic orientation. That is, rather than allowing a single wise individual to determine what is best for all, Mill says that "all or almost all who have experience of" two pleasures must prefer one for it to have greater utility. But he also says "If one of the two is, by those who are *competently acquainted* with both, placed so far above the other that they prefer it, even though knowing it to be attended with a greater amount of discontent, and would not resign it for any quantity of the other pleasure which their nature is capable of, we are justified in ascribing to the preferred enjoyment a superiority in quality, so far outweighing quantity as to render it, in comparison, of small account" (*Utilitarianism*, 139, emphasis added). This passage suggests that quality of preference can outweigh quantity considerations, and raises questions about freedom. For instance (in a twist on the common objection to Benthamite utilitarianism) if the only way to achieve a sublime pleasure for a minority is through the institution of slavery, could that be justified? And could it be justified by virtue of the fact that only a few have experienced the pleasure, and therefore are qualified to judge it "sublime," or that slaves are not "competent" to evaluate it?

On the face of it, one would have to say that slavery could not be justified on such grounds. Mill was an outspoken opponent of the enslavement of Africans, using the same incisive mockery of the standard arguments defending the practice as he used in the *Subjection* to debunk common prejudices about women. In both "The Negro Question" and "The Slave Power," Mill makes an uncompromising and vigorous defense of abolition and excoriates the practice of slavery in terms that recognize the full humanity of Africans and the unbearable suffering they have endured under slavery.[38] In this, the utilitarian argument could be the same he offers in the *Subjection*: that the happiness of Africans, like the happiness of women, needs to be counted.

But Mill also holds that liberty and democracy are not appropriate for "barbarians" or "backward" races who supposedly lack the ability to reason and think critically. Particularly in *On Representative Government* he maintains that such races require despotism to ensure their wellbeing, and that they are not fit subjects for liberty (232). Mill is speaking here of India more than Africa, and the enslavement of Africans is the practice to which he objects explicitly. But his utilitarianism offers less secure opposition to slavery than he seems to think. The issue of qualitative pleasure particularly challenges the logical consistency of Mill's argument. Mill notes that "all persons are deemed to have a right to equality of treatment, except when some recognized social expediency requires the reverse" (*Utilitarianism*, 200). For "the happiness which forms the utilitarian standard of what is right in conduct, is not the agent's own happiness, but that of all concerned." Accordingly, "the utilitarian morality does recognize in human beings the power of sacrificing their own greatest good for the good of others" (*Utilitarianism*, 148). Following this logic, a small minority of Africans—or white women, for that matter—could in principle be expected to sacrifice themselves for the greater good of social utility.

Furthermore, in *Representative Government*, Mill explicitly defends slavery as a necessary institution when people are not sufficiently advanced to be self-governing. Because "a slave, properly so called, is a being who has not learnt to help himself," then slavery may be necessary as a transitional institution from a barbarous society to a civilized one, because such a transition depends on productive labor, and most "uncivilized races . . . are averse to continuous labour of an unexciting kind. . . . Hence even personal slavery, by giving a commencement to industrial life, and enforcing it as the exclusive occupation of the most numerous portion of the community, may accelerate the transition to a better freedom than that of fighting and rapine" (*Government*, 232–33). The linkage here between slavery and freedom, and between freedom and industry, echoes Mill's description of poor laborers, who would not work if they were not forced to. The key difference for Mill is that in a civilized society, the economy is structured so as to require people to work. If "the first lesson of civilization [is] that of obedience" (*Government*, 260), then economic structures must also flow out of this lesson, and reinforce it daily. But Mill fails to see the analogy he has made between slavery and capitalism. Thus, Mill concludes, as if in justification, "It is almost needless to say that this excuse for slavery is only available in a very early state of society" (232).

The presence of this "excuse" in his argument supplements my more general point about the question of "competent acquaintance." For superiority of judgment is more complicated than simple experience. One might be exposed to opera and still obstinately prefer rock and roll. Indeed, a preference for pop over Puccini could be taken as *evidence* of one's incompetence. Mill acknowledges that it is easy to lose sight of the higher pleasures and prefer the lower ones: "Capacity for the nobler feelings is in most natures a very tender plant, easily killed" (*Utilitarianism*, 141). Most people "addict themselves to inferior pleasures, not because they deliberately prefer them, but because they are either the only ones to which they have access, or the only ones which they are any longer capable of enjoying" (141). It follows from this that most people are not in fact "competent" judges; if they have access only to the lower pleasures, they cannot evaluate the higher. And if they are not capable of enjoying the higher—if, after hearing Puccini, they still prefer pop—that would serve as evidence of their disqualification because *what* they prefer indicates an impoverished ability of preference evaluation.

It is precisely because the majority of people do not have elevated or educated tastes that Mill, much like Hume before him, advocates the utility of certain practices and of following certain rules, even when it might appear in individual cases that following the rule is nonutilitarian. "The rules of morality for the multitude, and for the philosopher until he has succeeded in finding better," will guide us in deciding which things produce utility and which do not (*Utilitarianism*, 156). Such "secondary rules"—keep your promises, respect others' property, tell the truth—are guides to the "first principle" of promoting happiness and minimizing pain, for following such rules will, in most cases, produce greater happiness. And such rules are also well set, not up for negotiation: "all rational creatures go out upon the sea of life with their minds made up on the common questions of right and wrong, as well as on many of the far more difficult questions of wise and foolish" (157). Indeed, it is only when two such rules conflict—for instance, stealing medicine to save a life—that I should appeal directly to the principle of utility.

But what is the relationship of such utility to freedom? Mill's utilitarianism concentrates the issues of choice, virtue, and diversity, for he says that people do not "voluntarily choose the lower description of pleasures in preference to the higher. . . . It may be questioned whether any one who has remained equally susceptible to both classes of pleasures, ever knowingly and calmly preferred the lower" (*Utilitarianism*, 141). Not only is the selection of a lower pleasure evidence of one's unsuitability to judge utilitarian value; it also indicates a lack of freedom. In this, of course, Mill's formula systematically favors the educated, professional, and wealthier classes, for their range of experience will of necessity be larger than that of laborers and the poor. Moreover, they will have the resources to sustain their interest in the higher pleasures and prevent their "youthful enthusiasm for everything noble" from degenerating "as they advance in years . . . into indolence and selfishness" (141). This bias suggests a tacitly elitist structure to his apparently democratic utilitarian framework. Like Locke and Rousseau, Mill emphasizes individual choice and freedom as the absence of external obstacles, but he also is afraid of what people will choose without "guidance." His theory of utility tries to provide such guidance, but this guidance conflicts with the strong notion of individual liberty of conscience and thought that is generally attributed to Mill.

The tensions between *Utilitarianism* and *On Liberty* have been explored by a number of scholars, producing Himmelfarb's aforementioned "two Mills" thesis, as well as other claims that Mill takes simultaneously opposing positions: for socialism and for laissez-faire capitalism; for populism and elitism; for women's equality and full-time housewifery. In his *Autobiography*, Mill says about his apparent abandonment of Benthamism after his emotional breakdown, "If I am asked what system of political philosophy I substituted for that which, as a philosophy, I had abandoned, I answer, no system; only a conviction that the true system was something much more comprehensive than I had previously had any idea of."[39] About this passage, John Gray says, "it is this self-critical and open-minded eclecticism of Mill's thought which has led many commentators, exasperated by the systematic elusiveness of his standpoint on the great philosophical and social issues of his time, to despair of finding any coherent view in his writings." However, Gray notes, "the construction of an integrated and comprehensive philosophy was not one of Mill's major aspirations. . . . the tolerance of uncertainty, and reverence for diversity . . . is the distinctive feature of Mill's intellectual personality."[40] So the apparent tensions per se do not make Mill unintelligible or even wrong; he is complex, and aware of contrary forces existing simultaneously in the human experience.

Gray may sell Mill short, however. When we read the bulk of Mill's texts together, utility emerges as the core value, the element that gives his apparently noncohesive theory coherence. Liberty is important to Mill, to be sure; but its primary theoretical importance is as a *means to utility*. If the point of freedom is to achieve truth, and if truth is key to people's wanting the right things and making the right choices, then it would seem not only that freedom serves the end of utility, but that freedom is the paramount utilitarian value. But utility itself is the core of Mill's theory. Admittedly, there is some circularity to that claim: why would liberty be important to utility for Mill if he did not believe that humans had some fundamental, perhaps even natural desire for freedom? Why would liberty produce the greatest happiness if it were not at some level essential to humanity? Fair enough. Mill asserts that "after the primary necessities of food and raiment, freedom is the first and strongest want of human nature" (*Subjection*, 576). But the reverse is also true: why is liberty important if it does not make people happy, and thereby produce utility? Mill claims in *Utilitarianism* that all other moral systems that place other things at their heart as a priori principles are at least tacitly relying on utility, which is the "one fundamental principle or law, at the root of all morality" (133).

If liberty serves utility, then the case that Mill is a strict negative libertarian is much more difficult to sustain, and his view of freedom becomes more complicated and nuanced. In order to be free, according to Mill's utilitarianism, we must want the right things; but because we often want the wrong things, Mill has to figure out a way to safeguard our freedom of choice from those incorrect desires. His social constructivism permits him to see that the existing laws, practice, and institutions force people, particularly women and the poor, to make bad choices. What he seeks through his theory of utility, I maintain, is to change the structure by changing laws, social policies, and economic practices to *enable* people to make good choices. In this, he may come out better than the other theorists considered in the foregoing chapters, who often seemed to force these good choices on people. But this is not because Mill has a simple confidence that the human spirit will triumph. Indeed, his optimism about human nature, if provided with the right conditions, often conflicts with his strong pessimism about the potential of workers and the poor under current conditions. Rather, Mill has confidence in the possibility of changing conditions so that social structures will produce people in the right way. The trick, then, is to produce the right structures to ensure the best construction of humanity. In this project, it is often the case that Mill's elitism and paternalism get the better of him, and he too falls into the paradox of forcing the right choice onto people.

DEMOCRACY, CLASS, AND GENDER

The ambiguity I have just described is particularly evident in Mill's writings on gender, where the complexity of his theory of freedom is most obvious, the interaction of positive and negative liberty themes most apparent. The supremacy of utility over freedom is a prominent theme in the *Subjection*. Not only must women be granted equality and freedom in order to obtain their own happiness—which must be counted in the calculation of utility (576)—but men themselves will be better off, in at least two ways. In the first place, individual men will be better off by having more intelligent and better-educated wives. Mill claims that

> A man married to a woman his inferior in intelligence finds her a perpetual dead weight, or, worse than a dead weight, a drag, upon every aspiration of his to be better than public opinion requires him to be. It is hardly possible for one who is in these bonds, to attain exalted virtue. If he differs in his opinion from the mass—if he sees truths which have not yet dawned upon them, or if, feeling in his heart truths which they nominally recognize, he would like to act up to those truths more conscientiously than the generality of mankind—to all such thoughts and desires, marriage is the heaviest of all drawbacks, unless he be so fortunate as to have a wife as much above the common level as he himself is. (*Subjection*, 568–69)

This warning might seem to appeal only to "exceptional" men who belong to the "clerisy." But in fact all of society benefits from women's equality, because all will benefit from the emergence of genius. If uneducated women are "perpetual drags," educated wives can provide men with intelligent conversation and spur them on to continual improvement. Furthermore, such women will be able to create a new generation of thinking citizens by being better, more intelligent, and more fulfilled mothers who can educate their children to be similarly analytical and stimulating (560–61). The costs to society of uneducated women cannot be exaggerated, Mill says, for "If the wife does not push the husband forward, she always holds him back" (575).

Mill's vision of women's role in the family is an obvious advance over Rousseau's, who wanted women to be "educated" only in modesty and obedience, or Kant, who thought education for women was a waste of time. It also should be kept in mind that men's benefit is not Mill's *primary* reason for educating women. It is an *additional* reason, and a rhetorical tool to convince men—who, Mill believes, will resist such radical social change as educating women, opening the professions to them, and granting them suffrage—that such change is in their own interest. Such a strategy similarly leads Mill to point out that removing barriers to women's participation in the public sphere would also result in "doubling the mass of mental faculties available for the higher service of humanity" such as "a public teacher, or an administrator of some branch of public or social affairs" (*Subjection*, 561). Given the "deficiency of persons competent to do excellently anything which it requires any considerable amount of ability to do" (561), increasing the number of people who can run for political office, enter a profession such as medicine or law, or even apply for a factory job, will thereby improve the quality of politicians, doctors, lawyers, and workers. Increased competition would also stimulate the current available applicant pool—namely men—to improve themselves. Thus, women's freedom will increase overall social utility.

At the same time, increased competition will likely result in men's greater unemployment: "Whoever succeeds in an overcrowded profession, or in a competitive examination . . . reaps benefits from the loss of others." Certainly, it would be consistent with his theory of equal liberty to argue that if women are to exercise an equal right to the same liberties as men, then it is morally incumbent on men to give up some of the privileges that result from women's subservience. If mediocre men are employed because of unfair labor practices that keep women out, then they enjoy unequal freedoms at women's expense; equality requires that men give some of that freedom up. But instead he argues that men will be better off through increased competition, and that the relevant trade-off is not between women's liberty and men's liberty, but between liberty and "wasted exertion and . . . disappointment." The market allows all to compete freely. Such freedom entails costs. "But it is . . . better for the general interest of mankind, that persons should pursue their objects undeterred by this sort of consequences" (*Liberty*, 105).

It is thus utility, rather than freedom, that justifies women's right to participate in the labor market, for the increased competition that women add will produce the best overall effects for society. A displaced unemployed worker may be out of a job, but he is better off living in a society in which the best people hold the appropriate positions. And such utility is consistent only with women's increased negative freedom to compete in the marketplace and enter the professions. But in making this argument, Mill clearly values the overall situation of society at the expense of particular individual men: utility over liberty. After all, while these newly displaced male workers may in one sense benefit from living in a society that now has the best doctors, lawyers, and factory workers, they most likely will be worse off because they are out of work and hence unable to afford those doctors and lawyers, unable to vote if they are unemployed and financially dependent on parish relief, and therefore unable to enjoy the qualitatively improved working environment that superior (female) colleagues have now created.

Yet perhaps these men should not worry too much. For in the middle of his exhaustive argument for removing legal barriers to women's participation in the economy, and their right to compete in the marketplace and the professions, Mill almost offhandedly asserts that most women will not in fact enter the labor force but will choose the "career" of wife and mother. "Like a man when he chooses a profession, so, when a woman marries, it may in general be understood that she makes choice of the management of a household, and the bringing up of a family, as the first call upon her exertions" (*Subjection*, 523). Indeed, he goes beyond simply predicting that women will make this choice; he recommends it. "The common arrangement, by which the man earns the income and the wife superintends the domestic expenditure, seems to me in general the most suitable division of labour between the two persons. . . . In an otherwise just state of things, it is not . . . I think, a desirable custom, that the wife should contribute by her labour to the income of the family" (522). He specifically says this about families that depend on "earnings" rather than "property." But at the end of chapter 3, where he is explaining women's apparent inferiority "even in the pursuits which are open to both" sexes already, he cites women's responsibility for "superintendence of the family . . . [and] household" as an important reason, for it leaves them "no time" for other pursuits. Then in passing he says that families "so rich as to admit to delegating that task to hired agency" suffer for it, "submitting to all the waste and malversation inseparable from that mode of conducting it" (*Subjection*, 551). The implication of this seems to be that women of all classes should do their own housework. This obligation should last until age "forty or fifty" at which point a woman could then pursue other interests.

Though this latter comment often escapes notice, Mill's argument at the end of chapter 2 has been discussed by many feminists, and can be read in several ways. In a favorable light, he can be seen as anticipating contemporary feminist arguments for "equality through difference"; just because women are better at nurturing than men is no reason to treat them as inferior, nor does it make sense to prevent them from engaging in caretaking activities.[41] Furthermore, given how much work is involved in being a wife and mother, women's participation in the paid labor force would give them a "double day" that is extremely burdensome and in the interest of no one, man, woman, or child. In *Political Economy*, Mill identifies the sexual division of labor as the first instance of division of labor in production; and division of labor, presumably even within the household, makes everyone better off because it is the most efficient way to maximize wealth.[42] Thus, he talks as much in *Political Economy* about the relationship of women's household labor to productive labor as he does about women in industrial production itself, though the latter is something that he acknowledges as a reality of the economic landscape.

Yet even if labor should be divided, why should it be divided in this way? If Mill truly held "strong convictions on the complete equality" of women "in all legal, political, social, and domestic relations," as he claimed in his *Autobiography*, then why should women be exclusively responsible for household labor and child care while men seek common subsistence?[43] This is an objection raised by numerous feminists, who take it as evidence that Mill was not as much of a feminist as he might appear at first glance. Leslie Goldstein calls it "a major exception to his argument for equality of individual liberty between the sexes—an exception so enormous that it threatens to swallow up the entire argument." Mary Shanley argues that Mill's maintenance of the sexual division of labor undercuts his advocacy of marital friendship. Julia Annas calls Mill's assumption "that most women will in fact want only to be wives and mothers . . . timid and reformist at best." And Linda Zerilli claims that Mill shared with conservatives "the view that women would work in the market only out of economic necessity; that unpaid domestic labor was unlike and preferable to wage labor; and that it was natural for a wife to be dependent on her husband's wage."[44]

Mill's political economy arguments may provide some insight; for any other redistribution of labor, such as equal sharing between husbands and wives, would not necessarily have solved anything from an efficiency point of view. Running a household was considerably more time-consuming in Mill's day than it is in the twenty-first century, and splitting these tasks between husband and wife so as to allow wives the equal chance to work for wages would still provide for an exhausting day for both partners. As Okin points out, "primitive contraceptive techniques, a high rate of infant mortality," combined with "onerous household chores," made it "far harder for Mill than it is for us to conceive of the sharing of child rearing and domestic duties."[45] So perhaps Mill should not be taken to task for failing to envision an entire restructuring of the family and gender roles: medical science had not yet caught up with progressive social ideals. He argues that it is enough to end the subjection of women that they have the *ability*—the educational skills, the opportunities, and the legal rights—to earn their living. Such an ability provides women with power in their marriages by providing the threat of an "exit option" that can effectively forestall husbands' domination and abuse, a problem with which Mill was particularly concerned (*Subjection*, 523). Given the rigors of nineteenth-century housekeeping, perhaps this was the most woman-friendly position.

The less generous interpretation that other feminists make of the *Subjection*, however, has greater support in "Marriage and Divorce," where

Mill explicitly argues that married women should not work outside of the household for income. Though Mill notes that "women will never be what they should be, nor their social position what it should be, until women, as universally as men, have the power of gaining their own livelihood," from this "It does not follow that a woman should *actually* support herself because she should be *capable* of doing so: in the natural course of events she will *not*." Indeed, what counts as "gaining their own livelihood" is that "every girl's parents [should] have either provided her with independent means of subsistence, or given her an education qualifying her to provide those means for herself."[46] That is, even single women need not work for a living if their parents can afford to give or bequeath them property. But the real point is that he argues here, as he argued in the *Subjection*, that most women will choose to marry, and for most women such a choice entails the choice of a "career" as wife and mother. In "Marriage and Divorce" the reasons Mill offers in favor of this limitation pertain as much to economic utility as to the family per se: in apparent contradiction to what he later argued in *On Liberty*, he maintains here that "It is not desirable to burthen the labour market with a double number of competitors. In a healthy state of things, the husband would be able by his single exertions to earn all that is necessary for both: there would be no need that the wife should take part in the mere providing of what is required to *support* life."[47] Here, he clearly advocates against women's paid employment.

Why does Mill express this apparent contradiction? Could it have been a change of mind brought about by longer association with Harriet Taylor? Possibly. Mill did not think that she should be "merely" a housewife, either while she was married to John Taylor or after she became his own wife. Perhaps she was an exception, a member of the clerisy, for whom individual liberty was so important. In their extensive correspondence over the *Political Economy*, Mill tried to resist Taylor's suggestions for altering and even cutting his criticisms of communism from the first edition, but he ultimately conceded to many of them because "I never should long continue of an opinion different from yours on a subject which you have fully considered."[48] However, the question of married women's working is more uncertain. Alice Rossi declares that there is no contradiction, and that Mill consistently held "that a woman's goal would continue to be marriage to a man she loved," which was "a view . . . not moderated with the passage of time. . . . Thirty-seven years later [i.e., after "Marriage and Divorce," in the *Subjection*] Mill was still arguing that he saw no benefit to a wife's contributing to the income of the family."[49] Hayek further maintains that women's equality "was not one of the subjects on which he was mainly indebted to her for his ideas."[50] Gertrude Himmelfarb suggests that we "compare the several editions of *Political Economy* ([volume] I, 394) in respect to the crucial passage on the employment of women. In 1852 the weight of the argument was in favor of their employment; after 1862 (the first edition to appear after his wife's death) it was heavily against it." Though Himmelfarb's general point is supportable, her wording is not quite precise. According to Robson's notation about the passage to which she refers, the change made in 1862 was a minor one. Specifically, in book 2, chapter 14, Mill discusses the depressing effect on income when women work with their husbands, for "the earnings of the whole family" will generally be no more than the man would have earned if he were the sole provider. In 1852, Mill says that even in such a situation, "the advantage to the woman of not depending on a master for subsistence is more than an equivalent." In 1862, he says it "may be more than an equivalent," a more hesitant endorsement. In 1865, however, Mill added the following sentence: "It cannot, however, be considered desirable as a *permanent* element in the condition of a labouring class, that the mother of the family (the case of single women [changed to "a single woman" in 1871] is totally different) should be under the necessity of working for subsistence, at least elsewhere than in their place of abode." These changes should be taken to support the argument that the passage in question in chapter 2 of Mill's *Subjection*, written in 1861 and published in 1869, can readily be interpreted as not supporting married women's work outside the home, and that the views he expressed in "Marriage and Divorce" were not all that different from those found in the *Subjection* on this question.[51] I have already shown Mill's inconsistency in the *Subjection* itself. Thus, while competition, according to Mill, is good for society, producing the best-quality workers, the best-quality products, and the greatest degree of free choice, women, it seems, should not compete, or should be eliminated from the competitor pool de facto by the social conditions of marriage and motherhood.

More sentimental and idealistic arguments about the family are made in "Marriage and Divorce," and these pose even greater difficulties for those readers who seek to rationalize Mill's views on women's working. For Mill claims in that essay that "The great occupation of woman should be to *beautify* life: to cultivate, for her own sake and that of those who surround her, all her faculties of mind, soul, and body . . . and to diffuse beauty, elegance, and grace, everywhere. . . . it will be for the happiness of both that her occupation should rather be to adorn and beautify [life, rather than support life]. Except in the class of actual day-labourers, that will be her natural task, if task it can be called, which will in so great a measure be accomplished rather by *being* than by *doing*."[52] Even among women who work, "the only difference between the employments of women and those of men will be, that those which partake most of the beautiful, or which require delicacy and taste rather than muscular exertion, will naturally fall to the share of women: all branches of the fine arts in particular." Such a claim would, of course, seem to leave not only the wives of day-laborers but working-class women employed in factories out of the picture altogether; even their status as "women" is implicitly called into question, as Mill seems to universalize a romantic vision of femininity. More broadly, the feminist Mill here is beginning to sound like the misogynist Kant of *The Beautiful and the Sublime* discussed in the previous chapter: women have an antirationalist connection to sentiment and moral goodness.

Thus, for instance, despite the sexual division of labor where the wife runs the household, Mill indicates that it is absurd to claim that mothers should take responsibility for educating their children. One might think Mill would advocate the contrary, as did precursors like Mary Wollstonecraft, for the emphasis that Mill places on education is often linked to women's role as educators of children. In *On Liberty* he argues that public education is a prescription for mediocrity and conformism, and that fathers should be responsible for children's education, receiving fines if their children do not pass a national examination. One might assume that mothers would share this responsibility, as equal partners in marriage. Yet in "Marriage and Divorce" Mill maintains that mothers' educating children in each individual household would be an extremely inefficient use of resources. Given that Mill wants women to stay out of the labor market, and that he believes that household labor is not productive and does not contribute to wealth, it is unclear what resources mothers would use up.[53] However, he clearly maintains in this essay that children should be taught in schools, a position he later again emphasized in his St. Andrews "Inaugural Address."[54]

The exception is moral education, "the training of the affections," which mothers should teach only by example. "She effects it by being with the child; by making it happy, and therefore at peace with all things; by checking bad habits in the commencement and by loving the child and by making the child love her. It is not by particular effects, but imperceptibly and unconsciously that she makes her own character pass into the child."[55] Again, character is the linchpin of Mill's better society, but women contribute to the character of their children by being—and specifically, by being around—rather than doing, as Mill seems inexplicably to fall back on quasi-mystical claims about women reminiscent of those we have seen in Rousseau and Kant. Women become less than individuals; they become almost magical creatures with powers of moral phoresis.

That he expressed these ideas in an essay written in response to Taylor—"she to whom my life is devoted," as he says in its opening sentence, though this was written twenty years before their marriage—makes them even more noteworthy. Harriett Taylor asked in her companion essay,

"Would not the best plan be divorce which could be attained by any *without any reason assigned*, and at small expence but which could only be finally pronounced after a long period?" (thereby requiring a two-year waiting period before one could remarry). Indeed, Taylor is not particularly supportive of the institution of marriage: "when the whole community is really educated, though the present laws of marriage were to continue they would be perfectly disregarded, because no one would marry." Even better than a liberal divorce law, therefore, would be to abolish marriage altogether: put "women on the most entire equality with men, as to all rights and privileges, civil and political, and then [do] away with all laws whatever relating to marriage." Marriage would become, as some contemporary advocates suggest it should be, only a religious ceremony, not one endorsed or controlled by the state.[56]

By contrast, Mill does not seem favorably disposed to divorce. He worries that liberalizing divorce might simply allow people to choose badly, because the consequences of a bad choice would be remediable, rather than motivating them to choose wisely in the first place: "it is highly desirable changes should not be frequent, and desirable that the first choice should be, even if not compulsorily, yet very generally, persevered in: That consequently we ought to beware lest in giving facilities for retracting a bad choice, we hold out greater encouragement than at present for making such a choice as there will probably be occasion to retract." Yet he notes that many marriages are bad. Thus, the right to divorce should be legally guaranteed, primarily to provide women with a way to escape abusive marriages. Though in the past the "indissolubility of marriage" used to help women by giving them a hold on men, and thereby some control, he argues, now it works against them, keeping them in servitude, making them vulnerable to abuse of various kinds.[57]

He particularly blames the fact that people marry when they are too young to choose wisely, and is thus pessimistic about the ability of first marriages to be happy. He recommends that people wait until they are thirty to marry, suggesting that at that age they will make better spousal choices, and thus have more successful marriages, though he does not go so far as to recommend legal prohibitions. Again, we find Mill addresses both the principled conception of what he thinks should be the case—enduring marriages—and the pragmatic recognition of what is the case: namely, as long as women are virtually compelled to marry and forced by inadequate education into bad choices, then liberal divorce laws must exist to allow them to escape. By contrast, if women and men were truly equal, women would be free to wait for good choices, to the point of choosing not to marry at all. And if women were equal within marriage, with control over property, the right and ability to earn their own living if they needed to, then divorce would not need to be so accessible except in cases of abusive spousal behavior. Again, Mill concerns himself with the productive possibilities of legal and social change. On the one hand, liberalizing divorce laws could empower women and exert a controlling force over men's abuse of power. But at the other extreme, it could promote a casual and careless approach to marriage, thus further deepening what he sees as an already irresponsible attitude toward the institution. Of particular importance is the damage to children that frequent divorce and casual marriage would inflict.[58]

Thus, feminists who are deeply suspicious of Mill's feminist ideals have reason to doubt. But I think that the story is even more complicated; gender must be considered together with class to understand Mill's position. Contra Rossi, I believe Mill did want *some* women to work, and suggest that he resolved this apparent tension through the class distinction that underlies the *Subjection*. That is, perhaps it is not necessary to keep all women out of the labor market to avoid the economic costs of increasing the size of the labor pool; perhaps it is enough to keep working-class women out. When considering doctors, lawyers, or government leaders, it might be important to ensure that society has recruited the best possible persons, so permitting women to compete makes eminent sense: exceptional human beings could come in either gender. However, when considering unskilled positions, it makes less sense for women to compete with men, for women's participation in such labor does not increase any marginal utility. In fact, it could decrease utility for individual women who had to work a double shift at factory and at home. After all, the double day of which he indirectly speaks would be particularly relevant to working-class women; professional women could afford to hire other women to do the housework and child care, as he notes (disapprovingly) in both the *Subjection* (523) and "Marriage and Divorce."[59]

Thus, perhaps Mill is less concerned with enhancing choices for women per se than in protecting them from exploitation and abuse. He is not interested in figuring out how women can "have it all" but rather seeks to find a way for women to continue in the sexual division of labor under better conditions. This concern crosses class lines: though he almost resignedly acknowledges that wealthy women hire servants to do the work they should do themselves, he would prefer that wealthy women also stay at home, and do their own housework. I have already noted his remarks in the *Subjection* concerning the "waste and malversation" caused by the employment of domestic servants. Likewise, in "Marriage and Divorce" Mill says, "As for household superintendance [*sic*], if nothing be meant but merely seeing that servants do their duty, that is not an occupation; every woman that is capable of doing it at all can do it without devoting anything like half an hour every day to that purpose peculiarly. . . . But if it be meant that the mistress of a family shall herself do the work of servants, *that* is good." However, Mill recognizes that this "will naturally take place in the rank in which there do not exist the means of hiring servants; but nowhere else."[60] If wealthy women hire servants, he wants them to be able to take a profession or be socially useful in some other way. Like Locke before him, Mill is as intolerant of the idle rich as he is of the lazy poor; but Mill explicitly recognizes that wealthy women can be just as idle as their masculine counterparts. By contrast, Locke seemed to imply that women's supervising a household of servants was itself sufficient to establish their industry.

Class affects his views on domestic violence as well. In a series of articles for the *Morning Chronicle* that Mill coauthored with Harriet Taylor between 1846 and 1851, they note that most people, in all classes, are "impressed with the belief of their having a *right* to inflict almost any amount of corporal violence upon *their* wife or *their* children."[61] But it is particularly "the universal belief of the labouring class, that the law permits them to beat their wives—and the wives themselves share the general error."[62] Thus Mill and Taylor decry "the frightful brutality which marks a very large proportion of the poorest class, and no small portion of a class much above the poorest."[63] How much "above the poorest class" is, of course, unspecified. But in discussing the case of a woman who was sentenced to death for poisoning her abusive husband, Mill and Taylor note that men are routinely acquitted from murder of their wives, and ask, "Is it because juries are composed of husbands in a low rank of life, that men who kill their wives almost invariably escape—wives who kill their husbands, never?"[64] As this is the closing sentence of that letter, one assumes the answer is yes.

It is possible that this apparent focus on the abusive behavior of lower-class men is a function of the cases that Mill and Taylor are analyzing; they abhor all violence but these sensational cases happened to occur among lower-class individuals. Presumably, class power might enable upper-class men to stay out of the newspapers. But we must remember that even in the *Subjection* Mill lambasts the "thousands" of men "among the lowest classes in every country, who, without being in a legal sense malefactors in any other respect, because in every other quarter their aggressions meet with resistance, indulge the utmost habitual excesses of bodily violence towards the unhappy wife, who alone, at least of grown persons, can neither repel nor escape from their brutality." He implies that upper-class men, as tyrannical as they might be, are more inclined to benevolence, or at least chivalry, that forestalls violence; by contrast, for men "among the lowest classes in every country," women's "excess of dependence inspires their mean and savage natures, not with a generous forbearance, and a point of honour to behave well to one whose lot in life is trusted entirely to their kindness, but on the contrary with a notion that the law has delivered her to them as their thing, to be used at their pleasure, and that they are not expected to practise the consideration towards her which is required from them towards everybody else" (*Subjection*, 508).

Even so, Mill and Taylor did not fail to recognize domestic violence in upper-class marriages. Their critique of the legal enforcement of domestic assault law in fact suggests an unspoken alliance among men across class: men of the upper classes who control laws and legal practices that tacitly condone all men's right to discipline their wives, and lower-class juries that put that right into practice by excusing murdering husbands. If judges, for instance, were more classist than they were sexist, they would ensure that working-class men were punished for violence by allowing evidence that would prevent lower-class juries from acquitting abusive husbands. It is this tacit acceptance of male prerogative by those who should know better, Mill suggests, that is responsible for the widespread practice of wife abuse among the lower classes. Indeed, it is the irresponsibility of judges, lawyers, and other political leaders to which Mill attributes the attitudes of lower-class men.[65]

Thus, class considerations affect Mill's understanding of gender in complicated ways that many readers miss. An important though subtle theme in Mill's work is that only upper- and upper-middle-class women can really qualify for full "liberty of choice" and hence for "equality" with men. So when he says that the benefit of education for women lies in the fact that women would be "equally capable of understanding business, public affairs, and the higher matters of speculation, with men *in the same class of society*" (*Subjection*, 562, emphasis added), the fact that he does not think that working-class men are particularly capable suggests the same for working-class women. He thus rather offhandedly accepts class divisions and location as given even as he challenges gender stratification in some significant ways.

Mill's account would also seem to foreshorten the liberty of working-class women vis-à-vis wealthier women. But as Mill presents it, that is not a function of gender bias as much as the logical outcome of class-structured society: those on the bottom rungs always have fewer choices than those on the top, and this hierarchy of freedom is necessary to the sustenance of the overall greatest freedom for everyone, even the least well off, as Locke argued. For women on those lower rungs, the traditional sexual division of labor is not only efficient, Mill notes in *Political Economy*, but productive of the greatest overall utility. Thus, class may be as much a barrier to women's freedom as gender.

Yet Mill turns this relationship on its head, for he seems to think that economically privileged women are in many ways *more* restricted than women from the laboring classes: "Society makes the whole life of a woman, in the easy classes, a continued self-sacrifice; it exacts from her an unremitting restraint of the whole of her natural inclinations, and the sole return it makes to her for what often deserves the name of martyrdom, is consideration" (*Subjection*, 570). It is not clear what Mill means by this. Given his apparent beliefs that most people in the lower classes are lazy and unintelligent, whether by nature or by circumstance, one must assume that part of the sacrifice of women in the "easy classes" is that they have to give up more: for an unintelligent (lower-class) woman, cleaning a house may be a fine occupation, but for a woman of talent it would be a sacrifice. However, since Mill has urged all women to be full-time wives and mothers, explicitly in "Marriage and Divorce" and more ambiguously in the *Subjection* and *Political Economy*, the sacrifice is not made simply by doing housework per se; it is by virtue of subjecting themselves to their husbands in the current state of affairs that women sacrifice themselves.

But even this argument does not quite track Mill's commentary; after all, most women who are in the easy classes are there not because of their own abilities but rather because of the abilities of their fathers or husbands. If women are forbidden from working, then they cannot logically take credit for their economic luck. One could assume that girls and women in the upper classes are exposed to more literature and artistic influences, philosophical ideas and so forth, which would thereby stimulate their intellectual abilities, but that would contradict the very criticisms that he makes against women's subjection, namely, that they are not encouraged to develop their intellects and talents, which are thus wasted. Could it be that he measures what women in these classes *are* against what they *might be* in the absence of gender discrimination? That would allow him greater freedom in his argument, for he could conclude that a working-class woman will never amount to much, regardless of whether she works for wages or cooks for her husband, whereas gender is the only barrier to upper-class women's availing themselves of all of the educational and professional opportunities of which men in their class can avail themselves. Such an argument would be difficult to reconcile with his clear urging, in "Marriage and Divorce," that wealthy women do their own housework. But insofar as Mill maintains his contrapuntal balance between the ideal and the real—the legal provision of opportunities for women to succeed at whatever economic endeavor they wish, versus the practical reality that most women want to marry and have children—he can ignore the tensions that his arguments pose.

THE CLASS OF EDUCATION

When we consider Mill's views of gender, the negative libertarian Mill who emphasizes individuality, eccentricity, choice, and freedom of thought becomes seriously challenged. As I have already suggested and will discuss further in the present section, class may pose as profound a challenge to Mill. But both of these cohere with a more general elitism that undergirds Mill's theory. This elitism is a function of his belief that his contemporaries are living in "an age of transition." In a series of essays written for the *Examiner* titled "The Spirit of the Age," Mill says that in most periods of history, there is an elite who can "dedicate themselves to the investigation and study of physical, moral, and social truths, as their peculiar calling" by whom others should, and normally do, let themselves be guided.[66] However, "In an age of transition, the divisions among the instructed nullify their authority, and the uninstructed lose their faith in them." As a result, "the multitude are without a guide; and society is exposed to all the errors and dangers which are to be expected when persons who have never studied any branch of knowledge comprehensively and as a whole attempt to judge for themselves upon particular parts of it." This reliance on private judgment is disastrous for social progress; "men who place implicit faith in their own common sense are . . . the most wrong-headed and impracticable persons." One must not follow the guidance of people who cannot see, but leading yourself when you cannot see is no better. Yet "in an age of transition . . . the exercise of private judgment" is the only resource people have.[67]

If Mill believes that private judgment is so unreliable, then why should he advocate freedom of thought? If lack of agreement among the elite is the problem, would not the ideals of discussion and intellectual exchange exacerbate that? To answer those questions, we must understand that the age of transition is not a result simply of disagreement; the transition is not a function of ideas per se. Rather, disagreement among the learned and leaders is a function of the fact that the *world* is changing. Economic, social, and political relationships are in material transition, and it is up to the superior members of society to figure out the new truths that apply to this new world as it emerges. Thus, Hamburger argues that freedom of thought would loosen the grip of formalized religion on morality, so that intellectuals—all of whom should by rights be atheists, or at least agnostics—could pursue a true morality based on the good of humanity rather than arbitrary religious dictates. The key, according to Hamburger, was to create circumstances that would allow the superior to develop new ideas. That required Mill to advocate a strong philosophy of individual liberty. As he notes in *On Liberty*, "Genius can only breathe freely in an *atmosphere* of freedom. Persons of genius are, *ex vi termini, more* individual than any other people—less capable, consequently, of fitting themselves, without hurtful compression, into any of the small number of moulds which society provides in order to save its members the trouble of forming their own character. . . . I insist thus emphatically on the importance of genius, and the necessity of allowing it to unfold itself freely both in thought and in practice" (72). If people of genius are "more indi-vidual," then average men and women must be less so, and ignorant la-borers even less. Thus, freedom of thought was aimed at the mentally superior, not the masses. Though affording such freedom to the latter might allow some to emerge from the pack with fresh ideas, the majority primarily needed to be prevented from hamstringing their superiors.

The fact that Mill zeroes in on "the tyranny of the majority" so early in *On Liberty* indicates that it is the true focus of the essay. Mill com-plains of "the tendency of society to impose, by other means than civil penalties, its own ideas and practices as rules of conduct on those who dissent from them; to fetter the development, and, if possible, prevent the formation, of any individuality not in harmony with its ways, and compel all characters to fashion themselves upon the model of its own" (9). He seems less concerned with the restrictions on freedom imposed by law than with how individuals have to battle common opinion in order to achieve their individuality. For "The majority have not yet learnt to feel the power of the government their power, or its opinions their opinions. When they do so, individual liberty will probably be as much exposed to invasion from the government, as it already is from public opinion" (13). Thus, "diversity [is] not an evil, but a good, *until mankind are much more capable than at present of recognizing all sides of the truth*" (63, emphasis added). When they are so capable, this pas-sage implies, diversity might not be so welcome.

So for Mill, individualism was not really about all individual prefer-ences per se, because many of those preferences were the product of un-thinking conformity. Rather, the ideology of individualism was the mecha-nism by which leaders could be developed who could help show the way for the masses to achieve truth and a better society, "a transformation of moral values and social institutions."[68] For the rest of the people, the challenge was how to turn them into beings who could recognize superior-ity of wisdom and choose to follow it, thereby adhering to duty and think-ing of the good of the society rather than selfish interest. This was key, for "No government . . . ever did or could rise above mediocrity, except in so far as the sovereign Many have let themselves be guided . . . by the counsels and influence of a more highly gifted and instructed One or Few" (*Liberty*, 74). In an age of transition, this is less likely to happen, so Mill must serve as midwife to the new age of truth that should emerge next.

Developing character is the way to ensure that people defer to their superiors and make the right choices, enhancing qualitatively superior utility and therefore freedom. A goal of Mill's *System of Logic* was to develop an "Ethology, or the Science of Character"; but as Hamburger notes, in *On Liberty* as well as other writings, "Mill provided more de-tailed and concrete accounts of how to promote wholesome and how to prevent depraved qualities of character."[69] It was not simply the more intelligent who should serve as guides, however; it was those who had superior character as defined by "the religion of humanity." An idea that Mill got from Comte, the religion of humanity "held up duty as an ideal and sought to fundamentally change motives and habits to generate widespread altruism. . . . The goal was to discourage selfishness by making private motives coincide with the public good. . . . ethology . . . would form the desires so that those which were selfish would be diminished and those which were altruistic would become predominant."[70]

As was the case for other theorists considered here, education is an important strategy for reconciling this apparent tension between making your own choice and making the right choice; or more specifically, making the right choice your own. Education should produce better-thinking citizens who are less likely to consider solely themselves and their immediate short-term interests and pleasures, more likely to approach the truth, and thus to want the right things and make the right choices. Though Mill never wrote a general treatise on education as Locke, Rousseau, and Kant did, several of his essays reveal a theory of education that echoes these other theorists in important ways. Indeed, his *Autobiography* is revealing, for Mill's own childhood education was extremely intense. Tutored at home by his father, he learned Greek, Latin, and mathematics at a very young age. He also had a nervous breakdown at sixteen, but this apparently did not shake his faith in extraordinary education. Rather, he believed that his father had left out an essential aspect of education, namely, sentiment.[71] Mill saw his own education as nothing remarkable, nor a result of any particular talents or intelligence on his part: "what I could do, could assuredly be done by any boy or girl of average capacity and healthy physical constitution." Rather, the credit was to go to the time and attention his father took to bestow this education on him. Hence, an important point in Mill's *Autobiography* was to show "how much more than is commonly supposed" can be achieved through a more demanding education.[72]

But as Collini suggests, the *Autobiography* "reads more like Rousseau's *Emile* than his *Confessions*" because of the attention that Mill pays to education's role in the development of character.[73] In his inaugural address to St. Andrews University, Mill defines education extremely broadly as "whatever helps to shape the human being, to make the individual what he is, or hinder him from being what he is not."[74] Given Mill's problematization of the concept of "nature," which I discussed earlier, what an individual is and what she is not might seem to be up for grabs; but this passage implies that education helps us realize our "true potential," whatever that might be. Furthermore, what I am may be something that is not good: perhaps I am a natural-born safe cracker, because of a particular sensitivity in my fingertips. Yet that is hardly a talent that Mill would want me to develop. So Mill is saying that a proper education ought to make us what we *should* be, namely, people who will prefer the higher pleasures, eschew mediocrity and conformity, seek the truth, and become "effective combatants in the great fight which never ceases to rage between Good and Evil."[75] But if education includes many aspects of experience, then the construction of character would seem to take place in those many aspects as well, and not merely through formal academic learning; education would be part of a larger process of social construction, rather than the indoctrination that it sometimes seems for Rousseau and Locke. Although in *On Liberty* and the *Subjection*, as well as "The Negro Question," Mill often views the social construction of desire and identity as a negative force, a result of oppression that squeezes out hope of accomplishment or elevation, his views on education consistently suggest a more positive construction of individuals. Garforth maintains that Mill's "associationism," which he inherited from his father—the notion that ideas come from sensory experience, and ideas that persist must come from repeated experiences—meant that he favored nurture over nature in his understanding of education and human identity.[76] As Mill says about women, what is "natural" is difficult to discern given the powerful constructing forces of poorly organized and run social institutions (like schools), not to mention the frequently mind-deadening requirements of industrial labor.

Much like Rousseau, Mill holds that what is "natural" to humans is both good and bad, and education must encourage the development of the former and the atrophy of the latter. His method of education, like Locke's, therefore involves the formation of the right habits, for as Garforth notes, "repetition . . . is essential to the formation of associations."[77] Mill asserts in his inaugural address to St. Andrews that the end product of education should be free-thinking citizens, rather than minds "hopelessly filled full with other people's conclusions," and the university should be "a place of free speculation." Despite these assertions, however, Mill's prescription for what should be taught in universities, as well as in the common schools, is quite rigorous and demanding, and the outcome of such free thinking should be fairly consistent agreement on ethical and political issues. Disagreement should occur only within reasonable parameters.[78] If education was key to creating the essential characteristics of a self-governing people, namely, the ability to engage in reasoned discourse to the end of discovering truth, then those people needed to be properly equipped. As Cowling maintains, when Mill claims that "the proper business of an university" is to provide "information and training," he says this "with a view to forming men's beliefs about the right way to infuse the right content into their moral principles."[79]

At the same time, however, this may be the point of education only for some people, and this is where gender and class make particular entry. In *Political Economy* Mill notes that "the aim of all intellectual training for the mass of the people" is only "to cultivate common sense; to qualify them for forming a sound practical judgment of the circumstances by which they are surrounded. Whatever, in the intellectual department, can be superadded to this, is chiefly ornamental" (375). Such an education might help workers be productive, but it does not sound like the kind of education that Mill advocates in his "Inaugural" as necessary for a vibrant democracy. There may be little point in giving workers a more elaborate education, in Mill's view. In an essay written for the *Morning Chronicle*, some twenty years before the "Inaugural," Mill suggests that a "day labourer who earns his wages by mere obedience to orders may become a good artificer in his particular manual operation, but his mind stagnates. He is not paid for thinking and contriving but for executing,"[80] and so a nonthinking automaton is what society gets. Educating workers per se is not the answer, however; in an echo of Locke's *Conduct*, Mill implies that it would be rather beside the point. This was not because he thought that workers were innately unintelligent, but rather because of the conditions in which they lived:

> I go, perhaps, still further than most of those to whose language I so strongly object, in the expectations which I entertain of vast improvements in the social condition of man, from the growth of intelligence among the body of the people; and I yield to no one in the degree of intelligence of which I believe them to be capable. But I do not believe that, along with this intelligence, they will ever have sufficient opportunities of study and experience, to become themselves familiarly conversant with all the inquiries which lead to the truths by which it is good that they should regulate their conduct. . . . the great majority of mankind will need the far greater part of their time and exertions for procuring their daily bread.[81]

As Locke argued in *Of the Conduct of the Understanding*, the limit on education for laborers was time and resources, not innate capacity. In contrast to Locke's "working schools," however, Mill advocated national education, so that workers would achieve enough education to decide intelligently how to vote, to increase productivity, and to think about the common good. This was not an overt hierarchical philosophy, as I suggested Locke's was. Like Locke, however, Mill thought that the point of education was not just to teach academic subjects per se, but rather to develop morals and character; indeed, he thought the former was likely to aid the latter. For Mill, education serves "the purpose . . . of altering the habits of the labouring people," and so it therefore must be "directed simultaneously upon their intelligence and their poverty." And because the habits that they display are easier to change if they can be disrupted when young, "effective national education of the children of the labouring class, is the first thing needful" (*PE*, 374). Hamburger notes that "the term 'education,' associated with cognition and schooling, fails to capture his deeper and more important goal—to shape moral feelings and beliefs." Thus, education required a "'restraining discipline' which would create the habit of subordinating personal impulses and aims to what were considered the ends of society."[82]

As such comments suggest, the place of class in Mill's conception of education is significant. Just as in the *Logic*, where Mill's circular views of character indicate that the desire to improve oneself will only occur to individuals who already appreciate the value of "better" characters, so in *Political Economy* Mill says, "Education is not compatible with extreme poverty . . . it is difficult to make those feel the value of comfort who have never enjoyed it, or those appreciate the wretchedness of a precarious subsistence, who have been made reckless by always living from hand to mouth" (375). That is, the poor will not really be able to benefit from education until poverty is ended, yet education is key to ending poverty. In Mill's view, however, the circularity lies not in his argument, but in the circumstances that motivate his argument. The trick is to figure out ways to reduce poverty *while* educating children, to provide them with alternative ways of seeing themselves than their experience at home teaches them. As long as the experience of poverty at home persists, however, it is doubtlessly stronger than the self-image they might learn in school; so the vicious circle can be broken only by "extinguish[ing] extreme poverty for one whole generation" (374) all at once.

One way to do that is through emigration: "a grant of public money, sufficient to remove at once, and establish in the colonies, a considerable fraction of the youthful agricultural population" (*PE*, 376). This would benefit the poor who emigrated, because there would be greater opportunity for them, but it would also help those who remained, because the supply of labor would decrease. Mill sees overpopulation as the primary cause of poverty: too many workers competing for too few jobs drive down wages. Emigration would reduce the population of the poor in England in one fell swoop, thus increasing wages and reducing poverty levels across the board. This puts the pieces in place for a population, both at home and abroad, more receptive to education, which should thereby be more effective.

But given the logistical difficulties of such a massive effort (not to mention the likelihood that the most highly motivated poor would seek to emigrate, leaving behind the laziest and least industrious),[83] Mill turns his attention more directly to control of reproduction. "Poverty, like most social evils, exists because men follow their brute instincts without due consideration," reproducing at will without regard to whether they can support their children, much less considering the long-term effects of too many workers on the economy (*PE*, 367–68). Unregulated sexual reproduction among the poor and laboring classes is both a moral problem and a political economy one. Mill compares someone who "has a large family and is unable to maintain them" to "a man who is intemperate in drink." The latter "is discountenanced and despised by all who profess to be moral people," yet the former is seen as justified in asking for charity (368). This sort of illogical reasoning is morally wrong, Mill claims, and destructive to society. Thus, "if a man cannot support even himself unless others help him, those others are entitled to say that they do not also undertake the support of any offspring which it is physically possible for him to summon into the world" (358).

Mill claims that if this opinion gained popularity, then "the respectable and well-conducted" of the laboring classes "would conform to the prescription, and only those would exempt themselves from it, who were in the habit of making light of social obligations generally" (*PE*, 372). In other words, Mill here says that public opinion could be a useful tool, in contrast to his disparagement of public opinion in *On Liberty*. But if the crux of his argument is that poverty itself exacerbates the tendencies toward corrupt dissolution, one might be rather dubious about the success of public opinion; the very characteristics that make the change in attitudes about reproduction necessary are the very same features that would make it extremely difficult to instill. That may be why he supported public policies controlling reproduction. "Society can feed the necessitous, if it takes their multiplication under its control; or (if destitute of all moral feeling for the wretched offspring) it can leave the last to their discretion, abandoning the first to their own care. But it cannot with impunity take the feeding upon itself, and leave the multiplying free" (359). Mill thus approved of "Restrictions on marriage, at least equivalent to those existing in some of the German states, or severe penalties on those who have children when unable to support them" (359). More strongly, Mill says that "It would be possible for the state to guarantee employment at ample wages to all who are born. But if it does this, it is bound in self-protection, and for the sake of every purpose for which government exists, to provide that no person shall be born without its consent" (358–59). Similarly, in *On Liberty*, Mill argued that "the laws which, in many countries on the Continent, forbid marriage unless the parties can show that they have the means of supporting a family, do not exceed the legitimate powers of the State" (120).

Given these views, it makes sense that Mill was a strong supporter of the Poor Law of 1834, which sent the able-bodied poor to the workhouse, where they were "stigmatized by loss of civil rights and strongly discouraged from procreation," in contrast to the disabled, who received "outdoor relief," that is, cash assistance or food, and were not stigmatized.[84] The trope of the "deserving" and "undeserving" poor thus took a particular form for Mill: desert was not a function solely of how one became poor (whether through laziness, disability, or fraud) but also of one's ability to labor to raise oneself out of poverty. Labor was key to improving character. Accordingly, Mill's reform efforts provided for more "indoor" relief, because it would ensure that the able-bodied would work, whereas "parish allowances" end up "subsidizing him [the laborer] in a mode which tends to make him careless and idle" (PE, 358). Outdoor relief also produced the opposite result of its intent; that is, it motivated the energetic and industrious poor to emigrate, where their industry would be better rewarded, and provided the lazy with a reason not to emigrate. "So long as the poor-rate is available to him, he will accept of nothing which is only to be obtained by real work."[85]

For most twenty-first-century liberals, such views, particularly of reproduction, smack of the worst kind of paternalism, completely inhibitive of personal liberty. Indeed, these views might make Mill sound like a late-twentieth-century neoconservative; for like them, Mill believed that the poor were encouraged to be irresponsible by misguided public and economic policy.[86] Mill in fact excoriates those who advocate reproduction as a fundamental right, who "see hardship in preventing paupers from breeding hereditary paupers in the workhouse itself. Posterity will one day ask with astonishment, what sort of people it could be among whom such preachers could find proselytes" (PE, 358). For such attitudes implicitly accepted "the base doctrine, that God has decreed there shall always be poor" (369). Mill instead believed that poverty could be ended if the poor could be reconstructed to make the right choices. Echoing his particular take on free will and determinism, he argues that even if poverty is a response to humans' "brute instincts," humans are not determined by those instincts; "society is possible, precisely because man is not necessarily a brute. Civilization in every one of its aspects is a struggle against the animal instincts" (367). Hence, Mill claimed that support of reproductive freedom for the poor involved "misplaced notions of liberty," for true liberty required not just doing what one wants, but recognizing what one should want and what is in one's long-term interest, which poverty often prevents one from seeing. Even though the circumstances of poverty create bad characters that result in bad choices that perpetuate poverty, it is possible to change the character of the poor and the choices they make. Accomplishing this, however, clearly requires the government to create better public policy as well as to oversee and administer poor relief more effectively. Private charity might enable people to survive poverty, but would not end it, in part because the charitable wealthy took a fatalistic attitude about the poor, needed to feel superior to them, and had an interest, though generally unrecognized, in perpetuating poverty precisely to sustain those feelings of superiority. Moreover, the toughness that was required of an efficient poverty policy was not in keeping with the presumed sentiments of charity.

The "positive liberty" implications of Mill's views of poverty are thus obvious, for he holds up the "true interests" of the poor, which they themselves cannot see, as the measure of their freedom. But there is a different "negative liberty" angle to Mill's argument that is often unnoticed by his interpreters, which is that the "individual" Mill is thinking about is not just the reproductive adult, but the resulting children who will likely live in illness and hunger. Certainly starvation is not a happy condition to be born into, and Mill's criticism of selfish and thoughtless parents is less a rejection of their freedom than a plea that children be born into conditions that will enable them to realize their own freedom to pursue "their own good, in their own way." On this reading, parents would be included in those with "distinct and assignable duties," like the police officer, for whom the bar of individual liberty is raised. The damage that irresponsible or careless parents will do to their children is, like that done by the drunk policeman, a "definite risk" and therefore subject to greater limitation:

> The existing generation is master both of the training and the entire circumstances of the generation to come; it cannot indeed make them perfectly wise and good, because it is itself so lamentably deficient in goodness and wisdom; and its best efforts are not always, in individual cases, its most successful ones; but it is perfectly well able to make the rising generation, as a whole, as good as, and a little better than, itself. If society lets any considerable number of its members grow up mere children, incapable of being acted on by rational consideration of distant motives, society has itself to blame for the consequences. (*Liberty*, 91)

Advocacy of mandatory education is the logical outcome of such a belief in social responsibility for children, but putting restrictions on parents is even precedent to that. Control of reproductive behavior among people who cannot afford to raise children, thus, is one of the kinds of behavior that "may be legitimately controlled," much like restricting the sale of poisons (*Liberty*, 106).

Of course, children are not the only ones whose liberty Mill is thinking of in recommending limitations on reproduction. This longtime advocate of birth control is also speaking about the women who are forced to give birth. In fact, shortly after criticizing "those [i.e., not just "men"] who have children when unable to support them," Mill notes that "It is seldom by the choice of the wife that families are too numerous; on her devolves (along with all the physical suffering and at least a full share of the privations) the whole of the intolerable domestic drudgery resulting from the excess. To be relieved from it would be hailed as a blessing by multitudes of women who now never venture to urge such a claim, but who would urge it, if supported by the moral feelings of the community" (*PE*, 372). Indeed, Mill goes so far as to say that "there would be no need . . . of legal sanctions" against reproduction if women were granted equality. "Let them cease to be confined by custom to one physical function as their means of living and their source of influence, and they would have for the first time an equal voice with men in what concerns that function" (372–73).

Why Mill thinks that it is so self-evident to women is not explained; after all, if the poor are unable to appreciate "the value of comfort" because they "have never enjoyed it," would not poor women suffer from that inability as well? Why would it not be equally difficult for women to enjoy the value of liberty, or economic independence, or control over their fertility, if they have never enjoyed it? Mill seems to believe that the solution to poverty must lie in the poor themselves, whereas the solution to women's subordination must lie in men. Women are victims of others' bad behavior; the poor are victims of their own bad behavior. That leaves poor women in an oddly ambiguous position, but it highlights a key distinction. To end the subjection of women Mill does not propose the kind of drastic action he suggests for ending poverty, such as colonial deportation, because for him class is naturalized, whereas gender is socially constructed. Thus, changing laws will produce social change in gender relations much more easily and readily than it will in class relations.

But that only makes the legal equality of women that much more important, for on Mill's account the liberation of women will result in the liberation of the working class; that is, women's legal independence is likely to result in reduced population, and thereby improve conditions for workers. Women's negative liberty—their freedom to control their bodies by limiting their pregnancies, their freedom to work for a living and thereby delay marriage—is crucial to ending poverty. But so is their positive liberty—their ability to desire these things, to exert self-control and to trade short-term for long-term desires—as gender and class are intertwined. Women, Mill sees, are uniquely situated to make the right choice their own choice. That is, whereas working-class and poor men have little reason to recognize the seriousness of their plight as long as they have money to buy beer, the immediate self-interest women have in reducing their childbearing coincides with the longer-term economic interests of the family and of society. It is both the ability to see this coincidence and the power to enact it that animate the need for women's equality.[87]

Class and gender also overlap on the issue of education. The ineducability of the poor suggests that employed laborers may have at least a compromised educability; and this also raises questions about that of women. Insofar as education is key to women's equality, Mill's differentiation of women by class, where only women of the upper classes will likely be working, raises the question whether it really makes sense to educate women who will not use their learning. For if the ineducability of workers and the poor is not a function of natural intelligence, but of the situation of poverty, how is most women's situation any different? As Betty Friedan was to argue a century later, housework and child rearing do not make serious demands on the intellect;[88] and if Mill's argument against married women's paid work hinges on the argument that it will overburden them, the implication is that they will have no more time or energy to devote to intellectual pursuits than will their working-class husbands.

As I have shown, in some places Mill suggests that the market should determine women's labor-force participation, and of course the market cannot work if all women do not have a basic education. In other places, however, he clearly indicates that women should not enter the market at all. There is, of course, the "fail safe" argument that he offers in "Marriage and Divorce," that even if wives should not work, they should be able to do so in case they need to exit from marriage. But it seems like a rather inefficient use of social resources, at odds with utilitarianism, to educate all women when only a small minority will need such benefits. Mill does make the utilitarian argument, as I have noted, that educated women will be better mothers, and better wives who can help their husbands to be better individuals, though as I have noted, he does not think mothers should educate their own children. So the question of what purpose women's education would serve is a logical one. Just as Mill seems to differentiate between the kind of education that the elite should receive and the kind that the average worker needs, he must differentiate among women of different classes as well. Gender equality would seem to be not a universal or absolute, but regulated by class.

POLITICS, PARTICIPATION, AND POWER

A more persuasive ground on which Mill can consistently advocate for universal women's education is in his arguments for women's suffrage. Education is key to helping women of all classes, whether doctor, worker, or wife, form intelligent opinions about political matters and judge the character of their elected representatives, just as it is for men. Educated women, like educated men, would be better voters. Accordingly, Mill advised certain minimal educational requirements for voters, which included basic literacy and mathematics. As poor as he believed the public education system to be, he thought it at least guaranteed the availability of this rudimentary level of knowledge. But education was not merely an "input" to politics; it also was an "outcome." That is, given Mill's broad definition of education, and his class-divided vision of education's purpose, schools are not necessarily the primary locale for learning and forming appropriate political opinions. Indeed, politics, law, and government themselves are key educative tools, at least as Mill would like to construct them. Hence, Mill's theory of representative government advocates universal suffrage, based in part on the premise that people with a vote will have a stake in thinking through the issues they are voting on. Whatever Mill's despair over the ability of people to learn how to think critically, to change their habits so as to conform to virtuous or rational behavior, he clearly thinks that self-interest is an important motivator. The trick is to structure social organizations to help individuals recognize that their self-interest can be pursued through the political process. He believes that giving people a stake in the outcome of elections, and thereby of government more broadly, will stimulate them to pay attention to politics and try to make better choices.

A parallel line of thought leads Mill to criticize current modes of capitalist industrial production and urge instead the institution of cooperative ownership of industry. He advocates "placing the labourers, as a mass, in a relation to their work which would make it their principle and their interest—at present it is neither—to do the utmost, instead of the least possible, in exchange for their remuneration." Doing so would increase productivity, but that "is as nothing compared with the moral revolution in society that would accompany it" to improve society as a whole. Not only would cooperative ownership effect "the transformation of human life, from a conflict of classes struggling for opposite interests, to a friendly rivalry in the pursuit of a good common to all"; it would also "produc[e] a degree of intelligence, independence, and moral elevation, which raise the condition and character of" laborers "far above" their current level (PE, 792, 770).

The idea of cooperative ownership of industry is not often considered in the context of Mill's views on voting, but they bear particular relevance when we consider Mill's most radically democratic proposal, for universal suffrage and political participation. Mill urged suffrage for all adults, male and female, worker and professional, rich and poor. Or at least, he did so for all but the poorest; those on parish relief or in excessive debt should not be granted the franchise, for those who pay no taxes should not be entitled to have a say in how tax dollars are spent (Government,

331–32). But Mill supported suffrage for everyone else because he strongly endorsed the idea of equal power: "This is no justification for making the less educated the slave, or serf, or mere dependent of the other. The subjection of any one individual or class to another, is always and necessarily disastrous in its effects on both." Owing to the existing class hierarchy, however, "in the present state of society, and under representative institutions, there is no mode of imposing this necessity on the ruling classes, as towards all other persons in the community, except by giving to every one a vote."[89] Universal suffrage, that is, would equalize power and put a leash on political and social leaders.

This might seem to run contrary to Mill's argument in "The Spirit of the Age," particularly when we acknowledge that he also feared that mass suffrage would inevitably result in domination by the "special interests" of the laboring masses, who were unlikely to vote for their long-term interests and the common good. This was the double-edged sword of self-interest; it could motivate people to participate in politics, but such paticipation could run contrary to the political welfare of the people. As Cowling notes, "The clerisy may indoctrinate through education: elevated minds may infuse elevated sentiments. But infusion of principles does not ensure control of consequences. . . . the superiority of superior minds is not always accepted without questioning."[90] Mill thus needed a safeguard. Just as cooperative ownership does not mean that every decision is made by consensus, because certain people have greater experience, wisdom, and expertise in making the decisions that will maximize productivity (PE, 795), so Mill sought to give wisdom an advantage over populism in the democratic state by proposing a system of plural voting. Everyone must have one vote, but those who can and will put the common good ahead of their individual interests should have more than one vote. Universal suffrage, like cooperative ownership, gives everyone a stake in the laws, policies, and decisions made by a government; but because many people are likely not to make the best choices, the wise and expert must have greater input and sway.

In industry, of course, leadership positions are likely to attach to financial investment: all workers may be part owners in Mill's ideal enterprise, but not equal owners, and the class divisions within the workplace are likely to be sustained. After all, as Mill says in his critique of socialism, if there is no incentive to better yourself by aspiring to a position of greater power or wealth, then productivity will suffer. Competition is a natural process by which leaders will emerge.[91] But in the democratic state, how plural voters are to be chosen is a bit less clear cut. In keeping with his belief that education will produce better thinking citizens who are more likely to approach the truth because they are less likely to think solely of themselves, Mill ideally envisions a state-administered examination system to ensure that the most intelligent will receive the privilege of plural voting. So in theory, all citizens would have equal opportunity to attain the privilege and responsibility of plural voting. But Mill the pragmatist also recognized that the educational system at the time was inadequate, so in the meantime he advocated giving extra votes to those in the professions. Mill rejected money as the basis for superior political position, particularly inherited money, as it says nothing about the merits of the current holder. Further, Mill worried that inherited wealth would often produce moral dissolution, because those who do not work become lazy and self-indulgent (*Government*, 335). This was particularly problematic in Mill's era. In his essay "Perfectibility," he observes with dismay that superior intellect is no longer the object of public esteem; rather, wealth is.[92] He wishes to reverse that trend, for "the only thing which can justify reckoning one person's opinion as equivalent to more than one, is individual mental superiority." But wealth is not entirely irrelevant if it is the result of earnings: so he suggests that "the nature of a person's occupation is some test" (*Government*, 336). People in the professions, such as doctors and lawyers, or people who have succeeded in business, have already been tested by the process of competition in the marketplace. Many of them have also received a more complete education than the average worker. So, Mill believes, such people are in a better position to assess the common good. In his essay on "Parliamentary Reform," Mill spelled out the connection between profession, education, and voting more explicitly:

> If every ordinary unskilled labourer had one vote, a skilled labourer, whose occupation requires an exercised mind and a knowledge of some of the laws of external nature, ought to have two. A foreman, or superintendent of labour, whose occupation requires something more of general culture, and some moral as well as intellectual qualities, should perhaps have three. A farmer, manufacturer, or trader, who requires a still larger range of ideas and knowledge, and the power of guiding and attending to a great number of various operations at once, should have three or four. A member of any profession requiring a long, accurate, and systematic mental cultivation,—a lawyer, a physician or surgeon, a clergyman of any denomination, a literary man, an artist, a public functionary (or, at all events, a member of every intellectual profession at the threshold of which there is a satisfactory examination test) ought to have five or six. A graduate of any university, or a person freely elected a member of any learned society, is entitled to at least as many.[93]

The distinctions in Mill's account here exceed those he outlines in *Representative Government*, and create a hierarchy of gradations, from lawyer down to unskilled laborer. But the idea in both proposals is the same: if mental superiority is the foundation for plural votes, then profession is a marker of such superiority. Mill may be conflating education with intelligence, because he thinks that anyone could get the education he had; as we have seen, Mill did not think that he was special, but only the product of education and application. This ties to a further assumption that success in economic endeavors, or holding a job that pays more or has more responsibility, is proof that you must be smarter than the people who work under you. Finally, he assumes that intelligence leads people to think in terms of the common good. But these assumptions work from his more general argument that having a vote, like cooperative ownership of industry, gives people a stake in the outcome and hence motivation to think harder about their choices. Presumably, workers who are cooperative owners of the business in which they work are also capitalists and managers of a sort, and they will participate in management decisions and production policies. So, again presumably, this greater involvement in their workplace, as opposed to simply earning a wage, would better position them to be included among the plural voters.

But despite the concern for political equality that lies behind universal suffrage, Mill's idea still obviously depends on a hierarchy. If everyone, or even a majority, had the same number of multiple votes, there would be little point in the practice. If education levels rise in the general population, that is certainly good for democracy as well as production, but it does not eliminate a hierarchy of talent and intelligence in Mill's view. At any rate, because cooperative ownership was even more distant a possibility than national education was in Mill's day, his linkage between working, professional status, intelligence, and moral character leads him to assume that doctors, lawyers, and business leaders are not just more capable of discerning the truth, but morally superior as well, less inclined to think of self-interest and more inclined to think of the public good than are average workers. After all, even if cooperative ownership would give workers more of a stake in the outcome of their particular business, they could still be short-sighted about the relation of their business to the larger political economy. Because the short-sighted, self-interested masses will constitute a majority, and the superior public-minded people a minority, the latter must be given an advantage in the policy-determining process, which having plural votes does. The class elitism—not to mention naïveté—that such a scheme betrays is consistent with what I have already argued about Mill's work.

Mill's scheme shows that he resolves the tension between one's own choice and the right choice at the collective level: as long as there are enough plural voters to make the right choice through a process of democratic election, then less wise single voters will, in essence, end up choosing the right things. As long as suffrage is universal, Mill can cling to the democratic ideal that participation entails consent to the decision achieved through democratic process; thus workers and other inferior participants consent de facto to whatever choices the plural voters select, as in any other form of majoritarian politics. But although the wise will likely prevail if they convince a sufficient minority of the general population, in theory Mill would not give them the power to rule unilaterally, for that would contradict the logic of universal suffrage. If the proportions are correctly constituted, plural voters would always need to persuade a minimal number of single voters in order to win; if a sufficient number of single voters cannot be persuaded, they would prevail over the plural voters. Though people must choose for themselves, Mill also wants to increase the odds that they make the right choice. Liberty serves utility by providing the best system for the attainment of truth, for the realization of the higher pleasures and the greatest overall social utility. One might want to argue that Mill-the-individualist believes that it is better that people choose the wrong things than have the right things forced on them. But even this generous imputation does not mean that liberty is paramount over utility; to the contrary, it suggests that liberty must be allowed full play if it is genuinely to serve utility. His policies on the poor clearly indicate that individual liberty requires social control for the common good, as Hamburger argued.

The fact that Mill's solution is so obviously class-based, and class biased, supports the challenge that I have raised about Mill. One might assume that he does not wish to entrench the power of the educated—much less the economically privileged—because, as he argues in *On Liberty*, even experienced or superior people's views of utility must be balanced against the dangers of stagnation; even the most intelligent person needs to be challenged periodically, if for no other reason than to be forced to defend her position and to reaffirm its truth. Furthermore, as no idea or view can ever contain the entire truth, such challenges (and the single votes of laborers) may also serve the even greater purpose of contributing some sliver of truth to the superior person's view. Thus, Mill denies that "only persons of decided mental superiority" should exercise individual freedom, saying that anyone who "possesses any tolerable amount of common sense and experience" should determine their own lives (*Liberty*, 75). But what defines "common sense," or even a "tolerable amount," and what criteria Mill expects to draw on are as unspecified as are those for determining that pushpin is not as good as poetry. His failure to recognize that wisdom does not necessarily cohere with occupation compounds his failure to see that profession is no less class biased than inherited wealth but is simply a different form of class striation. He then fails to link gender to class in his political proposal, because no housewives—or only those who received a university education—could become plural voters as long as profession is the benchmark. All of these missteps indicate that the democratic and individualist dimensions of his theory of freedom are superseded by collectivist visions of the common good, higher-order utility, and an entrenched, if somewhat porous, hierarchy that largely follows lines of class and gender.

CONCLUSION

Thus, the theme that I have pursued in other chapters, that the canonical theories of freedom deploy a dualistic conception of freedom that cuts across positive and negative liberty but adheres fairly consistently to lines of class and gender, takes a particular twist for Mill. More than any other theorist considered in this book, Mill had a great deal to say directly about both class and gender. Class appears to be the most obvious dividing line for Mill, for his theory would seem to indicate a positive liberty conception of freedom for workers and the poor. In order to achieve negative liberties to do what you want, you must be situated in a particular context that will enable you to make the right choices; but the context for the poor and working classes is much less optimal than it is for the upper classes. Mill's emphasis on education as well as his evaluation of higher and lower desires—or more and less utilitarian ones—speaks once again to the prominence in his theory of internal barriers to liberty and a true will. As I have shown, the democratic orientation of his theory masks an elitist bias and suggests considerable substantive values hiding behind an apparently innocent and egalitarian procedure for determining utility. Even in *On Liberty*, where he seems the most radically egalitarian, Mill introduces both subtle and overt examples of his apparent ambivalence, as I have shown. His repeated comments about the inferior intellectual ability and moral character of the poor and even of laborers—those on parish relief are lazy; laborers like to drink a lot of beer and think only of their narrow short-term interests; they either beat their wives into submission or their wives want them to be like everyone else and thereby rob them of what little potential they might have had to rise above the common mass—seem to take such inferiorities as natural or at least unchangeable, despite his grand schemes for education and political participation.

Of course, as I have indicated already, what is natural and what is socially constructed is difficult to parse in Mill's work. Hence, in the *Political Economy* Mill defends capitalism by pointing out that "It is the common error of Socialists to overlook the natural indolence of mankind; their tendency to be passive, to be the slaves of habit, to persist indefinitely in a course once chosen" (795). So all humans may have the tendency toward laziness, though the social circumstances of the poor encourage that tendency to predominate, whereas humans born into middle-class families learn more industrious habits and thereby learn to suppress this tendency. But the effect is rather the same in Mill's view, for it is a circular problem that feeds itself.

Thus, class is an obvious line of demarcation for two levels of freedom. But gender complicates the picture I have painted here. On the surface, it might seem that gender and class diverge in the remedies Mill supports: whereas women must be liberated by legal rights and negative liberties, workers must be controlled through the strictest poor law. Although workers are less dependent than in the past, they still need to acquire "the virtues of independence. . . . The prospect of the future depends on the degree in which they can be made rational beings" (*PE*, 763). By contrast, women's oppression is so obvious to them that simply removing their shackles will produce great change. But I have shown that the relation of gender and class is more complicated than this when it comes to freedom.

In fact, women's situation might pose an inversion of men's situation, with class cutting across the lines of both genders in opposite ways. Though Mill may be advocating a quantitative equality in freedom for all women by removing legal barriers and providing them with economic possibilities, there is a decidedly qualitative difference in the unfreedom of women of different classes. In the lower classes, Mill's goal of gender equality focuses on ending the brutality of domestic violence, to make men respect their wives more generally and to make women better wives and mothers by educating them. In this, lower-class women need negative liberty, for the removal of external barriers is probably all that is necessary to "liberate" such women from their oppression: freedom from oppression by their individual husbands, freedom to vote, and freedom of divorce, education, and work, so that they have exit options from their marriages. By contrast, upper-class women need positive freedom, for the focus is less on simple external obstacles and more on internal ones, both in changing men's prejudiced attitudes that lead to women's physical barriers and in developing women's intellectual and professional abilities. Certainly, negative liberty goals for upper-class women are important: specifically to end coverture and allow married women to keep their property (obviously not a concern to lower-class women, who did not have property to begin with) and to facilitate economic and professional opportunities. But perhaps most important is the positive liberty goal of ending customary and socially restrictive *attitudes* that hinder the development of women's talents and intellectual abilities. Because the gap between where such women are and where they could be is so much greater than it is for lower-class women, these women's identities and self-conceptions need changing as well. Patriarchal attitudes, not just actions, need to be changed for these women to achieve freedom. If such attitudes are changed, then wealthy women could do their own housework, presumably, and still make valuable contributions to society through their ideas and political activity.

The situation of men would seem to be the reverse of this. That is, men of the upper classes need only negative liberty: they need freedom of thought and discussion and eccentricity of ideas so as to escape the shackles of common opinion and mediocrity. It is only by escaping social pressures of conformity that they can lead the rest of society to truth. Lower-class men, by contrast, need positive liberty; they need to be led to the truths that their superiors can find. Even if education would not enable them to discover the truth for themselves, it would enable them to recognize the truth when it is presented to them by the elite. That is, they need enough education to abandon their smug self-satisfaction and give "voluntary deference" to their superiors.

There are obvious challenges to this four-square formula, of course. In the first place, Mill states that laws preventing women from obtaining education and competing in various professions are a primary barrier to upper-class women's achievement. Although Mill recognizes the need to change men's attitudes and women's self-conceptions, he also at times seems to indicate that the only way to accomplish this is through changing the law. He invokes the liberal ideal that if the law requires men to act in ways that demonstrate respect for women (such as making wife-battering illegal), men will eventually start thinking in ways that cohere with such behavior; they will actually start to respect women. Thus, as I have suggested, changing law is key to changing the structure of society. Mill seeks through legal reform not simply the removal of external barriers, but the construction of different ways of thinking. So positive and negative liberty are relevant for everyone, regardless of gender and class, for the hierarchy of freedom is not exclusively determined by class, any more than it is by gender. It is determined, once again invoking Mill's argument in the *Logic*, by character. That certain character traits are more commonly found in women than men, or the lower classes than the upper, leads Mill to focus on gender and class as particular windows into these characteristics that impact freedom by affecting desire and will. How these characteristics become associated with particular classes and genders is primarily experiential, not essential, even if Mill is not entirely consistent on that point. The role of experience suggests that the key to Mill's conception of freedom is not simply the desire to control one's own life, to make one's own choices, "to pursue our own good, in our own way." Rather, the recognition that who we are, the desires we have, and the choices we make come from the social situatedness of individuals is the fundamental drive behind Mill's argument. Though Mill may not be more committed to social constructivism than the other theorists considered in this book, he is more obvious about it, and perhaps more aware of the role it plays in his conception of freedom.

Gender also illustrates the ways in which Mill's theory of freedom decenters the individual more than most commentators want to admit. His advocacy of women's choosing to be wives and mothers as their "careers" is a case in point. It could be an example of Mill's attempt to reconcile the ideal with the practical; that is, the argument that most women, given their socialization, may not seek to work for wages is no reason to bar them from doing so by law and thus preventing the odd woman from excelling at law, medicine, or business. Or it could be an illustration of Mill's attempt to defend himself against exaggerated interpretations of his argument; given our own twenty-first-century hysteria about "the family," one can easily imagine the conservative fearmongering of Mill's contemporaries that his proposals would force women to work. As Urbinati claims, "Mill wanted to assure his Victorian readers that even without formal obligation, women would choose to raise a family. . . . This prudent strategy was very common among the early emancipationists and not only in England."[94]

But such generous interpretations ignore the fact, as I earlier indicated, that Mill goes on to make a utilitarian rational calculation that sacrifices women's individuality to a greater collective good of political economy: namely, not "burthen[ing] the labour market with a double number of competitors." This apparent sacrifice of women's individual liberty for improved overall economic utility might seem to be abated by his efforts to allow women more options so that they may delay marriage and have fewer children, or even choose not to marry. Given the poor economic conditions of the working classes in Mill's day, however, his recommendation for delaying marriage until a couple is financially solvent is likely to remove the option of marriage altogether for many working-class women, as their entry into the labor force, by increasing competition among workers and depressing wages, will make conditions worse before they get better. Mill believes that reduced reproduction will bring about eventual improvement in working conditions, but these improvements may not occur until at least the next generation. That likelihood is not something that Mill confronts in terms of individual liberty; his collective view sacrifices the negative liberty of today's workers and women to the greater positive liberty of tomorrow's. That may be an unavoidable trade-off in Mill's view, however. That is, given that liberty is not just the absence of external obstacles but also involves the social construction of humans into beings who can make the right kinds of choices, such liberty is simply not within reach for most workers of the current generation. Little, perhaps nothing, can be done to change that. The age of transition, though leading to better times, is itself harsh: change is hard.

This insight applies no less to upper-class women, however. On the one hand, Mill indicates that women of property should be free to enter professions, lead society, contribute to the marketplace of ideas, and vote intelligently, perhaps more than once. On the other hand, such women have less reason to refrain from marriage (assuming that laws on property and divorce change), and once married, they are likely to reproduce. But once they are mothers women should, Mill claims, stay home and raise their children and set examples of virtue by cleaning their own houses rather than hiring servants. That Mill recognizes that most women who can afford servants are not likely to refrain from hiring them may again be a testimony to the age of transition: under current circumstances, when women lack social and economic power, where they are treated as less than human, who can blame them for taking advantage where they can and seeking to enjoy their lives? But once the transition is completed, and laws are changed to allow women the same freedom as men, particularly the freedom not to marry, then women who do marry and have children will have no reason not to want to raise them and keep house.

This, however, more than any other argument in Mill's corpus seems the most far-fetched, as history has proved Mill dead wrong. Once women received education equivalent to men's, why would, and should, they still choose motherhood as an exclusive occupation?[95] More to the point, why would they choose a form of motherhood where, instead of using their minds to educate their children, they lead only by virtuous example? Mill is conspicuously silent on this issue. He could have argued that women should home-school their children and participate in volunteer networks to bring about social improvements that the market cannot bring about on its own. Or he could have argued, as Rousseau did, that mothering is a special activity that only women can perform, and that is why most women will make such a choice. But he does not.[96] Rather, he simply makes his assertion that women will choose the career of wife and mother and leaves this choice unanalyzed. At most, he offers political economy arguments that women's widespread entry into the labor market will destabilize the economy, which is a rather sexist argument. Nor does he recognize the challenge women's housewifery poses to the entire structure of his argument about the "nature" of women being "eminently artificial." For although he maintains that education should instill certain kinds of values and ideals, that individuals need to develop their sense of social unity, and that all need to change their attitudes about women, attitudes cannot simply be changed by force of will. As Mill indicates in the *Logic*, circumstances must change first. Thus, removing external barriers in the form of laws should, Mill suggests, change attitudes, so that once women are allowed to pursue education, more will seek to pursue it. The more women seek it, the more general social attitudes about educating women will change to favor it; the more attitudes change, the greater access women will have to education and careers. The greater the access, the more likely it is that women will enter the workplace. Yet Mill fails to carry through the logic of this argument.

He also leaves unexplored where men will fit into this new order of gender equality: what happens to men who are displaced economically by women workers? Do men's role and participation in the family change? One would assume they might, but Mill's silence suggests that men do not change at all; it is women who must do the adapting, and this adaptation ironically involves changing very little of the daily structure of society in spite of what Mill obviously believes are quite radical arguments. Mill wants to allow women the option to make different choices, but those choices are still rather proscribed within the parameters he articulates as the most utilitarian. And those parameters, in turn, cohere with traditional gender norms to a significant extent. Again, freedom serves utility. A robust negative liberty that encourages diversity, even eccentricity, though important in an age of transition, is not a universal good.

These gaps in his argument may attest to the particular form of social constructivism that Mill deploys. As I have shown, the first two layers of social construction are clearly evident in Mill's work. He seeks to reveal the falsehoods in the dominant patriarchal ideology as tools to shore up male power. He then identifies the ways in which that ideology materializes itself by producing women too afraid to stand up to abusive husbands, too convinced of their inferiority to demand respect, too poorly educated to think intelligently. He also engages in his own ideological construction, however, utilizing the ideology of liberalism and capitalism to create new "truths" that I have suggested are similarly problematic, such as the laziness of the poor, the neutrality of markets in rewarding talent, equality of opportunity, the sexual promiscuity of the poor and, simultaneously, "the familiar Victorian figure of woman as helpless (asexual) victim."[97] He then seeks to create social practices and institutions, ranging from universal suffrage and plural voting to industrial cooperatives and parenting licenses, that operationalize those ideals. The third layer of social construction, however, seems less clearly evident than it was in the work of the other four theorists; Mill's social constructivism is more obvious at the level of producing people themselves, particularly through his theory of utility, education, and plural voting.

But I have suggested throughout this chapter that discursive construction is a subtle underlying factor at work in Mill's writings. Mill uses discourse in a somewhat less self-conscious though more obviously political sense, perhaps, than the other theorists considered here. That is, he is clearly agitating on these issues, seeking overtly to persuade others to agree with him and change their minds. He writes because he wishes to convince, to shape how people think and how they perceive and understand the world. His most famous writings are not scholarly works as much as they are political pamphlets. Though the same could be said of Locke (and has been),[98] Mill seems somewhat less aware of his role as a theorist, and less attentive to language than were the other theorists. The exception, perhaps, is the *Logic*, where Mill dedicates considerable space to articulating the philosophical meaning of various terms, such as "will" and "freedom." But this attention to meaning subtly pervades his other, more overtly political writings as well. Indeed, one could argue that his advocacy of freedom itself is primarily discursive. For despite the attention he gives to the negative liberty of thought and speech, this freedom is not necessarily connected to the freedom to choose. Although individuals should think and say what they want (though speech had certain limits), they cannot choose whatever they want and still be free. Perhaps a reflection of the fact that he made many speeches in Parliament and wrote hundreds of editorials and letters to the editor—together, they comprise a full six volumes of Mill's *Collected Works*[99]—Mill seems to uphold the freedom of thought and speech for its rhetorical and educative purposes as much as, if not more than, for its ability to foreground choice and action.

On its face, this might seem like an unfair assertion; Mill obviously had practical applications in mind for many of his ideas, particularly women's suffrage, plural voting, and education. But recall that he thought it was important to express ideas per se and that their free exchange was an important part of the process of achieving truths on which practical action could be based. The account he offers in his *Autobiography* of his parliamentary experience, for instance, including his refusal to do all but minimal campaigning, emphasizes ideas, particularly his speeches in support of or opposition to various issues such as slavery, women's suffrage, capital punishment and the national debt, rather than practical actions he took.[100] Mill seems to suggest that an important purpose of speech is to socially construct our understanding of social relations and politics. This is particularly the case in his writings on gender, for he seeks to get his contemporaries to think differently about women. He recognizes that the material and legal conditions under which women live cannot change until people reconceive women's status as human beings. Bringing about this significant change in the way men understand women and women understand themselves and each other is an "internal" change in the positive liberty sense, even if it is meant to bring about "external" change in the form of laws and policies that will enhance negative liberties. It is in changing this inner landscape of individual understanding that he hopes to change the social landscape by locating the individual in contexts of language and meaning. The three layers of social construction come together for Mill through the act of writing.

Central to what he seeks to construct is freedom. Viewing Mill's theory of free thought and speech as outlined in *On Liberty* in terms of its rhetorical and educative function, rather than its practical function, somewhat explains, if it does not resolve, the tension he displays between freedom and utility, and between negative and positive liberty ideals. It helps clarify why the expression of a wide, almost infinite variety of ideas is consistent with his view of freedom, but the range of choices consistent with freedom is considerably smaller. This may result in a rather more timid notion of freedom that is usually associated with Mill, because expressing ideas without being able to enact them has limited value to individuals. But instead, I believe, it reveals the complexities that arise from reconciling key aspects of negative liberty with positive liberty through the project of social construction.

Rethinking Freedom in the Canon

THE CONCEPT OF FREEDOM as it has developed in the modern canon, as illustrated by the five figures I have considered here, demonstrates considerable consistency and continuity over time, even as it displays substantive differences in conceptualization, realization into political form, and expression in the various theories. I warned the reader at the outset of this book that I was not interested in constructing one single unifying message out of these theories, but rather a series of themes and arguments that display considerable overlap but also significant variation. That should not be surprising, considering that the theorists considered here cover a time span of more than two hundred years and come from three different countries (though all loosely grouped together under "western Europe," a grouping that might be more difficult to sustain in an era prior to globalization). Even so, the three themes that I have pursued here—positive and negative liberty, social constructivism, and gender—have shown this same pattern of overall similarity in the goals, aims, and undertakings of the theories, and difference in the particulars of how those similar goals, aims, and undertakings are realized.

FREEDOM IN ITS TWO FORMS

For instance, it would seem, given my readings of these five theorists, that each eludes an easy categorization into either the positive or negative liberty model because they each demonstrate key elements of both models. I said at the beginning of this exploration that I was less interested in fitting these five theorists into negative or positive liberty "boxes" than I was in learning what they had to tell us *about* these two conceptions. That has sometimes led me to compare the theory under consideration to the admittedly often simplistic rendering that Berlin originally formulated. But my purpose in doing so, I hope it has been clear, has been to demonstrate that the theories from which Berlin ostensibly drew his typology are much more complicated than Berlin acknowledged. In tracing the two conceptions of freedom through their historical origins, my concern has not been to replicate the debates between positive and negative liberty partisans, nor to advocate positive or negative liberty as a "better," more philosophically coherent, or politically adequate conception of freedom. Rather, my point has been to understand the different models by understanding the origins and theoretical articulations of the visions they put forth. For I have suggested that these models provide a useful guide for reading the texts, and I believe my analysis here has borne that out.

For instance, I have argued that all of the theories present a dualistic conception of freedom, but the theorists do not create the exact same divisions and hierarchies. Their major similarity, indeed, is that their divisions do not track Berlin's two models. As I have argued, some seem to grant negative liberty to men, positive liberty to women, others do the reverse, but all in the end divide the models along lines of class and gender quite complexly. The most fundamental difference I have traced lies between the theorists who ostensibly focus primarily on external barriers and those who focus on the importance of the inner barriers to freedom, the compulsions and behaviors of the will that keep an individual from realizing her true desire, her true goals, her true will. Although, intellectually and conceptually, inner barriers are defined as opposed to external barriers rather than as interconnected, we have seen that such opposition is itself a construction of the theories, one that will not stand the test of deeper examination. Instead, the theories show despite themselves that inner and outer are interrelated, interdependent, and intertwined: not only practically, but epistemologically as well. At the most basic level, my (internal) will is not free if I cannot act on it because of external forces. But less obvious is the notion of how the external world influences the internal in a more proactive sense, that is, how desire and will are themselves constructed through social relations and social forces. Most theorists agree that I am unfree to do X if I want to do it but am prevented; but they are more likely to disagree about whether I am free to do X if I cannot develop the desire to do it in the first place because of my location in a particular social matrix or cultural context. Although all of the theorists considered here overtly concern themselves with the former, they are tacitly even more concerned with the latter. On the most basic, and perhaps superficial level, each has a theory of education, each stresses the importance of teaching values and morals, and each defines education not as the simple imparting of knowledge and "facts" but as the creation of character, the creation of an agent who will be able to make the right choices and assume his place in society and the duties of citizenship. Moreover, in the project of developing their political theories, each constructs a set of definitions and an understanding of humanity, relationship, society, and the family that feeds a particular conception of freedom governed by particular kinds of choices and choice makers.

A marked characteristic of freedom as it has developed in the modern era is that all of these theorists, in somewhat different ways, grant central importance to individual choice making, the expression of will and the ability to follow and act on it, and they recognize a serious danger to liberty in other people's interference with such action. The absence of external barriers is the main ingredient in theories associated with negative liberty, but I have shown that it is also an important starting point for those traditionally associated with positive liberty as well. Certainly, by focusing so heavily on the will and on the internal mechanisms that prevent one from exercising absolute control over the will, Kant and Rousseau seem to downplay the importance of external barriers altogether as irrelevant to freedom of the "true" self, the inner self. As Kant suggests at various points, the exercise of a priori reason should be independent of one's external circumstances. And yet if the "true will" is to cohere to independent standards such as "reason," then the will must be able to overcome external barriers that interfere with its realization. Otherwise, as Berlin pointed out, all I have to do is tailor my will to what I can have, and my will is thereby fulfilled. But both Kant and Rousseau clearly maintain that the search for true will is and must be a valiant struggle, not a facile rationalization.

Yet Rousseau and Kant did not simply reject external barriers as irrelevant to freedom; they argued instead that these were not a sufficient basis for it. Even if individuals had to make the right choices in order to be free, both theorists still insisted that individuals had to make such choices for themselves. Indeed, Rousseau—commonly lambasted as one of the "worst" of positive liberty theorists because of *forcer d'être libre*—actually resembles Mill, the supposed paragon of negative liberty, in this respect of individual choice. For like Mill, Rousseau argued that choice and virtue had to be reconciled; but when push came to shove, voluntarism had to take priority over virtue, at least for men. Certainly, external obstacles were the primary force confronting natural liberty; though even here Rousseau recognized that the individual's *perception* of others' strength and ability could serve to block my action if I anticipated defeat. But even in moral freedom, forcing you to be free had a logical limitation to it. For if the majority made a bad choice, that had to be accepted as if it were the general will until people could see their mistake and change it themselves. The minority, even if they could see the truth more clearly, were not entitled to impose it on the majority. Though most readers focus on the minority that is forced to be free to conclude that Rousseau's freedom is the worst form of positive liberty, they fail to recognize that such force is the necessary corollary of the majority's freedom to choose the laws and be self-determining. Although it is possible that some particular minority will be repeatedly silenced under this formula, most members of society are likely to be a part of a majority at some point. After all, if that minority is always silenced, Rousseau says that they can leave to form a new society with a new social contract, where their interpretation of the general will is more likely to prevail. But he believes that the elements of negative liberty, of making our own choices, are meaningless without the positive liberty elements of making the right choices.

Paradoxically, however, Rousseau's emphasis on individual choice is what yields his true absolutist tendencies, which lie not in the democratic assembly but in the home. For it was precisely the danger that voluntarism would forsake virtue—that individuals would make bad choices—that motivated his elaborate theory of the family and a constrained role for women. Rousseau starts from the belief that men's will cannot be self-determining in the face of overwhelming external obstacles, such as women's sexuality or "professional" politics: externalities that corrupt the internal self and establish the lure of false desire that the will is too weak to resist. By constructing social relations to contain these elements, Rousseau believes that all individuals, male as well as female, would be free from both external and internal obstacles to realizing the general will, which is every individual's true will.

In a similar vein whose logic is more familiar to twenty-first-century liberals, Kant argues for republican government as the necessary political condition for individual citizens' ability to understand their moral duty and reason through to the categorical imperative. This government must provide for conditions of suffrage and freedom of speech as essential conditions for this project: the state must protect men from external barriers to enable them to engage in the reasoning processes that will lead them to the categorical imperative, and hence to freedom. Certainly, because the will exists in the mind, which constitutes the true self, and which in turn must master the false or lower self represented by the body, the ultimate barriers to freedom are decidedly internal—most generally, insufficient rationality. But external barriers are also important, for they are likely to give way to, prompt, or feed an individual's internal barriers. For instance, a man's will may be put in jeopardy by physical proximity to a beautiful woman, stimulating the irrational but powerful impulse to have sex in contradiction to the calling of his true will.[1] The internal barriers themselves, the things preventing him from resisting his urges, are ultimately what matter, but Kant must always confront the fact that our noumenal selves are situated in bodies that are of the phenomenal realm.

Thus, Kant and Rousseau paid considerable attention to the concept of external barriers as an important part of freedom. What is perhaps more surprising is the central role that internal barriers play in the theories of Hobbes, Locke, and Mill. All three of these theorists, even the most unrepentant individualist Hobbes, recognize that individuals can and often do make choices that are at odds with what those individuals want, or more precisely, with what the theorists assert that those individuals want. As a result, the theorists all strive to set up external structures to shape, influence, and even coerce people into "choosing" what the theorist wants them to choose. Hobbes's rational fiat, Locke's tacit consent and right reason, and Mill's utilitarianism are importantly different from Rousseau's general will and Kant's categorical imperative in their implementation, workings, origins, significance, and meaning, but they are all methodologically and politically equivalent. Challenges to what the theorist thinks people should want are dismissed as false consciousness, irrationality, stupidity, emotional or psychological slavery: in short, as unfreedom.

Locke particularly falls prey to this apparent contradiction, for despite his emphasis on consent and the social contract, very few people in his political society actually end up being able to choose for themselves. The centrality of tacit consent ensures that no matter what one does short of rebellion, one consents to the government. But one does so only if that government is good. Thus, residence in a tyranny does not, indeed cannot by the logic Locke lays out, constitute consent to it; but residence in a constitutional monarchy does. His construction of freedom as the basis for obligation and political legitimacy gives way to the recognition that the form of government itself, rather than the fact that citizens choose the form, is the key ingredient to the Lockean state and is vital to making his theory of the social contract work. The fact that Locke privileged freedom to such an extent in his theory despite these contradictory indications supports the conclusion that certain segments of the population, namely propertied men, were the primary targets of his proclaimed dedication to natural individual liberty for all.

Hobbes's "rational fiat" may be saved from this criticism by virtue of the fact that Hobbes seems to believe that freedom, the basic building block in his definition of humanity, is not the ultimate goal to be preserved: it is the starting point for his theory, but not its end point. Rather, order and security take pride of place, and freedom is secondary to that. If that is the case, then there is no problem with the fact that obedience must be absolute, or at least less of a problem than there must logically be for Locke. But at the same time, Hobbes's insistence that order and security are obtained via contract and agreement between otherwise antagonistic and unrelated individuals suggests that freedom must persevere as *a* primary value, if not *the* primary value after all: if order was truly the primary value, Hobbes would not need the social contract or the state-of-nature mythology in the first place, but could lodge a Humean argument for first possession or usurpation as the foundation for political legitimacy. The fact that he does employ consent and contract as the foundation for individuals' obligations to obey the government and the government's right to command them raises questions about the place and role of freedom in his theory and ensures that the contradictory character of his rational fiat remains a substantial problem.

Similarly, Mill's emphasis on freedom of conscience and speech indicates a strong dedication to the principles of negative liberty; freedom can be preserved only by individuals' pursuit of their own interests and expression of their own views unrestrained by the interference of others, particularly the government. At the same time, however, what those interests and views are is not immaterial to Mill, whose conception of utility requires a recontextualization of his theory of liberty. Insofar as particular individual choices do not cohere with his prescription for desire, subtle—and sometimes not-so-subtle—checks on such choice may undercut people's negative liberty for the sake of a higher-order utility and positive freedom. That Mill may have seen the contradiction in this is to his credit. Despite his belief in human "progress," he maintains that "unprogressive" beings can, for the most part, remain free to make mistakes, that they can wallow in a less valuable freedom (getting drunk in their dingy boardinghouse rooms, for instance), and that this is the paradoxical price society must pay if it is to achieve the progress it desires. But the tension is strong, as I have shown; the fact that humanity is in an age of transition requires mechanisms, such as plural voting, mass deportation of the poor, and licenses for reproduction, to help ensure that those of superior intelligence will be able to determine truth and higher-order utility.

Thus, all five of these theorists share a similar ambiguity vis-à-vis the negative-positive typology, for each theorist displays key aspects of both models. But I have also suggested that the truly significant difference between the two models lies in more political considerations about what counts as a barrier and why, what counts as a goal and why, and who counts as an agent and why. In this, we see considerable differences in the answers these five theorists seek to outline. What these differences indicate is that it is not the definitions of liberty per se that signify so much as it is the "stories" that the theories tell about their creators: the values that they claim to promote and support may be undermined by tacit adherence to their opposite, but the claiming itself reveals the vision of humanity, social relations, politics, and the self that each theorist *wants* to commit to. In this, the central issue in all of these theories is revealed to be a battle between "internal" and "external" as they refer to both barriers and the free self. Does the self lie in the mind, as Kant asserts, or in the body, as Hobbes declares? Is the essence of humanity—and hence human liberty—mental or corporeal in nature? Does it lie in the individual per se or in the society and the social relations in which the individual is located? Should we pay primary attention to the "inner self" or the "outer self," and what is the relation between my inner and outer selves? The definition of "barriers" to freedom as either primarily internal or external will of course depend on the answers to such questions. The ostensible focus on external barriers found in Hobbes, Locke, and Mill often serves as a smoke screen to mask the ways in which the apparent importance of individuals' making their *own* choices is really secondary to the importance of their making the *right* choices. Indeed, it is perhaps for precisely that reason that the notion of a true will stands out as such a stark surprise in these theories.

Mill, perhaps alone among these five, does at times seem to recognize the interrelationship between the internal and external when he acknowledges the ways in which women are influenced by repressive and restrictive social norms to want and value only what it is customary to want and value. His insight in fact applies to most men as well, of course, because he declares that only the exceptional person, the eccentric, or the genius is capable of bucking the norm, seizing on an original idea, and genuinely directing her or his own life. But Mill nevertheless often seems to insist on a distinct line between the internal and external. Hence, education should instill certain kinds of values and ideals, individuals need to develop their sense of social unity, and men need to change their attitudes about women, but these changes must come about through individuals' altered will. Surely, such change is not direct—if we want to change our will, Mill argues, we must first change our characters by changing our external circumstances. But the motivation comes from a rather simplified understanding of the self's motivations: because bad character causes me to suffer, I will unequivocally respond in a particular way; it is given that humans will prefer to pursue higher-order pleasures. The only thing stopping them is their external circumstances. The difficulty in producing radical change through this rather circular method is obvious, unless Mill subscribes to a naturalistic impulse behind the desire for change and improvement. But he does not; instead, he maintains that removing external barriers in the form of laws is the way to change attitudes, as if restrictive practices were all that prevented attitude change. Hence, for instance, once women are allowed to vote and own property, men's attitudes about women will change to favor it. Though Mill starts *On Liberty* with declarations of human difference and individuality that must not be interfered with by the state, these differences give way in his writings to a romantic ideal of a better society in which everyone more or less agrees on what is good, better, and best.[2] Though the reader starts out with an impression that Mill posits the relationship between inner and outer as complicated, dynamic, and constitutionally interactive, we end up seeing that it is straightforward, clear-cut, and rational.

GENDER, CLASS, AND BERLIN'S TYPOLOGY

It is significant, I have tried to suggest, that many of these dilemmas concerning the relationship between the internal realm and the external world relate to the theorists' views of women, not only in the explicit remarks that specific theorists make about women and men, but in their supposedly "gender neutral" definitions of freedom as well. The analysis of gender shows that these definitions may not be gender neutral at all, but instead are premised on particular kinds of gender exclusions. The idea that male freedom is premised on women's unfreedom plays out differently for the various theorists, and seems most obvious in Hobbes, Rousseau, and Kant, somewhat less obvious in Locke and Mill. Furthermore, as I have suggested at various points throughout this book, the claim that men's freedom depends on women's unfreedom must be complicated and nuanced by sometimes competing, sometimes complementary vectors of class. For it is not necessarily obvious that the different conceptualizations of liberty presented by these five theorists are themselves threatened by the inclusion of women. Women could, in principle, be granted property rights and be entitled to negative liberty protections of the liberal state, just as they could, in principle, be admitted to the assembly and discover the general will for themselves. But my analysis in these chapters shows that underlying these apparently changeable dimensions of the theories are certain shared assumptions and characteristics that suggest that both positive and negative liberty are in important ways structured by gender. Gender is an important tool for examining freedom, for it is one of the major dividing lines that allows the theorists to manage the concept, to reduce its complexity into neat compartments. Yet bringing gender into the discussion, as I have shown, ironically complicates the question of freedom far more than most of the theorists realize.

For instance, the ways that political theorists structure the family to represent particular relations of gendered power form the relational and social background against which freedom is configured. Because the family is seen as a key foundation of the state in many of these theories, the structure of the family effects the structure of the state. And the state is invariably central to how the theorist conceptualizes and expresses his ideas of freedom. Women pose a dangerous difference to state power and authority. But is that because the state is founded on male power, which women challenge? Or does the state *become* allied with male power de facto, once women are eliminated because of their difference? That is, does sexism motivate the construction of these political theories, or does it result from the logic of their arguments? Do political theorists structure states to address anxiety about women, or does this anxiety emerge after the state takes its form and the challenge that sexual difference poses to it becomes apparent? These questions may be impossible to answer, but questions of cause and effect are in the end less important to my analysis than is the use to which the author puts gender. That is, why do the theorists tell the particular stories they do about gender? What purpose does it serve?

I have suggested that a key purpose is to address the tension between individuals' ability to make their own choices and the theorists' need for them to make the right choices, which I have characterized in terms of a tension between negative and positive liberty, and between individual difference and social order. The issue of being enabled to make the right choices is particularly important in relation to women, for they pose the most serious challenge to male liberty. All of the theorists—though some more explicitly than others—express a fear of female sexuality as likely to compromise men's freedom. Sexuality, either in and of itself or via the powers of reproduction, poses serious threats to men's independence and autonomy: it can jeopardize their safety and security (Hobbes); interfere with and confound their ability to pass on property to their sons through inheritance (Locke); disrupt the market and reduce utility (Mill); and result in the manipulation of men and their wills by women's direct use of sexual temptation (Rousseau) or by their more indirect use of charms and wiles (Kant). When widespread negative liberty for women is contemplated, social chaos threatens to ensue, and women must thereby be contained by assignment to the private sphere. They may be given freedom from external interference, but only over a narrow range of options. Thus, even Mill glosses over the radical implications of granting negative liberty to women through large-scale legal reform by offhandedly assuming that they will choose to remain in the private sphere as wives and mothers despite all the new opportunities he wishes them to have. When positive liberty is engaged, women may seem even more repressed, and certainly more repressed than men, for women are deemed to lack the key characteristics, such as reason or virtue, that are essential to freedom. Thus, positive liberty similarly entails women's limitation to the private sphere, to protect them from themselves and the unwise choices that they would otherwise make, seducing and corrupting men and thereby condemning all to unfreedom. Because women's power—of sex, of reproduction, of unreason and emotion—is so crippling, men have little hope of making the right choices, the choices that are necessarily expressive of their freedom, unless women are brought under their direct control. There is thus an inverse relationship between positive and negative aspects of liberty across genders. If men are to pursue their goals, women must be restrained from preventing them; women's domestic restraint and activity makes men's individualism possible. But women's powers within this restrained private realm also prevent men from selecting poor goals to begin with. In this, women serve the state better than do men, as we saw most clearly in Rousseau's *Julie* and less overtly in Locke's remarks on inheritance.

Yet it is clearly too forceful to claim that male freedom comes at the expense of female unfreedom. I acknowledge that at various points in this book I have made the kind of strong claims that I wanted to avoid, particularly in the Rousseau chapter, where women's denial of negative freedom seems so directly and intrinsically foundational to men's positive liberty in the assembly. But the idea that sexism "causes" the modern conception of freedom, though arguably defensible from an analytical perspective, is hardly sustainable from a historical perspective, given that sexism takes so many different forms throughout history and throughout the world, and given that freedom does not have a universal meaning across time and place. In order to establish such a claim, one would have to correlate the changes in forms of patriarchy and sexism to differences in the figurations of freedom. That is not my project in this book. Rather, I hope that I have opened up some questions about the ways in which gender and, to a lesser extent, class have related to the ways in which freedom has been conceptualized and theorized in the modern canon of western Europe. If that seems to end my analysis with a whimper rather than a bang, that could be good or bad. It is good if it attests to the growing normalization of gender as an accepted category of analysis. But it is bad insofar as too many readers are still resistant to such normalization. For them, if the case for gender is not earth-shattering, then it must be irrelevant, and my argument will be met with a sigh of relief that we do not need to worry about gender anymore.

Thus, it is important to reiterate that what I have argued instead is that gender is part of a larger puzzle that includes class, language, social relations and institutions like the family, forms of government, the state, law, and economic and labor relations, all of which feed into political theories, and particularly the conceptualizations of freedom that are an important, if not central, part of those theories. As I hope I have indicated throughout this book, women cannot be reduced to their gender, any more than can men. As human beings, women have many facets to their identities, their social locations, and their roles and memberships. Race, class, sexuality, nationality, ethnicity, and multiple subdivisions within those broad categories (the kind of work one does within one's class, for instance), as well as the fluidity of those categories and subdivisions (such as homosocial or homoerotic aspects of or moments in social relations among ostensibly heterosexual women and men) make the standard categories of feminist analysis complicated, complex, subtle, blurred.

Rather than positing a simplified causal relationship, it is better to say that the theoretical conceptualization of freedom and the definition of "woman" are tied up in one another. Insofar as each of these theorists ends up requiring women's subservience in order to make his conception of freedom work, gender becomes part of the conceptual structure of freedom. For even if women's subordination is not structurally required, and even if women's lesser freedom is a contingent fact of particular historical and cultural forces, it is still obvious that gender and freedom have a particular relationship that influences how we see and understand freedom as it has developed through the canon.

The sexual division of labor may be the most obvious way in which this relationship is visible. Through this distinction, women can be excluded by what they do rather than who they are, even if the latter is what determines the former in the social landscape. Women's assignment to the concrete daily activities of the home such as housework, managing the household budget, raising children, caring for husbands, and even serving as moral beacons to men and children is intimately tied to their roles in reproduction, specifically their status as mothers. And reproduction, of course, brings us back to sexuality. Not only is sexuality something that eludes control; it resists the abstraction that is so necessary to political theory. Abstraction makes things safe by bringing them under control: if reality is a construct of the reasoning, conscious mind, it can never have an independent existence. The definition of terms, the structuring of social relations and political forms, enable the mind to gain control over social phenomena through their construction in the image of the theorist. They become in part a creation of the theorist's will. The exercise of political theory, as I have suggested throughout this book, is in part an attempt to gain control by means of abstraction, to construct reality into a particular set of relations with particular meanings that put a specific picture of order into place.

Women's concreteness and sexuality, however, provide a visceral reminder that such order is an illusion, that the body and desire are constantly in danger of going out of control. That is why men must assert control over women; to assert control over the self, the internal, they must assert control over the other, the external. But precisely because this self-control is illusory, the control of women must take the *form of* illusion: women are simultaneously ignored, excluded, repressed, denied, made invisible, dehumanized, denigrated, and desexualized, on the one hand, *and* feared, obeyed, glorified, deified, depended on, and sexualized, on the other hand. Perhaps that is why the notion of a true will and desire intrudes even in Hobbes's theory; if women are made to represent the body, if women are the concrete representation and reminder of men's own physicality, then freedom must exist in the mind or will, because that is the only way to control women, by eluding their grasp altogether.

Accordingly, despite the ostensible respect many of the theorists proclaim to have for women—either as moral guardians (Rousseau), cultivators of society (Kant), physical equals (Hobbes), intellectual equals (Mill), or moral equals (Locke)—all of them, in different ways and to different degrees, express sexist assumptions about the nature, character, abilities, and civil standing of women that most likely reflect the values of their contemporaries. But underlying these apparently changeable dimensions of the theories are certain shared assumptions and characteristics that suggest both positive and negative liberty are partially structured by and on the exclusion of women. What is significant, however, is not just the particular myths and illusions the different theorists use to deny women freedom, but also the way in which the theorists try to ignore this denial, even hiding it from themselves behind the rhetoric of either radical free agency or objective truth. Thus, not only is the subject of liberty male; it is a masculinized ideal of man. It is an illusion of man's humanity based on a companionate illusion of woman's inhumanity.[3]

When one considers the place of class in relation to gender, the importance of illusion becomes more apparent; because the meaning of "woman" changes in relation to the class in which the female persons about whom the theorist speaks is located. For some, such as Locke, lower-class women have a looser relationship to the ideal of femininity than do women of the gentry and upper-class women; thus he suggests that they earn a living, rather than exclusively caring for a household and their children. For others, such as Mill, upper-class women are more likely to challenge the patriarchal feminine norm by succeeding in various professions or political life, but lower-class women fail to "beautify" life and thus fail a different feminine norm. The theorists' treatment of men who labor for a living often dovetails with what all but Mill say about women of all classes: that they have inferior rationality, intelligence, and strength of character, which for many disable them from active participation in politics. But even Mill shares this dim view of the lower classes, particularly men. It is not enough for "masculinity" that one be male: one must be a certain kind of male to count as a political subject of liberty.

What this suggests, however, is not just that lower-class men are also excluded along with women; it suggests, rather, that gender itself is affected by class in terms of freedom. The construction of desire, of subjectivity and selfhood, of the self-determining agent intersects with constructions of gender and class to create an understanding of freedom that appears to be universal but is in fact targeted to a specific identity. The political exclusion of women and lower-class men within the conceptual dimensions of these theories means that such people cannot merely be "added" to them without some radical rethinking of their political and theoretical enterprises, goals, and projects. At the same time, however, because the concepts central to these theories that I have articulated in the foregoing chapters are central to Western social and political life, they have helped to shape our understanding of gender and class. This centrality is what provides the tools and vocabulary to bring the freedom of women and the poor into the realm of conceptual possibility, and makes much of the present critique possible.

The consideration of gender in particular illuminates the problems that ensue when the relationship between the inner self and outer world is undertheorized—in particular, when the self is seen as only "inner" and the world as only "outer." It points to an understanding of how we come to be the "subjects" of liberty: agents with desires, wills, and preferences, who make choices. Attention to gender in the context of class helps us see how some choices or alternatives are consistently available and others systematically foreclosed, and how the processes of choice making are not themselves neutral but the function of particular conceptual and political contexts that frame the realm of possibility and action. In looking at the continuities and discontinuities between early-modern and nineteenth-century theory, in seeing what questions and problems persist and what gets forgotten, I have demonstrated not only the overt or "contingent" biases of these theories but, more importantly, the theoretical and thematic consistency in determining the subject of liberty: has this subject changed, or has "he" pretty much remained the same? My analysis has, for the most part, led to the somewhat depressing conclusion that he has not changed very much over the early-modern and modern era. Whether that remains true in the twenty-first century is beyond the scope of the present book, but the implication that "the subject of liberty" is today still of a particular gender, race, class, ethnicity, and sexuality is, presumably, fairly obvious.[4]

But what does remain within the scope of the present argument for contemporary theorists is the methodological issue that my consideration of class addresses. I have taken up class primarily to open up the analysis of gender, but it is the only other social category that I have considered. And of course gender contains much more than just class: race, ethnicity, and sexuality, for instance, are equally central to the project of developing a "feminist" interpretation of modern political theory, for all of these things affect the understanding and meaning of gender. Though considering those other categories is beyond what I have done here, I hope my approach might provide some suggestions to those interested in looking at the intersection of gender with other aspects of social identity in canonical political theory.

THE SOCIAL CONSTRUCTION OF FREEDOM

The issues of method and approach indicate one way in which social construction operates in these theories, and that is at the level of theory itself: how terms are defined, how gender and class are discussed, how freedom is conceptualized. Freedom itself is socially constructed: as a concept, as a practice, as a legal and moral principle, as a way of understanding the self and the self's relation to the world. As I have suggested in each of the chapters, the theorists' particular account of freedom enables an entire framework for constructing the reader's understanding of who we are as human beings, how we live and should live, what our aspirations should be, how we should think about the world around us. The theorists literally construct a vision of the world through their descriptions of how the world operates and through their interpretations of social relations and institutions. Such interpretations are located in particular agendas, motives, or desires for power that are not necessarily obvious to the theorist, but are so to the critical reader who encounters these texts. Consider, for instance, the idea of reason as a mode of thinking, which can lead to erroneous conclusions (garbage in, garbage out) versus right reason, which leads only to truth. Such a conception of right reason might be fine when we occupy the realm of mathematics and science (though as Hobbes noted, even some forms of science do not live up to the geometrical ideal). But these theorists seek to translate or import this notion of reason into morality and politics: they posit as objective truth ideas that are, from the perspective of historical hindsight, not objective, much less true, at all. That the poor are naturally lazy, that women are irrational or sexually immoral, that property is a sign of hard work and merit are all conclusions that are passed off by these theorists as "true" in the same way that the angles of a triangle add up to 180 degrees. But in fact they are the political ideals of particular men of a particular time: men with power to shape the world in the particular image they prefer.

This framework serves as the justification for the materialization of these ideas through the theorists' normative prescriptions for the construction of social relations and institutions, such as the family and the state. The ideological representation that occurs through the writing of the theory leads to the outline of how readers should produce their lives in concrete form. How children are educated, how citizens can or cannot participate in the activities of the state, the authority that the law gives husbands over wives, women's relationship and rights to property are all founded on ideology that is translated into material practice. This second form of social construction, with its links to the notion of "socialization," as I discussed in the introduction to this book, might seem to be the most obvious form; but to leave it at the level of socialization implies a change-ability that belies its relationship to ideology, which is rooted in the per-petuation of existing power relations. Understanding the relationship be-tween ideology and practice opens up critical spaces for pulling apart the rationale for social practices; why do theorists construct their theories as they do? Why do they want certain social institutions and practices, and not others, to define the political landscape?

Consideration of the question of *why* theorists tell the stories they do suggests a third way in which social construction operates in these theo-ries, and that is through the narrative and discursive representation of social relations; how the family is materially structured, that is, dovetails with how "the family," "women," and "men" are defined, articulated, and deployed in discourse, including most centrally the discourse of po-litical theory in which the theorist is actively engaged. Rousseau's defi-nition of feminine virtue, for instance, creates a set of social expectations that may be starkly at odds with social practice—to wit, the stark con-trast between Sophie and the ladies of the Parisian salons, not to mention his lover Thérèse. But through his particular method of representing these differences in language, Rousseau seeks to produce a particular material outcome: that is, if his theory is successful, women and men will act in ways that the theory prescribes. The same holds true for class; theories like Locke's take a social phenomenon of poverty and construct from that a particular story of laziness that is juxtaposed to middle-class industriousness. By basing their theoretical prescriptions on a particular narrative that they claim is itself merely descriptive (the poor are lazy; therefore we must force them to work), political theory becomes "a map that purports to be a mirror."[5] The act of writing political theory is itself an attempt to socially construct the world in which the author lives; it entails the use of language to persuade readers of what "is," and thereby to persuade them further of what "should be." But the description is itself normatively charged with particular visions of power that come out of previously constructed understandings of gender, as well as race and class; it is not "scientifically neutral" or "objective." This appar-ently proactive, conscious construction of social relations is always al-ready informed by a subtler social construction that occurs despite "au-thorial intent" as ideas enter into language and are read by various audiences to construct the representations of "reality" that dominate in particular eras. The three layers of social construction that I offered in my introduction, of ideology, materiality, and discourse, weave through all of these theories in complex ways that are sometimes difficult to sepa-rate, but nevertheless identifiable.

In the foregoing chapters, I have shown that attending to how the theorists write about gender, and to a lesser extent class, enables twenty-first-century readers to understand the social constructivism that is at work in all of these political theories; social construction is not an idea that was "invented" by Foucault or twentieth-century sociologists, but extends back at least to Hobbes. The ambiguities, tensions, and even contradictions that mark all five of the theorists considered here reveal them to have particular agendas in establishing gender and gender relationships—as well as in establishing common understandings of them—that relate to the creation of state authority founded in masculine power. That not all men benefit directly from this state system of masculine power—such as laborers, the poor, and men of color—does not negate the fact that the system is a masculine one, that the people who occupy the positions of power are all men. Freedom thereby is revealed as a construction of masculine power, as a concept that defines and articulates social and political institutions.

To say this does not make freedom a fiction, a ruse of patriarchy to subordinate women. As I have shown, freedom is a concept with importance for women as well as men, for poor as well as rich. What I mean is that the particular ways in which we think about freedom are socially situated. Insofar as our social situations are shaped by gender and class privilege, the meaning of freedom necessarily reflects that; but such reflection is never simply reflection. It also refracts, distorts, creates new images, and produces new relationships and new understandings of preexisting relationships. Understanding social construction as a complex process involving ideology, discourse, and material relations reveals freedom to be a much more complicated concept than it might seem to those, like Berlin, who seek to divide the world into two camps.

This, in the end, may attest that the early-modern theorists were correct about the concept: freedom is somehow fundamental to humanity, to human social relations, and hence to politics. Everything about our lives and being must come back to freedom as an inescapable reference point. But by showing that this reference point is more complicated than we may have thought, I hope that conclusion opens up new possibilities for thinking about our "lives and being." We in the twenty-first century certainly could benefit from remembering that.

Notes

Introduction: Gender, Class, and Freedom in Modern Political Theory

1. The use of "we" throughout this book does not deny that various readers have different reactions to and interpretations of the texts under discussion, as well as different understandings of the term "freedom." However, the canonical authors discussed here do assume that there is a "we"—a unified audience who will or should respond fairly uniformly to the texts—and my use of the term often rhetorically deploys their "we." If that still seems too strong for contemporary readers to whom "we" is a colonizing term, then perhaps they will accept Teresa Brennan's more moderate explanation that " 'we' . . . refers to the author and those who, even if they disagree, still follow the argument." Brennan (2000), viii.
2. Isaiah Berlin, "Two Concepts of Libery," in Berlin (1971), 123.
3. Thomas Hobbes, *Leviathan*, ch. 14, 189.
4. Berlin, "Two Concepts of Liberty," in Berlin, (1971), esp. 123–29.
5. Ibid., 122.
6. For example, ibid., 123, 133, 136–39, 142–44, 150–54.
7. Ibid., 121.
8. Berlin, "Introduction," in Berlin (1971), xlvi.
9. Ibid., xlix.
10. Ibid.
11. Ibid., xlvii.
12. Berlin, "Two Concepts," in Berlin (1971), 122.
13. Ibid., 147, 167.
14. Ibid., 166.
15. MacCallum (1973), 301. See also Patterson (1991), 296.
16. MacCallum (1973), 298.
17. Ibid., 301, 303.
18. Gray (1980), 510–13.
19. Thomas Hobbes, *On Man*, in Hobbes, *Man and Citizen*, 46.
20. Taylor (1979), 179; Jean-Jacques Rousseau, *The Social Contract*; Berlin, "Two Concepts," in Berlin (1971).
21. See my introduction to *The Subject of Liberty*, Hirschmann (2003).
22. Berlin, "Introduction," in Berlin (1971), xxxviii–xl.
23. Berlin (1979), 190.
24. Ibid., 193.
25. See Hirschmann, "Introduction," in Hirschmann (2003), 5–6.

26. Pettit (1997), 18.

27. These quotes from ibid. are from the following pages, in order: 21, 52, 5, 6, 22, 18.

28. Hirschmann (2003), ch. 1.

29. Pettit (1997), 44–45.

30. See Hirschmann (2003), ch. 4, for a discussion of the various forms that domestic abuse may take, aside from physical assault, such as property damage or psychological and emotional abuse. Such surrogates for physical assault may reinforce the fear of such assault in the victim's mind without such assaults actually taking place. That is different from the scenario I am hypothesizing here, where all kinds of abuse cease.

31. Because statistics on these matters are notoriously difficult to assess, owing to the added social cost to women of reporting such interference, I offer this claim only for rhetorical purposes. As I argue in *The Subject of Liberty* (2003), such interference probably happens to more women than we realize, but my point about the relationship between domination and interference does not require that to be the case. For my critique of Pettit in that book, see esp. 26–28.

32. Pettit (1997), 63.

33. See Hirschmann (2003), ch. 7, where I argue for "participation in the processes of social construction" as a key element of a feminist theory of freedom. However, I do not argue for that on a principled basis of the meaning of terms: I do not call women's exclusion arbitrary. Rather, I say that it is a function of power, and that as a political positioning, feminism demands that we argue for equality of power. In other words, I endorse Pettit's goals and values; what I dispute here is the way that he expresses them, for this means of expression has unfortunate theoretical consequences. In particular, his usage of "arbitrary" is highly charged and inaccurate, and I think ignores the political underpinnings of language: what appears arbitrary to the liberal is tradition to the fundamentalist. But that is why I argue that political theorists need to see "freedom as political, not philosophical" (Hirschmann [2003], 14).

34. Pettit (1997), 6.

35. Ibid., 18.

36. Ibid., 40. John Locke, *Two Treatises of Government*, 2.57. Throughout, in citations for this work, the first number identifies the book number; the second, the paragraph number.

37. Pettit (1997), 37.

38. Hobbes, *Leviathan*, ch. 30, 388.

39. Benson (1991), 385–408; Meyers (1987), 619–28.

40. These three layers were first articulated in *The Subject of Liberty* in greater detail, but they are important to the argument I deploy in this book, so I here undertake a brief summary of that earlier account. Also, in that earlier account I described them more as "levels" than "layers," though I think the latter is more accurate phrasing. See Hirschmann, Brison, and Frye (2006).

41. Though Harvard University president Lawrence Summers's comments about the scarcity of women among science faculty, which he suggested might be the result more of innate differences from men than discrimination or social factors, invoked this ideology as recently as 2005. See Bombardieri (2005).

42. MacKinnon (1987).

43. Particularly Butler (1993).

44. See Collins (1998); Hirschmann (2006).

45. Ferguson (1993), 129. See also Brown (1995), 145, for a similar contrast between socialization and social construction.

46. That is, I do not deny outright the possibility that testosterone or other biological factors may contribute to a proclivity among some, perhaps many, men for violence; however, if such a proclivity exists, why it takes particular forms in particular societies is a function of social construction. On the social construction of masculinity in domestic violence, see Hirschmann (2003), ch. 4.

47. Hobbes, *Leviathan*, ch. 21, 268.

48. See Erickson (1993); Mendelson and Crawford (1998); and Wright, Ferguson, and Buck (2004).

49. I owe this phrasing to Joan Tronto.

50. Okin (1979); Pateman (1988). The "Rereading the Canon" series features edited volumes of feminist interpretations of individual canonical figures, ranging from Plato to Wittgenstein. See http://www.psupress.org/cgi-bin/search.exe, and click "Rereading the Canon" under "series." See also Witt (2006), 537–52.

51. See Hirschmann (1989), (1992), (1997) and (2003); Hirschmann and Pateman (1992); and Hirschmann and Di Stefano (1996).

52. Crenshaw (1991), 1241–99.

53. Hull, Scott, and Smith (1982).

54. Immanuel Kant, *Anthropology from a Pragmatic Point of View*; John Stuart Mill, *On the Subjection of Women*; Jean-Jacques Rousseau, *Dissertation on the Origin and Foundation of the Inequality of Mankind*.

55. That does not mean that more subtle, and perhaps inferential, arguments cannot be developed: see Glausser (1990), 199–216; and Farr (1986), 263–89.

56. Fryer (1984); Tucker (1992); Shyllon (1977); and Walvin (1973).

57. Macpherson (1962).

CHAPTER 1: THOMAS HOBBES

1. Skinner (1990), 122.

2. Hobbes, *Leviathan*, ch. 14, 189. Unless otherwise indicated, all textual references will be to the Macpherson edition by chapter and page number.

3. Flathman (1987), 112–15. This is not to deny that Hobbesian man pursues desires for particular items, or more generally for "glory" and "power after power," but rather that the prevention of pursuit of those desires is no different in terms of freedom for Hobbes than the prevention of expressing a reflex action. See also Flathman (1993).

4. Skinner (1990), 123, 126.

5. Ibid., 125.

6. Thomas Hobbes, "The Questions Concerning Liberty, Necessity, and Chance," 72. As Bramhall says, "If his will do not come upon him according to his will, then he is not a free, nor yet so much as a voluntary agent." John Bramhall, "A Defence of True Liberty," 44.

7. Thomas Hobbes, *On Man* in *Man and Citizen (De Homine and De Cive)*, ch. 11, sec. 3.

8. Macpherson (1962).

9. Hobbes, "Of Liberty and Necessity," 31.

10. Ibid., 18. Though Hobbes is not always fair to Bramhall's argument, his critique provides insight into Hobbes's own definition of freedom, and so I focus on Hobbes's interpretation rather than Bramhall's essay here. But see John Bramhall, "Discourse of Liberty and Necessity."

11. Hobbes, "Of Liberty and Necessity," 31.

12. Ibid., 37; see also Hobbes, *Leviathan*, ch. 6, 127.

13. Hobbes, *The Elements of Law*, 1.12.1. Subsequently cited as *Elements* by part, chapter, and section number as given in the Tönnies edition. The Rogers edition prints the *Elements* as two separate essays, *Human Nature, or the Fundamental Elements of Policy*, and *De Corpore Politico, or the Elements of Law*. See Skinner (1996), 1 n. 2, for an assessment of the weaknesses of the Tönnies edition and the debate over whether Hobbes intended these two essays to be separate, or parts of a single work. The comparative layout, however, is straightforward: part 1, chs. 1–13 of Tönnies's *Elements* make up Rogers's *Human Nature*; part 1, chs. 14–19 make up part 1 of Rogers's *De Corpore Politico*; and part 2 of Tönnies's *Elements* corresponds to Part 2 of Rogers's *De Corpore Politico*.

14. Hobbes, "Of Liberty and Necessity," 30. The example of the bound and dragged prisoner is also invoked in ibid., 32. The example of throwing your possessions into the sea on the chance that it will help stop the boat you are on from sinking is also used, though somewhat less clearly, in *Leviathan*, ch. 21, 262.

15. Hobbes, "The Questions Concerning Liberty, Necessity, and Chance," 80–81; Hobbes, "Of Liberty and Necessity," 32.

16. Since we cannot choose to die, or be obliged to let someone else kill us, then the limit of a woman's choice would be if her partner tries to kill her. But the fact that women are often actually at greater risk of violence and murder when they leave would seem to further complicate this application of Hobbes's argument; it would not be a vacillation between different desires, but a calculation of which option is more likely to satisfy the same desire, namely, safety. See Mahoney (1991) and Giles-Simms (1983), both of which would challenge my simplistic initial juxtaposition of staying/violence versus leaving/poverty. See Hirschmann (2003), ch. 4, for a fuller discussion of domestic violence and freedom.

17. Flathman (1993), 97.

18. Hobbes, *De Cive* in *Man and Citizen (De Homine and De Cive)*, ch. 1, sec. 2, note on p. 110. Subsequently cited as *De Cive* by chapter and section number.

19. Schochet (1988), 12.

20. Hobbes, "Of Liberty and Necessity," 25.

21. Skinner (1990), 133, 135; Gauthier (1969).

22. Hirschmann (1992), 36.

23. Skinner (1996), 313.

24. In his "Introduction" to *Leviathan* (19–21), Macpherson dates *Elements* to 1640, *Leviathan* to 1651.

25. The difference between the thief and a sovereign may also demonstrate the difference between renouncing and conveying, the former being simple abandon-

ment of a right, "when he cares not to whom the benefit thereof redoundeth," as long as he keeps him safe (pick a sovereign, any sovereign); the latter being "when he intendeth the benefit thereof to some certain person, or persons" such as the thief who will otherwise kill him (*Leviathan*, ch. 14, 191).

26. Schochet (1988), 235.

27. Ibid., 237, 240.

28. See, for instance, Di Stefano (1986); Flax (1983); Hirschmann (1992).

29. Wright (2002). She also points out that this instrumentalism means that Hobbes is never really concerned to disrupt gender norms per se, any more than he particularly cares to reinforce them. He is no feminist hero. See also Wright (2004), ch. 3–4.

30. Wright (2002), 127, 136, 137, 125.

31. Mendelson and Crawford (1998), 275, 288, 327–28, 330, 326.

32. Ibid., 256, 308, 304, 306–7. Women of the upper classes often performed work of medical healers as charity work, which thereby undermined the professional designation of women who did such work for pay. Ibid., 319–20.

33. Ibid., 330. This finding directly contradicts Alice Clark's claim that though "the wife was subject to her husband . . . she was by no means regarded as his servant." A. Clark (1968), 12.

34. Mendelson and Crawford (1998), 344; on women's voting, see ibid., 56 and ch. 7.

35. *Leviathan*, ch. 20, 253. In *De Cive*, Hobbes puts it at once more strongly and more ambiguously: "the inequality of their natural forces is not so great, that the man could get the dominion over the woman without war" (9.3). But this could be interpreted in two ways: the obvious way is that, if there is a war, it is equal chances who would win. The less obvious interpretation is to take it as a warning: men would probably win such a war if it happened, but that outcome is not guaranteed, so they will not normally attack women because it is too contrary to self-preservation. The former interpretation is supported by the passage just cited in *Leviathan*; but the latter interpretation could be borne out through the elements I discuss below.

36. Pateman (2007), 79.

37. Hobbes, *De Cive*, 9.5; why Hobbes follows "himself" with "him or her" once again illustrates the ambiguity with which his texts are rife, but at least it indicates the possibility that the man may be subjected to the woman.

38. *Elements*, 2.4.10. Could Hobbes again be given an out by declaring that women could be "masters"? He is quite slippery on that question; in this quoted passage, he designates "the father *or* the mother, *or* both" as the "sovereign." The use of "or" here indicates that women could be "masters." But in *De Cive*, shortly after he says "every woman that bears children, becomes both a *mother* and a *lord*" (9.3), Hobbes also says, "the preserved oweth all to the preserver, whether in regard of his education as to a *mother*, or of his service as to a *lord*" (9.4), introducing with that "or" a decided differentiation, if not mutual exclusivity, between the two.

39. I should of course point out that this assumes that Schochet's patriarchal family is not yet set; after all, if it existed, Hobbes would have no need to engage this discussion at all, for the question of dominion would already be settled by

contract prior to all children's birth within a given family. My point is that Hobbes's discussion here implicitly challenges Schochet's assertion of the prior existence of the patriarchal family in the state of nature and contributes to the consideration of how it might have come to be.

40. But see O'Brien (1981) for a similar argument made about other political philosophers.

41. Hobbes, "Questions Concerning Liberty, Necessity, and Chance," 76.

42. Hobbes, *De Cive*, 8.1. Stanlick (2001) makes a similar point, as does Pateman (1991), 64. The latter, however, contradicts an earlier assertion made by Brennan and Pateman that the "possibility . . . that the wife has the same status as a servant . . . is unlikely . . . for the master-servant relationship, like slavery, originates in force." Brennan and Pateman (1979), 190. In this, they are clearly mistaken, for the key *difference* between a slave and a servant is force: the former is physically bound and restrained, the latter is free because of contractual "trust," as I discuss below in the text.

43. Schochet (1988), 233.

44. Pateman (1991), 65, 67.

45. See for instance McKinney (1993); Stanlick (2001); Brennan and Pateman (1979); Di Stefano (1990).

46. Green (1994, 461) notes this latter possibility but then argues that women who do not enter patriarchal marriage contracts would in effect be wiped out of the gene pool: "the women whose children survive will tend to be those who are prepared to accept submission in order to increase their children's chances of survival, and who are, in this sense, reasonably altruistic, at least towards their own children." Admittedly, it is somewhat difficult to determine whether Green herself advocates this position or is attributing it to Pateman, but in either case she is wrong. Pateman clearly does not argue this, and the argument itself is rather implausible given Hobbes's account of the state of nature. All Hobbesian women, like men, are created with the same impulse for self-preservation; if there is difference in the kinds of contracts they are willing to form, with some willing to submit to patriarchal marriages and others not, the difference must lie in the conditions that determine the available options in particular choice situations, not in the contractors themselves.

47. Green (1994), 460. Hobbes also includes "adultery" as one way in which people seek honor, which by definition presupposes marriage in the state of nature. Tarcov (1984), 42, 45, says this also indicates women's inequality, and categorizes it along with rape, but I believe he is also wrong, as adultery can be committed by women just as freely as by men.

48. Pateman (1988), 49.

49. Hobbes definitely says that women feel lust as well as men, thus undermining an implicit foundation of Pateman's thesis that the act of rape underlies the sexual, and hence social, contract. In her view, Hobbesian women would have to never agree to sex, because it risks subordination; but as I have suggested that seriously underestimates the strength and wit of Hobbesian woman.

50. Plotz (2001); Heywood (2001).

51. Green (1994), 461.

52. *Leviathan*, ch. 21, 271; see also Tarcov (1984), 45.

53. See also Hirschmann (1992), 42–44.

54. Although Hobbes also at one point defines vainglory as "the feigning or supposing of abilities in ourselves, which we know are not" (*Leviathan*, ch. 6, 125), the prideful conception of actually believing, rather than pretending to believe, in an exaggeration of one's value predominates in his references to human vanity and vainglory.

55. Wright similarly says Hobbes's account is "more descriptive than explanatory." Wright (2002), 124.

56. Mendelson and Crawford (1998), 219, 262, 268, 281, 332.

57. Wright (2002), 126; referring to Breitenberg (1996).

58. See David Hume, "Of the Original Contract," "Of the Origin of Justice and Property," "Of the Origin of Government," in Hume, *Political Essays*. On Hume's theory of obligation, see Hirschmann (2000).

59. Stanlick (2001).

60. Holmes (1990), xxviii n. 39, xi.

61. Gauthier (1969). See also Leijenhorst (2002).

62. Hobbes, *Thomas White's De Mundo Examined*, 1.1. Subsequent references will be made in the text by chapter and section number.

63. See Johnston (1986) and Skinner (1996) for two different discussions of the role of language, and particularly rhetoric, in Hobbes's theory.

64. Hobbes, *Behemoth*, 95.

65. Vaughan (2002), 34–35.

66. Holmes (1990), xlix. On the relationship of prudence to reason, see Ewasiuk (2007).

67. Vaughan (2002), 35.

68. Hobbes, *Behemoth*, 2–3.

69. Vaughan (2002), 38, 49; Tarcov (1984), 48.

70. Flathman (1993), 147.

71. Wright (2002), 124.

72. Hobbes, *De Cive*, 8.3, 8.5; see also *Leviathan*, ch. 20, 255, for the contrast between servant and "captive."

73. Kay (1988), 25–26.

74. Breitenberg (1996).

75. Hobbes, *Elements*, 1.9.17. Though in several places, love is equated with desire, not sympathetic emotion, the difference being only that "by Desire, we always signifie the Absence of the Object; by Love, most commonly the Presence of the same" (*Leviathan*, ch. 6, 119).

76. Wright (2002), 123.

77. In his *Autobiography*, 93–94, Hobbes attributes his own timidity to the fact that rumors of the Armada invasion spread as his mother went into labor: "Thus my mother was big with such fear that she brought twins to birth, myself and fear at the same time"; see also Di Stefano (1990), 94, who contrasts such "avowed timidity" in his self-conception to the "heroic" thematics of Hobbes's political theory.

CHAPTER 2: JOHN LOCKE

1. John Locke, *Two Treatises of Government*, 2.223. Subsequent references will be made in the text by book and section number.

2. Mehta (1992); Tarcov (1984); John Locke, *Some Thoughts Concerning Education*, cited in the text by section number as *Education*; *Questions Concerning the Law of Nature*, cited in the text by page number as *Questions*; *Of the Conduct of the Understanding*, cited in the text by section and page number as *Conduct*.

3. See also Ashcraft (1986), 51; Schochet (1988). See also Sir Robert Filmer, *Patriarcha: The Natural Power of Kinges against the Unnatural Liberty of the People*.

4. McClure (1996).

5. Kramnick (1990), for instance, sees Locke's vision of reason as solidly Protestant, and in keeping with the traditional liberal, negative liberty vision.

6. McClure (1996), ch. 1. Dunn (1969) similarly argues that Locke believed that God created a "divine order."

7. Locke, "Some Considerations of the Consequences of the Lowering of Interest, and Raising the Value of Money: In a Letter to a Member of Parliament." See also Kramnick (1990).

8. Kramnick (1990). Though Kramnick has a point about the importance of the Protestant work ethic to the late seventeenth and eighteenth centuries, he treats Protestantism as the answer to all questions of Locke's motivation. By contrast, I believe it is important to examine the philosophical underpinnings of Locke's philosophy that lead him to Protestant ideals, which were not the only ideals available to him at the time. As I have said before, "There are many ways to respond to divine right, the Exclusion Crisis, civil war. . . . why did [Locke] respond in the particular ways [he] did?" Hirschmann (1992), 128.

9. Macpherson (1962), 226.

10. Ibid., 246.

11. On the importance of mathematics, see Locke, *Conduct*, sec. 6, 178, sec. 7, 180; on the time constraints of laborers, see ibid., sec. 3, 171, sec. 4, 173, and secs. 6 and 7, 178–82.

12. tenBroeck (1964), 257.

13. I discuss this issue at greater length in Hirschmann (2002).

14. Locke's use of the word "capable" might confuse my distinction between ability and capacity, but because those two words are commonly synonyms anyhow, the reader will realize that the particular distinction I make between these terms is my own contrivance, not Locke's.

15. Letter from John Locke to Mrs. Mary Clarke, December 1683, in Rand (1927), 103.

16. Mehta (1992), 132.

17. Ibid., 132. In this, Mehta suggests Locke's emphasis on the notion of "discipline" is particularly significant; Mehta invokes a Foucaultian meaning of "discipline" to paint a picture of Locke as creating and establishing institutions—particularly the family and the state—that inevitably produce a particular kind of

person, that "disciplines" people so that they completely internalize and embody the standards and norms Locke wishes to promote (ibid., 143). By contrast, Kramnick (1990) argues that the notion of discipline is more basically a Protestant one; but why Protestantism could not be subject to the very same observation Mehta makes is unclear. Also see Tarcov (1984).

18. Butler (1978), 148. See also letter from Locke to Mrs. Clarke, December 1683, in Rand (1927), 102–3.

19. Locke to Mrs. Clarke, December 1683, in Rand (1927), 103.

20. Ibid., 102.

21. Ibid., 101. See also Wright (2007), who maintains that annual pregnancies were an "ideal" for upper-class women, in order to produce heirs.

22. Axtell (1968), 199 n. 1.

23. Locke to Edward Clarke, January 1, 1685, in Rand (1927), 121.

24. L. Clark (1977); Eisenstein (1981); R. Smith (1985).

25. Kant, *Observations on the Feeling of the Beautiful and Sublime*. See Hirschmann (2003), ch. 2, for a discussion of the similarities between Locke's and Kant's theories of education.

26. Locke, *The Reasonableness of Christianity*, 76. At the end of *A Discourse of Miracles*, 86, he takes another swipe at the intellectual capacities of "poor bricklayers," though does not mention women this time.

27. Astell, *Reflections upon Marriage*.

28. L. Clark (1977), 714. Erickson (1993) documents a higher degree of property ownership among women; but only because *feme sole* was used more frequently than previous scholars thought, not because women had widespread legal property "rights" in the Lockean sense. See also Waldron (2007a), who suggests that Locke did support property rights for women.

29. L. Clark (1977), 713.

30. Tarcov (1984), 10.

31. In the *First Treatise*, Locke argues against Filmer's claim that kings rule by the same right that God gives husbands over wives by pointing out that God does not give husbands the kind of absolute rule of life and death that Filmer wants to give kings, and that the existence of queens overthrows Filmer's logic. As Pateman (1988) has argued, however, this antipatriarchalist argument ends up, in the *Second Treatise*, being quite patriarchal in the structure of the family that underpins Locke's liberal state.

32. L. Clark (1977), 716. See Hirschmann (1992) for a fuller development of this argument.

33. Tarcov (1984), 76.

34. See Ashcraft (1986), 236.

35. Macpherson (1962); Dunn (1969). I discuss the differences between their explanations for men's leaving the natural state, as well as T. H. Green's, in Hirschmann (1992), 46–47.

36. Locke, *An Essay Concerning Human Understanding*, 2.21.22.

37. Ibid., 2.21.27.

38. Both Dunn (1969) and Pitkin (1965), (1966) make this case, though in different ways and for different reasons. Pitkin argues that Locke deploys hypothetical consent; that is, what we would consent to if we were rational is what we

are obligated to. If we were rational, we would not consent to tyranny. Dunn argues that consent is a necessary but not sufficient condition for obligation, and that the quality of the government is also a factor determining obligation.

39. See Simmons (1979); Pateman (1984); Hirschmann (1992); and Pitkin (1965).

40. McClure (1996), 63.

41. Simmons (1979) particularly attributes this understanding to Locke. But see Schochet (1988), 254.

42. Locke, *An Essay Concerning Human Understanding*, 2.21.67.

43. I first offered this interpretation of this passage, albeit in considerably briefer form, in Hirschmann (2003), ch. 2.

44. Working schools would also provide food for the children, which they otherwise would not obtain from their impoverished parents. Indeed, to combine cost savings with children's support, they would not be paid in wages—which would only be lost to drunken fathers—but in food: specifically, bread and water, and "in cold weather, if it be thought needful, a little warm water-gruel." For the efficient Locke noted, "the same fire that warms the room may be made use of to boil a pot of it" ("Poor Law," 191).

45. Locke, *Essay Concerning Human Understanding*, 2.21.8. Because of the frequency of references to this work in the next few pages, they will be made in the text by book, chapter, and section.

46. Tarcov (1984), 105.

47. Ibid., 89–90.

48. Ibid., 115.

49. Neil (1989), 240.

50. N. Wood (1983), 121, 140, 145.

51. Kramnick (1990), 112, 191.

52. Schochet (1988), 251.

53. Locke, *A Letter Concerning Toleration*, 19. Hereafter cited in the text as *Toleration*, by page number.

54. Wootten (1993), 99.

55. Ibid., 104.

56. See particularly Ashcraft (1986).

57. Another example of Locke's ability to exclude from toleration all non-Protestant views through an apparent neutrality of reason that actually betrays deep bias is his reference to the Chinese as atheists in the *Essay*: "in China, the Sect of the Litterati, or *Learned*, keeping to the old Religion of *China*, and the ruling *Party* there, are all of them *Atheist*" (88). Not only does this display a glaring Eurocentrism in his conception of "religion," but Locke conveniently undercuts all of the elements that he carefully builds to support the superiority of his own Protestantism. For instance, he does not say that the Chinese lack belief in God, only that their "old Religion" is mistaken; yet in the *Letter Concerning Toleration* he said that no one can know which country has the true religion. Further, whereas in England the well-educated are the saviors of the rest, by infusing reason into the workings of government and civil society and serving as an example to all, in China the intellectuals are precisely the problem, suggesting that there is no hope for China at all. Here it seems that Locke willfully ignores or

twists his own words to ensure that what does not meet his narrow prescription is excluded from consideration on apparently "reasonable" grounds.

58. Indeed, in Mehta's thematic concern with insanity and madness, it would seem that Locke's dismissal of "lunatiks and ideots" as incapable of giving consent is much more significant than Mehta grants; for rather than these unfortunates being aberrations or deviants who must be cared for, it would seem that we are all on a continuum with them.

59. Mehta (1992), 31.

60. Ibid., 147.

61. *Education*, sec. 78. On the probable age of the child, see Axtell (1968), 129 n. 1.

62. Mehta (1992), 148.

63. Ibid.

64. Ibid. 163.

65. See for instance Butler (1978), 135–40; Schochet (1988); Shanley (1979).

66. On "contingent" and "structural sexism," see Hirschmann (1992), 11–12 and 57–59.

Chapter 3: Jean-Jacques Rousseau

1. Pateman (1984), ch. 7.

2. Kukla (2002), 346.

3. Shell (2001), 274.

4. Jean-Jacques Rousseau, *Dissertation on the Origin and Foundation of the Inequality of Mankind*, in Rousseau, *The Social Contract and Discourses*, 92, 84. Subsequent references will be made in the text as it is commonly referred to, *Second Discourse*.

5. See Noone (1980), ch. 3.

6. Keohane (1980), 440.

7. Jean-Jacques Rousseau, *Of the Social Contract*, in Rousseau, *The Social Contract and Discourses*, bk. 1, ch. 6. Subsequent references will be made in the text as *Social Contract*. Because of the large number of editions in translation, citations will be by book and chapter rather than page number.

8. Levine (1976), 34.

9. Orbach (1978).

10. Pateman (1984), ch. 7.

11. C. Taylor (1979); Berlin (1971), 118–72.

12. Keohane (1980), 442.

13. This is a key argument for Pateman (1984) and one I also make in Hirschmann (1992), ch. 2. For an effective dismissal of the totalitarian interpretation of Rousseau, see Blum (1986), 32–33.

14. Wolker (2001), 425–26.

15. This is an argument I first made in Hirschmann (1992), which I described as the reconciliation of voluntarism and virtue (see 61–70).

16. Shell (2001), 275.

17. In *A Theory of Justice* (1971), John Rawls argues that it would be rational

to support measures that produce unequal benefits, as long as I benefit somewhat. For instance, it would be rational for me to support a proposal that raises your income by $100,000 per year but mine only $1,000 per year because I am better off, regardless of the fact that the benefits to us are unequally distributed. Selfishness, greed, and jealousy, according to Rawls, contradict self-interest. But Rawls tacitly assumes a background inequality that compels us to accept the rationality of the proposal. If we start from a position of true equality, there is no reason for me to accept the lower benefit instead of trying for the higher one. That is, if I had equal political power and access, rational self-interest would be more likely to make me vote against your proposal with the idea of resubmitting the same proposal such that I am the one to receive the $100,000 raise and you the $1,000. And of course, if we are all thinking the same way, we each will seek to be the one who benefits more, so everyone will vote against everyone else's proposal. The end result can only be an entirely different proposal that creates and distributes wealth in a more equitable manner.

18. Although Rousseau does not capitalize the term "legislator," I follow the frequent practice in the secondary literature of doing so here to distinguish this very specific figure from the legislative powers of the citizens in assembly. Indeed, because the Legislator cannot vote, he is in fact the only (male) member of the society who is *not* a "legislator."

19. Shklar (1969).

20. Blum notes that *The Social Contract*'s "Dedication to Geneva," "though designed to flatter Geneva . . . was a covert indictment of the existing city as compared with Rousseau's vision of its ideal form." Blum (1986), 55. There are other figures from ancient history who certainly could fit Rousseau's bill, however, in particular Lycurgus the Lawgiver.

21. Shklar (2001), 154–55.

22. Jean-Jacques Rousseau, *Political Economy*, in Rousseau, *Social Contract and Discourses*, 147.

23. Rousseau, *Emile*, 40. Subsequent references will be made in the text.

24. Keohane (1980), 190, 435–42, 310–11. *Amour de nous-mêmes* is not a term Rousseau uses, Keohane notes, but rather can be traced to Montaigne's translation from the Latin of fifteenth-century Spanish theologian Raymond Sebond's *The Book of Creatures, or Natural Theology*. But she indicates that it is a term that captures much of Rousseau's thinking about love of self, community, and virtue. I should also note that Keohane uses the sixteenth-century spelling of *mêmes*, namely, *mesmes*, in her own prose as well as in quoted material.

25. Rousseau, *The Government of Poland*, esp. ch. 4.

26. Blum (1986), 134; Rousseau, *Correspondance Complète* 39:226.

27. Zerilli (1994), 18.

28. Bradshaw (2002), 66.

29. Weiss and Harper (2002), 51.

30. A small sampling includes Ruddick (1989); Trebilcot (1983); Fineman (1995); Kittay (1999); and Hirschmann and Liebert (2001).

31. That Rousseau abandoned his five children might undermine such a possibility, of course, but he claims to have had their good at heart. See his *Confessions*, bk. 7, 354, 367–68.

32. Fox-Genovese (1984), 121; Fairchilds (1984), 107. See also Sussman (1982).

33. Weiss and Harper (2002), 58.

34. Fairchilds (1984), 98–99.

35. See for instance, Ormiston (2002). Also see Morgenstern (1996). Additionally, certain aspects of his thought that I have previously articulated—particularly the importance of sentiment to truth, that sentiment must work in tandem with reason—are compatible with some feminist theoretical arguments about epistemology. See Antony and Witt (2001).

36. Conner (1984), 50.

37. Goodman (1994).

38. Mittman (1984), 160.

39. Spencer (1984).

40. Applewhite and Levy (1984).

41. Rousseau, *Confessions*, bk. 3, 105 and passim; bk. 7, 340, 350.

42. Kukla (2002), 360–61; Rousseau, *Confessions*, bk. 2, 52.

43. Rousseau, *Confessions*, bk. 7, 339.

44. Ibid., bk. 9, 426.

45. Ibid., bk. 7, 354.

46. Rousseau offers three rationalizations. First, he needed to be free of bourgeois responsibility, such as fatherhood, to be able to continue to make the valuable contributions that his writings constituted. Second, if the state were not so corrupt and inadequate, it would provide for children much better than any individual father could, and in such a context (which his writings could lead us to), Rousseau's actions would be virtuous. Third, he did not intend to cause any pain or suffering: "I wished . . . that I had been reared and brought up as they have been." *Confessions*, bk. 7, 354, 367–68; Blum (1986), 80–81, 117–18. None of these reasons are particularly satisfactory, but at least he admits "remorse" in the final chapter of *Confessions*: "I had neglected duties from which nothing could excuse me" (bk. 12, 617).

47. Rousseau, *Confessions*, bk. 7, 327–30.

48. See John Locke, *Essay Concerning Human Understanding*, 279.

49. Okin (1979), 99.

50. Kukla (2002), 349.

51. Okin (1979), 124, 127.

52. Zerilli (1994); Weiss (1987); and Wingrove (2002), 315. The importance of social constructivism to contemporary feminist analyses of Rousseau is apparent in Lange's introduction to Lange (2002), as she describes essays by these authors as well as those by Ormiston, Marso, and Morgenstern as social constructivist (16–17, 20–21). It should be noted, however, that while Marso's and Morgenstern's respective books on Rousseau deploy social constructivist arguments, their articles in the Lange volume do not, nor does Ormiston's. Kukla (2002), by contrast, centrally deploys a social constructivist argument that Lange does not acknowledge.

53. Wingrove (2002), 319.

54. Kukla (2002), 349–50.

55. Zerilli (1994), 18.

56. Ibid. In this sense, Rousseau demonstrates even more strongly than I myself realized in *Rethinking Obligation* the developmental dynamic of the male infant's gender identity posited by object relations theory. See Chodorow (1978); and Hirschmann (1992), ch. 3.

57. *Emile and Sophie, or Solitary Beings*, 201–3. Emile never acknowledges that his behavior may be the result of his own grief.

58. The details of Sophie's pregnancy are vague. Elizabeth Wingrove (2000) maintains that Sophie was raped, a plausible interpretation of the following sentences, which provide our primary clue:

> She believed that she could not erase her sin without paying the penalty, nor that she could come to terms with justice without suffering all the evils that she deserved. It is for that reason that, fearless and harsh in her frankness, she told her crime to you [that is, the tutor], to my whole family, and at the same time said nothing about what would excuse her, what would perhaps justify her, hiding it, I say, with such obstinacy that she never said a word to me, and I found it out only after her death. (*Emile and Sophie*, 220)

Additionally, before she tells Emile of her pregnancy, Sophie goes through a sudden change of "mood," curtailing her social activities, "shut up in her room from morning till night, not speaking, not weeping, not caring about anyone." She even expresses cold contempt of her former "friend," and Emile, in retrospection, mentions "betrayals of false friendship," suggesting perhaps a set-up that exposed Sophie to sexual abuse (*Emile and Sophie*, 203–4). Furthermore, Emile later bemoans that Sophie "had to wage battles without respite, unceasing, against others, against herself. What invincible courage, what obstinate resistance, what heroic strength she needed!" (210). But we must recall that Rousseau indicates in *Emile* that rape is a logical impossibility: "for the attacker to be victorious, the one who is attacked must permit or arrange it; for does she not have adroit means to force the aggressor to use force? The freest and sweetest of all acts does not admit of real violence" (*Emile*, 359). Furthermore, Emile's behavior prior to Sophie's repudiation is similarly unclear; despite his protestations that Sophie's friend "frequently made advances to me that I did not always resist without difficulty," the "too attractive liaisons" for which Emile professes a "weakness" could indicate that Emile had an affair. At any rate, these liaisons and pleasures "dulled my desires by diffusing them," Emile writes; "my heart . . . was becoming incapable of warmth and vigor" (*Emile and Sophie*, 202). This loss of affection, if triggered by Emile's infidelity, would be a double blow to Sophie and might cause her to retaliate in kind. One could imagine her cultivating a lover whom she would not otherwise admire (though her alleged beauty suggests she might have had a number of potential suitors), or even simply giving in to opportunity, quasi-reluctantly, when an otherwise unattractive man took advantage of her self-destructive desire for retaliation. The society of females that Sophie associates with would reinforce the appropriateness of such behavior; popular television of the twenty-first century is rife with examples of sex used for revenge with less than desirable partners; one can hardly imagine that Rousseau's eighteenth-century Paris would be less tawdry. As Colmo says, "Sophie is seduced in the city, not by a man, but by a married couple" (Colmo 1996, 77). That is, Emile persuades Sophie to go to Paris with him by pointing out that she would have a companion in a female friend of hers who was also accompanying her husband to the city. This couple, it turns out, is corrupt in its attitudes about "the duties of their married state," that is, sexual fidelity (*Emile and Sophie*, 203). Thus, Sophie is placed by Emile in a social milieu that might well lead her to think in retaliatory terms when faced with Emile's own emotional, if not sexual, infidelity. Indeed, Emile admonishes himself that "she broke her promises only because of your example. If you had not neglected her, she never would have betrayed you" (209). "Betrayed" is not an appropriate term to describe Sophie's behavior if she was raped; though it is not clear from the text whether this statement expresses what Emile was thinking at the time or his retrospective reflection on those events.

59. By using the words "soon after," I admit that I am assuming that these events all occurred within a matter of months. Since Emile never mentions the birth of Sophie's illegitimate child, I infer that she died before giving birth. The son's removal from his mother, and his subsequent death, precede Sophie's death, since the son's death is what causes Sophie to seek out Emile for a kind of reconciliation (*Emile and Sophie*, 220).

60. Wingrove (2000), 99, 97.

61. Blum (1986), 130; Zerilli (1994), 18.

62. Neither should we forget that Emile has abandoned his son as well, to whom Emile's duty is even greater than that to his wife. At the end of *Emile*, the title character says to his tutor, "God forbid that I let you also raise the son after having raised the father," because it is the father's duty to raise the son: "God forbid that so holy and so sweet a duty should ever be fulfilled by anyone but myself" (480). Thus, in abandoning Sophie, he abandons his son and abdicates his duty to educate him, doing the son irreparable harm. Indeed, his primary thoughts for his son concern whether he should take him away from Sophie as a means of revenge. After a scene is related to him in which Sophie brings her son to where Emile now works and observes Emile without herself being seen, he realizes that he was about "to sacrifice the child to take revenge on the mother," and furthermore, that it would be a greater punishment to her to leave his son with her: "may he each day of his life recall to the faithless one the happiness of which he was the token, and the husband she cast away" (*Emile and Sophie*, 219–20). If Emile were the responsible father the tutor trained him to be, not only would he have thought first of the welfare of his son, but he most likely would have sought to deal with his heartbreak in a way that did not harm the child. His apparent lack of grief over the death of his daughter as well indicates that Emile never really measured up to the emotional responsibilities of fatherhood.

63. From a feminist perspective, of course, this statement seems completely illogical, particularly if Sophie was raped. But Rousseau, having said in *Emile* that rape is impossible (women always have the means to defend themselves), maintains that even when sex appears nonconsensual, women must want it or it would not happen (359). Thus, if Sophie is pregnant, it is by virtue of her own desire by definition; and if that desire runs against the economy of patriarchal control (Emile is not the father), it threatens such control and must be disciplined.

64. Marso (1999), 2.

65. Colmo (1996), 76, 80, 83.

66. *Emile and Sophie*, 209, 219, 220.

67. S.G. are the initials that the lover uses to sign a note "permitting" Julie to marry Wolmar, the only time in the novel in which the lover identifies himself. Following the norm, I will refer to the lover as Saint-Preux even when discussing a portion of the novel prior to his receiving his pseudonym (*Julie, or the New Heloise*, 268. Subsequent references made in the text).

68. The second letter contains a fuller explication of her "new" views, and thus some passages from that letter will be used here; but the first letter is what marks her "revolution." To avoid awkward phrasing in identifying which letter my text refers to, my discussion may seem to imply that all of these passages are from a single letter. This would be erroneous, because the second letter is more dispassionate, with less religious reference, than the first, as if Julie has acclimated herself to this new position of virtue, whereas in the first letter virtue has truly come as a revelation. Thus, the reader should note the page number references provided in the text; the first letter is contained on pages 279–301, the second letter on pages 304–10.

69. Shklar (2001), 156, 163.

70. Ibid. 169; Marso (2002), 266; Disch (1994); Morgenstern (1996).

71. Mary Wollstonecraft, *Vindication of the Rights of Women: With Strictures on Political and Moral Subjects*. See also Mary Astell, *Reflections upon Marriage*.

72. See also Starobinski (1988) on the struggle between passion and virtue in *Julie*.

73. Marso (2002), 267.

74. Schwartz (1984), 115.

75. Marso (2002), 274, 260.

76. As Shklar puts it, "when Saint-Preux has been liberated from his miseries and she has fulfilled her maternal functions no one needs her. She is indeed perfectly ready to die." At the same time, Shklar calls Julie's death a "sacrificial suicide" because Julie has never been able to completely "cure" herself of her passion for Saint-Preux. This, I have argued, is a mistaken reading of *Julie*. Shklar (2001), 164–65, 169; see also Marso (1999); Morgenstern (2002).

77. On this point, see also Starobinski (1988), 114.

78. The fact that it is five children the Spartan woman gladly sacrifices also echoes Rousseau's personal history, in forcing Thérèse to give up her five children, which, I have already noted, Rousseau constructs as a mark of civic virtue (see note 46 above; *Confessions*, bk. 7, 367–68).

79. Gilligan (1982); Kittay (1999). See Hirschmann (1992) for a discussion of the distortion of freedom stemming from the refusal of mutuality.

80. Zerilli (1994), 52.

81. Landes (1988), 69.

82. Certainly, once Julie dies, Clarens seems to be in a chaotic tumult of grief, which some readers have taken as evidence that Clarens will not survive without Julie (for instance, see Morgenstern [1996], [2002]). But I believe that misinterprets the final pages of the novel. Anyone who understands the stages of grief will realize that the intensity of pain expressed in those final pages will eventually give way to more rational order. Indeed, that begins to happen, as in Rousseau's view

community is a healing agent. Thus, Wolmar continues to seek order and keep the community going, and particularly tries to encourage Claire to gain control over her grief. He also, following Julie's final wishes, urges Saint-Preux to return to Clarens to take over the education of her children, and even to marry Claire. He thus seeks to continue to bind people together, using Julie's memory as a fulcrum to move them into the circle of Clarens. In the final letter of the novel, Claire asserts that she will not marry Saint-Preux, saying that even though "I have felt love for you, I confess; perhaps I still do. . . . a man who was loved by Julie d'Étange, and could bring himself to marry another, is in my sight nothing but a knave and a scoundrel" (611). Yet she urges him to return to Clarens, and it is clear that she, Saint-Preux, and Wolmar will help each other in their grief and form a stable triangle on which the order of Clarens will rest. Married to Saint-Preux, of course, she would be less able to take over Julie's role at Clarens than if she remains a widowed cousin. But Julie's memory still acts as the primary agent: Claire writes, "may her spirit inspire us: may her heart unite all of ours; let us live continually under her eyes. . . . No, she has not departed these premises which she made so charming to us. They are still quite full of her" (612).

CHAPTER 4: IMMANUEL KANT

1. Reiss (1991), 3.
2. A. Wood (1984), 49.
3. Bennett (1984), 102, 106.
4. O'Neill (1989), ix; Beck (1960), 191 n. 43.
5. Nagl-Docekal (1997), 109.
6. Reiss (1991), 5.
7. Carnois (1987), xiii.
8. See particularly Patton (1964), 49; also Kant, *Critique of Practical Reason*, 5:42–43. Subsequent citations will be made in the text, using academy pagination.
9. Velkley (1989).
10. Kant, *Groundwork*, 451. Subsequent citations will be made in the text, using academy pagination.
11. I also favor the terms "noumenal" and "phenomenal" rather than "intelligible" and "sensible" primarily because the use of "sensible" can be rather confusing to readers who think of "sensible" in terms of the more popular usage of "common sense." Another phrase that Kant deploys in an uncommon way is *sensus communis*, to mean "public reason" rather than the unreflective opinions of ordinary people. Kant described "the Idea of a communal sense" as "a faculty of judgement, which in its reflection takes account (a priori) of the mode of representation of all other men in thought; in order as it were to compare its judgement with the collective Reason of humanity, and thus to escape the illusion arising from the private conditions that could be so easily taken for objective, which would injuriously affect the judgement. This is done by comparing our judgement with the possible rather than the actual judgements of others, and by putting ourselves in the place of any other man, by abstracting from the limitations which contingently attach to our own judgement." See *Critique of Judgement*, sec. 40.

12. Hartsock (1984). See also Hirschmann (1992), ch. 4. In his *Critique of Judgement*, however, Kant does say that the second of the three "Maxims of common human Understanding," which is "Judgement," requires us "to put ourselves in thought in the place of every one else. . . . However small may be the area or the degree to which a man's natural gifts reach, yet it indicates a man of enlarged thought if he disregards the subjective private conditions of his own judgement, by which so many others are confined, and reflects upon it from a universal standpoint (which he can only determine by placing himself at the standpoint of others)" (sec. 40). This is still not the epistemological standpoint about which Hartsock speaks, but it does soften the radically individualistic aspects of Kant's concept of reason.

13. O'Neill (1989), 60.

14. Pippin (1982), 189.

15. Ibid., 192.

16. Ibid., 189.

17. Williams (1985), 64.

18. Kant, *Critique of Pure Reason*, A536/B564.

19. Allison (1990), 40.

20. O'Neill (1989), ix.

21. Allison (1990), 38.

22. Reiss (1991), 39.

23. Ibid., 22.

24. Kant, "An Answer to the Question: 'What Is Enlightenment?' " 35, academy pagination. Hereafter cited as "What Is Enlightenment?"

25. Kant, "What Is Orientation in Thinking?" 249n. The Reiss volume in which this essay appears does not use academy pagination.

26. Johnson (1994), 43.

27. Kant, "What Is Enlightenment?" 37.

28. O'Neill (1989), 33–34.

29. Kant, *Critique of Pure Reason*, A738 / B766.

30. Irwin (1984), 35.

31. Kant, *Perpetual Peace*, 349.

32. Ibid., 352.

33. Ibid., 352–53.

34. Locke allows a king to serve as the executive power but designates a representative body for the legislative power. Kant could thus be closer to Locke in constructing a constitutional monarchy; but Locke's emphasis on Parliament as the most important branch, and the key to representation, contrasts with Kant's emphasis on the monarch as the most important, and as itself "representative."

35. Kant, *Perpetual Peace*, 354–56.

36. Allison (1990), 60.

37. Gregor (1991), xx.

38. This quote is from Reiss's translation of Kant, "On the Common Saying, 'That May Be True in Theory, but It Does Not Apply in Practice,' " 85, because I prefer Reiss's translation of this particular passage. However, because Reiss does not use academy pagination, I rely on the Ted Humphrey translation, "On the

Proverb: 'That May Be True in Theory but Is of No Practical Use,' " in the remainder of this chapter. Hereafter referred to as "Theory and Practice."

39. O'Neill (1989), 33.
40. Reiss (1991), 39, 20, 21.
41. Kant, "Theory and Practice," 290.
42. Pateman (1984).
43. Kant, *Metaphysics of Morals*, 6:418. Subsequent references are in the text.
44. Kant, "Theory and Practice," 297.
45. Reiss (1991), 26. Also, Kant, *Metaphysics of Morals* 6:316–17.
46. Kant, "Theory and Practice," 304; O'Neill (1989), 33.
47. *Metaphysics of Morals*, 6:323. David Hume, "Of the Original Contract" and "Of the Origin of Justice and Property," in Hume, *Political Essays*. See also Hirschmann (2000).
48. Immanuel Kant, *Education*, sec. 16. Subsequent citations will be made in the text.
49. Kant, "Theory and Practice," 295n.
50. Mendus (1987), 28, also 26–29 more generally.
51. O'Neill (1989), 65.
52. Pippin (1982), 191.
53. Reiss (1991), 7.
54. O'Neill (1989), 49.
55. Moen (1997), 215.
56. O'Neill (1989), 54, 53, 57.
57. Baier (1997), 307.
58. Compare on the one hand Rumsey and Sedgewick, who maintain that Kant is a radical individualist, and on the other, Baron, Keller, and Moen, who maintain that Kant's theory supports a more communal vision consistent with feminist "ethic of care" theory. All in Schott (1997b).
59. Sedgwick (1997), 89.
60. Nagl-Docekal (1997), 101–2.
61. Rumsey (1997), 126.
62. Schott (1997a), 324.
63. Kant, *Lectures on Ethics*, 384–85.
64. Kant, *Anthropology from a Pragmatic Point of View*, 303.
65. Kant, *Metaphysics of Morals*, 6:278; *Lectures on Ethics*, 27:388–90.
66. Kant actually says this to explain why "sexual intercourse of parents with their children" is "unconditionally prohibited," for children must respect their parents. By contrast, incest between siblings is wrong only conditionally, for in a state of nature "the first men must have married among their sisters." Kant, *Lectures on Ethics*, 27:389.
67. Kant, *Anthropology*, 303–4.
68. Ibid., 303.
69. Ibid., 309–10.
70. Schroder (1997), 294.
71. Wollstonecraft, *Vindication of the Rights of Women*; Astell, *Reflections upon Marriage*.

72. Kant, *Observations on the Feeling of the Beautiful and Sublime*, 2:229, 231.

73. Kant, *Critique of Judgement*, secs. 40, 39.

74. Kant, *Beautiful and Sublime*, 2:231.

75. Ibid., 2:232, 230.

76. Kant, *Anthropology*, 307.

77. Ibid., 303.

78. Kant, *Beautiful and Sublime*, 2:253–54.

79. Ibid., 2:254–55.

80. Tuana (1992), 69, 65.

81. Kant, *Beautiful and Sublime*, 2:242, 232.

82. Ibid., 2:229–30, emphasis added.

83. Hall (1997), 264.

84. Tuana (1992) also makes this point, 65–66.

85. Kant, *Anthropology*, 306, 209.

86. Ibid., 209.

87. Particularly popular, but not engaged here, are critiques of Kantian philosophy within the context of the Gilligan/Kohlberg controversy. See Rumsey (1989); Sedgwick (1997); Dancy (1992).

88. Sedgwick (1997), 90; Tuana (1992); Okin (1979).

89. Kant, *Anthropology*, 308.

90. Mendus (1987), 22. Obviously—and as Mendus notes—women are not the only victims of this methodological strategy, for this is something that we have particularly seen in the blatant class bias of Kant's views on active citizenship. See also Hall (1997), 263.

91. Mendus (1987), 35, is obviously being somewhat sardonic. But see also Baier (1986); "The great moral theorists in our tradition not only are all men, they are mostly men who had minimal adult dealings with (and so were then minimally influenced by) women. With a few significant exceptions (Hume, Hegel, J. S. Mill, Sidgwick, maybe Bradley) they are a collection of gays, clerics, misogynists, and puritan bachelors" (247–48). That her "exceptions" include clear misogynists such as Hegel indicates that such contact does not guarantee a *feminist* "influence" (even Hume, in his remarks on "chastity," was fairly sexist).

92. Mendus (1987), 36.

93. Kant, *Beautiful and Sublime*, 77, 2:229, 232, 236.

94. Mendus (1987), 35–36.

95. Allison (1990), 135–36.

96. Reath (1997), xxv n. 20, xiii, xxv.

97. David-Menard (1997), 342.

CHAPTER 5: JOHN STUART MILL

1. Mill, *On Liberty and Other Essays*, 17. All references to Mill's four essays— *On Liberty, Utilitarianism, On Representative Government*, and *The Subjection of Women*—are from this volume and will be cited in the text by page number, with the essay title indicated when it is not otherwise clear.

2. Berlin (1971), 172–206. Other theorists and philosophers who associate Mill with negative liberty include Gray (1983); Kristjansson (1992); Rees (1985);

Skinner (1984). Similarly, in *Nomos IV: Liberty* (Friedrich, [1962]), seven out of sixteen essays (by William Ebenstein, Frank Knight, Henry Aiken, Elizabeth Flower, Margaret Spahy, David Spitz, and Harry Jones) are about Mill, and all consider him to be putting forth a notion of freedom consistent with Berlin's negative liberty.

3. This includes "The liberty of expressing and publishing opinions," which are "almost of as much importance as the liberty of thought itself, and resting in great part on the same reasons, as practically inseparable from it" (*Liberty*, 16–17).

4. Himmelfarb (1974). See also Rees (1977).

5. In addition to the sources discussed in the text, see Jones (1992); Semmel (1983); and Scanlon (1958).

6. G. W. Smith (1984), 190.

7. Baum (1998), 190.

8. Capaldi (1995), 230, 225.

9. Ibid., 219.

10. Urbinati (2002), 159.

11. Ibid., 6, 7, 10. From my earlier chapters, however, it will be obvious to the reader that I think Urbinati mischaracterizes the distinction between positive and negative liberty. I particularly maintain that "reasons" are important to both positive and negative liberty. See also Hirschmann (2003), ch. 1.

12. Hamburger (1999), xi, 5.

13. Cowling (1963), 97, xii.

14. Ibid., 93, 44.

15. John Stuart Mill, "The Spirit of the Age, I" in *Collected Works*, 22:230.

16. Cowling (1963), 10–12, 15–23 and passim.

17. Ibid., 28, 30.

18. Hamburger (1999), xii, though he makes this point about Fred Burger, not Baum or Capaldi.

19. Urbinati (2002), 12.

20. Though we do tend to share a critical view of liberalism; see Hirschmann (1992).

21. Hamburger (1999), 9.

22. Ibid., xii–xv.

23. Urbinati's book *Mill on Democracy* (2002) does not centrally incorporate gender into her argument about the influence of classical thought on Mill's republicanism, but see 180–89. Also her earlier article, "John Stuart Mill on Androgyny and Ideal Marriage" (1991), demonstrates that she sees gender as a vital category of Mill's political theory.

24. Jones (1992), 293.

25. Rees (1985) identifies this as a distinction between "harm produced" and "harm-producing behavior," although drunk driving is not Rees's example.

26. Fuller (1964); Hart (1965).

27. "The Evidence of John Stuart Mill, Taken before the Royal Commission of 1870, on the Administration and Operation of the Contagious Diseases Acts of 1866 and 1869," in *Collected Works*, 21:353.

28. John Stuart Mill, *Principles of Political Economy: With Some of Their Applications to Social Philosophy*, in *Collected Works*, 2:107, 112, 374–75, 763, 947. Hereafter cited in the text as *PE* with page number.

29. John Stuart Mill and Harriet Taylor, "The Case of Anne Bird," in *Collected Works*, 25:1156.

30. John Stuart Mill, "Nature," in *Collected Works*, 10:400, 380, 396, 381.

31. Ibid., 397, 381, 402.

32. John Stuart Mill, *A System of Logic*, in *Collected Works*, 8:836. Hereafter cited in the text as *Logic* with page number.

33. McPherson (1982), 262 makes a similar point.

34. Mill, *Autobiography*, in *Collected Works*, 1:177.

35. Hume, *A Treatise of Human Nature*, bk. 3; Hirschmann (2000); Urmson (1953).

36. In his essay "On Bentham" (*Collected Works*, 10:113–14), Mill confides that Bentham personally disliked poetry because it was a "misrepresentation" and therefore not real. This might undercut the force of Bentham's argument, but Mill claims that Bentham would have said the same if he had compared pushpin to the things "he most valued and admired." So the common interpretation of this aphorism as comparing high values to low is correct despite the fact that Bentham himself did not care for poetry.

37. I am not here factoring into consideration the exorbitant incomes collected by many pop music stars in contrast to classical musicians, as ticket prices for both kinds of performances are roughly equal and the cost/benefit ratio to the consumer would not therefore be markedly affected by such considerations. Mill would likely, however, argue against enormous salaries for pop performers and movie stars, as well as for chief executive officers of corporations, as economically inefficient and unjust. See *Political Economy*, 755.

38. Mill, "The Negro Question" and "The Slave Power" in *Collected Works*, vol. 21.

39. John Stuart Mill, *Autobiography*, in *Collected Works*, 1:169.

40. Gray (1979).

41. This is an idea that Annas (1977) particularly critiques, calling Mill "timid and reformist at best" (189). But see Burgess-Jackson's (1995) response to Annas, 380–81.

42. *PE*, 116–18. Nadia Urbinati has offered a similar defense of Mill on these grounds, arguing that Mill is "distinguishing between labor as a necessity and labor as a means of self-realization. . . . Wife and husband *must* labor to support their family," and presumably the sexual division of labor was the best way to achieve that. This did not rule out working "as a means of self-realization" for women who decided not to have children (or at least not too many), for Mill explicitly noted with approval that liberating women would produce the desirable effect of reducing the population. Urbinati (1991), 641.

43. Mill, *Autobiography*, in *Collected Works*, 1:253.

44. Goldstein (1980), 328; Shanley (1981), 240–42; Annas (1977), 189; Zerilli (1994), 114. See also Burgess-Jackson (1995) and Eisenstein (1981).

45. Okin (1979), 228. Burgess-Jackson similarly suggests that Mill is more likely making an efficiency argument about the sexual division of labor. But he then asserts that Mill would have no difficulty with a family in which the woman sought common subsistence while the man cared for the children and home. Bur-

gess-Jackson (1995), 385. It is clear from the textual evidence offered here, however, that this latter claim overreaches.

46. John Stuart Mill, "Essay on Marriage and Divorce," 77, 74.

47. Ibid., 75.

48. Letter from John Stuart Mill to Harriet Taylor, February 21, 1849, in *Collected Works*, 14:11.

49. Rossi (1970), 23.

50. Hayek (1951), 57. The passage to which Hayek refers, located in a footnote on page 253 of the *Autobiography* (in *Collected Works*, vol. 1), simply asserts that Mill's belief in women's equality predated his acquaintance with Taylor; to her he attributed "that perception of the vast practical bearings of women's disabilities which found expression in the book on The Subjection of Women." However, Mill does acknowledge that the *Subjection* would have gone farther than it did had Taylor been an active coauthor, "though I doubtless should have held my present opinions." As I argue in the text, the *Subjection* itself provides strong evidence of Mill's lack of enthusiasm for married women's working that suggests a consistency with the earlier essay.

51. Himmelfarb (1974), 186; *PE*, 394; see also Jacobs (2002), 217.

52. Mill, "Marriage and Divorce," 76, 77.

53. In *Political Economy* Mill notes, "Every human being has been brought up from infancy at the expense of much labour to some person or persons, and if this labour, or part of it, had not been bestowed, the child would never have attained the age and strength which enable him to become a labourer in his turn." But he then says that "this labour and expense are usually incurred from other motives than to obtain such ultimate return, and, for most purposes of political economy, need not be taken into account as expenses of production" (40). See Hirschmann (2005) for a discussion of whether women's household and family labor has productive value in Mill's view.

54. The timeline for these changes cannot explain them as an evolution in Mill's thinking either, for *On Liberty* was published in 1859, in between the other two essays ("Marriage and Divorce" in 1832, the "Inaugural" in 1867). However, he did say in an 1868 letter that "nothing can replace the mother for the education of children." Mill to Princess Marie Stcherbatov, December 18, 1868. In *Collected Works*, 16:1528.

55. "Marriage and Divorce," 75, 76.

56. H. Taylor (1970), 85, 86; Fineman (1995).

57. Mill, "Marriage and Divorce," 80, 70.

58. Ibid., 78–79, 81.

59. Ibid., 75.

60. Ibid. In the *Subjection*, by contrast, Mill says that supervising servants is "onerous to the thoughts," requiring "incessant vigilance" (551), suggesting that housework is not merely physically demanding, but psychologically so. This position seems more sympathetic to wealthier women, and one can readily imagine that Taylor had a role in changing Mill's mind on that score. But this does not necessarily establish a change in his views about whether women who supervise servants should instead do more of the physical housework themselves, as his comment that utilizing servants produces "waste and malversation" is made in

the previous sentence. Presumably, women's supervision is part of that "waste" precisely because of its psychological cost.

61. John Stuart Mill and Harriet Taylor, "The Law of Assault" in Mill, *Collected Works*, 25:1173. Though Taylor is not named as coauthor in the *Chronicle* or Mill's bibliography, Robson indicates that the series of essays were coauthored by Taylor. See prologue to "The Acquittal of Captain Johnstone," in *Collected Works*, 24:865.

62. Mill and Taylor, "The Law of Assault," in *Collected Works*, 25:1174.

63. Mill and Taylor, "The Case of Anne Bird," in *Collected Works*, 25:1156.

64. John Stuart Mill and Harriet Taylor, "The Case of Susan Moir," in *Collected Works*, 25:1170.

65. Mill and Taylor, "The Case of Anne Bird," in *Collected Works*, 25:1156–57. See also John Stuart Mill and Harriet Taylor, "The Punishment of Children," in *Collected Works*, 25:1176–78; and "Wife Murder," in *Collected Works*, 25:1183–86.

66. John Stuart Mill, "The Spirit of the Age II," in *Collected Works*, 22:242.

67. Ibid., 238, 243, 239.

68. Hamburger (1999), 150.

69. Ibid., 118; Mill, *System of Logic*, 869.

70. Hamburger (1999), 108.

71. John Stuart Mill, *Autobiography*, in *Collected Works*, 1:141–45; Garforth (1971). See also Di Stefano (1991).

72. Mill, *Autobiography*, in *Collected Works*, 1:32, 5.

73. Ibid., 41; Collini, "Introduction," *Collected Works*, 21:xlix.

74. John Stuart Mill, "Inaugural Address Delivered to the University of St. Andrews," in *Collected Works*, 21:217.

75. Ibid., 256.

76. Mill, "The Negro Question," in *Collected Works*, vol. 21; Garforth (1979), 65–66, 123–24; Mill, *Autobiography*, in *Collected Works*, 1:140.

77. Garforth (1979), 143.

78. Mill, "Inaugural," in *Collected Works*, 21:217, 250, 244.

79. Cowling (1963), 117.

80. Mill, "The Condition of Ireland," in Mill, *Collected Works*, 24:975; see also Garforth (1979), 131.

81. Mill, "Spirit of the Age II," in *Collected Works*, 24:241.

82. Hamburger (1999), 20, 194.

83. Mill, "The Proposed Irish Poor Law," in *Collected Works*, 24:1072.

84. Editor's note, *Political Economy*, 444.

85. Mill, "The Proposed Irish Poor Law," in *Collected Works*, 24:1072.

86. See Hirschmann (2001) for an account of contemporary neoconservative perspectives on poverty. See also Hirschmann (2002).

87. Linda Zerilli argues that Mill's thinking here ignored material reality, for poor women's reproduction was less a product of thoughtless sexual indulgence than a response to "proletarianization." That is, because of the high infant mortality among working classes in the new industrialized city, and because children could be an economic resource once they started working, women had multiple pregnancies out of economic self-interest. Of course, Mill also opposed child

labor, but he does not make that issue part of his argument here (Zerilli 1994, 105). A similar argument is at work in Mill's testimony against the Contagious Diseases Act. Mill's objection to the act stems from the unequal distribution of liberty that it resulted in; female prostitutes were subjected to brutal treatment ("medical exams" in which they were tied down and their legs were forced open by mechanical restraints) whereas male clients were left alone. The wording of the act, moreover, permitted the police to force an examination on any woman on whom a man filed a report, including women who were not prostitutes, some of whom were in fact virgins. Mill, "Contagious Diseases Act," in *Collected Works*, 21:351–52. He was also concerned about public health, but again according to Zerilli, in applying his "harm principle" to the justification of state interference, Mill was concerned less about the husband's contracting venereal disease—for the husband sought out the prostitute—than about the man's "innocent" wife and children, to whom the disease could be passed. What Mill "neglected," according to Zerilli, was that the man often passed on the disease to the prostitute. Presumably, Mill did not include prostitutes in his scope of concern because, like male customers, they were "voluntary" participants, ignoring the very forces of social coercion that he recognizes in the *Subjection*, that women in dire economic straits had limited options for employment. Zerilli (1994); see also Waldron (2007b).

88. Friedan (1963).

89. Mill, "Parliamentary Reform, in *Collected Works*, 19:324.

90. Cowling (1963), 110.

91. John Stuart Mill, "Chapters on Socialism," in *Collected Works*, 5:739–41.

92. John Stuart Mill, "Perfectibility," in *Collected Works*, vol. 26.

93. Mill, "Parliamentary Reform, in *Collected Works*, 19:324–25.

94. Urbinati (1991), 640. On twenty-first-century conservative views about women's paid employment and the family, see, for instance, Santorum (2005).

95. Despite recent hysteria in the press about college women aspiring to full-time motherhood, rates of women's employment in the United States and Europe are currently close to an all-time high. However, women still lag behind men in pay and opportunities and disproportionately bear the burden of child care, resulting in more part-time work. Story (2005); Aliaga (2005); Lantz and Sarte (2000).

96. In a letter to Isabella Beecher Hooker on September 13, 1869, evidently in response to her remarks about his *Subjection*, he concedes that there is an "infinitely closer relationship of a child to its mother than to its father," and that this relationship has "important consequences with respect to the future legal position of parents & children. . . . But I do not perceive that this closer relationship gives any ground for attributing a natural superiority in capacity of moral excellence to women over men. I believe moral excellence to be always the fruit of education & cultivation." *Collected Works*, 17:1640.

97. Zerilli (1994), 108. She argues that this image "denies whatever social power women held in the working-class family—a power that was, on some accounts, not only considerable but considerably more than that held by middle-class women."

98. See particularly Ashcraft (1986). On Mill's political rhetoric, see Urbinati (2002).

99. In addition to two volumes titled *Public and Parliamentary Speeches* (vols. 28 and 29), and four volumes of Mill's newspaper writings (vols. 22–25), there are six volumes of his letters (vols. 12–17), a key means by which Mill engaged debate and discussion of his ideas. Additionally, the *Collected Works* include two volumes that contain Mill's "debating speeches," along with his journals (vols. 26 and 27). And of course there are many other volumes containing the many essays, short and long, that Mill wrote on an incredibly wide variety of subjects, from Coleridge to prostitution. There are, in all, thirty-three volumes.

100. Mill, *Autobiography*, in *Collected Works*, 1:272–79.

CONCLUSION: RETHINKING FREEDOM IN THE CANON

1. This sexist example, I hope it is obvious, is meant to reflect Kant's thinking, not mine.

2. See Rosenblum (1987) on Mill and "romantic liberalism."

3. See Hirschmann (2003).

4. Ibid. See Hirschmann (1992) on "contingent sexism."

5. Though MacKinnon (1987, 162) said this about pornography, I find the phrase particularly useful to understanding the complex relationship of materiality and language.

References

Aliaga, Christel. 2005. *Statistics in Focus, Theme 3, Population and Social Conditions: Gender Gaps in the Reconciliation between Work and Family Life*. Luxembourg: Eurostat, the Statistical Office of the European Communities.

Allison, Henry. 1990. *Kant's Theory of Freedom*. New York: Cambridge University Press.

Annas, Julia. 1977. "Mill and the Subjection of Women." *Philosophy* 52: 179–94.

Antony, Louise, and Charlotte Witt, eds. 2001. *A Mind of One's Own: Feminist Essays on Reason and Objectivity*. Boulder, CO: Westview Press.

Applewhite, Harriet B., and Darline Gay Levy, 1984. "Women, Democracy, and Revolution in Paris, 1789–1794." In *French Women and the Age of Enlightenment*, ed. Samia I. Spencer. Bloomington: Indiana University Press.

Ashcraft, Richard. 1986. *Revolutionary Politics and Locke's "Two Treatises of Government."* Princeton, NJ: Princeton University Press.

Astell, Mary. 1996. *Reflections upon Marriage*. In *Astell: Political Writings*, ed. Patricia Springborg. New York: Cambridge University Press.

Axtell, James L., ed. 1968. *The Educational Writings of John Locke: A Critical Edition with Introduction and Notes*. London: Cambridge University Press.

Baier, Annette. 1986. "Trust and Antitrust." *Ethics* 96:231–60.

———. 1997. "How Can Individualists Share Responsibility?" In *Rereading the Canon: Feminist Interpretations of Immanuel Kant*, ed. Robin May Schott. University Park: Pennsylvania State University Press.

Bailyn, Bernard. 1967. *The Ideological Origins of the American Revolution*. Cambridge, MA: Belknap Press of Harvard University Press.

Ball, Terence. 2000. "The Formation of Character: Mill's 'Ethology' Reconsidered." *Polity* 33 (1): 25–48.

Baum, Bruce. 1998. "J. S. Mill on Freedom and Power." *Polity* 31:187–216.

Beck, Lewis White. 1960. *A Commentary on Kant's "Critique of Practical Reason."* Chicago: University of Chicago Press.

Bennett, Jonathan. 1984. "Commentary: Kant's Theory of Freedom." In *Self and Nature in Kant's Philosophy*, ed. Allen Wood. Ithaca, NY: Cornell University Press.

Benson, Paul. 1991. "Autonomy and Oppressive Socialization." *Social Theory and Practice* 17 (13): 385–408.

Berlin, Isaiah. 1971. *Four Essays on Liberty*. New York: Oxford University Press.

———. 1979. "From Hope and Fear Set Free." In Isaiah Berlin, *Concepts and Categories: Philosophical Essays*. New York: Viking Press.

Blum, Carol. 1986. *Rousseau and the Republic of Virtue: The Language of Politics in the French Revolution*. Ithaca, NY: Cornell University Press.

Bombardieri, Marcella. 2005. "Summers' Remarks on Women Draw Fire." *Boston Globe*, January 17, A1.

Bradshaw, Leah. 2002. "Rousseau on Civic Virtue, Male Autonomy, and the Construction of the Divided Female." In *Feminist Interpretations of Jean-Jacques Rousseau*, ed. Lynda Lange. University Park: Pennsylvania State University Press.

Bramhall, John. 1999. "Discourse of Liberty and Necessity" and "A Defence of True Liberty." In *Hobbes and Bramhall on Liberty and Necessity*, ed. Vere Chappell. New York: Cambridge University Press.

Breitenberg, Mark. 1996. *Anxious Masculinity in Early Modern England*. New York: Cambridge University Press.

Brennan, Teresa. 2000. *Exhausting Modernity: Grounds for a New Economy*. New York: Routledge.

Brennan, Teresa, and Carole Pateman. 1979. "Mere Auxiliaries to the Commonwealth: Women and the Origins of Liberalism." *Political Studies* 27:183–200.

Brown, Wendy. 1995. *States of Injury: Power and Freedom in Late Modernity*. Princeton, NJ: Princeton University Press.

Burgess-Jackson, Keith. 1995. "John Stuart Mill, Radical Feminist." *Social Theory and Practice* 21 (3): 380–81.

Butler, Melissa. 1978. "The Early Liberal Roots of Feminism: John Locke and the Attack on Patriarchy." *American Political Science Review* 72 (1): 135–50.

Capaldi, Nicholas. 1995. "John Stuart Mill's Defense of Liberal Culture." *Political Science Reviewer* 24:205–50.

Carnois, Bernard. 1987. *The Coherence of Kant's Doctrine of Freedom*, trans. David Booth. Chicago: University of Chicago Press.

Chodorow, Nancy. 1978. *The Reproduction of Mothering*. Berkeley: University of California Press.

Clark, Alice. 1968. *Working Life of Women in the Seventeenth Century*. London: Frank Cass.

Clark, Lorenne M. G. 1977. "Women and John Locke: Or, Who Owns the Apples in the Garden of Eden?" *Canadian Journal of Philosophy* 7 (4): 699–724.

Collini, Stephan. 1984. "Introduction." In John Stuart Mill, *Collected Works, Vol. 21: Essays on Equality, Law, and Education*, ed. John M. Robson. Toronto: University of Toronto Press.

Collins, Patricia Hill. 1998. *Fighting Words: Black Women and the Search for Justice*. Minneapolis: University of Minnesota Press.

Colmo, Ann Charney. 1996. "What Sophie Knew: Rousseau's *Emile et Sophie, ou Les Solitaires*." In *Finding a New Feminism: Rethinking the Woman Question for Liberal Democracy*," ed. Pamela Grande Jensen. New York: Rowman and Littlefield.

Conner, Susan P. 1984. "Women and Politics." In *French Women and the Age of Enlightenment*, ed. Samia I. Spencer. Bloomington: Indiana University Press.

Cowling, Maurice. 1963. *Mill and Liberalism*. Cambridge: Cambridge University Press.

Crenshaw, Kimberle. 1991. "Mapping the Margins: Intersectionality, Identity Politics, and Violence against Women of Color." *Stanford Law Review* 43: 1241–99.

Dancy, Jonathan. 1992. "Caring About Justice." *Philosophy* 67:447–66.

David-Menard, Monique. 1997. "Kant, the Law, and Desire," trans. Leslie Lykes de Galbert. In *Rereading the Canon: Feminist Interpretations of Immanuel Kant*, ed. Robin May Schott. University Park: Pennsylvania State University Press.

Disch, Lisa. 1994. "Claire Loves Julie: Reading the Story of Women's Friendship in *La Nouvelle Heloise.*" *Hypatia: Journal of Feminist Philosophy* 9 (3): 19–45.

Di Stefano, Christine. 1986. "Masculinity as Ideology in Political Theory: Hobbesian Man Considered." *Hypatia: Journal of Feminist Philosophy* 1: 633–44.

———. 1990. *Configurations of Masculinity*. Ithaca, NY: Cornell University Press.

Dunn, John. 1969. *The Political Thought of John Locke: An Historical Account of the Argument of the 'Two Treatises of Government.'* London: Cambridge University Press.

Eisenstein, Zillah. 1981. *The Radical Future of Liberal Feminism*. New York: Longman.

Erickson, Amy Louise. 1993. *Women and Property in Early Modern England.* New York: Routledge.

Ewasiuk, Craig. 2007. "Rethinking Recurrence in Hobbes, Hegel, and Nietzsche." Ph.D. diss., Cornell University.

Fairchilds, Cissie. 1984. "Women and Family." In *French Women and the Age of Enlightenment*, ed. Samia I. Spencer. Bloomington: Indiana University Press.

Farr, James. 1986. " 'So Vile and Miserable and Estate': The Problem of Slavery in Locke's Political Thought." *Political Theory* 14:263–89.

Ferguson, Kathy. 1993. *The Man Question: Visions of Subjectivity in Feminist Theory*. Berkeley: University of California Press.

Filmer, Sir Robert. 1999. *"Patriarcha" and Other Writings*, ed. Johann P. Sommerville. Cambridge: Cambridge University Press.

Fineman, Martha. 1995. *The Neutered Mother, the Sexual Family, and Other Twentieth Century Tragedies*. New York: Routledge.

Flathman, Richard E. 1987. *The Philosophy and Politics of Freedom*. Chicago: University of Chicago Press.

———. 1993. *Thomas Hobbes: Skepticism, Individuality, and Chastened Politics*. Newbury Park, CA: Sage Publications.

Flax, Jane. 1983. "Political Philosophy and the Patriarchal Unconscious." In *Discovering Reality: Feminist Perspectives on Epistemology, Metaphysics, Methodology, and Philosophy of Science*, ed. Sandra Harding and Merrill B. Hintikka. Boston: D. Reidel.

Fox-Genovese, Elizabeth. 1984. "Women and Work." In *French Women and the Age of Enlightenment*, ed. Samia I. Spencer. Bloomington: Indiana University Press.

Friedan, Betty. 1963. *The Feminine Mystique*. New York: Norton.

Friedrich, Carol, ed. 1962. *Nomos IV: Liberty*. New York: Atherton Press.

Fryer, Peter. 1984. *Staying Power: Black People in Britain since 1504*. Atlantic Highlands, NJ: Humanities Press.

Fuller, Lon. 1964. *The Morality of Law*. New Haven, CT: Yale University Press.

Garforth, Francis W., ed. 1971. *John Stuart Mill on Education*. New York: Teachers College Press, Columbia University.

———. 1979. *John Stuart Mill's Theory of Education*. New York: Harper and Row.

Gauthier, David. 1969. *The Logic of Leviathan: The Moral and Political Theory of Thomas Hobbes*. Oxford: Clarendon Press.

Giles-Simms, Jean. 1983. *Wife Battering: A Systems Theory Approach*. New York: Guildford Press.

Gilligan, Carol. 1982. *In a Different Voice: Psychological Theory and Women's Development*. Cambridge, MA: Harvard University Press.

Glausser, Wayne. 1990. "Three Approaches to Locke and the Slave Trade." *Journal of the History of Ideas* 51 (2): 199–216.

Goldstein, Leslie. 1980. "Mill, Marx, and Women's Liberation." *Journal of the History of Philosophy* 28:319–34.

Goodman, Dena. 1994. *The Republic of Letters: A Cultural History of the French Enlightenment*. Ithaca, NY: Cornell University Press.

Gray, John N. 1979. "John Stuart Mill: Traditional and Revisionist Interpretations." *Literature of Liberty* 2 (2): 7–37.

———. 1980. "On Positive and Negative Liberty." *Political Studies* 28 (4): 507–26.

———. 1983. *Mill on Liberty: A Defense*. London: Routledge and Kegan Paul.

Green, Karen. 1994. "Christine De Pisan and Thomas Hobbes." *Philosophical Quarterly* 44 (177): 456–75.

Gregor, Mary. 1991. "Introduction." In Immanuel Kant, *Metaphysics of Morals*, ed. and trans. Mary Gregor. New York: Cambridge University Press.

Hall, Kim. 1997. "*Sensus Communis* and Violence: A Feminist Reading of Kant's *Critique of Judgement*." In *Rereading the Canon: Feminist Interpretations of Immanuel Kant*, ed. Robin May Schott. University Park: Pennsylvania State University Press.

Hamburger, Joseph. 1999. *John Stuart Mill on Liberty and Control*. Princeton, NJ: Princeton University Press.

Hart, H.L.A. 1965. *The Concept of Law*. Oxford: Clarendon Press.

Hartsock, Nancy C. M. 1984. *Money, Sex, and Power: Toward a Feminist Historical Materialism*. Boston: Northeastern University Press.

Hayek, F. A. 1951. *John Stuart Mill and Harriet Taylor: Their Friendship and Subsequent Marriage*. London: Routledge and Kegan Paul.

Heywood, Colin. 2001. *A History of Childhood: Children and Childhood in the West from Medieval to Modern Times*. Cambridge: Polity Press.

Himmelfarb, Gertrude. 1974. *On Liberty and Liberalism: The Case of John Stuart Mill*. New York: Alfred A. Knopf.

Hirschmann, Nancy J. 1989. "Freedom, Recognition, and Obligation: A Feminist Approach to Political Theory." *American Political Science Review* 83: 1227–44.

———. 1992. *Rethinking Obligation: A Feminist Method for Political Theory*. Ithaca, NY: Cornell University Press.

————. 1997. "Feminist Standpoint as Postmodern Strategy." *Women and Politics* 18 (3): 73–92.

————. 2000. "Sympathy, Empathy, and Obligation: A Feminist Reading of Hume." In *Rereading the Canon: Feminist Interpretations of David Hume*, ed. Anne Jacobsen. University Park: Pennsylvania State University Press.

————. 2001. "A Question of Freedom, a Question of Rights? Women and Welfare." In *Women and Welfare: Theory and Practice in the United States and Europe*, ed. Nancy J. Hirschman and Ulrike Liebert. New Brunswick, NJ: Rutgers University Press.

————. 2002. "Liberal-Conservativism Once and Again: Locke's *Essay on the Poor Law* and U.S. Welfare Reform." *Constellations: An International Journal of Critical and Democratic Theory, Special Issue on Property* 9 (3): 335–55.

————. 2003. *The Subject of Liberty: Toward a Feminist Theory of Freedom.* Princeton, NJ: Princeton University Press.

————. 2005. "Mill, Carework, and Productive Labor." Paper presented at the annual meeting of the American Political Science Association, Washington, DC. PDF file available at http://64.112.226.77/one/apsa/apso05/index.php (search under title).

Hirschmann, Nancy J., Susan Brison, and Marilyn Frye. 2006. "Symposium on Nancy J. Hirschmann's *The Subject of Liberty*." *Hypatia: Journal of Feminist Philosophy* 21 (4): 178–211.

Hirschmann, Nancy J., and Di Stefano, Christine. 1996. "Introduction: Revision, Reconstruction and the Challenge of the New." In *Revisioning the Political: Feminist Reconstructions of Traditional Concepts in Western Political Theory*, ed. Nancy J. Hirschmann and Christine Di Stefano. Boulder, CO: Westview Press.

Hirschmann, Nancy, and Ulrike Liebert. 2001. *Women and Welfare: Theory and Practice in the United States and Europe.* New Brunswick, NJ: Rutgers University Press.

Hirschmann, Nancy J., and Carole Pateman. 1992. "Political Obligation, Freedom and Feminism." *American Political Science Review* 86:179–88.

Hobbes, Thomas. 1958. *Autobiography*, trans. Benjamin Farrington. In *Rationalist Annual 1958*.

————. 1969. *The Elements of Law, Natural and Politic*, ed. Ferdinand Tönnies. London: Frank Cass and Co.

————. 1976. *Thomas White's "De Mundo" Examined*, trans. Harold Whitmore Jones. London: Bradford University Press.

————. 1985. *Leviathan*, ed. C. B. Macpherson. New York: Penguin.

————. 1990. *Behemoth: Or, the Long Parliament*, ed. Ferdinand Tönnies with an introduction by Stephen Holmes. Chicago: University of Chicago Press.

————. 1991a. *De Cive*. In *Man and Citizen: De Homine and De Cive*, ed. Bernard Gert. Indianapolis: Hackett.

————. 1991b. *De Homine*. In *Man and Citizen: De Homine and De Cive*, ed. Bernard Gert. Indianapolis: Hackett.

————. 1999a. "Of Liberty and Necessity." In *Hobbes and Bramhall on Liberty and Necessity*, ed. Vere Chappel. New York: Cambridge University Press.

Hobbes, Thomas. 1999b. "The Questions Concerning Liberty, Necessity, and Chance." In *Hobbes and Bramhall on Liberty and Necessity*, ed. Vere Chappel. New York: Cambridge University Press.

Holmes, Stephen. 1990. "Introduction." In Thomas Hobbes, *Behemoth: Or, the Long Parliament*, ed. Ferdinand Tönnies. Chicago: University of Chicago Press.

Hull, Gloria T., Patricia Bell Scott, and Barbara Smith, eds. 1982. *All the Women Are White, All the Blacks Are Men, but Some of Us Are Brave: Black Women's Studies*. Old Westbury, NY: Feminist Press.

Hume, David. 1953. *Political Essays*, ed. Charles W. Hendel. Indianapolis: Bobbs-Merrill.

———. 1978. *A Treatise of Human Nature*, ed. L.A. Selby-Bigge. New York: Oxford University Press.

Irwin, Terence. 1984. "Morality and Personality: Kant and Green." In *Self and Nature in Kant's Philosophy*, ed. Allen Wood. Ithaca, NY: Cornell University Press.

Jacobs, Jo Ellen. 2002. *The Voice of Harriet Taylor Mill*. Bloomington: Indiana University Press.

Johnson, Pauline. 1994. *Feminism as Radical Humanism*. Boulder, CO: Westview Press.

Johnston, David. 1986. *The Rhetoric of Leviathan: Thomas Hobbes and the Politics of Cultural Transformation*. Princeton, NJ: Princeton University Press.

Jones, Herbert S. 1992. "John Stuart Mill as Moralist." *Journal of the History of Ideas* 53:287–308.

Kant, Immanuel. 1960. *Education*, trans. Annette Churton. Ann Arbor: University of Michigan Press.

———. 1964. *Groundwork of the Metaphysics of Morals*, trans. H. J. Patton. New York: Harper and Row.

———. 1965. *Critique of Pure Reason*, trans. Norman Kemp Smith. New York: St. Martin's Press.

———. 1980. *Critique of Judgement*, trans. James Creed Meredith. Oxford: Clarendon Press.

———. 1983a. "On the Proverb: 'That May Be True in Theory, but Is of No Practical Use.'" In *Perpetual Peace and Other Essays,* trans. Ted Humphrey. Indianapolis: Hackett.

———. 1983b. "Perpetual Peace." In *Perpetual Peace and Other Essays*, trans. Ted Humphrey. Indianapolis: Hackett.

———. 1983c. "An Answer to the Question: 'What Is Enlightenment?'" In *Perpetual Peace and Other Essays*, tran. Ted Humphrey. Indianapolis: Hackett.

———. 1991a. "What Is Orientation in Thinking?" In *Political Writings of Immanuel Kant*, ed. Hans Reiss. 2nd ed. Cambridge: Cambridge University Press.

———. 1991b. "On the Common Saying, 'That May be True in Theory, but It Does Not Apply in Practice.' " In *Political Writings of Immanuel Kant*, ed. Hans Reiss. 2nd ed. Cambridge: Cambridge University Press.

———. 1991c. *The Metaphysics of Morals*, trans. Mary Gregor. Cambridge: Cambridge University Press.

———. 1997a. *Critique of Practical Reason*, trans. and ed. Mary Gregor. New York: Cambridge University Press.

———. 1997b. *Lectures on Ethics*, trans. Peter Heath, ed. Peter Heath and J. B. Schneewind. Cambridge: Cambridge University Press.

———. 2006. *Anthropology From a Pragmatic Point of View*, trans. and ed. Robert B. Louden. Cambridge: Cambridge University Press.

———. 2007. *Observations on the Feeling of the Beautiful and Sublime*, trans. Paul Guyer. In Kant, *Anthropology, History, and Education*, ed. Robert Louden and Günter Zöller. Cambridge: Cambridge University Press.

Kay, Carol. 1988. *Political Constructions: Defoe, Richardson, and Sterne in Relation to Hobbes, Hume, and Burke*. Ithaca, NY: Cornell University Press.

Keohane, Nannerl. 1980. *Philosophy and the State in France: The Renaissance to the Enlightenment*. Princeton, NJ: Princeton University Press.

Kittay, Eva Feder. 1999. *Love's Labor: Essays on Women, Equality, and Dependency*. New York: Routledge.

Kramnick, Isaac. 1972. "Reflections on Revolution: Definition and Explanation in Recent Scholarship." *History and Theory* 11:26–63.

———. 1990. *Republicanism and Bourgeois Radicalism*. Ithaca, NY: Cornell University Press.

Kristjansson, Kristjan. 1992. "What's Wrong with Positive Liberty?" *Social Theory and Practice* 18 (3): 289–310.

Kukla, Rebecca. 2002. "The Coupling of Human Souls: Rousseau and the Problem of Gender Relations." In *Feminist Interpretations of Jean-Jacques Rousseau*, ed. Lynda Lange. University Park: Pennsylvania State University Press.

Landes, Joan B. 1988. *Women in the Public Sphere in the Age of the French Revolution*. Ithaca, NY: Cornell University Press.

Lange, Lynda, ed. 2002. *Feminist Interpretations of Jean-Jacques Rousseau*. University Park: Pennsylvania State University Press.

Lantz, Carl, and Pierre-Daniel Sarte. 2000. "A Study of U.S. Employment Rates with Emphasis on Gender Considerations." *Economic Quarterly* 86 (3): 1–26.

Leijenhorst, Cees. 2002. *The Mechanization of Aristotelianism: The Late Aristotelian Setting of Thomas Hobbes' Natural Philosophy*. Leiden: Brill.

Levine, Andrew. 1976. *The Politics of Autonomy: A Kantian Reading of Rousseau's Social Contract*. Amherst: University of Massachusetts Press.

Locke, John. 1824. "Some Considerations of the Consequences of the Lowering of Interest, and Raising the Value of Money: In a Letter to a Member of Parliament in the Year 1691." In *The Works of John Locke in Nine Volumes*. 12th ed. London: Rivington.

———. 1955. *A Letter Concerning Toleration*, trans. William Popple, with an introduction by Patrick Romanell. Indianapolis: Bobbs-Merrill.

———. 1958a. *A Discourse of Miracles*. In *The Reasonableness of Christianity and a Discourse of Miracles*, ed. I. T. Ramsay. Stanford, CA: Stanford University Press.

———. 1958b. *The Reasonableness of Christianity*. In *The Reasonableness of Christianity and A Discourse of Miracles*, ed. I. T. Ramsay. Stanford, CA: Stanford University Press.

———. 1963. *Two Treatises of Government*, ed. Peter Laslett. New York: New American Library.

Locke, John. 1975. *An Essay Concerning Human Understanding*, ed. Peter H. Nidditch. Oxford: Clarendon Press.

———. 1990. *Questions Concerning the Law of Nature*, ed. Robert Horwitz, Jenny Strauss Clay, and Diskin Clay. Ithaca, NY: Cornell University Press.

———. 1996a. *Some Thoughts Concerning Education*. In *Some Thoughts Concerning Education and Of the Conduct of the Understanding*, ed. Ruth Grant and Nathan Tarcov. Indianapolis: Hackett.

———. 1996b. *Of the Conduct of the Understanding*. In *Some Thoughts Concerning Education and Of the Conduct of the Understanding*, ed. Ruth Grant and Nathan Tarcov. Indianopolis: Hackett.

———. 1997. "An Essay on the Poor Law." In John Locke, *Political Essays*, ed. Mark Goldie. London: Cambridge University Press.

MacCallum, Gerald. 1973. "Negative and Positive Freedom." In *Concepts in Social and Political Philosophy*, ed. Richard E. Flathman. New York: Macmillan.

MacKinnon, Catherine A. 1987. "Not a Moral Issue." In *Feminism Unmodified: Discourses on Life and Law*. Cambridge, MA: Harvard University Press.

Macpherson, C. B. 1962. *The Political Theory of Possessive Individualism: Hobbes to Locke*. Oxford: Oxford University Press.

———. 1968. "Introduction." In Thomas Hobbes, *Leviathan*, ed. C. B. Macpherson. New York: Penguin.

Mahoney, Martha R. 1991. "Legal Images of Battered Women: Redefining the Issue of Separation." *Michigan Law Review* 90 (1): 1–94.

Marso, Lori Jo. 1999. *(Un)Manly Citizens: Jean-Jacques Rousseau's and Germaine de Staël's Subversive Women*. Baltimore: Johns Hopkins University Press.

———. 2002. "Rousseau's Subversive Women." In *Feminist Interpretations of Jean-Jacques Rousseau*, ed. Lynda Lange. University Park: Pennsylvania State University Press.

McClure, Kirstie M. 1996. *Judging Rights: Lockean Politics and the Limits of Consent*. Ithaca, NY: Cornell University Press.

McKinney, Audrey. 1993. "Hobbes and the State of Nature: Where Are the Women?" *Southwest Philosophical Studies* 15:51–59.

McPherson, Michael. 1982. "Mill's Moral Theory and the Problem of Preference Change." *Ethics* 92:252–73.

Mehta, Uday Singh. 1992. *The Anxiety of Freedom: Imagination and Individuality in Locke's Political Thought*. Ithaca, NY: Cornell University Press.

Mendelson, Sara, and Patricia Crawford. 1998. *Women in Early Modern England, 1550–1720*. Oxford: Clarendon Press.

Mendus, Susan. 1987. "Kant: An Honest but Narrow-Minded Bourgeois?" In *Women in Western Political Philosophy*, ed. Ellen Kennedy and Susan Mendus. New York: St. Martin's.

Meyers, Diana T. 1987. "Personal Autonomy and the Paradox of Feminine Socialization." *Journal of Philosophy* 84 (11): 619–28.

Mill, John Stuart. 1965. *Principles of Political Economy: With Some of Their Applications to Social Philosophy*. In *Collected Works*, Vols. 2 and 3, ed. J. M. Robson. Toronto: University of Toronto Press.

———. 1967. *Collected Works, Vol. 5: Essays on Economics and Society*, ed. J. M. Robson. Toronto: University of Toronto Press.

———. 1969. *Collected Works, Vol. 10: Essays on Ethics, Religion and Society*, ed. John M. Robson. Toronto: University of Toronto Press.

———. 1970. *Essay on Marriage and Divorce*. In John Stuart Mill and Harriet Taylor Mill, *Essays on Sex Equality*, ed. Alice S. Rossi. Chicago: University of Chicago Press.

———. 1972. *Collected Works, Vol. 14: The Later Letters of John Stuart Mill, 1849–1873*, ed. Francis E. Mineka and Dwight N. Lindley. Toronto: University of Toronto Press.

———. 1974. *A System of Logic, Ratiocinative and Inductive*. In *Collected Works, Vol. 8*, ed. J. M. Robson. Toronto: University of Toronto Press.

———. 1981. *Autobiography*. In *Collected Works, Vol. 1*, ed. J. M. Robson and Jack Stillinger. Toronto: University of Toronto Press.

———. 1984. *Collected Works, Vol. 21: Essays on Equality, Law, and Education*, ed. J. M. Robson. Toronto: University of Toronto Press.

———. 1986a. "The Spirit of the Age." In *Collected Works, Vol. 22: Newspaper Writings, December 1822–July 1831*, ed. Ann P. Robson and John M. Robson. Toronto: University of Toronto Press.

———. 1986b. *Collected Works, Vol. 24: Newspaper Writings, January 1835–June 1847*, ed. Ann P. Robson and John M. Robson. Toronto: University of Toronto Press.

———. 1986c. *Collected Works, Vol. 25: Newspaper Writings, December 1847–July 1873*, ed. Ann P. Robson and John M. Robson. Toronto: University of Toronto Press.

———. 1988. *Collected Works, Vol. 26: Journals and Debating Speeches, Part I*, ed. J. M. Robson. Toronto: University of Toronto Press.

———. 1991a. *On Liberty*. In *On Liberty and Other Essays*, ed. John Gray. New York: Oxford University Press.

———. 1991b. *Utilitarianism*. In *On Liberty and Other Essays*, ed. John Gray. New York: Oxford University Press.

———. 1991c. *On Representative Government*. In *On Liberty and Other Essays*, ed. John Gray. New York: Oxford University Press.

———. 1991d. *On the Subjection of Women*. In *On Liberty and Other Essays*, ed. John Gray. New York: Oxford University Press.

Mittman, Barbara G. 1984. "Women and the Theatre Arts." In *French Women and the Age of Enlightenment*, ed. Samia I. Spencer. Bloomington: Indiana University Press.

Moen, Marcia. 1997. "Feminist Themes in Unlikely Places: Re-reading Kant's *Critique of Judgement*. In *Rereading the Canon: Feminist Interpretations of Immanuel Kant*, ed. Robin May Schott. University Park: Pennsylvania State University Press.

Morgenstern, Mira. 1996. *Rousseau and the Politics of Ambiguity*. University Park: Pennsylvania State University Press.

———. 2002. "Women, Power, and the Politics of Everyday Life." In *Feminist Interpretations of Jean-Jacques Rousseau*, ed. Lynda Lange. University Park: Pennsylvania State University Press.

Nagl-Docekal, Herta. 1997. "Feminist Ethics: How It Could Benefit from Kant's Moral Philosophy," trans. Stephanie Morgenstern. In *Rereading the Canon: Feminist Interpretations of Immanuel Kant*, ed. Robin May Schott. University Park: Pennsylvania State University Press.

Neil, Alex. 1989. "Locke on Habituation, Autonomy, and Education." *Journal of the History of Philosophy* 27 (2): 225–46.

Noone, John. 1980. *Rousseau's "Social Contract:" A Conceptual Analysis*. Athens: University of Georgia Press.

O'Brien, Mary. 1981. *The Politics of Reproduction*. Boston: Routledge and Kegan Paul.

Okin, Susan Moller. 1979. *Women in Western Political Thought*. Princeton, NJ: Princeton University Press.

O'Neill, Onora. 1989. *Constructions of Reason: Explorations of Kant's Practical Philosophy*. New York: Cambridge University Press.

Orbach, Susie. 1978. *Fat Is a Feminist Issue: The Anti-Diet Guide to Permanent Weight Loss*. New York: Paddington Press.

Ormiston, Alice. 2002. "Developing a Feminist Concept of the Citizen: Rousseauian Insights on Nature and Reason." In *Feminist Interpretations of Jean-Jacques Rousseau*, ed. Lynda Lange. University Park: Pennsylvania State University Press.

Pateman, Carole. 1984. *The Problem of Political Obligation*. Berkeley: University of California Press.

———. 1988. *The Sexual Contract*. Stanford, CA: Stanford University Press.

———. 1991. " 'God Hath Ordained to Man a Helper': Hobbes, Patriarchy and Conjugal Right." In *Feminist Interpretations and Political Theory*, ed. Mary Lyndon Shanley and Carole Pateman. University Park: Pennsylvania State University Press.

———. 2007. "Afterword: Mere Auxilliaries to the Commonwealth in an Age of Globalization." In *Rereading the Canon: Feminist Interpretations of John Locke*, ed. Nancy J. Hirschmann and Kirstie M. McClure. University Park: Pennsylvania State University Press.

Patterson, Orlando. 1991. *Freedom: Freedom in the Making of Western Culture*. New York: Basic Books.

Patton, H. J. 1964. "Analysis of the Argument." In Immanuel Kant, *Groundwork of the Metaphysics of Morals*, ed. H. J. Patton. New York: Harper and Row.

Pettit, Phillip. 1997. *Republicanism: A Theory of Freedom and Government*. New York: Oxford University Press.

Pippin, Robert. 1982. *Kant's Theory of Form: An Essay on the "Critique of Pure Reason."* New Haven, CT: Yale University Press.

Pitkin, Hanna Fenichel. 1965. "Obligation and Consent: I." *American Political Science Review* 59 (4): 990–99.

———. 1966. "Obligation and Consent: II." *American Political Science Review* 60 (1): 39–52.

Plotz, Judith A. 2001. *Romanticism and the Vocation of Childhood*. New York: Palgrave.

Rand, Benjamin, ed. 1927. *The Correspondence of John Locke and Edward Clarke*. Oxford: Oxford University Press.

Rawls, John. 1971. *A Theory of Justice.* Cambridge, MA: Harvard University Press.

Reath, Andrews. 1997. "Introduction." In Immanuel Kant, *Critique of Practical Reason,* trans. and ed. Mary Gregor. New York: Cambridge University Press.

Rees, John C. 1977. "The Thesis of the 'Two Mills.' " *Political Studies* 25: 369–82.

———. 1985. *John Stuart Mill's "On Liberty."* Constructed from published and unpublished sources by G. L. Williams. Oxford: Clarendon Press.

Reiss, Hans. 1991. "Introduction." In *Kant's Political Writings,* ed. Hans Reiss. 2nd ed. Cambridge: Cambridge University Press.

Riley, Patrick, ed. 2001. *The Cambridge Companion to Rousseau.* New York: Cambridge University Press.

Rosenblum, Nancy. 1987. *Another Liberalism: Romanticism and the Reconstruction of Liberal Thought.* Cambridge, MA: Harvard University Press.

Rossi, Alice. 1970. "Sentiment and Intellect: The Story of John Stuart Mill and Harriet Taylor Mill." In John Stuart Mill and Harriet Taylor, *Essays on Sex Equality,* ed. Alice Rossi. Chicago: University of Chicago Press.

Rousseau, Jean-Jacques. 1945. *The Confessions of Jean-Jacques Rousseau.* New York: Modern Library.

———. 1960. *Politics and the Arts: Letter to M. D'Alembert on the Theatre,* trans. with notes and an introduction by Allen Bloom. Ithaca, NY: Cornell University Press.

———. 1967. *Correspondance Complète,* ed. R. A. Leigh. Geneva: Institut et Musée Voltaire.

———. 1979. *Emile: or On Education,* trans. Allan Bloom. New York: Basic Books.

———. 1985. *The Government of Poland,* trans. Willmoore Kendall. Indianapolis: Hackett.

———. 1989. *The Reveries of the Solitary Walker.* In *The Collected Writings of Rousseau,* vol. 8, ed. Christopher Kelly, trans. Charles Butterworth, Alexandra Cook, and Terence Marshal. Hanover, NH: Dartmouth College Press.

———. 1991a. *The Social Contract.* In *The Social Contract and Discourses,* trans. G.D.H. Cole, revised and augmented by J. H. Brumfitt and John C. Hall. Everyman's Library. London: J. M. Dent-Rutland, VT: Charles Tuttle.

———. 1991b. *Dissertation on the Origin and Foundation of the Inequality of Mankind.* In *The Social Contract and Discourses,* trans. G.D.H. Cole, revised and augmented by J. H. Brumfitt and John C. Hall. Everyman's Library. London: J. M. Dent-Rutland, VT: Charles Tuttle.

———. 1991c. *Political Economy.* In *The Social Contract and Discourses,* trans. G.D.H. Cole, revised and augmented by J. H. Brumfitt and John C. Hall. Everyman's Library. London: J. M. Dent–Rutland, VT: Charles Tuttle.

———. 1996. *Emile and Sophie, or Solitary Beings,* trans. Alice W. Harvey. In *Finding a New Feminism: Rethinking the Woman Question for Liberal Democracy,* ed. Pamela Grande Jensen. New York: Rowman and Littlefield.

———. 1997. *Julie, or the New Heloise: Letters of Two Lovers Who Live in a Small Town at the Foot of the Alps,* ed. Roger D. Masters and Christopher

Kelly, trans. and annotated by Philip Stewart and Jean Vache. Hanover, NH: Dartmouth College Press.

Ruddick, Sarah. 1989. *Maternal Thinking: Toward a Politics of Peace*. London: Women's Press.

Rumsey, Jean P. 1989. "The Development of Character in Kantian Moral Theory." *Journal of the History of Philosophy* 27:247–66.

———. 1997. "Re-Visions of Agency in Kant's Moral Theory." In *Rereading the Canon: Feminist Interpretations of Immanuel Kant*, ed. Robin May Schott. University Park: Pennsylvania State University Press.

Santorum, Rick. 2005. *It Takes a Family: Conservativism and the Common Good*. Wilmington, DE: ISI Books.

Scanlon, James P. 1958. "J. S. Mill and the Definition of Freedom." *Ethics* 68 (3): 194–206.

Schochet, Gordon. 1988. *The Authoritarian Family and Political Attitudes in Seventeenth Century England: Patriarchalism in Political Thought*. New Brunswick, NJ: Transaction.

Schott, Robin May. 1997a. "The Gender of Enlightenment." In *Rereading the Canon: Feminist Interpretations of Immanuel Kant*, ed. Robin May Schott. University Park: Pennsylvania State University Press.

———, ed. 1997b. *Rereading the Canon: Feminist Interpretations of Immanuel Kant*. University Park: Pennsylvania State University Press.

Schroder, Hannelore. 1997. "Kant's Patriarchal Order," trans. Rita Gircour. In *Rereading the Canon: Feminist Interpretations of Immanuel Kant*, ed. Robin May Schott. University Park: Pennsylvania State University Press.

Schwartz, Joel. 1984. *The Sexual Politics of Jean-Jacques Rousseau*. Chicago: University of Chicago Press.

Sedgwick, Sally. 1997. "Can Kant's Ethics Survive the Feminist Critique?" In *Rereading the Canon: Feminist Interpretations of Immanuel Kant*, ed. Robin May Schott. University Park: Pennsylvania State University Press.

Semmel, Bernard. 1983. *John Stuart Mill and the Pursuit of Virtue*. New Haven, CT: Yale University Press.

Shanley, Mary Lyndon. 1979. "Marriage Contract and Social Contract in 17th Century English Political Thought." *Western Political Quarterly* 32 (1): 79–91.

———. 1981. "Marital Slavery and Friendship: John Stuart Mill's *The Subjection of Women*." *Political Theory* 9 (2): 229–47.

Shell, Susan Meld. 2001. "*Emile*: Nature and the Education of Sophie." In *The Cambridge Companion to Rousseau*, ed. Patrick Riley. New York: Cambridge University Press.

Shklar, Judith. 1969. *Men and Citizens: A Study of Rousseau's Social Theory*. New York: Cambridge University Press.

———. 2001. "Rousseau's Images of Authority (Especially in *La Nouvelle Héloïse*)." In *The Cambridge Companion to Rousseau*, ed. Patrick Riley. New York: Cambridge University Press.

Shyllon, Folarin. 1977. *Black People in Britain, 1555–1833*. London: Oxford University Press.

Simmons, A. John. 1979. *Moral Principles and Political Obligation*. Princeton, NJ: Princeton University Press.

Skinner, Quentin. 1984. "The Idea of Negative Liberty: Philosophical and Historical Perspectives." In *Philosophy in History*, ed. Jerome Schneewind and Quentin Skinner. New York: Cambridge University Press.

———. 1990. "Thomas Hobbes on the Proper Signification of Liberty: The Prothero Lecture." *Transactions of the Royal Historical Society* 40:121–61.

———. 1996. *Reason and Rhetoric in the Philosophy of Hobbes*. New York: Cambridge University Press.

Smith, G. W. 1984. "J. S. Mill and Freedom." In *Conceptions of Liberty in Political Philosophy*, ed. Z. Pelczynski and J. Gray. New York: St. Martin's Press.

Smith, Rogers M. 1985. *Liberalism and American Constitutional Law*. Cambridge, MA: Harvard University Press.

Spencer, Samia I. 1984. "Women and Education." In *French Women and the Age of Enlightenment*, ed. Samia I. Spencer. Bloomington: Indiana University Press.

Stanlick, Nancy A. 2001. "Lords and Mothers: Silent Subjects in Hobbes's Political Theory." *International Journal of Politics and Ethics* 1 (3): 171–82.

Starobinski, Jean. 1988. *Jean-Jacques Rousseau: Transparency and Obstruction*, trans. Arthur Goldhammer, with an introduction by Robert J. Morrissey. Chicago: University of Chicago Press.

Story, Louise. 2005. "Many Women at Elite Colleges Set Career Path to Motherhood." *New York Times*, September 20.

Sussman, George. 1982. *Selling Mother's Milk: The Wet-Nursing Business in France, 1715–1914*. Urbana: University of Illinois Press.

Tarcov, Nathan. 1984. *Locke's Education for Liberty*. Chicago: University of Chicago Press.

Taylor, Charles. 1979. "What's Wrong with Negative Liberty." In *The Idea of Freedom: Essays in Honor of Isaiah Berlin*, ed. Alan Ryan. New York: Oxford University Press.

Taylor, Harriet. 1970. "Marriage and Divorce." In John Stuart Mill and Harriet Taylor, *Essays on Sex Equality*, ed. Alice Rossi. Chicago: University of Chicago Press.

tenBroeck, Jacobus. 1964. "California's Dual System of Family Law: Its Origin, Development, and Present Status: Part I." *Stanford Law Review* 16 (2): 257–318.

Trebilcot, Joyce, ed. 1983. *Mothering: Essays in Feminist Theory*. Totowa, NJ: Rowman and Allanheld.

Tuana, Nancy. 1992. *Women and the History of Philosophy*. New York: Paragon House.

Tucker, Joan. 1992. *Resistance, Change and Continuity: Britain and the Black Peoples of the Americas, 1550–1930*. London: JET.

Urbinati, Nadia. 1991. "John Stuart Mill on Androgyny and Ideal Marriage." *Political Theory* 19 (4): 626–48.

———. 2002. *Mill on Democracy: From the Athenian Polis to Representative Government*. Chicago: University of Chicago Press.

Urmson, J. O. 1953. "The Interpretation of the Moral Philosophy of J. S. Mill." *Philosophical Quarterly* 3: 33–39.

Vaughan, Geoffrey M. 2002. *Behemoth Teaches Leviathan*. Lanham, MD: Lexington Books.

Velkley, Richard L. 1989. *Freedom and the End of Reason: On the Moral Foundation of Kant's Critical Philosophy*. Chicago: University of Chicago Press.

Waldron, Jeremy. 2007a. "Locke, Adam and Eve." In *Feminist Interpretations of John Locke*, ed. Nancy J. Hirschmann and Kirstie M. McClure. University Park: Pennsylvania State University Press.

———. 2007b. "Mill on the Contagious Diseases Act." In *J. S. Mill's Political Thought: A Bicentennial Reassessment*, ed. Nadia Urbinati and Alex Zakaras. New York: Cambridge University Press.

Walvin, James. 1973. *Black and White: The Negro and English Society, 1555–1945*. London: Penguin.

Weiss, Penny. 1987. "Rousseau, Antifeminism, and Woman's Nature." *Political Theory* 15:81–98.

Weiss, Penny, and Anne Harper. 2002. "Rousseau's Political Defense of the Sex-Roled Family." In *Feminist Interpretations of Jean-Jacques Rousseau*, ed. Lynda Lange. University Park: Pennsylvania State University Press.

Williams, Bernard. 1985. *Ethics and the Limits of Philosophy*. London: Fontana Press/Collins.

Wingrove, Elizabeth. 2000. *Rousseau's Republican Romance*. Princeton, NJ: Princeton University Press.

———. 2002. "Republican Romance." In *Feminist Interpretations of Jean-Jacques Rousseau*, ed. Lynda Lange. University Park: Pennsylvania State University Press.

Witt, Charlotte. 2006. "Feminist Interpretations of the Philosophical Canon." *Signs: Journal of Women in Culture and Society* 31 (2): 537–52.

Wolker, Robert. 2001. "Ancient Postmodernism." In *Cambridge Companion to Rousseau*, ed. Patrick Riley. New York: Cambridge University Press.

Wollstonecraft, Mary. 1985. *Vindication of the Rights of Women: With Strictures on Political and Moral Subjects*, ed. Miriam Brody Kramnick. New York: Penguin.

Wood, Allen. 1984. "Kant's Compatibilism." In *Self and Nature in Kant's Philosophy*, ed. Allen Wood. Ithaca, NY: Cornell University Press.

Wood, Neal. 1983. *The Politics of Locke's Philosophy*. Berkeley: University of California Press.

Wootten, David. 1993. "Introduction." In *The Political Writings of John Locke*. New York: Mentor Books.

Wright, Joanne. 2002. "Going against the Grain: Hobbes's Case of Original Maternal Dominion." *Journal of Women's History* 14 (1): 123–48.

———. 2004. *Origin Stories in Political Thought: Discourses on Gender, Power, and Citizenship*. Toronto: University of Toronto Press.

———. 2007. "Recovering Locke's Midwifery Notes." In *Feminist Intepretations of John Locke*, ed. Nancy J. Hirschmann and Kirstie M. McClure. University Park: Pennsylvania State University Press.

Wright, Nancy E., Margaret W. Ferguson, and A. R. Buck. 2004. *Women, Property, and the Letters of the Law in Early Modern England*. Toronto: University of Toronto Press.

Zerilli, Linda. 1994. *Signifying Woman: Culture and Chaos in Rousseau, Burke and Mill*. Ithaca, NY: Cornell University Press.

Index

ability: vs. capacity for Kant, 190, 191, 196–97, 203–4; vs. capacity for Locke, 85–88, 95, 254, 298n14; vs. capacity for Mill, 231, 232, 241, 254, 259–60; and choice for Mill, 215, 216, 239; and choice for Rousseau, 128, 130, 133–34, 135, 147, 154, 158, 167; and cooperation for Rousseau, 121, 122; vs. freedom in Hobbes, 30, 32–33; internal vs. external source of, 3, 276–77; and reasoning for Kant, 170, 173, 176, 190, 191, 201

abuse, domestic. *See* domestic violence

agency: and freedom, 5; Hobbes on, 29–30, 31, 33, 39; Locke on, 81, 107; Mill on, 220–21; and perfectibility of humans, 145–46; Rousseau on, 128

Allison, Henry, 172–73, 183, 208

Annas, Julia, 241

Applewhite, Harriet, 142

autonomy: Kant on, 173, 178, 180, 181, 193–94, 195, 210; Locke on, 108, 219; Mill on, 216–17, 219; Rousseau on, 153–54. *See also* moral freedom

Axtell, James L., 93

Baier, Annette, 195

Baum, Bruce, 216

beautiful, the, and canon's sexism, 201, 203–4, 206–7, 243

Beck, Lewis White, 168

Bennett, Jonathan, 168

Bentham, Jeremy, 10, 232, 233–34, 312n36

Berlin, Isaiah: and gender, 22; and Mill's complexities on freedom, 214, 217, 220, 223, 274; on positive and negative freedom, 1–13

biologism in Hobbes, 29, 31

birth control, 139–40, 258–59

Blum, Carol, 136

bourgeois, the. *See* class issues

Bramhall, John, 32, 33, 294n10

Butler, Judith, 15

Butler, Melissa, 91–92, 93, 94

capacity. *See* ability

Capaldi, Nicholas, 216–17

capitalism: and Mill, 213, 235, 261, 266, 271; and social construction, 15, 19, 26

categorical imperative, 172–78, 182, 183, 184, 190–91, 193, 205–6

Catholicism and toleration, 111–12

character, building of: and canon's biases, 285; importance in education, 275; Kant on, 190–91, 194; Locke on, 82, 88, 91, 109, 113–14; Mill on, 221–22, 230–31, 244, 253, 257, 258, 268, 280; and Mill's elitism, 251–52, 254–55; Rousseau on, 133, 137. *See also* virtue

children/child rearing: and divorce, 98, 116, 246; Hobbes on, 48, 49, 50–51, 54–55; Kant on, 190–91, 309n66; Locke on, 86–91, 93–96, 98, 105–6, 109, 112–16, 300n44; Mill on, 244, 312n42, 313nn53–54, 314–15n87; parental responsibility for character of, 258; and Rousseau, 120, 135, 138–41, 143, 147–49, 155, 157, 302n31, 303n46, 306n78. *See also* mothers

choice: and Berlin's typology, 6–7; complexities in canon, 276, 277–78; and domestic violence, 294n16; free vs. right, 18–19, 21, 27–28, 282; Hobbes on, 30–33, 36, 39–40, 59, 65, 78, 296n46; Kant on, 177–78, 180, 209, 210; Locke on, 89, 99–106, 108, 110, 299–300n38; Mill on, 215, 216, 220, 229–30, 231, 236, 239; Rousseau on, 119–20, 128, 129, 132–34, 135, 147, 154–55; social construction of, 65, 228–29. *See also* true will

citizenship: and gender and class, 285; Hobbes on, 72–73; Kant on, 189–90, 195, 205; Locke on, 88–91; Mill on, 234, 260–66; Rousseau on, 133–38, 152–61, 162–64, 303n35

civil freedom: Kant on, 182–85, 208; Rousseau on, 123–24, 126, 179. *See also* negative liberty